THE COMPLEXITY OF HUMAN RIGHTS

This book provides the first systematic assessment from a human rights law perspective of the landmark contributions of the renowned legal anthropologist, Sally Engle Merry.

What impact does over-simplification have on human rights debates? The understandable tendency to present them as a single, universal, and immutable concept ignores their complexity and by extension only serves to weaken them.

Merry and her colleagues transformed human rights thinking by highlighting the process of 'vernacularization', which sees rights discourse as being unavoidably dependent upon translation and interpretation. She also warned of the pitfalls of excessive reliance upon statistical and other indicators, through the process of quantification. Here the leading voices in the field assess the significance of these contributions.

The cover shows Judith Mason's painting The Man Who Sang and the Woman Who Kept Silent (known as 'the Blue Dress'), part of a triptych which hangs in the South African Constitutional Court. The work symbolizes accounts of the killings of two freedom fighters under the apartheid system that emerged in the hearings of the Truth and Reconciliation Commission.

The Complexity of Human Rights

From Vernacularization to Quantification

Essays in Honour of Sally Engle Merry

Edited by
Philip Alston

•HART•
OXFORD • LONDON • NEW YORK • NEW DELHI • SYDNEY

HART PUBLISHING

Bloomsbury Publishing Plc

Kemp House, Chawley Park, Cumnor Hill, Oxford, OX2 9PH, UK

1385 Broadway, New York, NY 10018, USA

29 Earlsfort Terrace, Dublin 2, Ireland

HART PUBLISHING, the Hart/Stag logo, BLOOMSBURY and the Diana logo are trademarks of Bloomsbury Publishing Plc

First published in Great Britain 2024

Copyright © Philip Alston, and Contributors 2024

Philip Alston, and Contributors have asserted their right under the Copyright, Designs and Patents Act 1988 to be identified as Authors of this work.

All rights reserved. No part of this publication may be reproduced or transmitted in any form or by any means, electronic or mechanical, including photocopying, recording, or any information storage or retrieval system, without prior permission in writing from the publishers.

While every care has been taken to ensure the accuracy of this work, no responsibility for loss or damage occasioned to any person acting or refraining from action as a result of any statement in it can be accepted by the authors, editors or publishers.

All UK Government legislation and other public sector information used in the work is Crown Copyright ©. All House of Lords and House of Commons information used in the work is Parliamentary Copyright ©. This information is reused under the terms of the Open Government Licence v3.0 (http://www.nationalarchives.gov.uk/doc/open-government-licence/version/3) except where otherwise stated.

All Eur-lex material used in the work is © European Union, http://eur-lex.europa.eu/, 1998–2024.

A catalogue record for this book is available from the British Library.

A catalogue record for this book is available from the Library of Congress.

Library of Congress Control Number: 2023947598

ISBN: PB: 978-1-50997-286-9
HB: 978-1-50997-290-6
ePDF: 978-1-50997-288-3
ePub: 978-1-50997-287-6

Typeset by Compuscript Ltd, Shannon
Printed and bound in Great Britain by CPI Group (UK) Ltd, Croydon CR0 4YY

To find out more about our authors and books visit www.hartpublishing.co.uk. Here you will find extracts, author information, details of forthcoming events and the option to sign up for our newsletters.

Every effort has been made to trace copyright holders and to obtain their permission for the use of copyright material. The publisher apologises for any errors or omissions and would be grateful for notification of any corrections that should be incorporated in future reprints or editions of this book.

Preface

THE ESSAYS IN this volume are dedicated to Sally Engle Merry, a renowned anthropologist who made major contributions in areas as diverse as popular justice, the cultural power of law, colonialism, gender, human rights and the ethnography of international institutions. The essays focus primarily on her work on the process of vernacularization in relation to human rights norms and on the seductions of quantification, especially in the form of indicators.

Sally, as she was known by all who worked with her, taught at New York University until her untimely death in September 2020. She was the Julius Silver Professor of Anthropology, taught regularly in the School of Law and was an active co-director of the Center for Human Rights and Global Justice.[1]

Among the many prizes and honours that she won was the Franz Boas Award for Exemplary Service to Anthropology, presented at the American Anthropological Association annual meeting in 2019. The first winner of the award was Margaret Mead in 1976. The award is given to a person whose career demonstrates extraordinary achievement and who has 'made exceptional contributions to anthropology with respect to the increase and dissemination of humanistic and scientific knowledge and/or service to the profession'.

Sally was a great many things to those who knew and worked with her. As a scholar, she was creative, incorrigibly intellectually curious and rarely failed to challenge the received wisdom. Her prodigious work unfailingly enhanced the world's understanding of every issue that she explored in any depth. As a teacher, she was exceptionally committed and very talented. She cared deeply for her students and gave generously of her time to anyone who sought her advice or help. As a colleague, she was superb and could never do enough for others, was never 'busy' when demands were made on her time and was an enthusiastic participant in all scholarly and related endeavours. She was always thoughtful: thinking deeply about any topic, no matter how mundane; thinking of others and how she might help them; and thinking about how the world might be a better place. But above all, Sally was a delightful human being.

Particular thanks are due to Lucy Forbes, Katarina Sydow and Helen Jennings for their invaluable roles in preparing the manuscript for publication, and to Raja Dandamudi for outstanding research assistance.

---

[1] For a detailed and insightful account of her career, see M Goodale, 'Sally Engle Merry (1944–2020)' (2021) 123 *American Anthropologist* 724.

© NYU Photo Bureau: Thomas.

Contents

Preface v
List of Contributors ix

1. *Acknowledging the Complexity of the Human Rights Regime* 1
   Philip Alston

PART I
VERNACULARIZATION AND HUMAN RIGHTS

2. *'A Very Murky Process': Embracing the Indeterminacy of International Justice and Human Rights* 43
   Richard Ashby Wilson

3. *Vernacularizing Rights: Indispensable but Dangerous* 61
   Jack Snyder

4. *Globalising the Indigenous: The Making of International Human Rights from below* 75
   César Rodríguez-Garavito

5. *Rites of Culture: Legal Frameworks, Indigenous Protocols, and the Circulation of Culture in Australia* 93
   Fred Myers

6. *Vernacularization as Anthropological Ethics* 101
   Mark Goodale

7. *The Vernacularization of Transitional Justice: Is Transitional Justice Useful in Pre-conflict Settings?* 117
   Pablo de Greiff

PART II
QUANTIFICATION AND HUMAN RIGHTS

8. *Beyond the Vanishing Point: Quantification as Rhetoric in Today's Anti-slavery Campaigns* 153
   Samuel Martínez

9. *The Competitive Pressures of Rankings: Experimental Evidence of Rankings' Influence on Domestic Priorities* 173
   Rush Doshi, Judith Kelley and Beth A Simmons

10. *Between Conduct and Counter-conduct: Human Rights Translation at the Universal Periodic Review*..187
    Julie Billaud

11. *Recommendations in Words and Numbers: Thinking with Sally Engle Merry at the Universal Periodic Review*...203
    Jane K Cowan

12. *Visualising the 'Women, Peace and Security Agenda'*...........................229
    Hilary Charlesworth

13. *The Seductions of Quantification Rebuffed? The Curious Failure by the CESCR to Engage Water and Sanitation Data*...247
    Margaret L Satterthwaite

14. *Strategising the World: Uncounted People in the Sustainable Development Goal on Health*..273
    Sara LM (Meg) Davis

Index..283

List of Contributors

Philip Alston is the John Norton Pomeroy Professor of Law at New York University and a faculty director of the Center for Human Rights and Global Justice at NYU School of Law. He served as UN Special Rapporteur on extreme poverty and human rights from 2014 to 2020 and Special Rapporteur on extrajudicial executions from 2004 to 2010. Alston was a member of the Security Council Commission of Inquiry into the Central African Republic, the Independent International Commission on Kyrgyzstan and the UN Group of Experts on Darfur. Previously, he served as special adviser to the UN High Commissioner for Human Rights on the Millennium Development Goals; Chairperson and Rapporteur of the UN Committee on Economic, Social, and Cultural Rights (1987–98); and UNICEF's senior legal adviser on children's rights. He was editor-in-chief of the *European Journal of International Law* (1996–2007).

Julie Billaud is an Associate Professor of Anthropology and Sociology at Geneva Graduate Institute. She has previously held positions at the University of Sussex, Ecole des Hautes Etudes en Sciences Sociales and Humboldt University and Max Planck Institute for Social Anthropology. Billaud is the author of *Kabul Carnival: Gender Politics in Postwar Afghanistan*, an ethnographic study of the 'reconstruction process' in post-9/11 Afghanistan carried out among various groups of women targeted by 'emancipatory' projects. More recently, she collaborated with Jane K Cowan on an ethnographic study of the Universal Periodic Review, a mechanism of human rights monitoring within the UN Human Rights Council in Geneva.

Hilary Charlesworth is a judge of the International Court of Justice, elected in 2021. She was previously Harrison Moore Professor of Law and a Melbourne Laureate Professor at Melbourne Law School, and a Distinguished Professor at the Australian National University. She has been a visiting professor at various institutions, including Harvard Law School, New York University, UCLA, Paris I and the London School of Economics. She is an associate member of the Institut de Droit International.

Jane K Cowan is an Emeritus Professor of Anthropology at the University of Sussex. Until her retirement in 2020, she was Co-director of the Sussex Rights and Justice Research Centre (SRJRC), which she co-founded in autumn 2015. Cowan was the Jane and Aatos Erkko Visiting Professor at the Helsinki Collegium for Advanced Studies in 2018–19 and is currently President of the Society for the Anthropology of Europe. While her early work investigated gender, power, performance and embodiment in ritual and celebratory events in northern Greece, in later work she has been exploring the nexus of rights claiming, transnational activism and international supervision, first in the context of minority petitioning to the League of Nations, and more recently at the Universal Periodic Review (with Julie Billaud). Her publications include *Dance and the Body Politic in Northern Greece* (Winner of the Chicago Folklore Prize), *Macedonia: The Politics of Identity and Difference* and *Culture and*

Rights: Anthropological Perspectives (with Marie-Bénédicte Dembour and Richard A Wilson).

Sara LM (Meg) Davis is Professor of Digital Health and Rights at the Centre for Interdisciplinary Methodologies, University of Warwick and principal investigator of the Digital Health and Rights Project. She was founding executive director of Asia Catalyst, as well as the first senior advisor on human rights at the Global Fund to Fight AIDS, TB and Malaria. Her work focuses on human rights, data and digital technologies in global health. Her latest book is *The Uncounted: Politics of Data in Global Health*.

Rush Doshi is the founding director of the Brookings China Strategy Initiative and a fellow in Brookings Foreign Policy. He is also a fellow (on leave) at Yale's Paul Tsai China Center, special advisor to the CEO of the Asia Group and an adjunct senior fellow at the Center for a New American Security. Doshi has also served as a member of the Asia policy working groups for the Biden and Clinton presidential campaigns, an analyst at the Long Term Strategy Group and Rock Creek Global Advisors, an Arthur Liman Fellow at the Department of State and a Fulbright Fellow in China. His research focuses on Chinese grand strategy as well as Indo-Pacific security issues.

Mark Goodale is Professor of Cultural and Social Anthropology and Director of the Laboratory of Cultural and Social Anthropology (LACS) at the University of Lausanne. For the year 2023–24, he is a Leverhulme Trust Visiting Professor at the University of Oxford and a member of St Antony's College. He is the founding series editor of *Stanford Studies in Human Rights* and the author, editor and co-editor of a number of books on human rights, anthropology and law, justice, and legal history, including *The Practice of Human Rights: Tracking Law between the Global and the Local* (co-edited with Sally Engle Merry) and *Reinventing Human Rights*.

Pablo de Greiff is Senior Fellow and Director of the Transitional Justice Program and Prevention Project at the Center for Human Rights and Global Justice at New York University School of Law. Prior to joining NYU, he was the Director of Research at the International Center for Transitional Justice (2001–14), Associate Professor in the Philosophy Department at SUNY Buffalo (1992–2001) and Laurance Rockefeller Faculty Fellow at the Center for Human Values at Princeton University (2000–01). He served as the first UN Special Rapporteur on the promotion of truth, justice, reparation and guarantees of non-recurrence (2012–18), and is currently one of the Commissioners in the UN's Independent Commission of Inquiry on Ukraine. De Greiff is the editor or co-editor of 10 books and has written extensively on democratic theory and the relationship between politics, morality and law.

Judith Kelley is Dean of the Sanford School of Public Policy at Duke University. She serves on the editorial board of International Organization and other journals, as well as the boards of the Hunt Institute, the Government Accountability Office Board of Academic Advisors, the Electoral Integrity project, the International Foundation for Electoral Systems, the Nicholas Institute and the advisory board of the 2023 United Nations Human Development Report. Her work focuses on human rights and democracy, international election observation, and human trafficking.

Samuel Martínez is an Emeritus Professor of Anthropology and Latin American Studies at the University of Connecticut. In 2016, he was awarded the American Anthropological Association's (AAA) President's Award for outstanding service to the Association. In 2005, he contributed an extensive expert affidavit to the Inter-American Court of Human Rights, in support of the plaintiffs in the case of *Yean and Bosico v Dominican Republic*, later recognised as a landmark ruling in the area of statelessness. His main area of research expertise is the migrant and minority rights mobilisations of undocumented Haitians and Dominicans of Haitian descent. His current research examines the visual culture and discourse of the global movement to end human trafficking and modern slavery.

Beth A Simmons is Andrea Mitchell University Professor of Law and Political Science at Penn Law, University of Pennsylvania. She researches and teaches international relations, international law and international political economy. Simmons spent a year working at the International Monetary Fund, has directed the Weatherhead Center for International Affairs at Harvard, is a past president of the International Studies Association and has been elected to the National Academy of Sciences and the American Academy of Arts and Sciences. Key areas of her research include international political economy during the interwar years, policy diffusion globally and illustrating the influence that international law has on human rights outcomes around the world.

Fred Myers is the Silver Professor of Anthropology at New York University. He is a past editor of the journal *Cultural Anthropology* and President of the American Ethnological Society. Myers has been involved in research with, and writing about, Western Desert Aboriginal people since 1973. He has written two monographs, *Pintupi Country, Pintupi Self: Sentiment, Place and Politics among Western Desert Aborigines* (1986) and *Painting Culture: The Making of an Aboriginal High Art* (2002). He has also edited books including *The Traffic in Culture: Refiguring Anthropology and Art*, *The Empire of Things* and *Experiments in Self-Determination: Histories of the Outstation Movement in Australia* (co-edited with Nicolas Peterson).

César Rodríguez-Garavito is Professor of Clinical Law and Chair of the Center for Human Rights and Global Justice at NYU School of Law. He is the founding director of the Earth Rights Advocacy Clinic, the Future of Rights and Governance Program, the Climate Litigation Accelerator and the More Than Human Rights (MOTH) project at NYU Law. He is the editor-in-chief of *Open Global Rights* and has published widely on international human rights, climate litigation, socio-economic rights, global governance, Indigenous rights, and business and human rights. He has served as a board member or strategy advisor to leading international and domestic human rights organisations in different parts of the world, and has been an expert witness of the Inter-American Court of Human Rights, an adjunct judge of the Constitutional Court of Colombia and a member of the Science Panel for the Amazon.

Margaret L Satterthwaite is the faculty director of the Robert and Helen Bernstein Institute for Human Rights and a director of the Center for Human Rights and Global Justice (CHRGJ). She is a Professor of Clinical Law and director of the Legal Empowerment and Judicial Independence Clinic. She is currently serving as the

UN Special Rapporteur on the independence of judges and lawyers, and previously served as a consultant to the Special Rapporteur on the human right to safe drinking water and sanitation, the Special Rapporteur on the promotion and protection of human rights while countering terrorism, the World Health Organization, and the World Bank. Satterthwaite has served as an adviser or member of the board of directors of a range of human rights organisations, including Amnesty International USA, Digital Democracy, the Global Initiative for Economic and Social Rights, and the International Justice Resource Center. Her recent scholarship has involved legal empowerment, access to justice and cross-disciplinary work aimed at advancing the evidence base for human rights advocacy.

Jack Snyder is the Robert and Renée Belfer Professor of International Relations in the Department of Political Science and the Saltzman Institute of War and Peace Studies at Columbia. He is a Fellow of the American Academy of Arts and Sciences and editor of the WW Norton book series on world politics. He has authored and edited a number of books on conflict, human rights and international relations, and has published articles in the *Journal of Democracy* and *American Political Science Review*. His most recent book is *Human Rights for Pragmatists: Social Power in Modern Times* (2022).

Richard Ashby Wilson is a Board of Trustees Distinguished Professor of Anthropology and Law, Gladstein Chair of Human Rights and founding director of the Human Rights Institute at the University of Connecticut. He has authored or edited 11 books on anthropology, international human rights, truth and reconciliation commissions, and international criminal tribunals. His latest book, *Incitement on Trial: Prosecuting International Speech Crimes*, examines how international courts have handled hate speech and incitement to genocide. He currently serves on the Hate Crimes Advisory Council of the State of Connecticut.

1
Acknowledging the Complexity of the Human Rights Regime

PHILIP ALSTON

I. LINKING VERNACULARIZATION AND QUANTIFICATION

AT FIRST GLANCE, vernacularization and quantification might seem to have little to do with one another; in fact, they both serve to emphasise the importance of a nuanced and sophisticated understanding of the complexities of human rights. Simplicity and neatness are often sought by those who wish to ensure that human rights norms are understood and respected, that compliance can be measured and that countries' performance can be judged and compared. But there are limits to simplification, whether it applies to the normative framework or to the evaluation of compliance. This volume explores the limits of two of the most prominent techniques for promoting what might be termed the 'de-complexification' of human rights. The first is an insistence that human rights norms represent a universally valid and accepted consensus and that they do, or should, have the same meaning everywhere in the world (the universalising technique). While the aspiration to achieve universality in certain respects is integral to the international regime, that term is often understood and invoked in ways that are both inappropriate and counter-productive. The second is the rapidly increasing use of quantification, and especially of composite indicators, to capture the essence of complex rights issues, to evaluate compliance and to rank the human rights performance of states or other actors (the quantification technique). Again, while indicators are potentially important to developing a deeper understanding of what is happening in practice, it is important to recognise their limitations and their potential to distort reality.

This book, inspired by Sally Engle Merry's path-breaking work on both issues, shows how the clarity and straightforwardness sought by using such techniques can be deeply problematic. These qualities can end up masking or hiding complexity that it is essential to acknowledge and integrate if the human rights regime is to succeed in its diverse goals. Vernacularization, which Merry defined as the process through which 'an idea or norm is redefined and represented in a way that is more or less compatible with the existing social world',[1] is about the need to recognise that communication about human rights involves important elements of interpretation or translation. This process occurs in the most elevated diplomatic contexts, in which states' representatives negotiate in a range of languages while trying to understand culturally loaded concepts and terminologies being proposed by different delegates. At the opposite end of the spectrum, it also takes place at the community or village level, where individuals try to make sense of human rights language that has been imported from the international stage but is assumed to be capable of resonating with them in important ways.[2] Merry stressed the central role of intermediaries or translators, especially in the space in between these two far-apart groups, but in fact there are a great many such intermediaries working within many different parts of the human rights enterprise, all seeking to make the relevant norms comprehensible, relevant and accommodating. Some of these intermediaries will be working at cross purposes, some unconsciously and others very deliberately. Cacophony is no doubt too strong a term to describe the resulting conversation, but it captures the diversity, untidiness and iterative nature of human rights discourse.

While Merry's use of the concept of vernacularization has been widely cited in the literature, it has also provoked considerable scepticism on the grounds that it is, or might become, a Trojan horse for smuggling a degree of relativism and open-endedness into the concept of human rights. The fear is that such relativism will invite abuse and even appropriation of human rights norms by those whose aims are actually antithetical to the enterprise. One of the principal goals of this volume is to respond to such concerns by exploring what vernacularization means and seeking a deeper understanding of when and by whom rights might need to be translated into other languages.

The other main goal of this volume is to explore the implications of Merry's insight that many of the ways in which quantification is pursued in today's world, especially in the sphere of human rights, involve problematic endeavours to de-complexify or simplify large bodies of data. What often results is a process that loses, distorts or mystifies much of the essential meaning of the original data, even while claiming to make it more accessible, digestible and readily able to be acted upon. There is a point at which such approaches to quantification result in the aggregation of data and issues that should remain granular, in acknowledgement of the complex reality that they represent.

Vernacularization focuses especially, although not exclusively, on the processes of translation downwards, so that concepts and principles can be better understood at the local level. Quantification and 'indexisation' often work in the opposite direction, with the effect of obscuring or fundamentally recasting qualitative data that is heterogeneous and complex into highly simplified indexes used for ranking the 'performance' of countries, sectors of society or the economy.

---

[1] SE Merry, 'The State of Human Rights Consciousness: Not Yet Endtimes' in N Bhuta et al (eds), *The Struggle for Human Rights* (Oxford, Oxford University Press, 2021) 62, 63.

[2] See, eg MB McKenna, 'Feminism in Translation: Reframing Human Rights Law through Transnational Islamic Feminist Networks' in R Gould and K Tahmasebian (eds), *The Routledge Handbook of Translation and Activism* (Abingson, Routledge, 2020) 317.

While there are many reasons why a more sophisticated understanding of these issues is needed, the various contributions contained in this volume are especially timely by way of a partial response to some recently published critiques challenging the validity, plausibility, defensibility and effectiveness of the international human rights regime.[3] Close examination of many of these critiques reveals a conception of human rights that is largely lacking in complexity. The authors tend to oversimplify, whilst failing to offer a transparent definition of exactly what it is they are referring to when they address 'human rights', the 'human rights system', the 'human rights movement' or whatever other terms are used to describe the complex interactions of a very wide range of actors, processes and institutions.[4] It is, of course, difficult, if not impossible, for a single book to capture the essence of a regime that spans the global, regional and local levels; that is institutionalised in international courts and councils, as well as local ombuds offices and a great deal in between; that is driven by the work of large and powerful civil society groups, as well as by millions of smaller groups and grassroots advocates; and that involves many more diverse narrative forms than the legal discourse in which it is often expressed. But instead of acknowledging the complexity of the regime and conceding that their analytical lens is narrow and limited, some authors seek to ground wide-ranging conclusions on an analysis that is focused only on a narrow slice of a very large pie that becomes a proxy for the regime as a whole: for example, the way in which a handful of international civil society groups understand and approach human rights; the workings of a body like the United Nations Human Rights Council; the ability of the human rights system to respond to atrocities; or shortcomings in the jurisprudence of one of the regional court systems. That narrow focus is then used as the basis for sweeping generalisations as to the utility or otherwise of the regime as a whole.

The focus on vernacularization, in particular, provides a powerful antidote to these approaches. In contrast, it highlights that the normative aspirations of the regime as a whole are transmitted through a vast array of intermediaries and interpreters, and that they take a great many forms that are not captured meaningfully by global or big-picture analyses of the type that have tended to dominate much of the literature in the field in recent years. As Kapczynski has noted, much of this literature ignores 'forms of human rights practice, particularly at the periphery, that exist beyond' the purview of these authors, and yet it is 'in these marginal places that hope for human rights lies, and to these places that we should look if we want to build a human rights adequate to our times'.[5] It is in such diverse, under-researched and often overlooked settings that the process of vernacularization is at its most vibrant and plays its most significant role.

---

[3] See, eg S Moyn, *The Last Utopia: Human Rights in History* (Cambridge, MA, Harvard University Press, 2010); S Hopgood, *The Endtimes of Human Rights* (Ithaca, NY, Cornell University Press, 2013); E Posner, *The Twilight of Human Rights* (Oxford, Oxford University Press, 2014); S Moyn, *Not Enough: Human Rights in an Unequal World* (Cambridge, MA, Harvard University Press, 2018).

[4] On the polycentric nature of the regime, see P Alston, 'Does the Past Matter? On the Origins of Human Rights' (2013) 126 *Harvard Law Review* 2043, 2078.

[5] A Kapczynski, 'The Right to Medicines in the Age of Neoliberalism' (2019) 10 *Humanity* 79, 95.

II. UNIVERSALITY AND THE ORIGINS OF THE INTERNATIONAL REGIME

In order to understand the significance of vernacularization, it is important to locate it within the overall human rights regime and to understand the ways in which the latter has evolved in its quest to reconcile universality with responsiveness to local cultural practices. The starting point for such an overview is the set of challenges to universality that confronted the UN Commission on Human Rights in the late 1940s, when it embarked upon the process of drafting a bill of rights.

The Universal Declaration of Human Rights (UDHR) that emerged from that process proudly proclaimed universality in its title and described itself in its Preamble as 'a common standard of achievement for all peoples and all nations'. But the claim to universality was something of a fiction, albeit one that was necessary to conclude the urgent and worthy task of bridging deep cultural, philosophical and political differences in the aftermath of the genocidal and systematic brutality of World War II.

The Commission began this monumental process in 1946. In principle, the idea was to commit every state, every culture and even every community to a single, concise, negotiated statement of the fundamental moral, ethical and perhaps natural law; principles that would be promoted and adhered to by the international community. The enterprise was promoted by a range of civil society groups in the West and in Latin America, and drew strong support from prominent groups of both domestic and public international lawyers.[6] The process was brought to a successful conclusion when the draft, elaborated by a small group of diplomatic representatives, was endorsed by governments in the UN General Assembly in December 1948.

But while the representatives of the 58 states that were then UN members were prepared to bury, or at least not insist upon, their disagreements, this did not mean that the resulting consensus miraculously dissolved the many misgivings and qualifications that surrounded the drafting process. These misgivings were cogently expressed at the time by, among others, prominent groups of philosophers, anthropologists and economists. While those groups were not speaking in formal representative capacities and reflected highly diverse opinions, they nonetheless presented the views of important segments of their respective professions, and posed strong challenges to some of the assumptions that underpinned the UDHR enterprise.

Philosophers were, inevitably, particularly divided. The clearest expression of that division came from a distinguished group of individuals convened by the United Nations Educational, Scientific and Cultural Organization (UNESCO) in 1947 to give their views on what could or should be covered in a proposed declaration of rights. The group, somewhat haphazardly chosen, almost entirely male and far from being truly representative in cultural or philosophical terms, made it clear that there could be no consensus beyond a very thin set of formulations carefully designed to

---

[6] American Law Institute, *Statement of Essential Human Rights* (New York, Americans United for World Organization, 1945); M Charles De Visscher (Rapporteur), *Les droits fondamentaux de l'homme, base d'une restauration du droit international* (Lausanne, Institut de Droit International, 1947).

paper over deep differences.⁷ The introduction to their survey was written by the renowned French Catholic philosopher Jacques Maritain. He used his impressive verbal acrobatic skills to convey the message that, while fundamental ideological and philosophical differences could never be bridged, this did not preclude the emergence of 'a sort of common denominator ... at the point where in practice the most widely separated theoretical ideologies and mental traditions converge'. This, he said, would require a pragmatic approach and the recasting of accepted formulae in order that they would be acceptable 'as points of convergence in practice, however opposed the theoretic viewpoints'. He sought to end on an optimistic note by observing that, despite 'the clash of theory' reflected in the views of the various contributors, one could nevertheless hope that 'a few scanty features of ... a practical ideology ... are in the course of taking root in the conscience of the nations'.⁸

Maritain's effort to discern a practical convergence of ideas is reminiscent of John Rawls's later contention that it is possible in a liberal society for there to be an 'overlapping consensus' in relation to principles of justice even where there remain 'considerable differences in citizens' conceptions of justice provided that these conceptions lead to similar political judgements'.⁹ In fact, a careful reading of the many contributions to the UNESCO volume does not easily lead to the conclusion that there existed even the limited convergence of ideas discerned by Maritain. The small 'UNESCO Committee on the theoretical bases of Human Rights' given the task of drawing practical conclusions from the musings of the philosophers was equally guarded in its formulation. It concluded that while UN member states shared 'common convictions', those had necessarily to be 'stated in terms of different philosophic principles and on the background of divergent political and economic systems'.¹⁰

Subsequently, the chairman of the Committee – the prominent British historian EH Carr – criticised the final text of the UDHR as being 'pale, eclectic and unconvincing'. In his view, it reflected the outcome of a 'political sparring match' rather than a 'common agreement among men of good will'. He lamented its striking 'emptiness' and the fact that 'political expediency' had led the drafters to keep the 'real issues' 'decently out of sight'.¹¹ But neither Maritain nor Carr's UNESCO Committee had any interest in being on the wrong side of history by challenging the feasibility of the overall enterprise.

Many anthropologists also had deep misgivings. In 1947, the American Anthropological Association submitted a statement to the UDHR drafters asserting that

> [s]tandards and values are relative to the culture from which they derive so that any attempt to formulate postulates that grow out of the beliefs or moral codes of one culture must to

---

⁷ UNESCO, 'Human Rights: Comments and Interpretations: A Symposium Edited by UNESCO, with an Introduction by Jacques Maritain' (25 July 1948) UNESCO/PHS/3 (rev).
⁸ ibid.
⁹ J Rawls, *A Theory of Justice* (Cambridge, MA, Harvard University Press, 1971) 399.
¹⁰ UNESCO (n 7) Appendix II, 2.
¹¹ EH Carr, 'Rights and Obligations', *The Times Literary Supplement* (11 November 1949) 725–26.

that extent detract from the applicability of any Declaration of Human Rights to mankind as a whole.[12]

While the statement was apparently written solely by Melville Herskovits, who was also a contributor to the UNESCO volume,[13] it nonetheless reflected a relativist position shared by many of his professional colleagues.

Prominent economists at the time were also in clear disagreement as to whether issues of economic justice should form part of a declaration of rights. The emphasis on 'freedom from want', proclaimed in the 1941 Atlantic Charter outlining the Allies' war aims and again in President Franklin Delano Roosevelt's 1944 proposal for a second Bill of Rights in the USA, placed this issue squarely on the agenda for the drafters of the UDHR. EH Carr, writing in 1949, described the issue as 'a profound problem which dogs those who embark on the discussion of human rights in our time' and chastised those who pretended that the fundamental conflict between a laissez-faire approach and freedom from want could be reconciled by 'a formula that makes the best of all worlds'.[14] But Carr's concerns were mild and potentially negotiable, unlike the positions reflected in the Statement of Aims adopted by the Mont Pèlerin Society convened in 1947 by Friedrich von Hayek and Ludwig von Mises. The Society's economists proclaimed that the 'central values of civilization' were in danger as a result of creeds that reflected 'a decline of belief in private property and the competitive market'. In particular, they saw 'danger in the expansion of government, not least in the welfare state, in the power of trade unions and business monopoly'.[15] In spelling out their philosophy, carefully grounded in affirmations of freedom of thought and expression, property rights and the rule of law, these early neoliberals were also laying down a fundamental challenge to the economic and social rights that were at that very time being enshrined in the draft UDHR. Hayek considered social justice to be a mirage and the term itself to be both 'nonsense' and 'empty and meaningless'.[16] He reserved particular scorn for the economic and social rights recognised in the UDHR, arguing that they were fundamentally incompatible with civil rights, were incapable of being meaningfully designed and would require a totalitarian system for their implementation.[17] Von Mises shared this contempt for so-called 'basic economic rights'.[18]

The purpose of this brief survey is to demonstrate the extent to which, at the time of drafting of the UDHR, even Western elite opinion was unable to agree on

---

[12] American Anthropological Association, 'Statement on Human Rights' (1947) 49 *American Anthropologist* 539.

[13] M Goodale, *Anthropology and Law: A Critical Introduction* (New York, New York University Press, 2017) 99.

[14] Carr (n 11) 726.

[15] 'Statement of Aims' (Mont Pelerin Society, 8 April 1947) www.montpelerin.org/event/429dba23-fc64-4838-aea3-b847011022a4/websitePage:6950c74b-5d9b-41cc-8da1-3e1991c14ac5.

[16] A Lister, 'The Mirage of "Social Justice": Hayek Against (and For) Rawls' (2013) 25 *Critical Review* 409, 410.

[17] FA von Hayek, 'Justice and Individual Rights: Appendix to Chapter Nine' in FA von Hayek, *Law, Legislation, and Liberty: A New Statement of the Liberal Principles of Justice and Political Economy*, revised edn (Abingdon, Routledge, 1982) 101–06.

[18] L von Mises, *Socialism: An Economic and Sociological Analysis* (Indianapolis, Yale University Press, 1951) 56–63.

any deep conception of the universality of human rights. This, in turn, set the scene for a continuing struggle between those who prefer to adopt a fairly rigid approach in order to protect the claim that the standards in the Declaration are universally applicable and those who accept the need for a degree of flexibility that recognises the complex realities within which the UDHR was constructed.

III. THE NEED FOR FLEXIBLE UNIVERSALITY

Some have always viewed an uncompromising or rigid approach as essential if fundamental standards are to be secured in the face of inevitable efforts to dilute, distort or undermine them, especially through self-serving interpretations advanced by governments. Flexibility, on the other hand, is important if the system is going to be acceptable to a heterogeneous group of states and peoples, if the norms are to be relevant in dramatically different situations and if the overall corpus is to adapt to changing circumstances and challenges.

Before proceeding, a brief note on terminology is warranted. The term 'flexibility' is used here in opposition to the concept of rigidity. It is not intended to suggest that our understanding of human rights should be infinitely adaptable, lacking a core or backbone, or susceptible to accommodating whatever content might be proposed for it. Many philosophers have sought to convey this sense of non-rigidity or non-simplicity by using terms other than flexibility. In his 1989 Tanner Lectures, Michael Walzer argued in favour of a non-standard version of universality which he suggested could encompass 'and perhaps even [help] to explain the appeal of moral particularism'.[19] He suggested that universalists and relativists had long argued against one another without pausing to see that both perspectives had something important to offer, and that they might not need to be viewed as incompatible polarities. Klaus Günther premised a somewhat different approach on his view that 'the idea of universal human rights ... has a long history of misreading, selective interpretation, and wrong application'.[20] This led him to contrast what he termed 'simple universalism', which was abstract, epistemic and essentialist, with 'complex universalism', which is procedural, deliberative and determinedly inclusive.[21]

The need for flexibility is reflected in various characteristics of the human rights regime that has emerged since 1948. Some of these are expressly provided for in the UDHR or the relevant treaties. Thus, reservations can be lodged by states, making specific provisions inapplicable in the state concerned; limitations upon rights are specifically provided for, often in the very formulation of the right; in exceptional circumstances, states may derogate from, or suspend the operation of, some rights; and the treaties can be amended. In addition, the overall system remains open to

---

[19] M Walzer, 'Nation and Universe' (The Tanner Lectures on Human Values, Brasenose College at Oxford University, 1 and 8 May 1989) 509.
[20] K Günther, 'The Legacies of Injustice and Fear: A European Approach to Human Rights and their Effects on Political Culture' in P Alston (ed), *The EU and Human Rights* (Oxford, Oxford University Press, 1999) 117.
[21] ibid 119–23.

formal revision. New treaties can be adopted and new rights can be added to the overall corpus, as demonstrated most recently by the recognition of a right to a clean, healthy and sustainable environment.[22] And, perhaps most significantly, the implementation provisions have evolved to recognise that treaties are 'living instruments' and that various mechanisms such as courts, treaty bodies and others can contribute to evolutive interpretations of the texts, thereby generating new jurisprudential understandings.[23]

But these flexibility mechanisms are not inevitably conducive to progressive outcomes, in the sense of always expanding the protection offered by human rights. Those who wish to prevent the evolution of the body of human rights law, freeze it at a particular historical moment or claim that it has gone too far in certain respects are equally able to turn to these mechanisms to vindicate their preferred approaches. The advent of the Cold War at around the same time that the UDHR was adopted led various actors to move to block off flexibility. This was true of both the Union of Soviet Socialist Republics and its allies and the USA and its supporters. It was from this particular historical and political context that three misconceptions of the human rights regime emerged, driven primarily by groups in the West, in an effort to limit the scope for flexibility and adaptation. They centred around claims that human rights were: (i) apolitical; (ii) characterised by normative certainty; and (iii) incontestably universal.

The first claim is that human rights are above or somehow apart from politics, and thus able to claim objectivity and neutrality in order to circumvent many of the heated challenges with which their proponents would otherwise have had to engage. As Michael Ignatieff put it, human rights were a sort of 'antipolitics' that could be used to counter or delegitimise ideological or sectarian justifications for violating rights.[24] This argument was reinforced by insisting that processes of interpretation and application can, and indeed must, be pursued through legal means that are separate and divorced from political considerations. Treating human rights as trumps, in the sense popularised by Ronald Dworkin, and then arguing that the policy prescriptions said to flow from them are not subject to negotiation was another way in which flexibility could be closed off.

Martti Koskenniemi has long criticised efforts to portray human rights as being independent 'from the political passions of the day' and present them as though they were 'ahistorical and universal'.[25] More recently, he characterised human rights as

---

[22] UN Human Rights Council, 'The Human Right to a Clean, Healthy and Sustainable Environment' (New York, adopted 8 October 2021) UN Doc A/HRC/RES/48/13; UNGA, 'The Human Right to a Clean, Healthy and Sustainable Environment' (adopted 28 July 2022) UN Doc A/RES/76/300. See 'Introduction to Symposium on UN Recognition of the Human Right to a Healthy Environment' (2023) 117 *American Journal of International Law Unbound* 162.

[23] D Moeckli and ND White, 'Treaties as "Living Instruments"' in D Kritsiotis and M Bowman (eds), *Conceptual and Contextual Perspectives on the Modern Law of Treaties* (Cambridge, Cambridge University Press, 2016) 136.

[24] M Ignatieff, *Human Rights as Politics and Idolatry* (based on the Tanner Lectures on Human Values, delivered at Princeton University's Center for Human Values on 4–7 April 2000) (Princeton, Princeton University Press, 2003) 292.

[25] M Koskenniemi, 'The Effect of Rights on Political Culture' in Alston, *The EU and Human Rights* (n 20) 99.

an 'attractively apolitical alternative' to political parties.[26] Amnesty International reflected this mindset in its first decades by framing its advocacy efforts around packages that included comparable cases from the West, the East (the Communist countries) and the Third World (the Global South) in order to demonstrate that it was taking an approach that transcended politics, or was at least politically neutral.

The second misconception of the human rights regime that has resisted the scope of flexible or adaptive approaches is what I term 'normative certainty'. It is the idea that human rights, or at least civil and political rights, must have the same content and meaning in every country of the world. This over-simplified conception can take various forms, but perhaps the most recognisable version is that promoted by Aryeh Neier, the lawyer and activist whose views largely shaped the approach promoted by Human Rights Watch from the late 1970s onwards and came to be shared by much of the activist community in the West. Neier approached human rights as though they had a hard and fast content which could be identified with some precision and which must be uncompromisingly defended against competing visions. Any concession that might take account of local circumstances or considerations would potentially open the door to chaos and abusive interpretations, thus undermining the essence of the norms. Neier professed himself to be 'a believer in very strong civil and political rights' and insisted that this strength depended on those rights meaning 'exactly the same thing every place in the world'. This, in turn, meant that 'compromise should not enter into the adjudication of civil and political rights'.[27]

The fact that this proposition, when applied by Western human rights advocates, concealed a clear double standard was apparently neither here nor there. The USA has long made clear that international human rights standards are not only judicially unenforceable, but could hardly even be mentioned in domestic courts without their relevance being harshly dismissed. Even in 1948, when Eleanor Roosevelt's central role in drafting the UDHR was being celebrated, a prominent Harvard professor dismissed demands for equal rights for African Americans and religious rights for Jehovah's Witnesses, writing that 'the people of the United States would not readily submit to the readjustment of the relations between saints or Negroes and the rest of our people' by the United Nations. He added that 'To impose any but an American version of freedom would be an even more hazardous undertaking'.[28] The UK was no better. There, as Brian Simpson explained in considerable detail, 'human rights were for foreigners, who did not enjoy them, not for the British, who enjoyed them anyway. They were for export.'[29] The upshot was that the sort of fundamentalism advocated by Neier and many others in the West was largely applicable in the Global South and the communist countries. Vernacularization was unacceptable if invoked in relation

---

[26] M Koskenniemi, 'Rocking the Human Rights Boat: Reflections by a Fellow Passenger' in N Bhuta, F Hoffmann, S Knuckey et al (eds), *The Struggle for Human Rights* (Oxford, Oxford University Press, 2021) 51, 56.

[27] A Neier, 'Social and Economic Rights: A Critique' (2006) 13 *Human Rights Brief* 1.

[28] AN Holcombe, *Human Rights in the Modern World* (New York, New York University Press, 1948) 122.

[29] AWB Simpson, *Human Rights and the End of Empire: Britain and the Genesis of the European Convention* (Oxford, Oxford University Press, 2004) 347.

to those countries, and it was not an issue in the West because there was no conversation to be had.

The third, and most all-encompassing, misconception is that there is one 'universal' version of human rights which must be determinedly defended against those who would adapt or adjust their interpretation to take account of local considerations of a cultural or other kind. As expressed by Ignatieff, 'human rights activists take it for granted that they represent universal values and universal interests'.[30] And while there is an indispensable universal dimension to human rights, this does not mean that every right must be applied in exactly the same way in every community around the world. In the regime's normative aspirations and its goal of engaging all states, such nuance is not always reflected.

These three misconceptions proved to be powerful, especially in the 1970s and 1980s, when the human rights regime was beginning to matter in global and domestic politics. When combined with the distortions fostered by the Cold War, the preoccupation of many post-colonial states with issues other than the interpretation of human rights and the dominant influence of organisations such as Amnesty International, with its narrow focus on political prisoners, torture and the death penalty, very little space remained in which to engage in the challenging task of cultural adaptation. In fact, the very concept was anathema to many of the most influential actors in the West, who saw it as being politically inspired and ungrounded in genuine demands. This is not the place to review, for example, the animated struggles that surrounded the debates over 'Asian values' as promoted by Singapore, China and others in the early 1990s.[31] However, the compromise resolution that emerged from the 1993 Vienna World Conference was at best an unsatisfactory holding position that failed to generate a particularly subtle or convincing understanding of the role played by cultural considerations in the implementation of international human rights standards.[32]

IV. THE ANTHROPOLOGY/LAW DISCONNECT

As the cultural relativism debate played out from the 1980s onwards, there emerged an ever-larger disconnect between the assumptions shared by many anthropologists, and other social scientists, and those that continued to dominate in the legal sphere. In a recent book, Julie Fraser conducts an extensive survey of relevant literature before concluding that 'scholars and practitioners have called for more culturally sensitive approaches to human rights, greater respect for cultural diversity and protection of cultural rights. Such calls advocate cultural sensitivity in the conceptualisation,

---

[30] Ignatieff (n 24) 292.

[31] K Engle, 'Culture and Human Rights: The Asian Values Debate in Context' (1999) 32 *New York University Journal of International Law and Politics* 291.

[32] Vienna Declaration and Programme of Action (adopted on 25 June 1993 at the World Conference on Human Rights in Vienna) para 5: 'All human rights are universal, indivisible and interdependent and interrelated ... While the significance of national and regional particularities and various historical, cultural and religious backgrounds must be borne in mind, it is the duty of States, regardless of their political, economic and cultural systems, to promote and protect all human rights and fundamental freedoms.'

interpretation, implementation and adjudication of rights'.[33] But there has been a surprising division between this growing body of scholarly consensus among anthropologists and other social scientists and the continuing domination of international advocacy and interpretive communities by lawyers and legalism. While the former emphasise the importance of considerations like social mobilisation, decolonising approaches, community-based interpretations and grassroots advocacy, the leading international advocacy groups continue to focus heavily on courts and judicial interpretations, on state-based institutions and on formal structures and frameworks. This legalistic approach takes little account of the anthropological insights that have emerged so consistently in recent decades.

Similarly, while United Nations treaty bodies now refer much more frequently to cultural considerations and even to the right to culture, such allusions rarely stray far beyond calls for greater sensitivity and awareness. To take but one example, the UN Committee on Economic, Social and Cultural Rights has, for well over two decades, insisted that rights to (for example) education and food need to be implemented in ways that are culturally appropriate and acceptable, and has belatedly adopted a General Comment on the right to culture. But it has done little to encourage states to promote economic and social rights through community-based endeavours, and rarely focuses on any other than formal institutional arrangements in its analyses of state reporting or avenues for rights promotion. This oversight risks undermining the effective implementation of these rights, especially in cultural contexts in which their formal legal incarnation might be relatively alien.[34]

Similarly, an analysis of the broad thrust of the UN Human Rights Council's work reveals an overwhelming preoccupation with formal legal and other institutions and actors, with little attention given to local, informal, grassroots or community initiatives.[35] Indeed, despite the intensity of the arguments about cultural values that surrounded the Vienna World Conference, the message taken away from the debates, even by some of the most enlightened participants, was that culturally based arguments for nuanced or calibrated approaches to the legal interpretation and application of international norms were simply not compelling. For example, Rosalyn Higgins, a highly influential member of the UN Human Rights Committee who went on to become President of the International Court of Justice, made a strong effort in the 1990s to get to grips with the challenges to universality. Her subsequent analysis warrants extensive quotation:

> It is sometimes suggested that there can be no fully universal concept of human rights, for it is necessary to take into account the diverse cultures and political systems of the world. In my view this is a point advanced mostly by states, and by liberal scholars anxious not to impose the Western view of things on others. It is rarely advanced by the oppressed, who are only too anxious to benefit from perceived universal standards. The non-universal,

---

[33] J Fraser, *Social Institutions and International Human Rights Law Implementation: Every Organ of Society* (Cambridge, Cambridge University Press, 2020) 41.
[34] P Alston, 'The UN Committee on Economic, Social and Cultural Rights' in F Mégret and P Alston (eds), *The United Nations and Human Rights: A Critical Appraisal*, 2nd edn (Oxford, Oxford University Press, 2020) 439.
[35] R Freedman, 'The Human Rights Council' in Mégret and Alston (n 34) 181.

relativist view of human rights is in fact a very state-centred view and loses sight of the fact that human rights are human rights and not dependent on the fact that states, or groupings of states, may behave differently from each other so far as their politics, economic policy, and culture are concerned. I believe, profoundly, in the universality of the human spirit. Individuals everywhere want the same essential things: to have sufficient food and shelter; to be able to speak freely; to practise their own religion or to abstain from religious belief; to feel that their person is not threatened by the state; to know that they will not be tortured, or detained without charge, and that, if charged, they will have a fair trial. I believe there is nothing in these aspirations that is dependent upon culture, or religion, or stage of development. They are as keenly felt by the African tribesman as by the European city-dweller, by the inhabitant of a Latin American shanty-town as by the resident of a Manhattan apartment.[36]

Even a decade later, Louise Arbour, speaking in her capacity as United Nations High Commissioner for Human Rights, expressed concern at the extent to which 'we have unduly embroiled our normative discourse in unnecessary clashes of vision', one of which was the question 'Are human rights universal or culturally specific?' She concluded that

[s]uch questions serve, in practice, as little more than a series of diversions to the real task in hand. They become the theoretical playground within which we demonstrate our irrelevance and justify our inaction, whether that inaction is borne of indifference, shrewd calculation, or despair.[37]

These reactions are entirely understandable when viewed as expressions of frustration at what were, and still are, seen as politically motivated manipulations of culture-based arguments by governments seeking to discourage scrutiny and avoid accountability. In this mould, leading figures in contemporary international human rights courts and institutions remain sceptical of the need for deep engagement with different cultural traditions in order to shape a human rights-based message that resonates with local understandings and makes sense in local languages.

V. EXPLAINING RESISTANCE

Various factors help to explain why these three misconceptions exercised such an important sway over the evolution of the regime. The most important is the 'slippery slope' argument: ie, if space were opened up for interpretative processes that accommodate or even invite local cultural considerations to be taken into account, there would be no way to resist interpretations that – while advanced on the basis that they make the relevant norms more sensitive to, or better aligned with, local culture – are fundamentally incompatible or inconsistent with established international norms. Purists fear that conceding room for interpretative flexibility would open a Pandora's

---

[36] R Higgins, *Problems and Process: International Law and How We Use It* (Oxford, Oxford University Press, 1994) 96.
[37] Louise Arbour (UN High Commissioner for Human Rights), 'Remarks on the Opening of the 61st Session of the Commission on Human Rights' (Geneva, 14 March 2005).

Box, inevitably destroying legitimate aspirations to protect an essential normative core of the relevant rights.

A principal thrust of the present volume of essays – to which many of the contributors are anthropologists, and which is dedicated to the work of one of the world's most respected and influential legal anthropologists, Sally Engle Merry – is that these fictions close off the space that is required for the international human rights regime to accommodate and reflect the true complexity of the task in which it is engaged. Processes of translation and interpretation are not only unavoidable but also indispensable if human rights are to fulfil their mission of mobilising and empowering groups and individuals who live in widely different cultural contexts. Merry's understanding reflected the results of ethnographic research that she and many others had undertaken and that showed the ways in which human rights are already 'widely appropriated, adopted, and redefined to fit particular social issues and struggles'.[33]

It was always going to be necessary to 'translate' the norms proclaimed in the UDHR. However, in addition to fears of a slippery slope, there were various other reasons why some principal actors in the international regime were reluctant to recognise that need explicitly. Because the multifaceted translation process was inevitably complicated, fraught and messy, many opted instead to downplay or ignore these complexities. Sometimes this was done not because of a lack of awareness of the minefields that exist, but because of the fear that such complexification might undermine or jeopardise the overall enterprise. Instead, the default option was to pursue an approach characterised by simplicity, or what others might have considered dogmatism, as the best way to 'sell' the approach being advocated. Diplomats and other government representatives drafting statements of rights or negotiating political positions understandably opted to prioritise consensus rather than seeking to expose troublesome lacunae or acknowledge significant disagreements. This papering over of important differences can also make sense for advocates who do not wish to be diverted into theoretical or doctrinal debates, which they fear might derail their advocacy. And at least in the early decades after World War II, scholars working in this field often seemed more intent on building and shoring up the edifice of human rights law than on exploring or exposing its vulnerabilities or weaknesses.[39]

This failure to probe the foundations of the human rights regime was not confined to its relationship to culture. There was, for many years, a reluctance to explore in any sophisticated way the philosophical foundations of human rights or to draw conclusions from the complex picture that emerged.[40] Similarly, the economics of human rights law was a subject quickly swept off the table by Western proponents of the legal regime. When this issue was raised by countries of the Global South in the context of demands for a New International Economic Order, or a right to development, resistance was strong and remarkably effective.

One of the consequences of settling for a monochrome image of human rights was a simplistic understanding of how change was to come about. Most human rights

---

[38] Merry, 'The State of Human Rights Consciousness' (n 1) 63.
[39] L Henkin, *The Age of Rights* (New York, Columbia University Press, 1990).
[40] CR Beitz, *The Idea of Human Rights* (Oxford, Oxford University Press, 2009).

proponents seemed to assume that the consolidation of legal norms at both the international and domestic levels would provide the necessary foundations upon which respect for human rights could be built in all societies. The construction of regional and international coalitions, reinforced by political and economic pressures, would gradually spread support for human rights – at least in the form of democracy and a substantive, rights-based notion of the rule of law. Regional courts would also come to play a key role in the overall enterprise. Similarly, at the domestic level, the adoption of national constitutional and legislative norms would set the scene for judges and lawyers to build the necessary infrastructure for implementation.

But this theory of change was conveniently divorced from messy questions relating to the indispensable role of social movements, the importance of political mobilisation, the influence of religion and the significance of local cultural values. While anthropologists would inevitably foreground such complex issues, lawyers and others who tended to dominate the early human rights movement preferred to downplay their importance and concentrate instead upon the legal framework.

Even today, many mainstream actors within the international human rights regime tend to avoid certain forms of complexity when they can. Examples include debates over the philosophical coherence and foundations of human rights; the extent to which governmental obligations, especially in relation to civil and political rights, are effected by resource availability; whether rights should be seen as trumps that automatically exclude consideration of other factors; the nature of the claim to universality that is inherent in the overall project; the response to relativist arguments, whether based on moral, cultural or other considerations; and the nature of the relationship between the two sets of rights – civil and political rights on the one hand and economic, social and cultural rights on the other. There are, of course, understandable reasons why advocates might opt for a simpler and more straightforward approach. For example, the philosophical debate might reasonably be viewed as unwinnable, leading to the conclusion that it will suffice to assert that human dignity is as good a foundation as any. Or the debate over the relationship between resources and rights might be dodged on the basis that it is so complicated that it is important to avoid getting into the weeds. But avoidance does not make the challenges or concerns disappear.

The explosion in recent years of critical, deconstructionist, feminist, post-colonial and other critiques of human rights, as well as more determined and engaged pushback from certain governments and conservative activists, has forced the mainstream to confront these complexities in a more open and systematic way. It is, however, somewhat ironic that the same tendency to over-simplify issues, or to downplay their complexity, also afflicts many of the critiques to which the human rights regime has been subjected in recent years. Some of the major ideational battles have been fought with sweeping arguments that minimise or ignore the nuances and subtleties that should characterise such debates. The result is impressive if judged by the extent of the scholarly fireworks that have been ignited and the number of citations chalked up by the leading contenders. But this volume seeks to take the debate in a different direction: to promote the recognition of complexity, in order to deepen and strengthen the understanding of human rights in all of its multifarious dimensions.

VI. VERNACULARIZATION AND DEBATES OVER LEGAL TRANSLATION AND INTERPRETATION

Understandings of the role played by interpretation have changed significantly as a result of new approaches to language which are embodied in different strands of twentieth-century philosophy. At the same time, anthropologists and other social scientists have attached even greater significance to the contexts in which interpretation takes place, as well as to the role played by the translators themselves. Growing use of the concept of vernacularization was one part of these trends.

International lawyers and human rights advocates were slower to take notice of these theoretical advances in linguistics, although this is now beginning to change. In earlier decades, major challenges relating to interpretation had been highlighted but little was done to absorb the resulting lessons. One such early example was the way in which General Macarthur and his lawyers transposed provisions from the American Bill of Rights into a new Japanese Constitution in 1946, which the Japanese authorities were prevailed upon to accept with minimal adaptation or debate.[41] As one study has noted, this outcome was possible because of the 'ambiguities of cross-linguistic and cross-cultural communication' that were involved. In other words, the democratic principles that were being embraced were actually understood very differently by the two sides.[42] In retrospect, it became apparent that the very different expectations generated served to make the draft acceptable, and explained its subsequent longevity.

In the example of the Japanese Constitution, the same text was construed in different ways, depending on the cultural and linguistic traditions of the interpreter. But documents may also be substantively revised and altered under the guise of translation into different languages. A significant example of this phenomenon, particularly for human rights proponents, arises in relation to Chinese-language versions of the International Covenants on Civil and Political Rights (ICCPR) and Economic, Social and Cultural Rights (ICESCR). As adopted in 1966, both the ICCPR and the ICESCR set out the law in five languages (including Chinese); each of these languages is equally binding and authentic. However, the Chinese-language versions of both covenants that are currently widely available (including on official UN websites) are not the original, authoritative texts. Instead, as described by James D Seymour and Patrick Yuk-tung Wong in 2015, these are 'ersatz *revisions* of the original covenants' that 'mysteriously appeared in 1973'.[43] These scholars observe that, although some revisions are merely stylistic, many are substantive, and some even reverse the position set out in the original covenants.[44] They do not suggest that these differences

---

[41] P Alston, 'Transplanting Foreign Norms: Human Rights and Other International Legal Norms in Japan' (1999) 10 *European Journal of International Law* 625.

[42] K Inoue, *MacArthur's Japanese Constitution: A Linguistic and Cultural Study of its Making* (Chicago, University of Chicago Press, 1991) 269.

[43] JD Seymour and PY Wong, 'China and the International Human Rights Covenants' (2015) 47 *Critical Asian Studies* 514, 515–16.

[44] eg by providing that the recognition of certain rights is within the discretion of the state, or by converting 'mandatory language regarding governmental responsibility into mere recommendations or vague suggestion'. Of particular concern, the revised covenants deny civil, political and economic rights that might otherwise accrue to ethnic groups. ibid 522–24.

arose through a conspiracy to subvert the principles of the covenants.[45] However, China is responsible for continuing to treat as authentic revised documents that do not, in fact, reflect the covenants.

> Of course, Beijing still has every right to object to any provisions of the Covenants it wants to. In signing or ratifying them, it could do so with reservations, or it could try to go through proper procedures to have the wording of the Covenants 'corrected' and perhaps brought in line with current thinking in Beijing. With one non-substantive exception, China has never made any attempt to officially change the wording of the actual Covenants, but Beijing has quietly attempted to withdraw rights that the covenants granted. Has it succeeded? … [I]f people know anything about the Covenants, they know only the revised drafts. More disturbing is the way that the revisions have slid through beneath the radar internationally. Beijing has been surprisingly successful in getting the drafts it prefers tolerated by the international community.[46]

It is arguable that any simplistic arguments regarding the universality of human rights are dealt a further blow when China, which comprises almost one-fifth of the world's population, regards as authoritative texts that diverge in important respects from the foundational human rights treaties relied on by the rest of the world.

In recent years, there has been a much greater awareness of the extent to which international law in general, and human rights in particular, are affected by the vagaries and uncertainties surrounding legal translation and interpretation.[47] Not so long ago, international lawyers confronted by challenges in this regard would have been content to resort for their answers to formal procedural rules. Thus, an argument that different meanings were conveyed in different language versions of the same text would have been met by noting the rule that the different language versions of human rights treaties are equally authentic. Or, when complex questions of interpretation were raised, the response was to resort to the rules laid out in the Vienna Convention on the Law of Treaties.

Today, there is a deeper understanding of the complexities involved in interpretation, and of the roles played by many different actors. But the question that arises in the present context is: where does Merry's understanding of vernacularization fit within this broader awareness? One potential answer is that the process of translation and vernacularization described by Merry may give rise to multiple legitimate cultural variations in human rights norms. Julie Fraser argues that bringing abstract international human rights norms down to earth and making them meaningful to diverse communities around the world[48] may involve a process of refining those norms so that they are sufficiently appropriate and sensitive to a given culture. Culturally sensitive approaches 'rely on the legitimacy enjoyed by local norms and actors to promote

---

[45] They conclude that 'originally this was a simply a clumsy but guiltless process that took place at the United Nations Secretariat with little or no direction from Beijing'. ibid 528.

[46] ibid 526–27.

[47] See, eg AL Kjaer and J Lam, 'Introduction: The Dynamics of Law and Language in the Interpretation of International Legal Sources' in AL Kjaer and J Lam, *Language and Legal Interpretation in International Law* (Oxford, Oxford University Press, 2022).

[48] J Fraser, 'Challenging State-centricity and Legalism: Promoting the Role of Social Institutions in the Domestic Implementation of International Human Rights Law' (2019) 23 *International Journal of Human Rights* 974, 978.

human rights as consistent with their community's values'.⁴⁹ Fraser contends that this approach is likely to make human rights more effective, relevant and palatable, stating that 'As a matter of pragmatism as well as principle, human rights should not be smuggled into a cultural community like a Trojan Horse, but rather embedded in that community's norms and values'.⁵⁰

However, if we accept that human rights norms can take different forms depending on the culture in which they are embedded, when does human rights advocacy cease to be human rights-based? How far can an argument stray from the language or terminology of treaty rights and still be a human rights argument? When should religious, environmental or labour groups be considered to be part of the international human rights movement, broadly defined? There are, of course, no easy answers. But perhaps the most convincing response is that not a lot of time should be devoted to the question. It will sooner or later become apparent if the arguments invoked are intended to address human rights concerns and to what extent their legitimacy in that regard is important to them. At that stage, various assumptions, expectations and limits will kick in to influence the outcome.

VII. COMPLEXITY AND QUANTIFICATION

At first glance, quantification seems to lend itself to minimising the kinds of translation problems outlined above. Numbers appear universal, objective, technical, stateless and apolitical, and therefore well suited for communicating ideas on a global scale,⁵¹ with minimal need for interpretation or cultural variation. 'Complex social phenomena become legible by means of quantification, extrapolation, and simplification.'⁵²

Whether these characteristics justify a positive or negative view of quantification depends on multiple factors, including the accuracy and credibility of the data that is collected; the processes of collection and of selection of data categories; and the complexity of the underlying issues and their susceptibility to being expressed numerically. Some human rights violations lend themselves to reasonably accurate measuring or counting, based on statistics that are reliably maintained by governmental, intergovernmental or independent agencies. But in a great many of the most prominent areas of international discourse, the challenge of obtaining accurate data or even meaningful estimates of prevalence can be enormous. Consider issues such as the extent to which torture is used, the incidence of violence against women, the number of child soldiers, the number of 'illegal immigrants' and so on.

Despite these difficulties, human rights groups are under increasing pressure to be able to demonstrate results and to present 'statistics' that will attract media attention and mobilise public opinion. They are thus driven to compete both for influence and

---

⁴⁹ ibid 979.
⁵⁰ ibid 980.
⁵¹ See SP De Souza, *Designing Indicators for a Plural Legal World* (Cambridge, Cambridge University Press, 2022) 6.
⁵² A Broome and J Quirk, 'Governing the World at a Distance: The Practice of Global Benchmarking' (2015) 41 *Review of International Studies* 819, 821.

funding by quantifying the size of the problems that they are tackling and helping to 'resolve'. The emergence of 'philanthrocapitalism' has further increased the pressure and exacerbated the problem. By placing extensive reliance on a combination of metrics and results-oriented management approaches, wealthy philanthropists have helped to redefine problems and pioneer responses that are often based on highly creative interpretations of the relevant international legal standards and on problematic methods of calculating the prevalence of the abuses that are being tackled.

Data, including data about the prevalence of violations, the identity of violators and the violated, and the responses of those in power, may be a vital resource for human rights proponents. However, data may also be used to de-complexify the discourse around human rights, concealing points of contestation and nuance. Quantification may even undermine arguments about the prevalence of human rights abuses if the data is inconsistent, unreliable or unconvincing. The ambiguity of quantification was illustrated clearly to me in 2016 when, in my capacity as United Nations Special Rapporteur on extreme poverty and human rights, I undertook an official visit to Mauritania, a country with a long history of slavery. The practice was not abolished until 1981, and it was over a quarter of a century more – 2007 – before it was criminalised. The 2007 legislation was subsequently expanded and updated the year before my visit. But the problem was that the government was doing all too little to enforce the law. As I found from interviews (and as confirmed by other analyses), the authorities failed to take action when alleged instances of continuing enslavement were brought to their notice; the prosecutors failed to pursue with any vigour cases that were actually put before them; and the courts did all they could to downplay the issue by avoiding the conviction of slave-owners and issuing inadequate penalties for those few who were convicted.[53]

The intransigence that characterised the overall response was facilitated above all by the relatively concealed nature of the practice. Almost no victims were held in chains;[54] rather, they were enslaved in more subtle ways that left them with no viable alternative but to remain in a clearly abusive relationship. The problem was then compounded by a determination on the part of the government not to collect meaningful data. As a result, it was particularly challenging to estimate the exact number of 'slaves' in Mauritania, which, in turn, was a prerequisite to drawing sustained international attention. This is where an initiative funded by an Australian mining magnate, Andrew Forrest, came into the picture. His Walk Free Foundation produces a Global Slavery Index (GSI),[55] which estimates the number of victims of modern slavery in different countries and globally.

In 2014, the GSI reported that 155,600 Mauritanians, or four per cent of the population, lived in a situation of slavery. The estimate was based on pre-existing surveys

---

[53] P Alston, 'Report of the Special Rapporteur on Extreme Poverty and Human Rights on His Mission to Mauritania' (8 March 2017) UN Doc A/HRC/35/26/Add.1, para 34; Anti-Slavery International, 'Mauritania: Descent-Based Slavery', www.antislavery.org/what-we-do/mauritania/.

[54] I would argue that the term 'modern slavery' itself is an artificial creation that builds upon traditional definitions of slavery, updated to include new categories of abuses that can be defined more or less flexibly to suit the needs and purposes of the sponsoring organisation or government.

[55] Also referred to by S Martínez, 'Beyond the Vanishing Point: Quantification as Rhetoric in Today's Antislavery', ch 8 in this volume.

and unidentified secondary sources. Following various challenges to this data, the 2016 GSI lowered the number dramatically to 43,000, or 1.06 per cent of the population. The new figure was attributed to a change in methodology, which involved 1000 random-sample telephone or face-to-face surveys. The 2018 GSI reports that there were 90,000 victims of modern slavery in Mauritania, representing 2.1 per cent of the population,[56] and again invokes a change of methodology to explain the doubling of numbers in a two-year period.[57] The most recent GSI, published in 2023, again edges closer to the 2014 number in its estimate (149,000 people, or 3.2 per cent of the population).[58] Its methodology does not indicate any reason for the considerable increase in the number of people living in slavery since 2018.

While the government flatly denied the existence of any slaves in 2015, and strongly rebuffed requests by other UN special procedures mandate-holders to visit the country, the unrealistic, inadequately explained and apparently greatly exaggerated estimates put forward in the GSI made it easier for the government to dismiss all claims as to the continuing existence of slavery and to focus attention instead on their preferred subject of the 'vestiges of slavery'. This ploy was highly successful in the country's 2021 engagement with the UN Human Rights Council's Universal Periodic Review (UPR), in which a great many countries either congratulated it on its record or said nothing about slavery.[59]

The only credible estimates that were available to me and on which I could rely to at least some extent were those produced by researchers who had long studied the country and spent extensive periods of time interviewing alleged victims and others to assess prevalence. Their prudent conclusion was that 'thousands of people still remain enslaved',[60] which was a far cry from the wildly fluctuating estimates produced by the GSI. All I could say in my report was that reporting such as that undertaken by the GSI 'does little to establish credibility and can actually undermine international monitoring efforts'.[61]

The resulting confusion is well illustrated by a joint submission on the situation in Mauritania to the UPR in 2021 by three highly respected advocacy groups, the Minority Rights Group, Anti-Slavery International and the Mauritania-based SOS-Esclaves. They reported that 'Many Haratines [the population of slave descent] are still held in slavery today', and added that individuals who 'live under the direct control of their owners suffer various forms of exploitation, violence, are treated as objects of property, and do not receive remuneration for work'.[62] The statement reflects the reluctance of the groups to go down the quantification rabbit hole and risk losing credibility.

---

[56] Walk Free Foundation, *The Global Slavery Index 2018* (19 July 2018) 69.
[57] ibid 174.
[58] Walk Free Foundation, *The Global Slavery Index 2023* (19 June 2023) 78.
[59] Human Rights Council, 'Report of the Working Group on the Universal Periodic Review: Mauritania' (9 April 2021) UN Doc A/HRC/47/6.
[60] Anti-Slavery International, 'Mauritania: Descent-Based Slavery' (n 53).
[61] Alston, 'Report on Mauritania' (n 53) para 33.
[62] Minority Rights Group, SOS-Esclaves and Anti-Slavery International, 'UPR of Mauritania – 37th session – January 2021, Fact Sheet on the Situation of Slavery in Mauritania' (July 2020) https://minorityrights.org/wp-content/uploads/2020/07/UPR37_Mauritania_Slavery_MRG_SOS-Esclaves_ASI.pdf.

The problems inherent in attempts to quantify the scale of slavery went much deeper than I could explain in a necessarily short report to the UN Human Rights Council. Chuang has warned that one of the risks of relying on the large-scale quantification approach championed by leading philanthropists who are funding activities in this field is that the main focus is on a victim–saviour narrative that portrays the victims as needing to be rescued and the perpetrators punished. By characterising the problem in this way and highlighting the alleged deviant behaviour of individual actors, the deeper structural causes underlying much of the human trafficking, such as widely tolerated forms of labour exploitation and gross inequality in wealth distribution, are ignored.[63]

Merry gave an eloquent account of the approach required to ensure that quantification does not lead to unduly de-complexified or distorted results:

> Numerical knowledge is essential, yet if it is not closely connected to more qualitative forms of knowledge, it leads to oversimplification, homogenization, and the neglect of the surrounding social structure. Grounding quantitative knowledge in qualitative analysis of categories, meanings, and practices produces better indicators. The current rush to quantification risks sacrificing the insights of rich ethnographic accounts.[64]

Although maintaining a tie to qualitative forms of knowledge may sacrifice the ease and simplicity of purely numerical methods of communicating information, it is more likely to retain a higher level of nuance and accuracy. However, this task becomes ever more complicated when moving from matters of simple quantification to composite indicators made up of multiple categories of data.

VIII. FROM QUANTIFICATION TO INDICATORS

In September 2022, the *US News & World Report* downgraded Columbia University from number 2 to number 18 in its annual ranking of colleges in the USA. The demotion came after one of the university's mathematics professors, Michael Thaddeus, accused the institution of submitting inaccurate or misleading data in support of its rankings.[65] However, it appears that his aim in disclosing such information was to challenge the practice of ranking higher education institutions, rather than simply to alter Columbia's position in the pack. Thaddeus was subsequently quoted in *The Guardian* as saying

> I've long believed that all university rankings are essentially worthless. They're based on data that have very little to do with the academic merit of an institution and that the data might not be accurate in the first place … It was never my objective to knock Columbia

---

[63] J Chuang, 'Giving as Governance: Philanthrocapitalism and Modern-Day Slavery Abolitionism' (2015) 62 *UCLA Law Review* 1516; see also A Gallagher, 'What's Wrong with the Global Slavery Index?' (2017) 8 *Anti-Trafficking Review* 90.

[64] SE Merry, *The Seductions of Quantification: Measuring Human Rights, Gender Violence, and Sex Trafficking* (Chicago, University of Chicago Press, 2016) 1–2.

[65] M Thaddeus, 'An Investigation of the Facts behind Columbia's US News Ranking' (Columbia University Department of Mathematics, March 2022) www.math.columbia.edu/~thaddeus/ranking/investigation.html.

down the rankings. A better outcome would be if the rankings themselves are knocked down and people just stop reading them, stop taking them as seriously as they have.[66]

Numerous criticisms of the *US News & World Report* have been advanced, including that the rankings rely heavily on self-reported data, which can be manipulated; that rankings exaggerate the differences between colleges and encourage a fixation on status and prestige; and that higher education institutions are too complex to be reduced to a single number.[67] But the *US News & World Report* is far from the only university ranking system. Arguably, even more pervasive concerns exist in relation to global indices that compare universities from around the world. These indicators may be used to privilege certain regions, languages and cultures over others, usually to the detriment of those in the Global South.

Marion Lloyd and Imanol Ordorika observe that rankings serve to further the hegemony of a US-based model of higher education. In effect, they are 'Harvardometers', measuring how closely institutions adhere to the paradigm of an elite, private, Anglo-Saxon research university.[68] In so doing, other national or regional education traditions are ignored and undermined,[69] a market-oriented logic is promoted that views higher education as the subject of competition for funding and students, and countries invest billions of dollars to remodel their higher education systems to better fit the mould.[70] In turn, American institutions reap economic benefits from this cultural imperialism, attracting high-paying foreign students.[71]

Many of the arguments at issue in broader debates around the strengths and weaknesses of composite indicators are on display in these discussions around the ranking of higher education institutions. What are the qualities, characteristics or issues about which data will be collected? How will data be supplied? What will be the impact on those who choose (or are chosen) to be included in the ranking system? Who designs the indicators, and who stands to lose or gain from their creation and promotion?

Innumerable aspects of contemporary life, including business, rule of law, transparency, governance and human rights, have been made the subject of indicators that seek to rank performance between institutions, countries or other actors. What exactly is an indicator? Kevin Davis, Angelina Fisher, Benedict Kingsbury and Sally

---

[66] C McGreal, 'Columbia Whistleblower on Exposing College Rankings, "They are Worthless"' *The Guardian* (London, 16 September 2022) www.theguardian.com/us-news/2022/sep/16/columbia-whistleblower-us-news-rankings-michael-thaddeus.
[67] See, eg A Hartocollis, 'US News Dropped Columbia's Ranking, but Its Own Methods Are Now Questioned' *New York Times* (New York, 12 September 2022) www.nytimes.com/2022/09/12/us/columbia-university-us-news-ranking.html.
[68] M Lloyd and L Ordorika, 'International University Rankings as Cultural Imperialism: Implications for the Global South' in M Stack (ed), *Global University Rankings and the Politics of Knowledge* (Toronto, University of Toronto Press, 2021) 26.
[69] Such as the tradition of 'state-building universities' in Latin America, where emphasis is placed on values of autonomy, democracy, academic freedom and political responsibility for nation-building and defence of democracy: ibid 27.
[70] ibid.
[71] ibid 33.

Engle Merry observed in 2012 that there is no agreed meaning of 'indicator', but suggested the following:

> An indicator is a named collection of rank-ordered data that purports to represent the past or projected performance of different units. The data are generated through a process that simplifies raw data about a complex social phenomenon. The data, in this simplified and processed form, are capable of being used to compare particular units of analysis (such as countries or institutions or corporations), synchronically or over time, and to evaluate their performance by reference to one or more standards.[72]

Indicators may involve simple quantification ('counts' of data, such as a census) or ratios which compare two numbers against each other; or they may be composite indicators, which combine multiple sources and types of data into a single score. As Merry put it, the latter are 'the most widely known, persuasive and referenced kind of indicator'.[73] The *US News & World Report* and other college rankings are composite indicators. The kind of numerical data described in the preceding section may be used to compile such indicators, and such indicators may also be expressed in numbers by way of a rank or a numerical score. The creation of an indicator represents a kind of 'translation', by which different concepts and data points are combined and converted into a single standard. A potential cacophony of conflicting interpretations may be rendered manageable when an authoritative indicator is interposed to categorise, rank and compare information. Along with Davis, Fisher and Kinsbury, Merry outlined salient characteristics of indicators, including that (i) they can be used for evaluative purposes; (ii) they may simplify complex social phenomena; and (iii) they enable comparison, ranking and exerting pressure for 'improvement' (in accordance with metrics measured by the indicator).[74]

Sally Engle Merry's interest in indicators did not centre around the kinds of inaccurate or incomplete data highlighted by Mark Thaddeus in relation to Columbia's college ranking submissions, but rather focused on the 'social and political processes of indicator production and their effects on regulation and governance'.[75] In particular, she took the view that 'The production of indicators is itself a political process, shaped by the power to categorize, count, analyze, and promote a system of knowledge that has effects beyond the producers. In these respects indicators are comparable to law'.[76] To take the example of university rankings, the producers of the various indicators must decide what categories of information are relevant to determining university quality, what weight each factor should be given, what data should be included or excluded in support, and how that data should be collected and labelled. In so doing, they shape and reinforce a particular worldview about, for example, what activity is valuable (for example, publication in English-language journals)[77] and what is not. As Merry observed, 'In the end, those who create indicators

---

[72] KE Davis, A Fisher, B Kingsbury et al (eds), *Governance by Indicators: Global Power through Quantification and Rankings* (Oxford, Oxford University Press, 2012) 6.
[73] Merry, *The Seductions of Quantification* (n 64) 14–15.
[74] Davis et al (n 72) 7.
[75] Merry, *The Seductions of Quantification* (n 64) 4.
[76] SE Merry, KE Davis and B Kingsbury (eds), *The Quiet Power of Indicators: Measuring Governance, Corruption, and Rule of Law* (Cambridge, Cambridge University Press, 2015) 2.
[77] Lloyd and Ordorika (n 68) 28.

aspire to measure the world but, in practice, create the world they are measuring ... The technical is always political because there is always interpretation and judgment in systems of classification'.[78]

The indicator that is produced may disclose little or no information about how the judgements involved in its formation were made, or by whom. In this way, the process of development is akin to a 'black box'.[79] The indicator appears to be a mere technical product, the inevitable outcome of an objective and scientific review of the relevant evidence. Although this is far from the reality, this perception of indicators as impartial and authoritative is, of course, one of their great attractions, and a source of their power. Siddharth Peter de Souza contends that simplification and masking contestation 'provides the first lens to building "trust" through indicators because they allow for objects or phenomena to be studied devoid of the complexity around them'.[80] Although this approach may increase faith in indicators, such 'de-complexification' also risks marginalising legitimate debate and excluding important perspectives, particularly from less powerful actors.

This is particularly hazardous in light of the disciplinary function exerted by indicators. The more authoritative an indicator becomes, the more probable it is that states, institutions or other actors will change their behaviour in the hope of improving or maintaining their ranking. In this way, diverse voices may be excluded not only from the process of indicator production, but also, increasingly, from the world that is being shaped by the indicators. This phenomenon can be observed in relation to international or global legal indicator frameworks, such as the World Justice Project Rule of Law Index and the World Bank Worldwide Governance Indicators. All too often, these benchmarking exercises, used to generate pressure on governments to change their policies, reduce the complex problems involved in concepts such as democracy, freedom and the rule of law to a composite indicator which, despite the degree of contestation that surrounds the basic notion, makes the relevant concept appear instead as 'fixed, unproblematic, and reified categories'.[81]

While a great many examples could be cited, no set of statistical indicators has captured more global attention than the UN's Sustainable Development Goals (SDGs), adopted in 2015 and used to assess and evaluate progress in relation to the key components of 'development'. When the SDGs' predecessors, the Millennium Development Goals (MDGs), were introduced at the turn of the century, they were much lauded precisely because they were determinedly 'measurable'.[82] In a careful analysis of the impact of that approach, Fukuda-Parr and Yamin identified resulting distortions in terms of both policy priorities and norms. 'The translation of norms from words to numbers involved simplification, reification and abstraction of social conditions that are complex, intangible and location specific'.[83] In particular, the approach reflected

---

[78] Merry, *The Seductions of Quantification* (n 64) 21.
[79] De Souza (n 51) 45.
[80] ibid 37–38.
[81] Broome and Quirk (n 52) 821.
[82] S Fukuda-Parr and AE Yamin, *The MDGs, Capabilities and Human Rights: The Power of Numbers to Set Agendas* (New York, Routledge, 2015).
[83] S Fukuda-Parr, AE Yamin and J Greenstein, 'The Power of Numbers: A Critical Review of Millennium Development Goal Targets for Human Development and Human Rights' (2014) 15 *Journal of Human Development and Capabilities* 105, 106.

in the MDGs was both reductionist and exclusionary. They focused on outcomes and averages, and made no reference to distribution or to core principles such as equality, non-discrimination, and participation. As Fukuda-Parr and McNeil concluded, it was an agenda that 'served the purposes of the donor community ... and the neoliberal economic policy agenda of the IMF and World Bank'.[84]

Despite the lessons that might have been learned from that experience, essentially the same quality was sought for the SDGs, albeit for an expanded range of goals. Since civil and political rights issues per se were almost entirely avoided in the SDGs, the most relevant goal ended up being Goal 16, which commits governments and other relevant actors to 'promote the rule of law at the national and international levels and ensure equal access to justice for all'. The 'rule of law' is a conveniently vague surrogate term. Given its breadth and the range of considerations that this goal could (and should) encompass, the indicators chosen to measure compliance would inevitably assume major importance. But those finally adopted by the United Nations would seem to be at best exotic, and at worst, derisory:

> Indicator 16.3.1: Proportion of victims of violence in the previous 12 months who reported their victimization to competent authorities or other officially recognized conflict resolution mechanisms.
>
> Indicator 16.3.2: Unsentenced detainees as a proportion of overall prison population.
>
> Indicator 16.3.3: Proportion of the population who have experienced a dispute in the past two years and who accessed a formal or informal dispute resolution mechanism, by type of mechanism.[85]

In his research, de Souza opines that rule of law indicators in most contexts tend to focus on the functioning of formal, state-sponsored rule of law institutions, giving weight to factors such as the number of judges or the speed with which courts resolve cases. In so doing, there is a failure to engage with legal pluralism, overlooking the experience of justice users who interact with multiple legal systems with different capacities, rules and criteria for legitimacy.[86] This approach inevitably privileges the experience of those in the Global North, and may prioritise projects focused on formal institutions equivalent to the infrastructure in place in Global North countries, notwithstanding the 'repeated failure of development interventions that focus on an institutional, top-down approach to justice reform'.[87]

Do these criticisms spell the end of indicators as a useful tool? Not necessarily, although it is likely that the methodology of indicator production would need to be significantly transformed to meet such concerns. De Souza asks if it is possible for an indicator to represent the resolution of justice disputes as a messy, contested process, rather than one which is limited to the operation of formal legal proceedings.[88]

---

[84] S Fukuda-Parr and D McNeill, 'Knowledge and Politics in Setting and Measuring the SDGs: Introduction to Special Issue' (2019) 10 *Global Policy* 5, 8.

[85] 'SDG Indicators Metadata Repository (Goal 16)' (UN Statistics, 2023) https://unstats.un.org/sdgs/metadata/?Text=&Goal=16.

[86] De Souza (n 51) 9–10.

[87] ibid 10.

[88] ibid 14.

He draws on the approach popularised by Amartya Sen and Martha Nussbaum as well as on design theory, arguing that indicator production should centre the experience of the justice user, tracking the 'capabilities' that would permit that individual to have better and more meaningful access to justice to resolve their legal disputes.[89] De Souza concludes:

> [I]n an environment where the articulation of problems and solutions is made in terms of numbers, we must develop an imagination for how to use and produce these numbers differently to serve the objectives of acknowledging and evaluating a heterogenous and plural world, rather than the homogenous one often envisioned by existing indicators.[90]

The World Bank has been at the forefront of producing composite indicators and has used them to powerful effect. One of the classic examples of a highly influential (but controversial and apparently manipulated) dataset is the World Bank's Ease of Doing Business indicators, which are discussed below and in chapter nine, by Doshi, Kelley and Simmons. Another example is its annual publication *Women, Business and the Law*. The foreword to the 2023 report claims that the project

> shows how equal legal rights and freedoms for women can be achieved around the world. It tracks how the law affects women's decisions and opportunities at various stages in their lives – from the essentials of freedom of movement and safety to the reconciliation of work and parenting, from the ability to own assets and access credit to the ability to inherit their fair share of property. It works under the premise – well supported by economic evidence – that a legal environment in which women have the same rights and opportunities as men leads to economic prosperity for everyone.[91]

There are innumerable value judgements and assumptions built into this approach. In essence, the promotion of women's rights is presented in terms of market economics: the appeal to governments is not to empower women for their own sake in ways that they choose, but rather to stem the losses to productivity and income that result from lower labour force participation by women. Women's work is presented as a means of promoting greater national prosperity.[92] The report laments the fact that the type of reforms being promoted by the World Bank slumped to a '20-year low' in 2022:

> This 'reform fatigue' is a potential impediment to economic growth and resilience at a critical time for the global economy. As global economic growth is slowing, all countries need to mobilize their full productive capacity to confront the confluence of crises besetting them. Reforming in ways that encourage women to contribute to the economy as employees and entrepreneurs will both level the playing field and make the economy more dynamic and resilient in the face of shocks.[93]

Leaving aside the fact that the World Bank otherwise refuses to adopt human rights policies on the spurious grounds that to do so would amount to political

---

[89] ibid 13.
[90] ibid 207.
[91] World Bank, *Women, Business and the Law 2023* (Washington DC, World Bank, 2023) ix.
[92] For a critique, see R Russell, 'Women and the "Business" of Human Rights: The Problem with Women's Empowerment Projects and the Need for Corporate Reform' (2022) 7 *Business and Human Rights Journal* 84.
[93] World Bank, *Women, Business and the Law 2023* (n 91) xiii.

interference, the promotion of indicators that import such an array of neoliberal economic assumptions into discussions of how societies should be structured is an excellent example of the ways in which such composite indicators can be used without acknowledgement of the real agenda at play. As Broome and Quirk conclude, 'While it is in the interests of benchmarkers to rhetorically appeal to models of neutral, methodical, and technocratic assessment, their activities and outputs will always be inherently political'.[94]

The qualities that make quantification and indicators powerful – their clarity, their persuasiveness and the ease with which they permit monitoring and comparison across time and between actors – ensure that these tools will never be wholly abandoned. But it also means that human rights proponents ignore them at their peril. There is a vital need for advocates in this field to restore the complexity that has been concealed or lost by exposing the assumptions and agendas being promoted in these contexts. At present, there is remarkably little of this work being undertaken by human rights scholars and activists, despite the extent to which issues like the rule of law and women's empowerment go to the heart of their agendas. The tragic reality at present is that a detailed, meticulously researched and powerfully argued report on women's rights by a human rights NGO is certain to have less resonance that the claim that country X is performing much worse on the World Bank business index than one of its peers, or than it did in previous years.

IX. THE CONTRIBUTIONS TO THIS VOLUME

The contributions to this volume are divided into two parts, with the first set of authors dealing with aspects of the concept of vernacularization and the second set addressing the challenges of quantification.

In the opening chapter of Part I, Richard Wilson briefly describes the evolution of anthropologists' engagement with law and social ordering and then proceeds to locate the various contributions that Sally Engle Merry made to that field. He starts with her pioneering study of the ways in which working-class Americans made use of lower courts to sort out disputes that arose in their family and neighbourhood relations and then moves on to her work on the concept and practice of 'legal pluralism', in which he finds the beginnings of her theories about vernacularization and the application of a distinctive brand of 'legal realism' which emphasises that law is much more than formal law and is actually made up of a variety of social practices and the meanings attached to them. This insight applied as much in the unspecified lower courts of eastern Massachusetts as in international justice institutions.

Merry's application of these approaches in a variety of specific contexts resulted in the emergence of a 'theoretical model for conceptualizing human rights as a field of critical scholarly inquiry'. It was one that enabled scholars and practitioners to understand some of the ways in which the high politics of standard-setting and diplomatic engagement related to what actually happened on the ground. Accounts of

---

[94] Broome and Quirk (n 52) 840.

local culture that had once been 'nativist, romantic, and essentialist' could now be contextualised and reflect the many ways in which communities, as well as understandings of rights, evolved and changed.

Since much of Wilson's own pioneering ethnographic work has focused on international courts and tribunals working on issues of criminal justice, he starts by noting that Merry's foray into the international arena began with her study of the work of the 1993 People's International Tribunal for Hawai'i, which focused on the claims of indigenous Hawaiians to be protected from state-led development efforts and moved to assert a right to self-determination, inspired in part by the UN Declaration on the Rights of Indigenous Peoples. Her study foreshadowed many of the research questions that would soon come to be the focus of work by anthropologists on the international criminal tribunals that emerged around the same time.

In arguing that Merry's insights from the last couple of decades of the twentieth century remain highly relevant for a very different international community today, Wilson focuses on the competing perspectives developed in recent years by Samuel Moyn and Kathryn Sikkink. He notes that the work of each contains 'accurate observations' and important insights, but also points to their 'discernible frailties'. He suggests that both authors have been somewhat selective in marshalling evidence to support their overall theses, thereby avoiding the 'murky processes' described by Merry and the 'messiness of social life' that is the almost inevitable finding of anthropologists. It is this unpredictability and complexity in the results of ethnographic studies that stands in such contrast to the often-sweeping judgements made by lawyers, political scientists and historians.

His chapter finishes with an exploration of the ways in which studies of international justice institutions have provided rich insights that reflect the great diversity of the institutional designs used, the legal mandates on which they are based and the legal outcomes that they have produced. Instead of broad generalisations, most of which do not withstand closer scrutiny, such studies 'provide a precise and empirically grounded basis to understand both the benefits and inadequacies' of the work done by these courts and tribunals. Elements of contingency and fragmentation lead anthropologists to adopt a certain 'intellectual humility instead of magisterial pronouncements of a utopian or dystopian kind'.

Jack Snyder points to the impressive scholarly and practical impact that Merry's work on this theme has had, but also warns that, while vernacularization might be indispensable, it can also be dangerous. He picks up on a number of the potential pitfalls that Merry and her co-author in one of the most important analyses, Peggy Levitt, had themselves recognised. However, Snyder's main focus is on the risk of resorting to vernacular versions of rights in contexts in which there has been a backlash against the promotion of liberal values. He sees such advocacy as often reflecting legalism, moralism and universalism.

Merry and Levitt have suggested that vernacularization is something of a natural antidote to these approaches, in that it opens up different ways of understanding rights and of seeking to promote their realisation. But vernacularization as an antidote is not without its pitfalls, including the risk of diluting the essence of the message that human rights norms aim to convey and permitting those norms to be invoked by those who wish to 'justify and perpetuate abuse'. In other words, while the process of translating norms into a language that is more easily understood can be and often is used to achieve progressive goals, it can also be used in the opposite direction. Snyder draws on examples from the areas of religion and policing to illustrate some of these more problematic uses. He is particularly critical of the practice of 'naming and shaming' when used by outsiders in relation to the practices of other cultural groups: insiders might well be able to use this practice to their advantage, but when used by actors outside the community it can backfire badly. Snyder cites a range of examples to illustrate this dynamic, including the campaign led by Westerners against female genital cutting in many countries of the Global South. He adds, however, that pursuing the same goal through a more vernacularized approach that aims to speak to those engaging in the practice in terms of their own understandings and goals might also backfire, as this could help to develop a somewhat sanitised and thus more defensible version of the same practice.

Snyder concludes by drawing a parallel between Merry's culture-based approach to making international human rights norms more relevant and acceptable to local groups, and political science literature that highlights the benefits of using political processes that 'localise' international norms to make them more culturally attuned. He refers especially to the writing of Amitav Acharya on reconciling a strong attachment to sovereignty in the politics of South-East Asia with progressive evolution in relation to other norms. The technique involves incorporating a hybrid of these two approaches and presenting the resulting notion as a 'congruent, legitimate, beneficial, evolutionary development that resonates with previously accepted principles'. This approach leads Snyder to suggest a range of techniques through which discourse vernacularization can be combined with politically brokered localisation in order to find more widely acceptable 'solutions to cross-cultural dilemmas of human rights persuasion'.

In a similar vein to various other contributors, César Rodríguez-Garavito's chapter is framed in part as a response to the criticisms of the human rights movement put forward by some leading Western scholars, and especially by Stephen Hopgood and Samuel Moyn. While he concedes the validity of some of the challenges put forward by these authors, he suggests that they are focused on a relatively small part of a much more complex and contested set of practices. Rodríguez-Garavito points out that there are multiple human rights projects, and it is inevitable and appropriate that they manifest internal tensions and contradictions. They cannot be captured by the snapshots or caricatures that often seem to preoccupy the attention of many of the critics. He is dismissive of their 'armchair blanket dismissals of rights' and argues that Merry's approach, based on what she described as a 'deterritorialized ethnography', is a much richer and more revealing one.

Rodríguez-Garavito provides a brief elaboration of the three processes that Merry identified as enabling the unfolding of the process of vernacularization. He reviews the various ways in which the first of these, consensus building, takes place, primarily at the international level. The second involves the effort to transplant the agreed norms into domestic legal systems, often through techniques and approaches that have been adopted elsewhere. Intermediaries play an important role in facilitating this process of translation. The third process involves the localisation of the transnational knowledge, and is dominated by local actors, who give concrete meaning to the global norms through a wide variety of institutions, community interventions and other actions.

But his most important contribution lies in his suggestion that the process of vernacularization as identified by Merry is essentially unidirectional: it moves from the global, through the national, to the local level. While each stage involves many acts of translation or adaptation, there is no significant feedback loop that leads back up in the opposite direction. As a result, it 'captures only one half of the circuit through which human rights norms and practices are globalized'. Rodríguez-Garavito presents a detailed and important case study of the way in which this unidirectional process can be seen to have played out in relation to the rights of indigenous peoples, using the particular example of the peoples of the Amazon and their struggle against various forms of disruption and predation. But he suggests that whereas most models of vernacularization end once the global norms have been transmitted in whatever forms into local practice, this only reflects one half or one side of what very often occurs.

By using a framing theory, involving different phases of contestation, bridging and transformation, he shows how another process of what he terms 'legal globalization from below' has occurred. Through particularly interesting and revealing case studies of the evolution of the norm of free, prior and informed consultation, he shows how this process works in practice. The result is that local actors do not only receive and adapt or translate norms from above, but they 'also contest, resist, transform, and re-export new norms and interpretations of human rights'. The picture that emerges from his analysis is one in which the relevant norms are in a constant state of evolution, and the range of actors involved in what he terms the overall ecosystem extends far beyond the very limited picture painted by many of the critics. Instead, he sees a complex and diverse array of governments, NGOs, grassroots activists and other actors interacting in ways that shape and transform the overall system.

In the following chapter, Merry's longtime colleague at New York University, Fred Myers, builds upon the insights provided by Rodríguez-Garavito in relation to the rights of indigenous peoples by describing the ways in which international norms have interacted with domestic law and indigenous protocols in Australia in relation to the circulation of cultural forms. He focuses particularly on efforts to honour the traditions, interests and laws of Indigenous Australians in relation to photographic images depicting initiation ceremonies that are considered restricted knowledge that should never be divulged to certain groups and individuals. He traces the interactions involving the transposition of the international norms reflected in the United Nations' Declaration on the Rights of Indigenous Peoples, the interpretation by domestic courts of national law and the efforts by various actors to ensure respect for the rights and interests of Indigenous Australians. In all of this, Myers sees vernacularization at work, thus providing another illustration of the processes also described by Rodríguez-Garavito.

Mark Goodale emphasises that vernacularization should be understood as fulfilling two quite different functions or roles. The first is as a way of explaining or making sense of global norms that are expressed at a level of abstraction, thereby enabling them to be translated into terms that are meaningful and 'owned' by the local groups that seek to relate to these norms and make them relevant in the local context. The second is as a normative theory of what human rights practice actually entails, or at least should entail. In order to illustrate his understanding of these processes, he surveys the results of some of his own work in Bolivia and then provides an overview of relatively well-known case studies that show how human rights norms were made relevant in particular cultural contexts: the aftermath of the late-twentieth-century conflict in Chiapas, in Mexico; in arriving at shared understandings of human rights in a particular Indigenous community in Australia; and in relation to the rights of LGBT people in Myanmar.

Goodale combines the conclusions to be drawn from these diverse case studies with his own general understanding of the role that human rights norms play in today's scholarly discourses, many of which are deeply pessimistic about the likely future of rights. Like Wilson, he reviews the work of Kathryn Sikkink and Samuel Moyn, and identifies a commonality in their very different approaches and conclusions: they both adopt a narrow conception of human rights. This contrasts with his own conclusion that the quest for a single globalised or universal understanding of human rights is a lost cause. Instead, the content of the norms will always be open-ended and contested, and the meanings derived from them will always be in a 'state of becoming, through negotiation, resistance and reformulation'. It is simply impossible to forge 'a world order based in a common understanding of the form and content of universal human rights'. His vision is a very different one and is rooted in what he terms an 'anthropological ethics', which sees human rights as being 'animated by the values of pluralism, contingency, and translocal ... solidarity'.

Pablo de Greiff provides an additional example of this process, examining what he describes as 'an atypical case of "vernacularization"'. He considers recent calls to import a transitional justice model into new contexts, very different from the post-authoritarian transitions in which such measures were first developed. In particular, demand has come for these approaches to be used in the USA in the wake of the Black Lives Matter movement, and in other states with a legacy of 'historical injustice', particularly when associated with colonialism. De Greiff examines common social factors from these 'pre-conflict' situations (including polarisation, xenophobia, racism, and a decline in interpersonal and institutional trust) and traces their prevalence in more conventional transitional justice settings, demonstrating the existence of parallels that might make the transitional justice model a good fit.

One key question is whether a policy designed for redress purposes can be used preventively. De Greiff concludes that transitional justice methods that serve to induce trust and enhance social integration may be of value in these circumstances. These approaches include truth-telling, memorialisation, apologies, and consultative and participatory methods. By way of example, truth-telling could be used to undo the simplifying narratives that are at the heart of polarisation: the 'Us versus Them' dynamic. De Greiff observes that, 'In a sense, truth humanizes by complexifying, and it is in part this liberating process of complexification that allows for a more respectful and consensual form of social integration'.

However, the effectiveness of this endeavour depends upon the extent to which it reaffirms and reinforces shared norms and values, which may be particular to a given context. De Greiff cautions against 'isomorphic mimicry', observing that the same institutional forms do not work equally well regardless of circumstances. Therefore, although truth-telling may be of value in a pre-conflict context, truth commissions may not necessarily be appropriate. De Greiff applies Sally Engle Merry's insight that vernacularization falls along a continuum. Imported institutions may remain largely unchanged from their transnational prototypes or become hybridised, merging with local institutions and symbols. He concludes that some, although not all, of the lessons and tools of transitional justice can be applied in a 'pre-conflict' setting, but they must be appropriately translated into the relevant context. Replication is guaranteed to fail.

The contributions to the second part of this volume look at the practice of measuring or quantifying key phenomena in different areas of development and global governance.

Samuel Martínez's chapter starts by noting a paradox exposed by Merry's work, which is that information which is incomplete or sketchy, and thus open to question or challenge, can, when it is aggregated and condensed, be transformed into a powerful tool in the form of an easily understandable symbol, number or ranking. He describes this process as involving 'synoptising' or 'bundling' and distilling information into a different form that then enables it to be used as something akin to an 'information derivative'.

Martínez then applies Merry's insights in relation to the especially complex and troubling approaches used by some advocacy organisations in combating human trafficking and seeking to draw attention to that and other related forms of 'modern slavery'. This was an issue that had already been flagged by Anne Gallagher and Janie Chuang in a chapter they wrote for *Governance by Indicators*, one of the volumes on quantification co-edited by Merry,[95] but Martínez takes the analysis much further by applying an anthropologist's eye to the ways in which the 'new abolitionists' have combined equivocal numbers, with carefully chosen text and images, to mobilise public opinion. He brings his analysis to life by exploring the representations of modern slavery that are to be found on the internet and applying 'literary and image-textual techniques of close reading' to provide an understanding of the dynamics that are at work.

As a non-lawyer, Martínez does not dwell, as others have done, on the deeply problematic term 'modern slavery', which has been described as a 'legally empty but highly emotive and galvanizing term'. It is the open-ended, readily manipulable, and often subjective nature of this artificially constructed category that forms the backdrop of his analysis. He then shows the extent to which some of the key activist campaigns against modern slavery combine assertions that the phenomenon is hidden and elusive, but at the same time widely prevalent. It is, as he puts it, 'both indubitable and unknowable'.

Despite the hidden and elusive nature of the problem, the enormity of the claimed scale of modern slavery is often backed up by surprisingly precise statistics. It is not difficult to find examples of this approach online. The Australia-based Walk Free Foundation, for example, says concisely that 'In 2016, 40.3 million people were living

---

[95] A Gallagher and J Chuang, 'The Use of Indicators to Measure Government Responses to Human Trafficking' in Davis et al (n 72) 356.

in modern slavery. It exists in every corner of the world, yet is seemingly invisible to most people'.[96] UK-based Anti-Slavery International starts with a definition according to which

> we define modern slavery as when an individual is exploited by others, for personal or commercial gain. Whether tricked, coerced, or forced, they lose their freedom. This includes but is not limited to human trafficking, forced labour and debt bondage.
>
> ...
>
> Modern slavery is all around us, often hidden in plain sight. People can become enslaved making our clothes, serving our food, picking our crops, working in factories, or working in houses as cooks, cleaners or nannies.[97]

It goes on to say that '49.6 million people live in modern slavery', including 22 million in forced marriages, two-fifths of whom are children.[98] And US-based Polaris Project concludes that 'human trafficking is a $150 billion global industry that robs 25 million people around the world of their freedom'.[99]

Like many other scholars who have drawn attention to the fluffiness of these statistics and the accompanying claims, Martínez does not seek to downplay the importance of the human rights violations involved but argues that the exceptionally weak factual basis upon which most such prevalence estimates are based should give rise to far more probing and sceptical reactions than has generally been the case. He concludes that exposing the lack of credible facts or verifiable numbers alone will not succeed in countering an appeal that is based, not on facts, but on fear and intuition. The question he seeks to answer is how such a sense of scale and urgency has been built despite the absence of verifiable data.

He argues that the post-abolitionist equivocation is an example of post-truth politics, some of the hallmarks of which are 'equivocating about the facts; equating political positions with moral stances; appealing to intuitions and emotions; and defining truth as a matter of belief, and not evidence'. In illustrating the techniques used to promote this approach, he looks carefully at the combination of personal narratives about the suffering of individual victims, evocative photography and text images such as maps and flow charts, along with the use of didactic text analyses which 'favor shadows over light, put conjecture over facts, and more generally sustain a series of mutually contradictory characterizations of modern slavery'.

While Martínez's focus is on the use and abuse of quantification by civil society actors, the following chapter, written by Rush Doshi, Judith Kelley and Beth Simmons, uses the example of the World Bank's Ease of Doing Business (EDB) indicators to illustrate the powerful influence that Global Performance Indicators (GPI) can have, especially when they come with the imprimatur of a leading intergovernmental organisation. They begin by citing Sally Engle Merry's insistence that indicators

---

[96] Walk Free Foundation, *Global Slavery Index 2018* (n 56) i.
[97] Anti-Slavery International, 'What Is Modern Slavery?', www.antislavery.org/slavery-today/modern-slavery/.
[98] ibid.
[99] B Anthony et al, 'On-Ramps, Intersections, and Exit Routes: A Roadmap for Systems and Industries to Prevent and Disrupt Human Trafficking' (Polaris, July 2018) 5.

inevitably reflect political choices, and that the process of producing them is 'itself a political process, shaped by the power to categorize, count, [and] analyze'. In earlier work, two of the authors had defined GPIs as 'regularized public assessments that rate, rank, and categorize state policies, qualities and/or performance' and observed that such indicators are used for a wide range of purposes, including to shame states and to provoke a spirit of competition among them. The tools used in this endeavour include generating social pressure, stimulating competitive dynamics among states and undertaking 'performative nudges' to move policy-makers in the desired direction. They are thus very different from more traditional coercive policies, such as conditionality, but can be even more effective.

International organisations frequently employ such GPIs, and do so to encourage states to adopt policies that accord with the organisation's preferences. Thus, the United Nations Development Programme has been producing the Human Development Index since 1990 and has had a major impact in encouraging governments to attach greater importance to non-economic indicators such as literacy, health, participation and gender equality. In contrast, the World Bank's goal with the EDB indicators is to generate pressure on states to deregulate their economies. It does so by comparing countries' performance with others, by fostering reputations for business-friendliness or otherwise and by encouraging or even provoking competition. The measures used to assess when a state is making it easier to do business closely track the neoliberal goals of the Washington Consensus.

By the standards set by its authors at the World Bank, the Doing Business report was highly successful. But it was strongly criticised by a very large group of civil society organisations on the grounds that its rankings 'encouraged a race to the bottom between countries, who have turned to slashing labor regulations and relaxing social and environmental standards to climb up the rankings and better attract private investments'.[100] Ultimately, it was allegations of improper manipulation of the methodology and some data that led to the report's suspension in 2020 and its discontinuation in 2021. While civil society groups celebrated its demise,[101] the World Bank immediately began work on replacing it with a project that would assess the 'Business Enabling Environment (BEE)' of countries and would play a very similar role to the EDB index.[102]

In order to demonstrate the impact of the Ease of Doing Business index, Doshi, Kelley and Simmons undertook a case study of India, based on an online survey experiment that they designed and implemented. The study seeks to demonstrate two propositions. The first is that the index changes the perception of the situation not just for political and business elites, but also for broader constituencies within the relevant country. As a result, demands are directed at the government from both the

---

[100] Eurodad, 'Letter to the World Bank Executive Directors about Ceasing Publication of the Doing Business Report' (15 March 2021) www.eurodad.org/rights_not_rankings.
[101] Oxfam, 'World Bank Discontinues Problematic Doing Business Report: Oxfam Reaction' (16 September 2021) oxfam.org/en/press-releases/world-bank-discontinues-problematic-doing-business-report-oxfam-reaction: 'It's a welcome move and about time the World Bank scrapped its Doing Business report'.
[102] World Bank, 'Business Ready (B-READY)' (2023) www.worldbank.org/en/programs/business-enabling-environment.

elites and the grassroots to improve the country's rankings, especially vis-à-vis neighbouring countries with which there is ongoing competition. This is, at least in part, a bottom-up process. The second proposition reflects a top-down process whereby elites invoke the rankings in order to create political pressure to justify regulatory reforms. They then use improved rankings scores to gain political capital and claim significant progress in the overall economic environment.

The authors' goal is to demonstrate the extent to which global actors can 'capture governance spaces and exert influence' based on the promulgation of such GPIs. In other words, the goal of the indicators is not to reflect the reality, but rather to influence behaviour and change the reality.

The next two chapters focus on a complex bureaucratic/diplomatic procedure initiated in 2008 under the auspices of the newly formed UN Human Rights Council and termed the Universal Periodic Review (UPR). The fourth cycle of the process began in 2022. The name 'Universal Periodic Review' is partly self-explanatory insofar as it involves all UN Member States (the Universal element) engaging in a process in which one 'cycle' takes place over a fixed period of four and one half years, then gives way to the next cycle, the content of which is significantly informed by what happened in the preceding cycle (the Periodic element), in order to review the performance of states against international human rights standards, broadly defined (the Review element). Both chapters provide illuminating examples of the ways in which vernacularization and quantification interact in the human rights field in general and in the UPR in particular, and of the deeper appreciation of the process that can be gained by adopting an anthropologically informed analytical approach.

The UPR is important because it ensures that every state, rather than only those accused of serious violations, must account to the Council. It is a peer mechanism in the sense that the review is undertaken by states, rather than experts, and the reporting state retains significant control over the outcome. This makes it more acceptable to states and much less easy to wriggle out of. The review is carried out by all 47 Council members acting as a Working Group. Three states, chosen by lottery (the 'troika'), act as Rapporteurs in the review of a given state's report. In addition to (i) the National Report, there is (ii) a 'Compilation' by the Office of the High Commissioner for Human Rights of information from treaty bodies, special procedures and other UN sources and (iii) a 'Stakeholder Summary' of information submitted by civil society, researchers, national human rights institutions and others. Jane Cowan's analysis focuses especially on the method of preparation of the latter two documents.

To an uninformed observer, the UPR process would be puzzling at best, and at worst would seem like a bizarre piece of choreography designed only to appeal to and be understood by aficionados of the genre. But such rituals and the characters who perform them are ideal objects for anthropological scrutiny. After a brief but instructive overview of the procedure, Cowan argues that, among all the various inputs and outputs that the process involves, it is the 'recommendations' made by the states that comment on one another's performance that are the essence of the procedure. Her chapter explores the ways in which forms of vernacularization are involved and the extensive role played by quantification within the UPR.

While Sally Engle Merry attributed major importance to the role of intermediaries as translators of human rights language, her main emphasis was on the 'downwards' process of translating the norms formulated at the international level so that they could be understood and acted upon at the national and local levels. But Cowan's story is one in which local civil society actors are enabled to bring their understandings, concerns and perspectives to the Geneva-based diplomatic process by undertaking their own form of translation. By translating their concerns, they seek to make them comprehensible and palatable to governmental representatives, who are formulating the questions and recommendations that they will be addressing to the government of the country under review and from which the civil society groups in question have originated. She starts by describing how the formal procedure largely, and no doubt intentionally, allocated only a token opportunity for civil society actors to orally express their views. This 'omission' was however, ingeniously supplemented by an additional step introduced by a Geneva-based NGO called UPR Info, which exists in order to support the UPR process and to make it as effective as possible. It introduced a 'Pre-Session' opportunity, available only to civil society actors who wish to express their views on a country whose official review is imminent. Since it is public and states might learn a lot from the carefully formulated presentations, government representatives are often present as observers.

Cowan provides a fascinating account of the ways in which activists, especially those from countries of the Global South and those for whom the standard UPR languages of English and French are foreign, must engage in the 'complex labor of linguistic, conceptual and cultural translation'. As she puts it, 'they must learn how to articulate local concerns in ... UN language, in the appropriate emotional registers, and conforming to the precisely designated technical parameters of speaking time and space on the page'. In other words, 'local claims, grievances and experiences of suffering' must be reformulated into the technocratic language that is used and understood at the international level.

The more closely the recommendations that they formulate and advocate can be expressed in terms familiar to the diplomats, the more likely they will be picked up and reflected in the final outcome. She describes this process in considerable detail, but only alludes briefly at the end to another part of the circle of vernacularization: the recommendations that finally emerge from the UPR process in Geneva then need to be translated all over again when they are taken back 'home' to the country concerned. Again, there will be governmental translators, but also many others working at the local level who will need to convey to their constituencies what happened and what their government has been urged to do by other governments, albeit often at the behest of civil society actors who were able to influence and shape parts of the discourse in Geneva.

Cowan then turns her attention to the issue of quantification. She observes that despite the growing importance of indicators in other human rights contexts, as highlighted in Meg Satterthwaite's chapter, they are all but invisible in the UPR context. The global focus of the UPR, the acutely distilled nature of the dialogue, the unhelpfulness of complex formulations that require technical knowledge to be meaningful and the overall thrust of the procedure all combine to marginalise the utility and relevance of formal indicators. But this is not the end of the matter. The sheer numerical magnitude of the number of states involved, the number of recommendations made and the range of issues addressed and actors implicated means that some form of aggregation is highly desirable in order to make sense of the process and to take full advantage of the masses of data generated. She notes that in the second UPR cycle, between 2012 and 2016, over 36,000 recommendations were generated.

Based on the assumption that the best outcome was one that called for the state concerned to take some specific action, UPR Info collaborated with Edward McMahon, a political scientist, to develop a system that ranked the various recommendations to reflect the 'increasing levels of effort, including political and financial resource allocation' that would be required if the state were to implement a given recommendation. Five 'action' categories were identified: minimal, continuing, considering, general and specific. The last of these were connoted by the recommender's use of verbs such as eliminate, establish, investigate, abolish, adopt and implement. The reasonable assumption reflected is that the identification of a specific and tangible action that should be taken is far preferable to a broad, non-specific suggestion that consideration be given to something or other. But Cowan points out that this purportedly neutral ranking actually assumes that doing something new and different and expending additional resources will be more effective than other approaches.

In order to illustrate the ways in which such assumptions can distort outcomes, she takes the example of a group of Small Island Developing States in the Pacific region, all of which have low population numbers, are confronting existential challenges from climate change and have very limited resources. Given that many of them have refrained from ratifying some human rights treaties that would impose onerous reporting and other obligations, one of the easiest 'action' recommendations to address to them is to undertake ratification. Although the problematic nature of this course of action had long ago been identified in UN studies written by the present author,[103] the recommenders paid little heed to such concerns. As Cowan puts it, the Pacific island states 'were being guided by their peers toward devoting scarce resources to ratifying treaties and complying with reporting obligations, and away from human rights policies more appropriate to their size, specificities, capacities, and priorities'.

The second study of the UPR is provided by Julie Billaud, whose research originated in a joint project that she and Jane Cowan had initiated in 2010, and which has generated a significant scholarly output. Billaud's contribution focuses on the role of one particular group of intermediaries who play an important but largely hidden role in translating the various original source documents submitted under the UPR into the established templates that become part of the information base upon which the entire discussion is based. These intermediaries are the staff members of the UPR secretariat, who are UN civil servants or officials working for the Office of the High Commissioner for Human Rights. Billaud obtained most of her insights by volunteering to work as an intern in the secretariat and thus playing a role in producing some of the documents and gaining access to internal staff discussions.

UN officials are required to observe principles of neutrality and independence, and to follow the instructions provided by states, as reflected in various bureaucratic

---

[103] P Alston, 'Report to the World Conference on Human Rights, on Treaty Body Reform', UN Doc A/CONF.157/PC/62/Add.11/Rev.1, para 87.

standards and procedures. This is designed to eliminate, or at least greatly reduce, any scope for them to introduce their own views or biases into the documentation. But Billaud suggests that many of the relevant officials are deeply committed to what she terms 'the utopian principles of human rights and civil society participation', and that they are consistently seeking to promote those two agendas to the extent possible while following internal rules and instructions. She provides a detailed description of a process followed within the secretariat in the early years of the UPR, which was designed to ensure that no one voice was dominant and that various checks and balances were reflected in the drafting process. Ironically, the resulting degree of anonymity actually resulted in providing various entry points for staff members to tilt or frame the information in ways that promoted the goals they sought to achieve.

But the process she described and actually participated in was time-intensive. Eventually, managers within the secretariat who were not convinced that the output of the UPR was worth the immense amount of staff time that had been invested in it prevailed and brought about a change of approach. The new technique was far more centralised and vested most of the responsibility for drafting a given document in a single individual staff member. The result was to make the staff member more exposed to criticism if any imbalance or inappropriate emphasis or source was reflected in the document, thus reducing the scope for secretariat influence. This reform had the effect of partly eliminating the 'social dimension of their work' in favour of 'efficiency and productivity criteria'. They have thus been turned into 'more diligent bureaucrats', although it seems unlikely that their intermediary role has been entirely eliminated. There are always opportunities to exercise judgement and discretion in terms of what information to privilege, where to situate it and how to present it.

Hilary Charlesworth highlights Sally Engle Merry's use of ethnography to uncover power relationships and cultural constructions of social life, including in the social life of international institutions. Charlesworth uses the United Nations Security Council's 'Women, Peace and Security' (WPS) agenda as a case study of the use that international institutions make of visual images of women, and of the underlying attitudes that such use reveals. Images are not indicators in a strict sense, but they play a similar role. Both indicators and images seek to be representational, and both run the risk of simplifying and blunting complex ideas.

Charlesworth argues that the WPS agenda is 'built on contradictory and impoverished images of women and men, and of gender roles', typecasting women as both peacemakers and as a group with special needs requiring male protection. She asserts that these problematic power asymmetries are reproduced and reinforced in images associated with the agenda. The chapter reviews images associated with the WPS agenda and produced by the UN, Australia, the African Union's peacekeeping mission in Somalia and NATO's Parliamentary Assembly. In these images, women from the Global South appear peaceful, being presented with children, or as trainees or students. Women from the Global North are more often portrayed as professionals or peacekeepers, often wearing the same uniforms as their male counterparts. Men are infrequently depicted, but when they do appear, they represent 'a safe pair of hands'.

In these images, as in the WPS agenda itself, gender is simplified and elided with 'women'. Charlesworth opines that 'The relational nature of gender, the contestability of categories of femininity and masculinity, as well as the role of power relations and the ways that structures of subordination and inequality are reproduced are invisible'. This approach obscures gendered problems faced by men, and suggests that women's problems are attributable to certain cultures, particularly in the Global South.

Martínez examines the ways in which statistical estimates of the prevalence of modern slavery can be used as the basis for 'imagetexts' that present a problematic picture of reality, whilst Charlesworth focuses on the use of images to project a simplified narrative of gender issues. In both of these examples, complexity and detail are obscured. In contrast, Meg Satterthwaite's chapter emphasises the potential advantages of an international human rights body making more effective and concerted use of available statistics to evaluate compliance with the human rights to water and sanitation. She takes an especially relevant example, the United Nations Committee on Economic, Social and Cultural Rights. As she notes, the Committee itself went through a significant awakening in terms of the potential utility of statistical indicators for its own monitoring work early in the twenty-first century. Having focused mainly on 'benchmarks' during the 1990s, it adopted General Comments on the right to health and then the right to water in the early 2000s, which both emphasised the centrality of statistics. These General Comments went as far as to suggest that a failure to monitor realisation in this way might amount to a violation of a state's obligations under the Covenant on Economic, Social and Cultural Rights. The Committee followed up by revising its Reporting Guidelines in 2008 to specifically request that states provide statistical details, and further reinforced this emphasis in a Statement that it issued in 2010 on the right to sanitation.

But having set itself up to make meaningful use of statistics in evaluating states' performance in relation to the rights to water and sanitation, the Committee has made surprisingly little progress in that regard. Through detailed reviews of the reports submitted by governments, Satterthwaite shows that states were largely unresponsive to the Committee's requests for statistical indicators to reinforce their own self-assessment of progress. This, too, is surprising, since a separate UN programme, the Joint Monitoring Programme on Water Supply and Sanitation (JMP), had been producing detailed and reliable data since 2002. This data was available to states and could readily have been adapted and incorporated in their human rights reporting in order to provide precisely the type of indicators sought by the Committee. In fact, the JMP now 'routinely publishes data and analyses that are relevant for human rights monitoring' in order to generate information required by the SDGs to assess inequalities in access to water and sanitation.

Satterthwaite then poses the key question, asking why the UN Committee has not made effective use of data that is now readily available and could be used to greatly enhance their monitoring and assessment of the situation in human rights terms. She demonstrates this failure on the basis of a specially constructed database that examines the 'concluding observations' reached by the Committee over a 15-year period up to 2018. Despite regularly addressing issues relating to these two rights, the Committee made very disappointing use of statistical data. While not at all reluctant to refer to relevant statistics, it generally failed to explore or explain the significance of the statistic. She concludes that the Committee systematically failed in its concluding observations on different states 'to explain whether a given statistic was being cited as a baseline, an achievement, or a benchmark for continued improvement or monitoring for retrogression'. At the same time, it continues to call upon states to make effective use of disaggregated indicators for these purposes. Her depressing conclusion is that the Committee essentially refuses to 'engage in tailored and searching assessments of or with data'. The power that available statistical data could wield in this context is thus ignored, which means that the Committee is abdicating its responsibility to undertake effective monitoring in relation to these two key human rights.

Satterthwaite concludes her chapter by noting that leading civil society organisations are making increasingly effective use of indicators in this domain and suggests that they need to play a more strategic role in prompting the committee to do likewise. Her chapter thus provides a very different perspective than that provided by Martínez, but her emphasis is reinforced by the chapters that follow.

Sara Davis's chapter focuses particularly on the goal of ending acquired immunodeficiency syndrome (AIDS) by 2030, which is one of the goals contained in the SDGs. SDG 3 is the umbrella goal dealing with health issues and Target 3.3 sets the goal of ending the AIDS epidemic. Progress since the adoption of the SDGs in 2015 has lagged, and the goal now seems very unlikely to be met: this is true of many, if not most, of the SDGs, and was the case even before COVID-19 brought a further dramatic setback in 2020. Davis seeks to explain some of the reasons for the failure to bring the human immunodeficiency virus (HIV) infections under control, an aim that had previously attracted strong support and funding. She situates the goal within the broader trend of the 'audit culture', which has prevailed at the international level in recent decades and has been accompanied by the adoption of ambitious global strategies aimed at combating epidemics such as AIDS, tuberculosis and malaria.

She acknowledges the capacity of such strategies, combined with the tools of quantification such as target-setting, mathematical modelling and cost-effectiveness analysis, to mobilise resources, galvanise political action, promote prioritisation and facilitate evaluation. But she also exposes the extent to which such strategies, unless generously funded and strongly supported politically, will often involve trade-offs that are rarely acknowledged, let alone openly debated. In the case of HIV, this has led to important population groups in certain disfavoured countries being left behind, resulting in rising infection rates as a new lease of life is given to policies of criminalisation, stigmatisation and discrimination against those infected or at risk of being infected. These trade-offs are, in her view, particularly problematic because they are not based upon 'transparent, accountable and ethical' discussions.

Following in Sally Engle Merry's footsteps, and especially her pioneering studies of the processes involved in shaping, defining and implementing statistical indicators in the SDG context, Davis calls for detailed ethnographic analyses of the various practices and assumptions that influence the formulation of a global health strategy: of the discourses used, the authority invoked by different actors and the power accorded to international agencies in the process. Ultimately, hers is a call not for the abandonment or downgrading of statistical indicators and other forms of quantification, but for greater openness and transparency to accompany the processes that employ and invoke those indicators.

Part I

Vernacularization and Human Rights

2

'A Very Murky Process': Embracing the Indeterminacy of International Justice and Human Rights

RICHARD ASHBY WILSON

I. REORIENTING THE ANTHROPOLOGY OF LAW AND HUMAN RIGHTS

THE ETHNOGRAPHIC STUDY of human rights and international justice is now a vibrant field of academic inquiry, due in no small part to Sally Merry's inspiring scholarship and generosity as a colleague. She has been, to use the language of torts law, a substantial factor. To fully comprehend the scale and significance of Sally Merry's contribution, we need to situate it within the grand historical sweep of legal anthropology over the last century.

In the mid-twentieth century, many prominent anthropologists such as Malinowski[1] and Llewellyn and Hoebel[2] wrote about law and social ordering in non-Western societies. Their scholarship had a wide intellectual audience, and Llewellyn was a leader of an influential group of US legal scholars and practitioners who urged a re-evaluation of conventional theories of legal positivism. Their alternative theory, called 'legal realism', focused on how law actually functions in the day-to-day. Legal realists argued that legal outcomes could result from process, not solely from black-letter law. Experience, not doctrine, was their mantra.

After World War II, decolonisation movements gathered momentum in Africa and Asia, and anthropologists sought to understand the interactions between decentralised and often unwritten customary law and the centralised law of the colonial and postcolonial state.[3] Merry was a progenitor of the theory of 'legal pluralism', which arose from a desire to understand the interactions between overlapping, and sometimes competing and contradictory, legal orders. Legal pluralism also had something

---

[1] B Malinowski, *Crime and Custom in Savage Society* (New York, Harcourt, Brace & Co, 1926).
[2] K Llewellyn and EA Hoebel, *The Cheyenne Way* (Norman, University of Oklahoma Press, 1941).
[3] M Gluckman, *The Judicial Process among the Barotse of Northern Rhodesia* (Manchester, Manchester University Press for the Rhodes Livingston Institute, 1955); P Bohannan, *Justice and Judgment among the Tiv* (London, Oxford University Press, 1957).

to say about the relationship between legal and non-legal norms; it treated all forms of normative social ordering as 'law' and elevated customary law as equivalent to state law.[4] Communities in colonised or formerly colonised countries seldom managed their conflicts over property, or over family or religious matters, in state justice institutions; rather, they did so through village or religious courts (eg *qadi* courts) that operated on moral precepts and principles that were quite distinct from the rational, secular and proceduralist institutions of the modern nation-state.

In the late 1970s and 1980s, legal anthropologists studied the arc of local disputes and conflict resolution in settings outside of state courts.[5] In the USA, anthropologists embedded themselves in newly created Alternative Dispute Resolution (ADR) mechanisms, which they initially applauded but then criticised as being overly committed to a 'harmony ideology'.[6] Their findings were necessary as a palliative to the hubris of the ADR movement in the USA, but once the point was made, it was made, and there was not much more to say. By the late 1980s, with a few notable exceptions, legal anthropology had lost its pizzazz.[7]

When the Berlin Wall fell in 1989, legal anthropology was not especially well situated to respond nimbly to the resurgence of human rights and liberal constitutionalism that was occurring not only in Eastern Europe, but also in Africa and Latin America. In the early 1990s, post-conflict and post-authoritarian regimes across the world wrote new constitutions with bills of rights and signed and ratified international human rights instruments. To address the violence of the past, they established high-profile commissions of inquiry or 'truth and reconciliation commissions' (eg in Chile, El Salvador, Guatemala and South Africa). The United Nations created the first international criminal justice institutions since the Nuremberg and Tokyo Trials of 1945–46 to prosecute crimes against humanity, war crimes and genocide committed in Rwanda and the former Yugoslavia. Internationally sponsored criminal tribunals then followed in Cambodia, East Timor, Kosovo, Lebanon and Sierra Leone.

In this unique historical juncture, anthropologists seeking a theoretical and methodological basis to study international justice institutions such as truth and reconciliation commissions or national or international prosecutions for torture or genocide had very little to draw on. Previous theories of legal pluralism, regulating disputes in 'stateless societies' and ADR mechanisms in Western countries were not obviously applicable to the array of novel national and international institutions that arose to investigate and adjudicate mass atrocities committed by state and non-state

---

[4] F von Benda-Beckmann, 'Who's Afraid of Legal Pluralism?' (2002) 47 *Journal of Legal Pluralism and Unofficial Law* 37; J Griffiths, 'What Is Legal Pluralism?' (1986) 24 *Journal of Legal Pluralism and Unofficial Law* 1; SE Merry, 'Legal Pluralism' (1988) 22 *Law and Society Review* 869; F Snyder, 'Colonialism and Legal Form: The Creation of "Customary Law" in Senegal' (1981) 19 *Journal of Legal Pluralism* 49.

[5] L Nader and H Todd (eds), *The Disputing Process: Law in Ten Societies* (New York, Columbia University Press, 1978); L Nader (ed), *No Access to Law: Alternatives to the American Judicial System* (New York, Academic Press, 1980); J Comaroff and S Roberts, *Rules and Processes: the Cultural Logic of Dispute in an African Context* (Chicago, University of Chicago Press, 1981).

[6] L Nader, *Harmony Ideology: Justice and Control in a Zapotec Mountain Village* (Stanford, Stanford University Press, 1990).

[7] See, eg C Greenhouse, *Praying for Justice* (Ithaca, NY, Cornell University Press, 1986); SF Moore, *Social Facts and Fabrications: 'Customary' Law on Kilimanjaro 1880–1980* (Cambridge, Cambridge University Press, 1986).

actors during armed conflicts. If ethnographic researchers were to have something valuable and distinctive to say about this new era of accountability and global human rights, then they would have to renovate the theoretical and methodological tools of legal anthropology.

Sally Merry's monograph *Getting Justice and Getting Even: Legal Consciousness among Working-Class Americans* arrived at a propitious moment.[8] In her study of how working-class Americans litigate personal and family conflicts in lower courts, Merry observed that law is a form of social control that is compatible with, and advances, deep-seated cultural values of individualism and urban egalitarianism. At the same time, there are countervailing factors: for example, plaintiffs (especially women subjected to domestic violence) often engage with the legal process in order to restore a vision of community and forge a relational form of social life. American courts are therefore a site of contestation between the two sets of litigants over core values and community symbols. In the courtroom, legal values and societal norms are mutually constitutive. Merry's temporal and contingent theorisation of the legal process represents a departure from law's archetypal self-image as an enclosed, hermetically sealed adjudication model that is highly regulated by prior-stated rules.

As a study of the legal consciousness of working-class Americans, the subject matter of *Getting Justice and Getting Even* may have seemed tangential to pressing human rights issues in conflict zones, but in fact the monograph showcased many of the methodological and theoretical tools that would guide ethnographers in their investigations of the new global expansion of human rights discourses and institutions. The central lessons of *Getting Justice and Getting Even* were applicable to international justice institutions in a number of ways. First, the monograph transcended the doctrinalism and formalism of law to emphasise the contingent nature of the trial process, which is profoundly shaped by the personalities, strategies and narratives of legal actors (such as judges, prosecutors or advocates) and non-legal actors (plaintiffs or defendants). This was especially relevant at the international criminal tribunals for Rwanda and the former Yugoslavia because in the early phases of their existence the international criminal law they implemented was itself novel and rested on only a slender statutory basis and limited body of case law.[9] *Getting Justice and Getting Even* directed the attention of legal anthropologists away from international legal doctrine to scrutinise the experiences of victims/survivors and to understand how their engagement with international justice institutions transformed their legal and political subjectivity. Crucially, Merry's monograph fostered attentiveness to the encounter (or in some instances, the clash) between social norms of personhood and dignity held by survivors on the one hand and the positivised rules, specialised procedures and evidentiary standards of the courts on the other.

Merry's method animated ethnographers to write about the emotional character and affective dimensions of a legal process, topics that lawyers are usually trained

---

[8] SE Merry, *Getting Justice and Getting Even: Legal Consciousness among Working Class Americans* (Chicago, University of Chicago Press, 1990) 178–80.

[9] On the 'strongly improvisational' nature of international criminal law, see S Moyn, 'Judith Shklar versus the International Criminal Court' (2013) 4 *Humanity: An International Journal of Human Rights, Humanitarianism and Development* 473, 474.

to dismiss as legally irrelevant and as the domain of subjective personal bias.[10] In her analysis, Merry combined structure and agency to simultaneously comprehend the 'cultural domination' of people by the law, as well as the discursive resistance of plaintiffs to the interpretations of the court.[11] Her recent application of 'new legal realism' to international human rights law extended her earlier studies of legal consciousness and legal pluralism, and offered new insights into the 'indeterminacy' and 'incoherence' of law[12] and how law is a 'set of practices with histories, habitual ways of doing things, and systems of cultural meaning'.[13]

II. THE VERNACULARIZATION OF HUMAN RIGHTS AT INTERNATIONAL TRIBUNALS

In 1994, after reading *Getting Justice and Getting Even* and as the horror of the Rwandan genocide was being documented by the international media, I wrote to Sally Merry inviting her to participate in the first edited book on the anthropology of human rights. The central aim was to move away from a simple position of advocacy or rejection of human rights and instead to bring together rigorous ethnographic studies of concrete manifestations of human rights in the 'new world order'.[14] Sally responded warmly and positively, with a generosity of spirit that her many collaborators and colleagues are accustomed to and admire.

Sally Merry's chapter on 'Legal Pluralism and Transnational Culture' in the subsequent edited volume *Human Rights, Culture and Context* was the first statement of her now famous vernacularization thesis.[15] Benedict Anderson[16] had advanced the concept of vernacularization in his path-breaking analysis of nationalism, *Imagined Communities*, to explain how national languages rose to prominence in nineteenth-century Europe as public discourse (and especially religious doctrine and ritual) moved from Latin to colloquial English, French or German. Merry identified a similar process in transnational human rights talk as it circulated between United Nations' committees in New York or Geneva, regional agencies such as the Inter-American Court of Human Rights in San José and shanty towns in Mumbai, Nairobi or Lima.

Even though human rights laws and standards are produced in international agencies and institutions, they move through global networks to dispersed communities around the world. As globalisation extends the reach of human rights, local social

---

[10] For a pathbreaking ethnographic account of US law school education, see E Mertz, *The Language of Law School: Learning to 'Think' Like a Lawyer* (Oxford, Oxford University Press, 2007).

[11] Merry, *Getting Justice and Getting Even* (n 8) 180.

[12] TJ Miles and CR Sunstein, 'The New Legal Realism' (2008) 75 *University of Chicago Law Review* 831.

[13] H Klug and SE Merry (eds), *The New Legal Realism; Studying Law Globally* (Cambridge, Cambridge University Press, 2016) 3.

[14] See GHW Bush, '"New World Order" Speech', address before a joint session of the Congress on the Cessation of the Persian Gulf Conflict (1991) https://college.cengage.com/history/wadsworth_9781133309888/unprotected/ps/bushnwo.html.

[15] SE Merry, 'Legal Pluralism and Transnational Culture' in RA Wilson (ed), *Human Rights, Culture and Context: Anthropological Perspectives* (London, Pluto Press, 1997).

[16] B Anderson (ed), *Imagined Communities: Reflections on the Origin and Spread of Nationalism*, revised edn (London, Verso, 2006).

actors revise and adapt rights talk to mesh with local value systems and priorities; this localised rights talk may, in turn, be re-exported back to the metropoles. The process of cultural adaptation of universal human rights is undertaken by 'translators', or intermediaries such as civil society activists, cause lawyers and social movements leaders who play a critical role in connecting the local with the global and rendering their goals and values intelligible to each other. These 'knowledge brokers', as Merry called them, translate human rights talk into local argot and present human rights knowledge in cultural terms that are comprehensible and convincing to members of their local communities.

In the act of translation, human rights intermediaries must (re)frame the underlying concerns of their constituency in a way that is consistent with the core principles of the international human rights system in order to attract international funding and global media attention. Translators connect local struggles to international networks of activists who assist community actors in pressuring their governments. This process has its limitations and may be constraining in its emphasis on international legal institutions and juridical outcomes. The predominantly legal focus of human rights can be depoliticising and hinder grassroots and legislative approaches to political and structural change. Of course, it need not be either/or: civil rights scholars such as Epp[17] observe that major social change in the 1960s was propelled by a combination of legal precedent, legislative and policy reform, and pressure by social movements.

Merry's vernacularization theory facilitated a sea change in socio-cultural anthropology with respect to the universalism versus cultural relativism debate that it had been mired in for the previous 50 years. It is hard to overstate how groundbreaking this was at the time for the discipline. Up until to the mid- to late 1990s, most socio-cultural anthropologists adhered to the relativist principles laid out in the American Anthropological Association's 1947 statement on the United Nations' Declaration of Human Rights. At the time, the Association's position was a necessary cautionary statement about the need to respect local values and not impose universal standards created by an unaccountable committee in the metropole.

However, in the intervening four decades, the human rights movement had transformed from a merely elite project to a grassroots mobilisation against authoritarian regimes around the world. Human rights covenants and discourse provided a cogent and compelling language for indigenous groups to claim basic rights from nation-states in places like Bangladesh, Brazil, Canada, Ecuador, Guatemala and West Papua. An increasing number of anthropologists such as Terence Turner actively participated in campaigns led by groups like Survival International. Yet there seemed to be an unresolved contradiction between anthropologists' involvement in indigenous rights activism and the generally hostile predisposition towards human rights within the discipline. And what were distinctly lacking were ethnographic methods and analytical theories for studying human rights as a loose constellation of social movements and politico-legal institutions.

---

[17] CR Epp, *The Rights Revolution: Lawyers, Activists, and Supreme Courts in Comparative Perspective* (Chicago, University of Chicago Press, 1998).

Sally Merry's legal realism and vernacularization thesis offered an invaluable theoretical model for conceptualising human rights as a field of critical scholarly inquiry. In this respect, socio-cultural anthropology was ahead of most other social science and humanities disciplines, including history and sociology, which did not generate substantial literatures on human rights until about two decades later. As a result of Merry's timely intervention, anthropologists no longer had to choose between blindly endorsing human rights as formulated by United Nations drafting committees or adhering to nativist, romantic and essentialist accounts of local culture that often ignored how anthropological subjects were rapidly adapting to the modern world. Instead, Merry and other anthropological contributors to the *Human Rights, Culture and Context* volume offered a distinctively ethnographic path that began with the empirical study of what people actually say and do with human rights in everyday political struggles in their communities.[18] In the volume, Wilson advocated for a comparative and empirical anthropology of rights that examined how they are 'materialized, appropriated, resisted and transformed in a variety of contexts'.[19] This was a call for 'grounded theory' of the social and institutional lives of human rights in the classic Weberian sense.

What is frequently forgotten is that Sally Merry developed the theoretical concept of vernacularization in order to comprehend the involvement of an indigenous group with an international justice institution: the People's International Tribunal for Native Hawaiians (Hawaiian People's Tribunal). This tribunal drew inspiration from the model first established by the radical philosophers Bertrand Russell and Jean-Paul Sartre. It was led by locals linked to the Hawaiian sovereignty movement, which campaigned for self-determination, sovereignty and/or autonomy for Hawaiians of whole or part Native Hawaiian ancestry. At the Hawaiian People's Tribunal, Hawaiians appropriated the adjudicative model of Western criminal law to put the US government on trial for international crimes, including genocide, illegal annexation and appropriation of natural resources (also known in international criminal law as pillage or plunder).

In her essay on the Hawaiian People's Tribunal, Merry identified a number of pressing theoretical questions that are still being discussed and analysed in the anthropology of international justice. She asked, for example: how are international justice institutions shaped by legal pluralism and global asymmetries of power; through what investigative process is evidence of crimes created; how does the legal epistemology of the courtroom exclude or distort certain types of information and testimony; what do the plaintiffs/survivors get out of the process, if anything; and how is the legal outcome (eg the judgment) shaped by the contingent strategies, practices and associated meanings pursued by the legal actors in an adversarial process?

Merry's[20] legal realist move decentred the law to comprehend how law is 'constituted by social practices and meanings' that establish 'law's symbolic identity'.

---

[18] Wilson, *Human Rights, Culture and Context* (n 15).
[19] ibid 23.
[20] Merry, 'Legal Pluralism and Transnational Culture' (n 15) 45.

Law has many levels, and ethnographers ought not to privilege state law over other domains of norm-generation and regulation which may be more relevant to people's everyday lives. International justice in particular is a salient normative order, and its meanings are forged at the intersection of local (in this case, Hawaiian Kanaka Maoli law), national (US criminal law) and global (international human rights) legal systems. In a processual view, the representational formation of international justice is not stable and fixed, but is transformed by grassroots social movements as well as developments at the United Nations.

Subsequent generations of ethnographers from anthropology and other social science disciplines have benefited enormously from Sally Merry's theoretical ground-clearing and intellectual leadership, and there now exists a lively anthropology of international justice institutions. Ethnographers have written about international tribunals and reparations claims mechanisms relating to, inter alia, the Holocaust,[21] apartheid-era crimes in South Africa,[22] the Extraordinary Chambers of the Courts of Cambodia,[23] the International Criminal Court,[24] the International Tribunal for East Timor,[25] the International Criminal Tribunal for Rwanda and the gacaca courts,[26] the International Criminal Tribunal for the Former Yugoslavia,[27] the Special Court for Sierra Leone and the Sierra Leone Truth Commission,[28] British trials of soldiers

---

[21] S Slyomovics, *How to Accept German Reparations* (Philadelphia, University of Pennsylvania Press, 2014).

[22] R Kesselring, *Bodies of Truth: Law, Memory and Emancipation in Post-Apartheid South Africa* (Stanford, Stanford University Press, 2017); F Ross, *Bearing Witness: Women and the South African Truth and Reconciliation Commission* (London, Pluto Press, 2002); RA Wilson, *The Politics of Truth and Reconciliation in South Africa: Legitimizing the Post-Apartheid State* (Cambridge, Cambridge University Press, 2001).

[23] AL Hinton, *Man or Monster? The Trial of a Khmer Rouge Torturer* (Durham, NC, Duke University Press, 2016).

[24] KM Clarke, *Fictions of Justice: The International Criminal Court and the Challenge of Legal Pluralism in Sub-Saharan Africa* (New York, Cambridge University Press, 2009); KM Clarke, *Affective Justice: The International Criminal Court and the Pan-Africanist Pushback* (Durham, NC, Duke University Press, 2019); RA Wilson, *Writing History in International Criminal Trials* (Cambridge, Cambridge University Press, 2011); RA Wilson, *Incitement on Trial: Prosecuting International Speech Crimes* (Cambridge, Cambridge University Press, 2017).

[25] E Drexler, 'The Failure of International Justice in East Timor and Indonesia' in AL Hinton (ed), *Transitional Justice: Global Mechanisms and Local Realities after Genocide and Mass Violence* (New Brunswick, NJ, Rutgers University Press, 2010).

[26] MB Dembour and E Haslam, 'Silencing Hearings? Victim-Witnesses at War Crimes Trials' (2004) 15 *European Journal of International Law* 151; K Doughty, *Remediation in Rwanda: Grassroots Legal Forums* (Philadelphia, University of Pennsylvania Press, 2016); N Eltringham, 'Judging the "Crime of Crimes": Continuity and Improvisation at the International Criminal Tribunal for Rwanda' in Hinton, *Transitional Justice* (n 25); N Eltringham, '"Illuminating the Broader Context": Anthropological and Historical Knowledge at the International Criminal Tribunal for Rwanda' (2013) 19 *Journal of the Royal Anthropological Institute* 338; N Eltringham, *Genocide Never Sleeps: Living Law at the International Criminal Tribunal for Rwanda* (Cambridge, Cambridge University Press, 2019).

[27] RM Hayden, 'What's Reconciliation Got to Do With It? The International Criminal Tribunal for the Former Yugoslavia (ICTY) as Antiwar Profiteer' (2007) 5 *Journal of Intervention & Statebuilding* 313; Wilson, *Writing History* (n 24); Wilson, *Incitement on Trial* (n 24).

[28] G Anders, 'Testifying About "Uncivilized Events": Problematic Representations of Africa in the Trial against Charles Taylor' (2011) 24 *Leiden Journal of International Law* 937; R Shaw, 'Memory Frictions: Localizing the Truth and Reconciliation Commission in Sierra Leone' (2007) 1 *The International Journal of Transitional Justice* 183.

accused of torture in Afghanistan,[29] terrorism[30] and genocide trials in Guatemala.[31] All owe a substantial intellectual debt to Sally Merry.

III. CONTEMPORARY DEBATES IN INTERNATIONAL JUSTICE AND HUMAN RIGHTS

Sally Merry's theory of human rights emerged in the 1990s and early 2000s, at a time of rapid globalisation, not only of international law and human rights, but also of manufacturing and industrial supply chains, mining and resource exploitation, financial markets and cultural production. In the interregnum between the fall of the Berlin Wall and the September 11 terror attacks, human rights attained an exalted status that they had not held previously in world affairs. Multilateral institutions regained a legitimacy and influence they had not had since the heady days of the immediate post-World War II period. The European Union and NATO expanded rapidly to include eastern European countries. The International Criminal Court, World Trade Organization and Organisation for the Prohibition of Chemical Weapons were all established, and some international relations theorists boldly claimed that the world was moving towards creating a new global constitution under the aegis of a revitalised United Nations.[32]

The twenty-first century has proved a little less amenable to multilateralism and the project of international justice than many had hoped. Multilateralism is under siege, including from its erstwhile strongest advocates such as the USA and the UK. The number of populist governments has doubled worldwide since the early 2000s: populist leaders have been elected in, inter alia, Brazil, Guatemala, Hungary, India, the Philippines, Poland, Turkey, the UK, the USA and Venezuela.[33] Populists have risen to power by cultivating a nativist backlash to globalisation, by decrying established political parties and by inveighing against multilateral institutions and accompanying universal ideas such as liberal democracy and human rights.[34] In their place, populists extol the virtues of religious, racial or ethnic chauvinism, and propagate essentialist myths of race, religion and nation. They deny science (and, indeed, facticity itself) and climate change, and withdraw from environmental and climate treaties. They close borders, and impugn refugees and immigrants for any social ills and economic problems.

---

[29] T Kelly, *This Side of Silence: Human Rights, Torture and the Recognition of Cruelty* (Philadelphia, University of Pennsylvania Press, 2012).

[30] S Hirsch, *In the Moment of Greatest Calamity: Terrorism, Grief, and a Victim's Quest for Justice* (Princeton, Princeton University Press, 2006).

[31] ML García, 'Translated Justice? The Ixil Maya and the 2013 Trial of José Efraín Ríos Montt for Genocide in Guatemala' (2019) 121 *American Anthropologist* 311.

[32] D Held, *Democracy and the Global Order: from the Modern Nation-State to Cosmopolitan Governance* (Cambridge, Cambridge University Press, 1995).

[33] P Lewis et al, 'Revealed: The Rise and Rise of Populist Rhetoric', *The Guardian* (London, 6 March 2019) www.theguardian.com/world/ng-interactive/2019/mar/06/revealed-the-rise-and-rise-of-populist-rhetoric; RJ Heydarian, 'Understanding Duterte's Mind-Boggling Rise to Power' *Washington Post* (Washington, DC, 20 March 2019) www.washingtonpost.com/news/theworldpost/wp/2018/03/20/duterte/.

[34] RF Inglehart and P Norris, 'Trump, Brexit, and the Rise of Populism: Economic Have-Nots and Cultural Backlash' (2016) HKS Faculty Working Paper Series No RWP16-026, https://papers.ssrn.com/sol3/papers.cfm?abstract_id=2818659.

Is a theory of human rights like Merry's, developed in an era of globalisation, still relevant? For a number of reasons, it arguably is. First, the challenges facing the majority of societies are still global; pandemics, climate change and the refugees it creates, nuclear proliferation, the vagaries of markets, terrorism, hate speech online – the list goes on. Economies and polities are still deeply intertwined and interdependent, despite populists' best efforts to pretend otherwise. Even if this were desirable, there is simply no way to wall off a country and be unaffected by, say, a nuclear war or a global health pandemic.

And human rights still matter, both normatively and empirically. They matter normatively because no political system can claim to be democratic or even representational without constitutionalising and creating the necessary institutions to protect the basic rights of individuals and groups, and especially vulnerable minority groups. Empirically, human rights continue to be the foremost global language for speaking about politically motivated crimes committed by governments against their citizens. In the Latin American countries where I have conducted research – Colombia and Guatemala – there are many vibrant social movements campaigning for women's rights, LGBTQ+ rights, indigenous rights and legal accountability for genocide, all in the language of human rights. Civil society groups with a significant indigenous membership such as Asociación Minga (Colombia) or CONAVIGUA (Guatemala) embrace the values, discourses and practices of international human rights as they confront authoritarian measures imposed by their governments and non-state actors such as powerful multinational corporations. In so doing, civil society activists (Merry's 'intermediaries') translate international human rights into the local moral argot and pressure international human rights institutions to be more receptive to their specific needs. The concept of vernacularization still describes this process accurately. Sometimes, to be sure, human rights are imposed from above, rejected from below or completely lost in translation. The concrete outcomes of international justice institutions and the character of popular legal consciousness are still empirical questions to be studied through careful ethnographic inquiry. They will vary from locale to locale, undermining any easy generalisations about human rights.

The continued relevance of Merry's ethnographic empiricism and legal realism can be illustrated by reference to the contemporary debate between Samuel Moyn and Kathryn Sikkink over the character and efficacy of human rights and international justice. Over the past decade, the study of human rights has extended to nearly every discipline in the humanities and social sciences, and with this has come a number of trenchant critiques and spirited defences of human rights. The rivalry between Moyn and Sikkink has helpfully crystallised these positions and allowed us to better understand how Merry's approach offers a constructive third way to think about human rights and international justice.

In *The Last Utopia* and *Not Enough*, Samuel Moyn[35] extends a materialist critique of contemporary rights talk that, in my reading, has its intellectual roots in Marx's dismissal of human rights in 'On the Jewish Question'.[36] Moyn identifies a

---

[35] S Moyn, *The Last Utopia* (Cambridge, MA, Belknap Press, 2010); S Moyn, *Not Enough: Human Rights in an Unequal World* (Cambridge, MA, Harvard University Press, 2018).
[36] K Marx, 'On the Jewish Question'/"Zur Judenfrage"' in *Deutsch–Französische Jahrbücher* (1844).

'connivance' between political terror and the neoliberal economic model that rose contemporaneously with human rights starting in the 1970s.[37] As socialism declined, human rights became the central language of justice, and international justice institutions stigmatised dictatorship 'while turning a blind eye to galloping material inequality'.[38] Human rights institutions drew attention to individual violations, but they did not challenge the neoliberal policies that resulted in massive wealth for the few and immiseration of the many.[39] Human rights failed to articulate a coherent commitment to distributive equality[40] or connect meaningfully with social movements struggling for socio-economic rights[41] such as housing, healthcare or worker's rights.

Moyn pushes back against Naomi Klein's outright dismissal of the language of rights to build a more nuanced position, observing that even though human rights are not responsible for causing, or even for distracting from, neoliberal economic policies, they have been 'condemned to a defensive and minor role in pushing back against the new political economy'.[42] Human rights advocates may be able to point to certain advances, but these came at the cost of sacrificing material fairness and mounting a fully blown campaign against the economic exploitation and dramatic increase in global inequality resulting from the inexorable rise of 'market fundamentalism' in the late 1970s. Moyn concedes that human rights campaigns on gender inequality, sexual violence and women's rights have achieved a great deal, but counters that the human rights movement has simultaneously neglected the mounting material inequality, which has had an even greater impact on women's lives.[43]

In *The Justice Cascade* and *Evidence for Hope*,[44] Sikkink provides a rebuttal to Moyn and other critics of human rights. She reflects that, since the mid-1980s, human rights prosecutions have challenged impunity and ensured that the prospects of accountability for human rights offenders have steadily improved. She charts the rise of international accountability institutions, from Nuremberg/Tokyo to the trials of Argentine military leaders to the International Criminal Court, and argues that these developments have brought us to a point where heads of state such as Slobodan Milošević, General Augusto Pinochet and Charles Taylor can no longer shield themselves behind the medieval notion of sovereign immunity. The norm of accountability for political leaders who commit mass atrocities against their own populations has triggered a cascade effect. This 'justice cascade' has had a positive impact on democracy, economic growth and equality. It has a deterrent effect by sending the message to proto-authoritarian political leaders that pursuing a strategy of corruption and violence may land them in a national or international court. Over recent decades,

---

[37] Moyn, *The Last Utopia* (n 35) 173.
[38] ibid 176.
[39] ibid 186.
[40] ibid 192.
[41] ibid 198.
[42] ibid 176.
[43] ibid 204.
[44] K Sikkink, *The Justice Cascade: How Human Rights Prosecutions Are Changing World Politics* (New York, WW Norton, 2011); K Sikkink, *Evidence For Hope: Making Human Rights Work in the 21st Century* (Princeton, Princeton University Press, 2017).

Sikkink observes an increase in states ratifying human rights treaties and an overall decline in armed conflicts and battle deaths worldwide.[45] She explicitly refutes claims that the achievements of the human rights system are 'minimal' and that human rights are 'powerless' to address economic inequality.[46] Sikkink lists the ways in which human rights have effectively confronted status inequalities, improved global health (eg by expanding access to retroviral drugs in South Africa) and tackled corporate greed (eg by holding tobacco companies accountable in Uruguay).[47]

Although Moyn and Sikkink's arguments are self-consciously opposed to one another, both contain many accurate observations. *Pace* Moyn, neoliberalism and human rights did arise concomitantly and seemingly without open contradiction. Moreover, the two paradigms share a number of elements, including an individual rights ethos and a legal-proceduralist approach to politics. A number of prominent human rights organisations such as Amnesty International, at least until the last few years, did not mobilise human rights laws to close the yawning chasm of material inequality, or to classify the neoliberal economic model as the primary threat to human well-being. It is true that human rights laws are more effective at addressing individual criminal responsibility than economic exploitation and structural forms of violence, yet Sikkink is also justified in her assertion that human rights have made enormous strides in securing accountability for mass human rights violations since the 1970s. This is important not only for survivors, but also for the rule of law, the independence of the judiciary and the kinds of institutional checks on political power that are essential to the creation of post-conflict governments that do not commit mass atrocities against their own citizenry. Evidently, Moyn and Sikkink are talking past one another.

Both theoretical stances towards human rights also have discernible frailties. Sikkink is careful to recognise that merely ratifying international human rights treaties is insufficient, and that there can be much backsliding on commitments by regimes. At the same time, the 'justice cascade' is a metaphor, and like all metaphors, it occludes as much as it reveals. It implies a flow in one direction and a kind of domino effect that is teleological towards ever-deeper state compliance with human rights. Sikkink's writings are characterised by a Whiggish tone in their historiography of human rights, in the sense that they present a steady and inexorable progression towards ever greater human rights protections which culminates in modern forms of liberal democracy. There seems to be no palpable downside to, or severe ruptures in, the onwards march of human rights and accountability for perpetrators. However, as with any political platform, human rights (when conceived narrowly as accountability for alleged perpetrators) have trade-offs, setbacks and unintended consequences. For instance, too inflexible a commitment to retributive justice may jeopardise a delicately poised peace process, a concern expressed by humanitarian organisations working in Sudan in 2006 when President Al-Bashir was indicted for genocide in Darfur by the International Criminal Court.

---

[45] ibid 187–88, 203.
[46] ibid 235–36.
[47] ibid 237–38.

Criminal law is a blunt instrument and a full awareness of societal complexity, including discussions of racism and material inequality, can be lost in a criminal proceeding. International justice is not always the best forum for hearing the voices of victims or fathoming the structural conditions that gave rise to political authoritarianism and armed conflict. Sikkink's 'justice cascade' that emerges from human rights prosecutions and the expansion of human rights treaty ratification only has full applicability in two regions of the world: Latin America and Europe. This is because they have strong human rights movements, because of the 'neighborhood effects' of human rights convention ratifications[48] and because they have reasonably robust regional human rights mechanisms – such as the Inter-American Court and Inter-American Commission of Human Rights and the European Court of Human Rights – that can hold recalcitrant regimes to account. As Sikkink has argued,[49] Latin American governments, social movements and regional organisations have played an outsized role in the formulation and implementation of the international human rights regime. Sikkink's arguments are on much shakier ground in Asia, where fewer states have ratified international treaties and only a handful have signed and ratified the Rome Statute of the International Criminal Court. In Africa, more states have ratified international treaties, but impunity for mass atrocities is the domestic norm; over the last 15 years, many African elites have turned to Pan-Africanism and rallied to shield political leaders from the International Criminal Court.[50] The justice cascade metaphor seems entirely inappropriate in the context of the flagrant and repeated flouting of international human rights law by the governments of Russia, China and the USA, not to mention Syria.

If Sikkink is over-reliant on Latin American examples for her defence of human rights, then Moyn seldom contemplates Latin American experiences except as a laboratory for neoliberalism. There are enough examples of social movements in that region campaigning for housing, healthcare and worker's rights and opposing mining and dam projects to disqualify Moyn's thesis that human rights movements have not meaningfully challenged neoliberalism or material inequality or have been unconcerned with socio-economic rights. In Guatemala alone, robust anti-mining campaigns at La Puya and El Estor and indigenous groups opposing the massive hydroelectric dams at Ixquisis and Rio Chixoy embrace international human rights as a central aspect of their struggle.[51] Many more examples of socio-economic rights movements that also appeal to international human rights can be found in Colombia, Ecuador, Mexico, Peru and other Latin American countries.[52] One of the problems in this discussion is that Moyn sets the bar impossibly high by saying that

---

[48] On theories of compliance with human rights, see B Simmons, *Mobilizing for Human Rights: International Law in Domestic Politics* (Cambridge, Cambridge University Press, 2009) 112.
[49] K Sikkink 'Latin America's Protagonist Role in Human Rights' (2015) 12 *Sur – International Journal on Human Rights* 207.
[50] Clarke, *Affective Justice* (n 24).
[51] SR Munzer, 'Dam(n) Displacement: Compensation, Resettlement, and Indigeneity' (2019) 51 *Cornell International Law Journal* 823.
[52] S Hertel and L Minkler (eds), *Economic Rights: Conceptual, Measurement, and Policy Issues* (Cambridge, Cambridge University Press, 2007); S Sawyer and E Gomez (eds), *The Politics of Resource Extraction: Indigenous Peoples, Multinational Corporations and the State* (London, Palgrave Macmillan, 2012).

'No human rights NGOs, northern or southern, emphasised inequality for its own sake',[53] which shows little awareness of how grassroots movements are compelled by practical considerations to mobilise marginalised communities against concrete manifestations of inequality rather than the abstract conceptualisation of economists and other learned analysts.

There are yet more unrealistic expectations in Moyn's critique. That resounding victories of human rights movements are few, and that they have not succeeded in single-handedly thwarting the rise of neoliberalist policies since the 1970s is undeniable. But this failure is hardly exclusive to human rights movements: it also applies to many more powerful actors, such as the Soviet Union and other socialist regimes, political parties of the left, trade unions and the labour movement, and progressive social justice-oriented social movements in liberal democracies. Neoliberalism crushed all in its path, backed as it was by the world's most powerful governments (principally the USA and the UK), the world's biggest multinational corporations, global financial markets, the International Monetary Fund and the World Bank. One could add to this list the most powerful military forces in the history of the planet, which acted aggressively to protect rapidly expanding global markets.

Human rights, on the other hand, have been backed intermittently by a handful of liberal governments when it suits them, international civil society organisations and philanthropic foundations, vulnerable grassroots social movements and the institutional agency structure of the United Nations. Nation-states and corporations possess vastly more resources than civil society groups and international institutions. The United Nations, it should be noted, has a budget a little more than half that of the New York Police Department. The mandate of the latter is to police the five boroughs of New York City, whereas the mandate of the United Nations is to ensure peace, security and human rights in the entire world.[54] Moyn's frustration at the uncontested supremacy of neoliberal economics is understandable, and I share it, but laying the blame at the door of human rights for our current condition of colossal global inequality seems misplaced.

Despite the occasional hubris of some advocates in the human rights field, human rights are not well designed to usher in a political utopia; they are designed to respond in fairly narrow legal and policy ways to a violent dystopia. They are most effective when they set minimum standards for governments and private actors, not when they articulate aspirational targets for the realisation of humanity's full potential. Achieving healthcare for all, eradicating poverty or promoting social mobility are more productively pursued through legislative and policy means, that is, through the political process, than through rights-claiming in law courts, although the latter can play a supporting role.

---

[53] Moyn, *Not Enough* (n 35) 195.
[54] The budget of the New York Police Department for 2020 was $5.6 billion and the UN's budget was $3 billion: Council of the City of New York, 'Report to the Committee on Finance and the Committee on Public Safety on the Fiscal 2020 Executive Plan, the Ten-Year Capital Strategy for Fiscal 2020–2029, and Fiscal 2020 Executive Capital Commitment Plan: New York Police Department' (15 May 2019) https://council.nyc.gov/budget/wp-content/uploads/sites/54/2019/05/NYPD.pdf; UN Affairs, 'General Assembly Approves $3 Billion UN Budget for 2020' (*UN News*, 27 December 2019) https://news.un.org/en/story/2019/12/1054431.

Sikkink and Moyn's diverging conclusions about human rights are in part the outcome of their respective theoretical models and methods of inquiry. In the quantitative data analysis favoured by Sikkink, it is hard to see anything that has not been coded into a dataset and for which you are not already looking, and this can elide an understanding of the unintended consequences and imperfections of international justice institutions. Moyn's legal, historical and philosophical approach is informed by a review of texts, archives and theory; here again, there is a tendency to marshal the evidence and cast aside the messiness of social life that is commonly encountered in ethnographic and empirical inquiry.

Ethnographic inquiry into international justice is quite a different and more uncontrolled undertaking. Ethnographers of international justice institutions regularly experience the demise of their research design and theoretical platform immediately upon entering the field and commencing fieldwork and interviews.[55] Political science, law and history are more insulated from the fragmentation and incoherence of qualitative empirical social research. Ethnography can be unpredictable and unnerving, but it is exactly this characteristic that is generative of original ideas and perspectives. Perhaps this is the reason why lawyers, historians and political scientists have been more willing than ethnographers to make sweeping judgements about the emancipatory or shackling implications of human rights institutions. Generalisations are good for promotional soundbites, but they have their intellectual drawbacks.

IV. THE ETHNOGRAPHIC STUDY OF INTERNATIONAL JUSTICE INSTITUTIONS

The current terms of the Moyn–Sikkink debate about human rights are pitched at such a high level of abstraction that they hinder a full understanding of international human rights laws, discourses and institutions, not to mention popular discourses on human rights as they are manifested globally. If we just concern ourselves with one domain of human rights – international criminal tribunals – there is wide variation in institutional design, underlying case law and legal outcomes. For instance, the Nuremberg trials were sponsored by only four nations (France, the Soviet Union, the UK and the USA) and employed an Anglo-American adversarial courtroom model. They had little basis in international law, which was incipient at the time, and instead relied on British and American legal theories (such as conspiracy) and novel concepts that had yet to be adjudicated in a court of law (eg crimes against humanity).

In contrast, the current International Criminal Court has a lengthy and detailed international law statute that has been signed and ratified by a majority of states and applies predominantly civil law rules of procedure and evidence in the courtroom. In between, there were the United Nations-sponsored ad hoc tribunals of former

---

[55] On the experiential dimensions of international legal ethnography, see J Meierhenrich and RA Wilson, '"The Life of the Law Has Not Been Logic; It Has Been Experience:" International Legal Ethnography and the New Legal Realism' in H Klug et al (eds), *Handbook on New Legal Realism* (Cheltenham, Edward Elgar Publishing, 2021).

Yugoslavia and Rwanda, as well as hybrid in-country models such as the Special Court for Sierra Leone and the Extraordinary Chambers of the Courts of Cambodia that integrate national and international legal procedures and personnel. While the ad hoc tribunals were quite disconnected from the populations and countries in which the crimes occurred, the Special Court for Sierra Leone launched an ambitious public outreach programme that succeeded in informing many Sierra Leoneans about the legal process.[56] This variance in design and outcomes makes it very difficult to generalise about international justice, much less Moyn's compendious concept of 'human rights law and politics', which would bring into view public international law and a host of other human rights settings and institutions.

In Sally Merry's new legal realism, we can identify a nuanced and grounded approach to human rights and international justice that allows us to navigate past the Scylla of utopian optimism and the Charybdis of dystopian pessimism.[57] As Merry sets out, its methodology 'includes transnational and multi-sited ethnographic research that tracks the flows of people, ideas, laws, and institutions across national boundaries and examines particular nodes and sites within this field of transnational circulation'.[58] Theoretically, Merry's legal realism promotes an attentiveness to 'how human rights law works in practice' and the production and global circulation of legal knowledge.[59]

Merry illustrated her method in her groundbreaking study of the process at the United Nations that governed the review, implementation and enforcement of the Convention on the Elimination of All Forms of Discrimination against Women (CEDAW), which she concluded was 'a very murky process'. States may sign the Convention but not ratify it, or both sign and ratify it but apply reservations (essentially, opt-outs) on certain contentious provisions. Some states sign, ratify and pass domestic legislation to implement all provisions and then enforce them, whereas others sign, ratify and implement but then ignore the provisions. When states fail to live up to their obligations under public international law, there is no international enforcement mechanism apart from shaming in diplomatic circles, although this can be surprisingly effective in shifting state behaviour. In her study of CEDAW implementation at the local level in five Asia-Pacific countries, Merry found that different approaches to violence against women – including international human rights law, national concepts of rights and feminist social services – coexist in marked tension with one another. Merry's new legal realist method leads her to conclude that human rights 'do not constitute a coherent system but are contingent, fragmented, and unevenly supported by the general public ... the articulation of rights does not guarantee performance'.[60] This is a far cry from Sikkink's 'justice cascade' or Moyn's blanket condemnation of the congenitally milquetoast nature of human rights.

---

[56] R Kerr and J Lincoln, 'The Special Court for Sierra Leone Outreach, Legacy and Impact: Final Report' (War Crimes Research Group at the Department of War Studies, King's College London, 2008) www.rscsl.org/Documents/slfinalreport.pdf.
[57] SE Merry, *Human Rights and Gender Violence; Translating International Law into Local Justice* (Chicago, University of Chicago Press, 2006); Klug and Merry (n 13).
[58] Merry, *Human Rights and Gender Violence* (n 57) 976.
[59] ibid 977.
[60] ibid 979.

Ethnographic studies of international justice provide a precise and empirically grounded basis to understand both the benefits and inadequacies of international accountability institutions. Overall, we can say that ethnographers have been broadly critical of these tribunals' efforts at accountability and documenting the past. Retributive justice has a restricted mandate and framing of events: to ascertain the guilt or innocence of the accused on the basis of whether the actions sufficiently match the elements of the crimes (*actus reus* and *mens rea*) as formulated in the statutes of international criminal law. The scope of international tribunals is limited to the actions or inactions of the defendant and those with whom the defendant was working in concert (through concepts such as 'joint criminal enterprise'), and whether these actions or inactions imply individual criminal responsibility. The wider structural conditions driving the conflict (eg religious discrimination, racism, material exploitation) are often overlooked, as are the actions of those who may have tolerated, benefited from or been complicit in structures of violence.[61] Even as they document the criminal actions of corrupt elites, courts generally neglect the role of international markets, corporations and other powerful global actors in fomenting conflict.

With respect to legal knowledge production, criminal law has a unique, limited and highly regulated set of criteria for investigating events and pronouncing on the validity of arguments.[62] The rules of evidence and procedure at an international tribunal and how the court comprehends the relationship between factors (ie causation) are tightly regulated. International courts often struggle to combine evidence from different systems of knowledge such as medicine, social science, historical inquiry and legal and forensic investigations.[63] In sum, if deep comprehension of why the conflict occurred in the first place is the goal, then international tribunals often fall short: they view events through a narrow legal prism, which often excludes the context, motivation and structural factors that shaped the violent patterns of behaviour in society. And as is true of criminal law generally, international courts have not always been receptive to the narratives of survivors, especially women speaking about their experiences of sexual assault.[64]

At the same time, ethnographic studies have also recognised the constructive contributions of international justice institutions in documenting and prosecuting past atrocities.[65] After mass crimes, there is intense contestation over the past. Powerful perpetrators (who may still hold high political office) often seek to erase or distort evidence of their crimes and evade accountability. International tribunals, by virtue of their liminal interstate position, often allow the introduction of more evidence of a historical or cultural nature than would be permitted in a national criminal court. Anthropologists and historians have proved to be effective expert witnesses

---

[61] Clarke, *Affective Justice* (n 24).
[62] Eltringham, *Genocide Never Sleeps* (n 26); Wilson, *Incitement on Trial* (n 24).
[63] Kelly (n 29).
[64] Dembour and Haslam (n 26).
[65] EL Lutz and C Reiger (eds), *Prosecuting Heads of State* (Cambridge, Cambridge University Press, 2009); L Nettelfield, *Courting Democracy in Bosnia and Herzegovina: The Hague Tribunal's Impact in a Postwar State* (Cambridge, Cambridge University Press, 2010).

in the international criminal courtroom, with a surprising ability to sway the judges' thinking and legal decisions.[66] International courts have produced comprehensive accounts of conflicts that are authoritative and resistant to historical revisionism by perpetrators, and thereby played a vital role in national projects of constructing collective memory and memorialising the past.

International courts have responded to criticisms that they diminish the testimony of survivors. The International Criminal Court now allows survivors and their legal representatives to be actual parties to the trial and participate in the legal proceedings: for instance, to scrutinise the evidence presented before the trial chamber and to cross-examine the defendant and other witnesses. In particular, the testimony of women about sexual assault has been handled more sensitively, and international tribunals have established, through key decisions such as *Akayesu*[67] (International Criminal Tribunal for Rwanda, ICTR) and *Kunarac*[68] (ICTY), the precedent that sexual violence is a war crime and a crime against humanity. Even if the outcome of a trial is not what the survivors hoped for, ethnographic studies have shown that international trials represent a focal point for survivors' groups to organise around, and this process can create new forms of sociality that are healing in themselves.[69]

In sum, international tribunals play an important role in pursuing accountability for perpetrators of mass crimes, although they represent only one element in a necessarily holistic response to an era of violence. Despite their flaws, international courts perform a valuable function when they articulate the moral values of a community and reject, for instance, the anti-Semitism of the Holocaust or sexual slavery during the conflict in eastern Congo. Merry's account of how working-class Americans approach courts in *Getting Justice and Getting Even* is directly applicable to understanding survivors' engagements with international courts. Even though law is constituted as a form of social control and cultural domination, there is always a process of resistance and struggle over the history and meaning of mass crimes. At international tribunals, survivors and their legal representatives demand recognition and reparations for harms, articulate a moral discourse of repudiation of violence and, in so doing, help to construct a new image of social relationality.

V. CONCLUDING REMARKS

Human rights movements, laws and discourses operate in so many settings globally that most generalisations about them crumble on closer scrutiny. Human rights may motivate a social movement protesting a dam project in Colombia or a women's maternal health campaign in India, or they may propel an international criminal tribunal adjudicating charges against an accused. They may also be distorted and

---

[66] Wilson, *Writing History* (n 24).
[67] *Prosecutor v Akayesu* (Judgment) ICTR-96-4-T, T Ch I (2 September 1998).
[68] *Kunerac et al* (Sentencing Judgment) IT-96-23 & 23/1, A Ch (12 June 2002); *Kunerac et al* (Judgment) IT-96-23 & 23/1, T Ch II (22 February 2001).
[69] Kesselring (n 22).

misused by powerful actors seeking to legitimate their ideological project of violent domination.[70]

These are all distinctive contexts, with diverse outcomes that challenge any sweeping assessments of the success or failure of human rights as a paradigm of law or politics. Instead, we are better advised to try to understand the particular instantiations of human rights in their social contexts (or what I call the 'social life of rights'). For this, we require grounded theories and empirical methodologies that will furnish insights into the concrete effects of human rights. This case-by-case approach to 'how law works in practice' focuses on process as much as outcome, and recognises the contingency and fragmentation of human rights. It inclines scholars towards intellectual humility instead of magisterial pronouncements of a utopian or dystopian kind about human rights.[71]

Throughout her career, Sally Merry argued for a complex and sophisticated approach to understanding human rights and international justice, one that encompasses the multiple influences of global, national and local law, and that is aware of law's coercive power while still reserving a place for contingency, social resistance and agency. She charted high-level diplomatic negotiations in New York and Geneva, as well as the local impact of human rights at a women's centre in Delhi. Her intellectual style of writing and analysis embraced the unexpected, and was comfortable with indeterminacy and a lack of analytical closure. To my mind, this is one explanation of the long-standing salience and influence of Sally's work; she did not insist dogmatically on a single template of analysis or a set of hard and fast conclusions about human rights. She was willing to dwell on the unsettling and murky nature of the process of creating and enforcing human rights and to recognise that what happens in Geneva may have entirely different effects on the ground in Hong Kong or Hawaii. Sally Merry was a legal realist without ignoring the strong inertial effects of legal doctrine and law's unique and specialised rules and procedures. She was a legal pluralist without falling into the arid formalism of some forms of legal pluralism. She was a feminist without focusing solely on gender. The suppleness and sophistication of her research and analysis, and the inclusive and open manner in which she collaborated and exchanged ideas with other scholars in the field, is a model for us all.

---

[70] On the Guatemalan military's appropriation of human rights discourse, see J Schirmer, *The Guatemalan Military Project: A Violence Called Democracy* (Philadelphia, University of Pennsylvania Press, 1999); on how the communist dictatorship in the German Democratic Republic portrayed itself as a champion of human rights, see N Richardson-Little, *The Human Rights Dictatorship: Socialism, Global Solidarity and Revolution in East Germany* (Cambridge, Cambridge University Press, 2020).

[71] Mark Goodale also makes the case for humility in the study of human rights, in *Surrendering to Utopia: An Anthropology of Human Rights* (Stanford, Stanford University Press, 2009).

3

Vernacularizing Rights: Indispensable but Dangerous

JACK SNYDER

A HIGH BAR for academic success is the reception of a scholar's work outside its home discipline. The enthusiasm of political scientists for Sally Engle Merry's concept of vernacularization of human rights discourse passes this test with flying colours. Its impact is all the more surprising in light of the inevitable stumbling over the pronunciation of this pretentious term, or what Americans might call a 10-dollar word.[1]

Speaking to local audiences about human rights in terms that resonate is indispensable for practitioners of human rights promotion. Whether or not they consciously adopt Sally's vernacularization approach, her research on women's rights around the world shows that activists and their audiences inevitably engage in a process of cultural translation. She underscores that her main task in this research is to describe the world – to show how vernacularization of rights actually happens. An important secondary task is evaluating the pluses and minuses of vernacularizing rights discourse from the standpoint of the activists' objective of persuasion.[2] Developing some of the ambivalent themes in Sally's work on vernacularization, I seek to locate her primarily cultural approach in relation to a nascent conversation in political science about the political dimension of the 'localization' of global norms.[3]

When human rights advocates attempt to mobilise the enthusiasm of supporters, volunteers and donors in wealthy, liberal societies, their discourse tends to feature legalism, moralism and universalism. Uncompromising clarion calls to act on principle serve the movement's organisational needs. Aryeh Neier's history of the human rights movement explains how the nineteenth-century campaigns to denounce Turkish atrocities against Bulgarians or to establish Red Cross medical protections on the battlefield gathered little momentum until such isolated efforts

---

[1] P Levitt and SE Merry, 'Vernacularization on the Ground: Local Uses of Global Women's rights in Peru, China, India, and the United States' (2009) 9 *Global Networks* 441.
[2] P Levitt and SE Merry, 'The Vernacularization of Women's Human Rights' in S Hopgood, L Vinjamuri and J Snyder (eds), *Human Rights Futures* (Cambridge, Cambridge University Press, 2017) 213.
[3] A Acharya, 'How Ideas Spread: Whose Norms Matter? Norm Localization and Institutional Change in Asian Regionalism' (2004) 58 *International Organization* 239.

were linked via the universalising ideology and organisation of the global human rights movement.[4]

Addressed to audiences in societies where rights concepts are unfamiliar, human rights talk can come off as alien and unpersuasive. It is legalistic in societies where concepts of justice and appropriateness are often not rule-based and impersonal, but rather relationship-based and communal. Rights talk sounds distinctively Western in societies that know the West mainly as a coloniser or a domineering rival. Rights advocates 'name and shame' entrenched local practices under the unconvincing banner of universality, which often reflects someone else's particular reality.

Beyond being unpersuasive, these ideas are provocative in a way that can backfire. Human rights shaming threatens powerful spoilers in the target society: religious and cultural elites, as well as privileged exploiter classes, including the patriarchy, dominant cultural groups, wealth-holders and other entrenched interests. The alien and demanding nature of human rights spurs these threatened groups to mobilise broad resistance around powerful cultural themes of communal self-defence and anti-imperialism. In Kenya, for example, former rivals in tribal mayhem managed to find common cause in successfully running for president and vice president on a platform of resisting the 'imperialist' International Criminal Court (ICC).[5] Once established in ideology and institutions, rights-resisting illiberalism can lock in and leave rights activism farther from its goal.

While examples of backlash against provocative rights discourse are not rare, Sally and her co-author Peggy Levitt point out that, rather than being a naturally occurring antidote, vernacularization is a common process at work in global human rights networks. They note that 'chains of actors stretch from the sites of the global production of human rights documents and ideas (in New York, Geneva, and Vienna) to localities where ordinary people around the world adopt them'.[6] This chain of vernacularizers includes 'centrally placed elite actors', 'global travellers' and locals who interact with them in settings such as 'leadership trainings', where locals 'talk back'. Also important are '"marginal actors" who can afford to go out on a limb because they are unconstrained by social norms'. Innovation, for good or ill, is facilitated by the suppleness of network connections and the cognitive flexibility of the people in the networks. Incentives in this networked system reward message content that is easily understood and 'culturally compatible with values already in place'.[7] For example, the formal language of the Convention on the Elimination of All Forms of Discrimination against Women gets translated in local NGO messaging as 'helping women to stand up for themselves' to be treated in ways that are 'fair' and 'just'.[8] Dramatisations and vivid narratives illustrate these points in a way that is concrete but schematic – packaged parables whose generalised lessons can be extracted in discussion with all participants. Through

---

[4] A Neier, *The International Human Rights Movement: A History* (Princeton, Princeton University Press, 2012) 42.
[5] L Vinjamuri, 'Human Rights Backlash' in Hopgood et al (n 2) 124.
[6] Levitt and Merry, 'Vernacularization on the Ground' (n 1) 446–47.
[7] ibid 444, 449.
[8] ibid 223, 225.

this process, Levitt and Merry say, 'identities, concepts, and categories' and 'practices' are diffused via a 'cultural act'.[9]

I. DILEMMAS OF VERNACULARIZATION

Levitt and Merry identify several dilemmas that are inherent to vernacularization from the standpoint of rights advocacy. Translating rights talk into the idiom of societies that do not think in terms of rights risks watering down the message. Even worse, vernacularization of rights discourse can slip into modes of thinking that justify and perpetuate abuse.

One common move, for example, is to shift from demands for the rights of victims to appeals to the duties that others owe them. This language of duties often fits better into the charitable concepts of entrenched religions, but it shifts agency away from the rights claimant to the provider of charity, which opens the door to the provider's judgements about the recipient's worthiness to receive charity. In many cultures, including even the Western concept of 'the deserving poor', rights may be seen as a privilege that is earned only when the recipient has fulfilled a duty or behaved in a manner deemed worthy.[10] For example, Indian police, even ones that have received human rights training, argue that it is acceptable to torture detainees who are suspected of violating community members' right to security, because the suspects have not earned the right to due process.[11] This justification for abuse becomes impervious to evidence when judgements about deservingness are based on an a priori group stigma: the suspects are not truly human, so there is no duty to grant them human rights.

The power of vernacularized messages can also get watered down when they are translated into everyday concepts like 'stand up for yourself'. As Neier argued, generalising the idea of rights was the key to its momentum over time and its spread across issues. Common-sense language by its nature fails to generalise into a critique of the whole system of exploitation. Thus, Levitt and Merry point out that what the common-sense vernacular gains in immediate intelligibility is lost in the depth and breadth of its impact.

Related to this, they argue that persuasive resonance is not based only on familiarity; it can also be based on a compelling message that shows a new way to resolve a tangle of seemingly insoluble, endemic problems. Oppressed minority audiences may see vernacular norms talk as part of the problem they want to escape.[12] Especially for downtrodden groups facing discrimination in their own society, universal human rights as part of the package of liberal modernity is 'imbued with the appeal, power, and legitimacy of the international'.[13] Vernacularization can water down this charisma.

---

[9] ibid 444–45.
[10] R Wahl, *Just Violence: Torture and Human Rights in the Eyes of the Police* (Stanford, Stanford University Press, 2017) 118; I Katznelson, *When Affirmative Action Was White* (New York, W.W. Norton & Company, 2005).
[11] Wahl (n 10) 118.
[12] Levitt and Merry, 'Vernacularization on the Ground' (n 1) 452, 458.
[13] ibid 446–47.

II. HUMAN RIGHTS AS A PACKAGE DEAL

A major barrier to successful vernacularization of rights talk is that ideas about specific rights are embedded in a comprehensive liberal worldview that is typically at odds with the worldview of the local vernacular. Levitt and Merry propose that human rights are part of what they call a 'neo-liberal package' that also promotes democracy, capitalism, rule of law, transparency, accountability and gender equity. This constitutes a 'global values package', which competes and coexists with a 'fundamentalist religious package' based on tradition, conservatism, authority and gender complementarity. They also argue that the framing of issues such as gender tends to be path dependent. Once a culture settles into a secular or a religious mode of discourse about an issue, it tends to stay on that track.[14]

Arguably, it is not just cultural inertia and institutional vested interest that pushes towards continuity of practice and discourse, but also the functional coherence of the packages of issues and the conceptual coherence of their frames. The liberal package hangs together because its elements share the taproot of individualism and ruled-based social relations, whereas the traditional package makes sense for societies that are organised around patron–client relations in an identity-based community.[15] It is no wonder that Levitt and Merry see 'more friction than flows' in attempts at vernacularized persuasion across the gulf between systems that have been coherently structured around antithetical logics.[16]

However, unpacking the gender component further in their empirical research, Levitt and Merry observe some variants and hybrids that integrate elements of each of the two global packages. Examples include 'Chinese social work ideology', a professional ethos that seeks many of the same practical outcomes as liberal gender advocacy while operating in an authoritarian setting; liberation theology in Peru, which adapts religion to the pursuit of typically liberal social justice aims; Gandhian thought and socialism in India, which draw on religious or non-liberal concepts to advance progressive objectives in a democratic state; and LGBT and 'people of color' activism in the USA, which adopts a liberal formula for identity politics.[17] It is worth noting that these hybrids, though drawing on strands of liberal modernity in circulation in global discourse and practice, were all forged locally by actors native to a particular culture. They were not crafted as pedagogical performances of vernacular persuasion by outsiders.

While Levitt and Merry show that vernacular hybrids can serve progressive ends, there is no guarantee of this. Rachel Wahl's study of Indian police torture shows how the struggle among contending frames can produce perverse hybrids. Not only do police with human rights training continue to torture detainees, they readily justify torture as protecting the 'human rights' of people in the community who criminals prey upon, which they say becomes necessary where an ineffective court system and

---

[14] ibid 452–53.
[15] C Tilly, *Contention and Democracy in Europe, 1650–2000* (Cambridge, Cambridge University Press, 2004) 17–20.
[16] Levitt and Merry, 'Vernacularization on the Ground' (n 1) 448.
[17] ibid 447–48.

limited investigative capacity rules out conventional methods. This perversion of human rights terminology cannot be blamed on inept use of the vernacular by the human rights trainers, since the formal language of the Indian police bureaucracy is already the liberal rule of law.[18] Nonetheless, Wahl shows that the tendency of police to understand human rights through the prism of local vernaculars subverts the intentions of the human rights trainers in ways that echo themes put forward by Levitt and Merry.

Wahl's extensive interviews document how police view human rights precepts through two sets of alternative, non-liberal cultural lenses. One of these, as in the Levitt and Merry package concept, is traditional religion. Wahl says that police assimilate human rights training through the ethical prism of the Hindu value of compassion based on personal relationships, not through the liberal prism of impersonal procedural equality. Compassion goes out to the victims of crime, not to suspects. Procedural protection is granted not to all humans, but only to those who deserve it.[19]

The other lens, again reflecting one of the concepts of Levitt and Merry, is professionalism. A perhaps superficial influence is that British colonial policing routines accustomed Indian police to the use of torture as a necessary expedient. At a deeper level, the comparative policing literature suggests that this made the Indian police similar to the vast majority of police forces worldwide, who gravitate to the excessive use of force through self-selection of personnel, professional socialisation to inherently confrontational tasks of policing and an embattled ethos of needing to control unruly classes through intimidation.[20]

Wahl argues that the professional culture of policing is a more fundamental influence than traditional religious culture. Indian police recognise the practical cross-pressures between strict rule of law and the security of the community under actually existing conditions. As a matter of professional duty, they prioritise the security of the community, which demands that they use torture to extract information and confessions and to punish perpetrators who will not be effectively punished by the courts.[21] Wahl acknowledges that the corruption of police and their political bosses also contributes to torture, but she shows that this cannot explain many routine abuses. These findings are echoed by the anthropological research of Daniel Goldstein, who studied the rivalry of Bolivian police with vigilante groups who insisted that the community's 'right to security' justified their lynching of neighbourhood criminals.[22]

These examples show how rights language can be twisted, amalgamated with abusive practices and weaponised to serve illiberal agendas that are the antithesis of the liberal rights project. In the US context, where rights talk is deeply embedded in

---

[18] Wahl (n 10) 123.
[19] ibid 131–41.
[20] ibid 117; R Wilson, *Human Rights, Culture, and Context: Anthropological Perspectives* (Sterling, Pluto Press, 1997).
[21] Wahl (n 10) 142–45.
[22] DM Goldstein, *Outlawed: Between Security and Rights in a Bolivian City* (Durham, NC, Duke University Press, 2012) 205, 219–36.

cultural practice, illiberal movements often employ a contrarian rhetoric of rights to serve the purposes of the traditional, conservative, religious, authoritarian package: the unrestricted individual right to have a gun; the right to absolute free speech for conservative provocateurs on the internet and on campus; 'states' rights' to gerrymander election districts in a way that takes voting power away from minorities; the 'right to life'; and the right to freedom of religion, including the religious right to discriminate against gays in providing public services. Like any effective cultural revival movement, when a powerful out-group has deployed a threatening technology of power, such as human rights shaming on issues of racial and gender equality, the funders and strategists of illiberal backlash have adapted and weaponised it for their own purposes.[23]

The stakes in such cultural revival movements are typically understood not as piecemeal policies, but as a showdown between alternative ways of life. In this contest, the targets of human rights shaming are rarely hapless retrogrades; they too trade on the charismatic power of modernity and even rights.

III. BACKLASH AGAINST SHAMING IN NORMATIVE CONFRONTATIONS BETWEEN CULTURES

One reason that friction sometimes overwhelms flow in cross-cultural rights discourse is the penchant of transnational rights advocates for the tactics of 'naming and shaming'. Shaming in itself is a dangerous tool for compelling compliance with social norms, especially norms that are aspirational rather than long-established. The social psychological literature finds that shame and shaming can lead to compliance in some situations, such as the socialisation of young people to the standards of their own culture, but it often leads either to hiding deviant behaviour or to denial, resentment, backlash and the glorification of a deviant counterculture.[24]

Shaming in the vernacular can have a positive role to play, but in most cases only when done by high-status, respected insiders to the cultural reference group. Thus, Human Rights Watch can shame US Democratic administrations, but not Trump, Xi or Putin, for committing or tolerating rights violations. Insiders may even have some leeway to shame in-group members on behalf of aspirational norms that step outside of the established vernacular. For example, Chinese nationalists successfully shamed parents who continued to practise foot binding, arguing that this was hobbling the power of the Chinese people and making China look backward and barbaric in the eyes of civilised outsiders. Sometimes even semi-outsiders may succeed in shaming an audience with appeals to common principles and an overarching identity, as with Martin Luther King's use of white moderates' established vernacular of legal equality to implicitly shame those who tolerated racial segregation.

---

[23] EM Hafner-Burton and H McNamara, 'United States Human Rights Policy: The Corporate Lobby' (2019) 41 *Human Rights Quarterly* 115.
[24] J Snyder, 'Backlash against Human Rights Shaming: Emotions in Groups' (2020) 12 *International Theory* 109.

In most cases, though, rights shaming by outsiders is playing with fire. In earlier days of human rights advocacy, shaming of widespread cultural practices in less developed societies was more common than it is now. On issues such as female genital cutting, tactics were sometimes starkly legalistic, moralistic and universalistic. These tactics typically led to hiding or backlash, so advocates experimented with a broader range of approaches. Even so, shaming widespread cultural practices remains a standard tool in the transnational rights advocacy playbook. I recently coded 10 randomly chosen Human Rights Watch reports on such subjects as Japan's new transgender law, Hindu vigilantism against Indian 'cow-killing' cultural minorities and Polish priests who are alleged to 'demonise' women for straying from strict Catholic precepts. In all 10 cases, the abusive policies or negligence of the government reflected underlying widespread mass attitudes (gender-based bias, neglect of the disabled, prejudice towards an out-group, religion-based opposition to women's health rights, toleration of child labour practices, opposition to immigration and popular support for policies enacted by elected legislators). These reports were scrupulous in making sure that the harshest rebukes were expressed through vernacular quotations from insiders to the culture being shamed. The tactic of shaming has adapted, but is still going strong.

The degree of cultural backlash to rights shaming by outsiders depends not only on the use of vernacular discourse, but also on a host of situational and practical factors. The history of transnational efforts to combat female genital cutting provides some insight into the contextual specificity of this.

Margaret Keck and Kathryn Sikkink's seminal *Activists beyond Borders*, which explicated the logic of norms-based transnational 'information politics', includes a telling chapter on the failure of British churches' efforts in the 1920s and 1930s to shame their Kenyan parishioners into abandoning the practice of female genital cutting. These shaming tactics played into the hands of independence leader Jomo Kenyatta, who exploited the issue as a prime example of British cultural imperialism, much as his son Uhuru exploited the ICC seven decades later.[25] In the Kabare region of Kenya, where British clergy employed an open-ended, deliberative approach to discussing the issue, the rate of cutting eventually went down to 35 per cent by the end of the millennium; but in the Kigare region, where shaming and excommunication were used, the rate remained around 60 per cent.[26]

When NGOs tried to combat genital cutting in the 1990s with blunt shaming tactics based on legalism and universalistic values, they ran into stiff resistance on grounds of religion and custom.[27] Many were initially guided by the influential *Hosken Report*'s exaggerated claims of medical consequences, which failed to distinguish among the various types of cutting, and inaccurately blamed the practice entirely on oppressive patriarchy.[28] Their persuasion campaigns often led with Western rights talk. They

---

[25] ME Keck and K Sikkink, *Activists beyond Borders* (Ithaca, NY, Cornell University Press, 1999) 66–72.
[26] EH Boyle, *Female Genital Cutting: Cultural Conflict in the Global Community* (Baltimore, JHU Press, 2002) 136–37.
[27] H Rajadurai and S Igras, *At the Intersection of Health, Social Well-Being and Human Rights: CARE's Experience Working with Communities towards the Abandonment of Female Genital Cutting* (Atlanta, CARE, 2005).
[28] FP Hosken, *The Hosken Report: Genital and Sexual Mutilation of Females*, 3rd and 4th edns (Lexington, Women's International Network, 1982 and 1993); B Shell-Duncan and Y Hernlund, 'Female

would ask what rights daughters should have, and parents would reply 'the right to be circumcised'.[29] Failing to get the knack of vernacularization, activists in one instance were evicted from a Somali refugee camp in Kenya at gunpoint.[30]

Faced with this kind of vivid feedback, programme design quickly improved. Activists switched to science-based health information rather than international human rights law as their initial pitch, often combined with the provision of actual health services. Even this was not an easy sell. Women in societies where everyone is cut lacked a baseline for comparison. They had no idea that fistulas and other dire gynaecological conditions were long-term consequences of cutting rather than just part of being female. Even when medical facts were accepted, activists usually found that this would change parents' views about the desirability of cutting their daughters, but not their decision to cut.

For Muslims, this was often due to the belief that Islam required cutting. Resourceful activists were ultimately able to convince local imams to allow them to show videotapes of prestigious Cairo religious authorities explaining that the Koran does not endorse, let alone require, cutting. Although local imams were reluctant to surrender their authority to interpret Islamic doctrine to their community, activists found that religious leaders were eager for NGO health clinics, and they would allow discussion of religious teachings that would be carried out in religiously appropriate ways.[31] Sometimes the stumbling block is not cutting per se but its implications for authority and status in the community.

Although some recalcitrants claimed that the requirement to cut was covered in a 'secret book' of the Koran, which was held to be all the more compelling precisely because it was secret, many accepted that they did not have to cut for religious reasons.[32] But most of those who were convinced on the religious argument did not change their behaviour because conformity to canons of ethnic identity and marriage eligibility still got in the way. Somewhat more effective were multidimensional programmes that combined non-directive rights discussions with health information, the provision of health services and – in a parallel tactic to the anti-foot-binding campaign – community pledging not to cut and not to marry girls who were cut.[33]

Behind the success or failure of these persuasion tactics, however, are structural facilitators. Elizabeth Boyle found that the strongest correlates of the intention not to

---

"Circumcision" in Africa: Dimensions of the Practice and Debates' in B Shell-Duncan and Y Hernlund (eds), *Female 'Circumcision' in Africa* (Boulder, CO, Lynne Rienner Publishers, 2000) 7.

[29] S Igras, J Muteshi, A WoldeMariam et al, 'Integrating Rights-Based Approaches into Community-Based Health Projects: Experiences from the Prevention of Female Genital Cutting Project in East Africa' (2004) 7 *Health and Human Rights* 251, 260.

[30] Rajadurai and Igras (n 27).

[31] Susan Igras interview (Washington, DC, 20 August 2008). See also Igras et al (n 29) 6–7.

[32] M Johnson, 'Becoming a Muslim, Becoming a Person: Female "Circumcision", Religious Identity, and Personhood in Guinea-Bissau' in Shell-Duncan and Hernlund, *Female 'Circumcision' in Africa* (n 28) 221–22.

[33] G Mackie, 'Ending Footbinding and Infibulation: A Convention Account' (1996) 61 *American Sociological Review* 999.

cut were the mother's income outside the home and access to world communications media.³⁴ Widespread awareness of anti-cutting campaigns could produce opposite effects, however, depending on the salience of cutting in the local ethnic identity and on levels of urbanisation and education.³⁵

Ylva Hernlund's field research in Gambia reported that the 'local and national debate' was 'becoming more polarized and acrimonious', with the reaction to international pressures ranging from 'relief that outside help is speeding up the elimination of genital cutting to rage at what is perceived as imperialist meddling'.³⁶ A more recent field interview reports that 'in some communities deep resentments over the "criminalization of culture" simmer just below the surface and boiled over when the subject was raised'.³⁷ Boyle concludes that

> the depiction of FGC as child abuse did little to generate local support for abandonment ... Rather than directly contest a practice from an outside perspective, successful approaches recruited and leveraged high status individuals who legitimized the abandonment of a long-standing practice.³⁸

If shaming by outsiders can often lead to unintended consequences, vernacularization is not without its own problems. The anthropologist Janice Boddy reports that the British women who founded Sudan's first midwifery school in the 1920s knew that native birth attendants also performed female circumcisions (what activists later called female genital mutilation). They

> took a pragmatic stance. They did not support a peremptory ban on the procedure but, controversially, taught a less damaging operation using sterile implements, local anesthetics, and antiseptic solutions. In this way they hoped to 'reduce harm', and gradually bring about abandonment of genital cutting as Sudanese became better educated. Because few midwifery trainees were literate, the sisters elected to work with rather than against local knowledge, taking heed of pupils' experiences and invoking their embodied memories. They used images that first summoned, then attempted to revise women's cultural dispositions. They taught in Arabic, incorporating words from 'women's vocabulary'. They built discursive bridges between local understandings and their own by creating scientific analogies to the objects and acts of Sudanese daily life with which women's bodies are metonymously linked ...

---

[34] Boyle (n 26) 120, 132.
[35] K Cloward, *When Norms Collide: Local Responses to Activism against Female Genital Mutilation and Early Marriage* (Oxford, Oxford University Press, 2016); B Shell-Duncan, D Gathara and Z Moore, 'Female Genital Mutilation/Cutting in Kenya: Is Change Taking Place? Descriptive Statistics from Four Waves of Demographic and Health Surveys' in *Evidence to End FGM/C: Research to Help Women Thrive* (New York, Population Council, 2017) 16.
[36] Y Hernlund, 'Cutting without Ritual and Ritual without Cutting: Female "Circumcision" and the Re-ritualization of Initiation in the Gambia' in Shell-Duncan and Hernlund, *Female 'Circumcision' in Africa* (n 28) 28, 242.
[37] B Shell-Duncan et al, 'Legislating Change? Responses to Criminalizing Female Genital Cutting in Senegal' (2013) 47 *Law & Society Review* 803, 831.
[38] EH Boyle and J Svec, 'Success in Reducing Female Genital Cutting: A Multilevel Framework for Social Change' in RE Anderson (ed), *Alleviating World Suffering: The Challenge of Negative Quality of Life* (Springer, 2017) 357–58.

For example, they referred to women's bodies as a 'house' or 'sealed tin' that needed to be closed off against germs.[39] Their lesson book advised:

> Should a midwife do circumcisions … she must perform the operation with all cleanliness just as she would a labour case, and attend the case daily for seven days, or more if necessary, in order to avoid infection of the wound.[40]

Boddy concludes, 'such counsel insinuated biomedicine into local practice, thereby wrapping "tradition" in biomedical mystique, lending it new authorizations (though it needed none), and fostering syncretisms that seemed likely to ensure the custom's resilience'.[41]

IV. POLITICAL AND MANAGERIAL APPROACHES TO CLASHES OVER RIGHTS

Human rights advocates generally prefer to portray their activities as apolitical, based not on power and bargaining, but on consensual international law and universal tenets of moral decency. In fact, human rights are supremely political in a way that challenges the fundamental legitimacy of authoritarian regimes and illiberal societies. Unless the goal of human rights activism is to provoke zero-sum conflict with the targets it threatens, political modalities are needed to find grounds for convergence and conciliation between global rights norms and local normative perspectives.

The political scientist who has written most promisingly in this vein is Amitav Acharya. Whereas Sally Merry discusses vernacularization in the vein of discourse and cultural practice, Acharya argues for 'localization' of international norms in a way that is more explicitly political, while retaining a focus on cultural difference.[42] Acharya is for the most part concerned with global norms such as the norm of sovereignty (for example, in his study of the Association of South East Asian Nations, ASEAN) rather than with human rights per se, but his approach can be applied to human rights norms as well.

Acharya is interested in the processes that can lead to 'congruence building' between global and local norms, not the 'wholesale acceptance' of global norms by localities. This, he suggests, can come about through 'local initiative' to 'prune' foreign ideas for 'fit with the [local] agents' cognitive priors and identities', to 'graft' local ideas onto the body of global norms and to 'frame' the global–local hybrid in a way that establishes its congruence.[43] The impetus for congruence building, he suggests, is typically a pressing stimulus such as war, economic depression or domestic change such as democratisation. The agents who provide the initiative are 'insider proponents', who come to see 'evolutionary assimilation' to global norms as a 'progressive' path that will lead towards 'expansion of the rulers' authority'.[44] Localising global

---

[39] J Boddy, 'The Normal and the Aberrant in Female Genital Cutting: Shifting Paradigms' (2016) 6 *Journal of Ethnographic Theory* 41, 54.
[40] ibid 55.
[41] ibid.
[42] Acharya, 'How Ideas Spread: Whose Norms Matter?' (n 3).
[43] ibid 244–46.
[44] ibid 248–52.

norms 'legitimizes and operationalizes' the agents' position, facilitates the expansion of the agents' tasks and draws in new members to the agents' working coalition. Plugging into the international normative order advances these goals by enhancing available means, including new policy instruments, procedures and institutions.

Acharya's approach has similarities to Merry's. The agents who seize the initiative to localise global norms seek to persuade audiences that the pruned, grafted hybrid is a congruent, legitimate, beneficial, evolutionary development that resonates with previously accepted principles. However, Acharya's localisation concept differs from Merry's in at least two important respects. First, Acharya is more explicit in insisting that the agent is trying not only to persuade the locality to buy into the global normative system, but also to persuade global actors that the localised elements are legitimate and worth importing into the global system itself.[45] Second, Merry describes vernacularization as a 'cultural act', whereas Acharya describes cultural persuasion as a process that serves the political end of enhancing the rulers' authority.

Merry's culture-based vernacularization and Acharya's more politically grounded localisation are complementary. Merry's own argument about the package nature of liberal and traditional cultural systems implies that the confrontation of their antithetical, self-reinforcing norms is likely to produce a culture war, notwithstanding the existence of some progressive and regressive hybrids. Vernacularization is needed in the first place to take the edge off this polarisation. But discursive code-switching is too limited a tactic to solve such socially embedded differences on its own.

Persuasion to reform a whole array of systemically reinforcing practices requires more basic sources of leverage, a more holistic strategy and considerable patience. Change in the cultural vernacular is sometimes best achieved indirectly as a side effect of material structural change. An interesting example is the debate over medicalisation of female genital cutting in Kenya and several other East African societies.[46] One response to rising awareness of the health consequences of cutting, and to its international stigma as barbaric, has been rising demand to medicalise the practice in the hands of doctors and clinics that would carry out a mild version of the procedure under safe conditions. Human rights activists and global medical circles have almost universally denounced this as an unprincipled abomination that would legitimise and prolong the heinous practice. Some ethicists, however, have taken the view that the slowness to abolish cutting justifies the expedient of medicalisation as a way to significantly reduce its ill effects. Moreover, detailed data available for Kenya shows that a significant rise in medicalisation has coincided with a large drop in the overall incidence of other forms of cutting in the most urbanised, educated areas of the country and in semi-modernised regions. One way to understand this is that medicalisation provides a transitional step for people who are moving out of the traditional cultural package through a hybrid waystation towards assimilation to liberal global culture.

A key feature of medicalisation in this adjustment is that it draws on the obvious comparative advantage of modern global culture in the area of scientific-technical

---

[45] A Acharya, *Rethinking Power, Institutions and Ideas in World Politics: Whose IR?* (Abingdon, Routledge, 2014).
[46] B Shell-Duncan, C Njue and Z Moore, 'Trends in Medicalisation of Female Genital Mutilation/Cutting: What Do the Data Reveal?' in *Evidence to End FGM/C: Research to Help Women Thrive* (n 35).

rationality. Locals can defer to unquestioned outsider expertise in a delimited technical area without abandoning traditional values in identity-related cultural realms. In contrast, a direct head-on assault by human rights legalists against local tradition in its own bastion of identity, religion and family is a battle fought on unfavourable terrain. Acharya's pragmatic political brokers might be more astute at devising such hybrid formulas that can succeed in assembling winning coalitions for reform.

The global human rights community itself is currently grappling with the question of how to adapt to growing pushback against the uncompromising legalism, cosmopolitanism and universalism of its mainstream approach. The United Nations system has been formally structured around the 10 legalistic treaty-body committees that are intended to review signatory states' compliance with their human rights treaty obligations. Foot-dragging by recalcitrant states has rendered these committees fairly dysfunctional. Recently, the United Nations has expanded the role of more politically attuned parallel structures, including of the Sustainable Development Goals (SDGs) mechanism, which presents rights compliance standards not as moral or even legal imperatives, but as technical advice for succeeding at the task of development. Ruling circles in developing countries who are sceptical about human rights are nonetheless keen to gain wealth, technological sophistication, advanced medical services and other desirable trappings of modernity, many of which flow from advanced liberal democracies and the global capitalist system that liberal states run. States with rights compliance shortfalls tend to be much more enthusiastic about the looser 'rights-based approach' of the SDGs, which link good governance targets and indicators to tangible development assistance.[47] This removes human rights advocacy from the realm of shaming and locates it nearer to management consulting. Chayes and Chayes argue that most violations of international law stem from incapacity.[48] Sometimes fixing organisational and technical problems can facilitate rights compliance.

V. COMBINING DISCOURSE VERNACULARIZATION AND POLITICALLY BROKERED LOCALISATION

Solutions to cross-cultural dilemmas of human rights persuasion can employ several mechanisms: vernacularizing persuasion, opening to two-way dialogue, strengthening social networks for cultural translation, investing in implementing institutions, brokering expedient coalitions and using pragmatic managerial techniques to create structural conditions that facilitate the development of a rights culture. Effective strategies in this realm tend to be incremental and multidimensional, based on building capacity to succeed at the modern liberal package of social relations. Persuasion and coalition-making work best in the short run in the local cultural idiom, though their long-run trajectory has to be kept consistent with the inclusive liberal package. In particular, strategies of persuasion and coalition-making need to show how rights improvements for powerful cultural majority groups are not only compatible with

---

[47] UNGA 'Transforming Our World: The 2030 Agenda for Sustainable Development' (22 September 2015) UN Doc A/RES/70/1.
[48] A Chayes and AH Chayes, 'On Compliance' (1993) 47 *International Organization* 175.

but actually depend on the development of institutions that also protect minority rights. Shaming is often counterproductive to this process and risks feeding backlash. Overall, human rights reform is most likely to thrive when political pragmatism fosters favourable structural conditions, and adeptly moves cultural discourse from tradition through the gauntlet of change to liberal modernity.

4

Globalising the Indigenous: The Making of International Human Rights from below

CÉSAR RODRÍGUEZ-GARAVITO

THE HUMAN RIGHTS field finds itself at a critical juncture. In addition to facing a formidable combination of challenges – the climate emergency, resilient populist-authoritarian governments, the impact of a global pandemic, rising socioeconomic inequalities, and polarising and invasive digital technologies – human rights have come under increasing scrutiny from scholars who view the current era as the 'end times' of the movement. Although critiques come from very different angles – from conservative social thought to postmodern critical legal studies – a distinctively progressive critique of human rights has been developed by some of the most influential contributors to this debate.[1] According to this line of argument, the simultaneous global expansion of neoliberalism and the rise of international human rights over the last five decades is not a historical coincidence. In this view, by focusing on civil and political rights rather than on socioeconomic rights and rising inequality, human rights actors have provided political and legal ammunition to neoliberal capitalism.[2] Given this diagnosis, critics tend to see little role for human rights in twenty-first-century progressive theory and politics.

A striking feature of this line of criticism is that it is based on a highly limited view of the actual practice of human rights. It is a perspective whose eyes are directed largely at the most visible actors in the Global North. For Hopgood, for instance, 'Human Rights are a New York–Geneva–London-centered ideology focused on international law, criminal justice, and institutions of global governance. Human Rights

---

[1] See, eg S Hopgood, 'Human Rights: Past Their Sell-By Date' (Open Global Rights, 18 June 2013) www.openglobalrights.org/human-rights-past-their-sell-by-date; S Moyn, *Not Enough: Human Rights in an Unequal World* (Cambridge, MA, Harvard University Press, 2018); S Moyn, 'How the Human Rights Movement Failed' *New York Times* (New York, 23 April 2018).

[2] See S Hopgood, *The Endtimes of Human Rights* (Ithaca, Cornell University Press, 2013); S Moyn, 'Trump and the Limits of Human Rights' (Open Global Rights, 14 November 2016) www.openglobalrights.org/trump-and-limits-of-human-rights/.

are a product of the 1%.'³ Moyn's criticisms are almost invariably focused on international non-governmental organisations (INGOs) such as Human Rights Watch, as if they were a proxy for the movement writ large.⁴ Therefore, paradoxically, the critics adopt a North-centric view of the field that is akin to that of the staunchest defenders of the traditional approach to human rights advocacy. This is the approach taken by some of those INGOs and other human rights actors that continue to operate along the lines of the intellectual, organisational and strategic paradigm of the second half of the twentieth century, which privileged the role of North-based NGOs in naming and shaming governments (mostly in the Global South) before receptive audiences (mostly in the Global North) in order to pressure the former to comply with international human rights norms. For defenders of this paradigm, naming and shaming is 'still the human rights movement's best weapon',⁵ regardless of the facts that today's populist authoritarian leaders are both shameless and eager to be named and that the world is undergoing epochal geopolitical, technological, ecological and economic transformations that render the traditional paradigm increasingly ineffective.

Critics like Hopgood are right to call out persistent inequalities within the movement – for instance, between Northern versus Southern organisations, professional NGOs versus grassroots movements, white-led versus non-white-led organisations. However, the practice of the human rights movement is considerably more heterogeneous, dynamic and contested than the views of both critics and defenders of the status quo would suggest.

Documenting and engaging with the everyday life of human rights requires broadening the field of vision well beyond Geneva, London or New York. This, in turn, calls for two conceptual and methodological moves. First, it entails tracking how the international standards developed in those sites are translated, implemented, indigenised, contested and even transformed at the national and local levels. Second, it involves looking into the active role of subaltern subjects, from racially oppressed communities to impoverished classes, women, undocumented migrants, indigenous peoples and other actors that are lumped together as 'victims' in the traditional view of rights. This expanded view creates analytical and empirical space to capture the myriad ways in which subaltern actors not only adopt or contest, but also often transform, create and re-export new human rights norms and frames that challenge not only the traditional paradigm of international human rights, but also the rules of neoliberal globalisation and capitalism themselves.

---

³ Hopgood, 'Human Rights: Past Their Sell-By Date' (n 1).
⁴ See, eg Moyn, *Not Enough* (n 1); Moyn, 'How the Human Rights Movement Failed' (n 1). Julieta Lemaitre and Gráinne de Burca have offered incisive critiques of Moyn's argument, including its geographic and historical selectiveness. See J Lemaitre, 'The View from Somewhere: On Samuel Moyn's Not Enough' (Law and Political Economy Project, 9 July 2018) https://lpeproject.org/blog/the-view-from-somewhere-on-samuel-moyns-not-enough/; G de Burca, 'Shaming Human Rights' (2018) Jean Monnet Working Paper 2/18, https://jeanmonnetprogram.org/paper/shaming-human-rights-a-review-of-samuel-moyn-not-enough-human-rights-in-an-unequal-world/.
⁵ A Neier, 'Naming and Shaming: Still the Human Rights Movement's Best Weapon' (Open Global Rights, 11 July 2018) www.openglobalrights.org/Naming-and-shaming-still-the-human-rights-movements-best-weapon.

In this chapter, I propose such an enlargement of the field of perception as a means to contribute to a more empirically accurate and strategically useful view of the human rights field. Rather than a homogeneous project, I understand the human rights field as an ecosystem for collaboration, contestation, synergies and competition among multiple political projects – from the expansion of neoliberal capitalism to anti-capitalist indigenous peoples' struggles, to the movement for accountability for crimes against humanity, to class-based mobilisation for social justice, to the youth movement for climate rights and many others. While they all use international human rights as one of their master frames, they do so in a selective and proactive way: they adopt, adapt, prioritise, contest, localise and globalise different pieces of the normative human rights umbrella, thus helping enforce and transform the master frame in equal measure.

In order to broaden and enrich the outlook of human rights that is predominant in the ongoing debate about the existential challenges in the field – as well as to offer a view about its future that differs from that of the critics and defenders alike – I draw on a combination of socio-legal and sociological tools. I build on Sally Merry's pioneer work on the vernacularization of human rights in order to capture the empirical details of the processes whereby international norms are translated, implemented and contested at the local level.[6] As shown in other chapters of the festschrift for Merry of which this essay is a part, the methodological and conceptual paths that her work opened cleared the way for a flurry of socio-legal studies that offer vibrant and nuanced accounts of the globalisation of human rights. Merry's 'deterritorialized ethnography' documented the making of human rights standards against gender violence in Geneva and New York, but also went well beyond those moments and locales. She tracked down the life of those norms and ideas as they were translated into the cultures and institutions of local settings around the world, from India to Fiji to Hong Kong to the USA, where local actors – including social service providers, feminist advocates, religious leaders and judges – reshaped international standards against gender violence even as they implemented them. All along, the picture emerging from Merry's work is one of a dynamic field, in which human rights are not a monolithic project imposed on the South by the North, but rather the result of engagement and contestation among governments, NGOs, grassroots activists and other social actors. Crucially, her sharp anthropological eye rightly exoticises human rights, thus viewing them as a cultural form in and of themselves, one that embodies the values and preferences, as well as the limitations and blind spots, of global modernity and liberalism. In doing so, her work encourages much-needed reflexivity in a field whose very accomplishments and daunting challenges have made many practitioners enter a defensive mode and double down on past ideas and strategies.

While the tradition of socio-legal studies – to which Sally Merry made a towering contribution – provides the conceptual and methodological tools to analyse the translation of international human rights into local cultures, it has paid considerably less attention to the process running in the opposite direction, from the local to

---

[6] See SE Merry, *Human Rights & Gender Violence: Translating International Law into Local Justice* (Chicago, University of Chicago Press, 2006).

the global and from the South to the North. Local subaltern actors and their allies not only engage, but also contest, transform and export back to the global arena alternative understandings of those rights. In a collective volume, I contributed to theorising and documenting movements, campaigns, and legal and political actions through which subaltern actors have advanced and globalised expansive interpretations of their rights.[7] This type of 'globalisation from below' can be seen at work, for instance, in the struggles of undocumented migrants for rights in the USA and Europe, indigenous peoples in Latin America, people deprived of food and shelter in South Africa or India, or patients whose lives depends on access to a brand-name vaccine or medicine around the world. In the terms used by Antonio Gramsci, one of the twentieth century's most influential Marxist writers, these forms of legal mobilisation advance counter-hegemonic understandings of rights that contest the limits and blind spots of the dominant modern, liberal paradigm, including the sanctity of property rights, the impermeability of national borders and the protection of the rights of present generations to the detriment of future generations.

In this chapter, I focus on this less visible, bottom-up side of legal globalisation. My aim is to offer both a diagnosis and a prognosis of the practice and relevance of human rights in the face of the aforementioned existential challenges. As for the diagnosis, I build on and go beyond Merry's vernacularization model by looking into the other half of the globalisation of human rights, the one running from the local to the global and from the South to the North (with the South including both the geographic South and excluded populations in the Global North).[8] The resulting picture is richer and more complex than the one offered by the critics and defenders of the dominant approach to human rights, which largely misses the wealth of ideas and practices through which Global South actors have not only shaped the meaning of human rights at the local level, but also developed and globalised counter-hegemonic interpretations of them.

Contrary to the critics' prognosis, I posit that human rights theory and practice can indeed contribute to progressive politics and thought in the twenty-first century. However, as I have argued elsewhere, the human rights field needs to be radically revamped in order to address the challenges of twenty-first-century geopolitical, technological and socio-environmental conditions.[9] Traditional strategies, narratives and organisational forms are no longer fit for the purpose of addressing the populist authoritarian challenge and other structural shifts in geopolitics, technology and ecology. As Yuval Harari has remarked, 'while human rights movements have developed a very impressive arsenal of arguments and defense against religious biases and human tyrants, this arsenal hardly protects us against consumerist excesses and technological utopias'.[10] I would add that it hardly protects us against the most

---

[7] See C Rodríguez-Garavito and B de Sousa Santos, *Law and Globalization from Below: Towards a Cosmopolitan Legality* (Cambridge, Cambridge University Press, 2005).

[8] This is what Santos calls 'the internal global South'. See B de Sousa Santos, *Toward a New Legal Common Sense: Law, Globalization, Emancipation*, 3rd edn (Cambridge, Cambridge University Press, 2020).

[9] See C Rodríguez-Garavito, 'Disrupting Human Rights: Existential Challenges and a New Paradigm for the Field' in S Knuckey et al (eds), *Festschrift for Philip Alston* (Oxford, Oxford University Press, 2021).

[10] YN Harari, *21 Lessons for the 21st Century* (New York, Penguin Random House, 2018) 215.

urgent planetary risks: the climate crisis and the unprecedented power of digital megacorporations thriving on the accumulation and sale of personal data and the manipulation of human behaviour. In terms of the literature on twenty-first-century capitalism, human rights ideas and practices need to squarely address the twin challenges of 'fossil capital'[11] and 'surveillance capital'.[12]

A striking, and rather frustrating, feature of the work of 'end-times' proponents is that they explicitly refuse to provide an alternative. Against the most famous of Marx's *Theses on Feuerbach*, they see their contribution as interpreting, not changing, the world. This chapter takes a different approach. Drawing on research and advocacy experience with movements in different parts of the world, I am interested in bringing to light and amplifying the potential of bottom-up legal mobilisation efforts for offering responses to fossil capital, surveillance capital and other existential threats to human rights. My goal is to find spaces between fatalism and defensiveness, spaces for reflexive reconstruction and constructive disruption of the dominant approach to human rights.[13]

The remainder of the chapter is divided into three sections. First, I set the scene by discussing how socio-legal studies have largely focused on only one half of the human rights circuit, namely the processes whereby international standards are adopted and implemented at the national and local scales. Since Sally Merry's work on vernacularization offers a particularly nuanced theory and empirical account of such processes, I unpack its view of the human rights field and the specific mechanisms it posits for explaining the circulation of human rights norms and cultural forms from the global to the local. I illustrate these mechanisms with evidence from my research on the trajectory of indigenous peoples' rights, one of the most active advocacy fields over the last three decades and one that displays with particular clarity the workings of legal globalisation from below. I pay particular attention to the globalisation of the key legal institution in this domain: the right to free, prior and informed consultation (FPIC), which requires governments to consult with indigenous peoples on any legislative or economic project that directly affects them. Introduced in 1989 by International Law Organization (ILO) Convention 169, FPIC has been incorporated, formally or informally, into legal standards and mobilisations through the world since.

Second, I hone in on the missing half of the circuit, the less visible processes whereby local actors reframe international norms and mobilise across borders to export alternative understandings of rights. Rather than a unidirectional arrow, the trajectory that emerges from this longer-term perspective is that of a spiral, going back and forth between the local and the global. I specify the framing mechanisms through which local actors carry out this reverse export and illustrate them with evidence from a case study of a 30-year struggle for indigenous peoples' rights: the legal and political mobilisation of the Sarayaku people of the Ecuadorian Amazon

---

[11] See A Malm, *Fossil Capital: The Rise of Steam Power and the Roots of Global Warming* (New York, Verso Books, 2016).
[12] See S Zuboff, *The Age of Surveillance Capitalism: The Fight for a Human Future at the New Frontier of Power* (New York, Hachette Book Group/Public Affairs, 2019).
[13] See Rodríguez-Garavito, 'Disrupting Human Rights' (n 9).

to protect their territory against oil exploration, in collaboration with national and international allies. Rather than a purely defensive campaign, the Sarayaku struggle explicitly reframed FPIC to mean not just consultation but *consent*, through an expanded understanding of indigenous self-determination and the rights of nature. Over three decades, the Sarayaku people and their allies successfully exported this expansive meaning of FPIC to the global level, as evident in the landmark ruling on the case by the Inter-American Court of Human Rights in 2012 and the more recent influence of the Sarayaku struggle on the global mobilisation for the protection of the Amazon and the rights of nature and future generations against global warming. Finally, I offer some conclusions.

I. FROM THE GLOBAL TO THE LOCAL: THE POTENTIAL AND LIMITS OF VERNACULARIZATION

Despite its normative commitment to equality, in practice, human rights, as all other social fields, are marked by multiple inequalities. Northern states and organisations tend to have a disproportionate influence on norm-making and agenda-setting.[14] Professional elites, especially those endowed with the requisite legal knowledge, have an outsized impact as experts in the language and the tools of a heavily legalised field. Funding structures and strictures give considerable leverage to North-based funders and to professional organisations with the language skills and social capital to navigate the world of global philanthropy.[15] These and other asymmetries help explain why some versions of the human rights project receive more visibility and support than others. For instance, a minimalist, procedural version of rights that privileged property and negative rights was part and parcel of the 'rule of law' and 'global governance' reforms that institutions like the World Bank and the US Agency for International Development promoted around the world during the turn of the century, at the high point of neoliberal globalisation.[16]

This hegemonic form of legal globalisation became the focus of attention in socio-legal and human rights scholarship. In one prominent example, Yvez Dezalay and Bryant Garth documented the role of lawyers and economists in institutionalising the neoliberal canon from Latin America to Asia.[17] In another, Hopgood critically examined the role of elite players like major INGOs (which he calls 'Human Rights', with capital initials) in prioritising issues like international criminal justice (as reflected in

---

[14] See C Bob (ed), *The International Struggle for Human Rights* (Philadelphia, University of Pennsylvania Press, 2009); C Carpenter, *'Lost' Causes: Agenda Vetting in Global Issue Networks and the Shaping of Human Security* (Ithaca, Cornell University Press, 2014).

[15] Barbara Klugman, Ravindran Daniel, Denise Dora, Maimouna Jallow & Marcelo Azambuja, "Addressing Systemic Inequality in Human Rights Funding," (Open Global Rights, 4 December 2017) www.openglobalrights.org/addressing-systemic-inequality-in-human-rights-funding/.

[16] See Rodríguez-Garavito and de Sousa Santos (n 7) 1–28.

[17] See Y Dezalay and BG Garth, *The Internalization of Palace Wars: Lawyers, Economists, and the Contest to Transform Latin American States* (Chicago, University of Chicago Press, 2002); Y Dezalay and BG Garth, *Asian Legal Rivals: Lawyers in the Shadow of Empire* (Chicago, University of Chicago Press, 2010).

the effort to establish the International Criminal Court) to the detriment of issues of social justice and others that featured prominently in the work of domestic actors and organisations ('human rights' in lowercase).[18]

While this perspective captures the workings of hegemony and uneven power, it misses, both analytically and empirically, the myriad connections between 'Human Rights' and 'human rights'. This includes the way in which domestic advocates network, collaborate and compete with international actors in the making and enforcement of human rights law, as well as the way in which subaltern actors weave diverse connections with elite domestic and transnational actors, even as they challenge and reframe the neoliberal understanding of human rights. To put it in Bourdieu's terms, human rights exhibit the internal tensions and contradictions of all socio-legal fields, as multiple players with different levels of economic, social and cultural capital strive to endow their worldview with the symbolic authority and coercive power of the law.[19]

The coexistence of multiple human rights projects has been a feature of the field since the very inception of the contemporary human rights architecture. It came alive, for instance, during the debates leading to the adoption of the United Nations Charter (1945) and the Universal Declaration of Human Rights (1948). At a moment of effervescence for post-colonial and social justice movements in the Global South, the inclusion of socioeconomic rights (SERs) in the new international agreements became a point of contention between the former and hegemonic powers like the USA. At the 1945 San Francisco conference, the USA endorsed the proposal to include human rights language in the Charter but stood in opposition to proposals to include SERs.[20] Since then, different human rights projects – postcolonial, postcapitalist, non-secular, democratic socialist and others – have unfolded alongside the modern liberal project, sometimes remaining on the margins of the latter, sometimes hybridising with it (as in the eventual international recognition of SERs in the 1960s and indigenous rights to FPIC in the 1980s)[21] and sometimes standing in direct opposition to it (as in the ongoing struggle of indigenous peoples against extractive capitalism in their territories). Despite power imbalances, Global South countries and subaltern actors have influenced the content of international human rights, as Steven Jensen has convincingly shown in his reinterpretation of the history of the field.[22] In a similar vein, Margaret Keck and Kathryn Sikkink conclude:

> Because international human rights policies came simultaneously from universalist, individualist, and voluntarist ideas *and* from a profound critique of how Western institutions

---

[18] See Hopgood, *Endtimes of Human Rights* (n 2).

[19] P Bourdieu, 'The Force of Law: Toward a Sociology of the Juridical Field' (1987) 38 *Hastings Law Journal* 814.

[20] K Sikkink, *Evidence for Hope: Making Human Rights Work in the 21st Century* (Princeton, Princeton University Press, 2017).

[21] International Covenant on Economic, Social and Cultural Rights (New York, 16 December 1966) 993 UNTS 3; Indigenous and Tribal Peoples Convention (Geneva, 27 June 1989), International Labour Organisation Convention No 169.

[22] See SLB Jensen, *The Making of International Human Rights: the 1960s, Decolonization, and the Reconstruction of Global Values* (Cambridge, Cambridge University Press, 2016).

had organized their contacts with the developing world, they allowed broader scope for contradictory understandings than might be expected. These critiques led in a very undetermined fashion to the emergence of human rights policy; theorists in the late twentieth century should not assume that the trajectory was predetermined by homogenizing global cultural forces.[23]

If the admonition applied to turn-of-the-century scholars studying the origins of human rights, it is even more relevant now, when twentieth-century institutions, including human rights institutions, are being profoundly challenged by external forces (such as populist authoritarianism and the climate emergency) and by internal ones (such as alternative understandings of human rights from different sides of the political spectrum). Not only the origins, but also the contemporary practice of human rights is laced with these tensions. Two well-known examples illustrate this point. During the 2000s, SERs were the object of lively debate among human rights NGOs. While most Global South organisations had a long history of advocating and litigating for the enforcement of constitutional and international norms recognising the justiciability of SERs (like the right to food in India, the right to housing in South Africa or the right to health in Latin America),[24] leading INGOs saw such a move as overstretching and imperilling the normative consistency and the strategic viability of a field that was already overwhelmed with the challenges of enforcing civil and political rights.[25] More recently, in the 2010s, environmental organisations such as Greenpeace and Earthjustice grew frustrated with human rights NGOs' resistance to taking on global warming as a matter of rights. Often in collaboration with indigenous peoples, environmental organisations disrupted the field from within by pioneering efforts to frame climate change as a human rights issue and translate that framing into binding rules in international negotiations and litigation before domestic courts around the world.[26] In both cases, the result of internal dialogue and contestation was the expansion of the field, as SERs and climate rights came to be perceived as part of the canon even by formerly recalcitrant organisations.

Apprehending the dynamic and contested life of human rights requires tracking the trajectory of rights-based norms as they transition from the halls of institutions like the United Nations in New York or Geneva to national government offices, domestic court hearings, social media, NGO offices, community centres, and the marginalised geographic and social territories that subaltern rights-holders inhabit. This is the crucial methodological contribution that legal anthropologists, Merry

---

[23] M Keck and K Sikkink, *Activists beyond Borders* (Ithaca, NY, Cornell University Press, 1998) 212.

[24] See C Rodríguez-Garavito and D Rodríguez-Franco, *Radical Deprivation on Trial: The Impact of Judicial Activism on Socioeconomic Rights in the Global South* (Cambridge, Cambridge University Press, 2015).

[25] See K Roth, 'Defending Economic, Social and Cultural Rights: Practical Issues Faced by an International Human Rights Organization' (2004) 26 *Human Rights Quarterly* 63.

[26] R Lock and L Vanhala 'International NGOs and the (Non) Mobilization of Human Rights in the Context of Climate Change: An Inconvenient Frame?' in G de Búrca (ed), *Legal Mobilization for Human Rights* (Oxford, Oxford University Press, 2022).

foremost among them, made to our understanding of human rights. A far cry from the armchair blanket dismissals of rights that has proliferated in the critical literature, the method of 'multisited ethnography' (in George Marcus's terms)[27] or 'deterritorialized ethnography' (in Merry's preferred terminology) entails undertaking prolonged fieldwork in multiple locales, conducting numerous interviews across countries and putting together the pieces of the global trajectory of key actors and networks. From this methodological perspective, the entry points are 'sites where global, national, and local processes are revealed in the social life of small groups'.[28] In Merry's classic study, those social interactions ranged from meetings of government representatives at the United Nations to negotiate the content of international norms against gender violence to court hearings in domestic courts that translated those standards into binding national decisions; NGO training programmes that disseminated the norms among civil society organisations; and the daily life of social workers, who, in providing support to victims of domestic violence, have to negotiate the often contradictory demands of the individual-centred culture of international women's rights and the community-centred culture of local dispute settlement mechanisms.

According to Merry, vernacularization proceeds through three processes: consensus building, transnational programme transplants and the localisation of transnational knowledge. The first one takes place largely at the global scale. It is the moment of creation of international standards, when, despite geopolitical asymmetries, Global South governments gain leverage over the precise language of rules thanks to the fact that decisions at the United Nations tend to be made by consensus. When confronted with the convoluted wording of treaties and the endless negotiations over the linguistic minutiae that result from this system, Merry's expert anthropological eye registers them with justified bewilderment, reminding practitioners that human rights are also a professional culture, as peculiar as the local cultures they seek to displace. Once norms are agreed upon, they are transplanted into legal systems around the world through replicable institutional arrangements, such as new criminal laws against gender violence. This is the stage of transition from the global to the national. Actors in this process include foreign funders and governments, as well as advocates and experts who, being conversant in the languages and cultures of international human rights and national institutions, serve as intermediaries and disseminators of transnational transplants. The third process takes place largely at the local scale. In addition to the intermediary actors, the localisation of the transnational knowledge and culture of rights features a host of local actors, from judges to community leaders to individual rights-holders, who give concrete content to rights in court proceedings, community mediations and counselling sessions. Figure 4.1 summarises the trajectory of vernacularization processes.

---

[27] GE Marcus, 'Ethnography in/of the World System: The Emergence of Multi-sited Ethnography' (1995) 24 *Annual Review of Anthropology* 95.
[28] Merry (n 6) 29.

Figure 4.1 Vernacularization processes

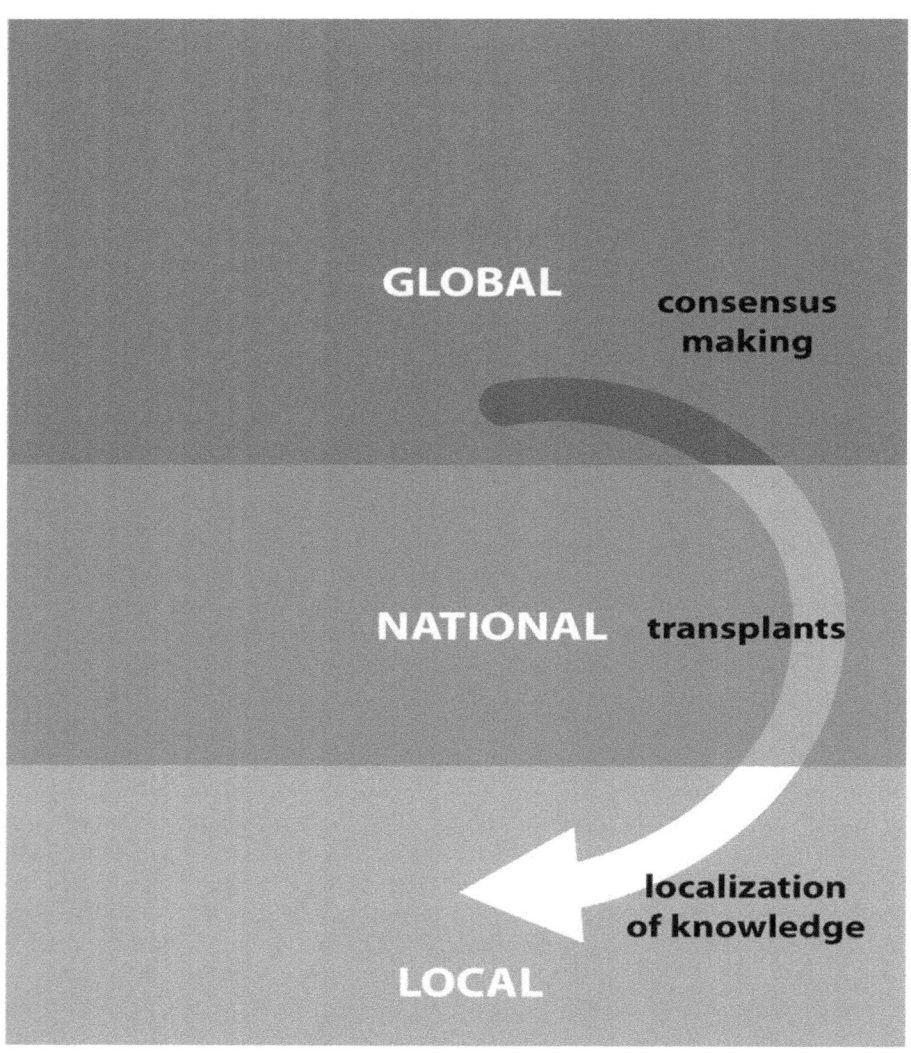

As the figure shows, the vernacularization model is largely unidirectional. The processes it encompasses run from the global to the national to the local. Although it plants the conceptual seeds for understanding the circulation of human rights norms and frames, it falls short of theorising and empirically examining the processes operating in the opposite direction, from the local to the national to the global. It offers a nuanced view of how global rights are actively adapted and contested by local actors, and insightfully concludes that rights claims, rather than superseding local culture, 'are layered over claims of social obligations of community'.[29] However, the

---

[29] ibid 216.

trajectory it describes stops at the local scale, thus leaving out the proactive role that local actors may play in transforming rights claims and re-exporting them back to the global scale.

Theorising and documenting the missing half of the globalisation of rights is the goal of the remainder of this chapter. I pursue this goal by inquiring into the trajectory of indigenous peoples' rights, an issue area that has gone full circle and illustrates the workings of legal globalisation from below.

II. GLOBALISING THE INDIGENOUS: FROM THE LOCAL TO THE GLOBAL

At first blush, globalising indigenous rights sounds like a contradiction in terms. After all, 'indigenous' and 'vernacular' are used interchangeably to refer to the local, the native, the particular – the inverse of the global, the cosmopolitan, the general. Just as the transnational adoption of a *lingua franca* (Latin, French, English) turns all other languages into vernacular, the globalisation of Western culture localises all other national cultures. Given that indigenous peoples have been further pushed to the margins of their national cultures, they are cast as the quintessential other, the vernacular par excellence.

This is indeed the way in which international law dealt with indigenous peoples until the late twentieth century. ILO Convention 107 (1959), the main international legal instrument on the matter, was squarely founded on the ideology of assimilationism. Indigenous peoples were defined as populations 'at a less advanced stage than the stage reached by the other sections of the national community'.[30] The fundamental right that the global legal order bestowed upon them was to right to have their governments promote 'their progressive integration into the life of their respective countries'.[31]

Against this background, the story of indigenous rights' profound transformation over the last three decades is a remarkable illustration of the processes underlying the globalisation of human rights. Indeed, it underscores not only the processes of vernacularization, but also those of bottom-up globalisation. The story validates the usefulness of the vernacularization model to understand the localisation of global norms. However, no account of indigenous peoples' rights would be complete without an equally careful analysis of the way in which the meaning of rights has been shaped by processes travelling in the opposite direction, from the local to the global. Indigenous peoples and their allies have engaged pragmatically with, transformed and ultimately reshaped the meaning of international norms – now demanding implementation of, contesting and ignoring or proposing alternatives to the rules of ILO Convention 169 of 1989, the legal framework that replaced Convention 107.

Elsewhere, I offer detailed accounts of the evolution of indigenous peoples' rights, namely of FPIC, its core institution.[32] Here, I limit myself to sketching pieces of that

---

[30] Indigenous and Tribal Peoples Convention (26 June 1957), International Labour Organisation Convention No 107, Art 1.
[31] ILO Convention 107, Art 2.
[32] C Rodríguez-Garavito, 'Ethnicity.gov: Global Governance, Indigenous Peoples, and the Right to Prior Consultation in Social Minefields' (2011) 18 *Indiana Journal of Global Legal Studies* 263;

story to the extent that they illustrate the two-way flow of human rights norms and frames between the global and the local. I begin by unpacking the workings of the three aforementioned processes of vernacularization: consensus making, transplantation and the localisation of knowledge. I then move on to formulate and illustrate the processes that constitute the reverse trajectory, that of globalisation from below: frame contestation, frame bridging and frame transformation.

III. LOCALISING THE GLOBAL

With respect to *consensus making*, ILO Convention 169 was the product of three years of negotiations between representatives of the sectors with voice and vote in ILO's peculiar tripartite structure: governments, employer associations and worker organisations. Since the very beginning of the negotiations, in 1986, the three sectors converged on the need to pivot from assimilation to participation as the key frame for indigenous peoples' rights.[33] FPIC was slated as the specific institutional mechanism whereby indigenous participation would be guaranteed. However, it soon became clear that very different conceptions of participation and consultation were at play. While most states and employers supported a thin, procedural conception of FPIC, worker organisations (in cooperation with indigenous and civil society organisations) advanced a more robust, substantive view of FPIC derived from indigenous peoples' right to self-determination. Every word of ILO Convention 169 was debated on several occasions (especially Articles 6 and 15, on FPIC); the textual differences, however, were not a matter of phrasing preferences. The states' and employers' positions effectively meant that, while governments were expected to consult with indigenous peoples when a proposed regulation or an economic project would have a distinct impact on indigenous communities, decision-making remained fully in the hands of government, even when indigenous people had expressed their opposition to the decision or project during the consultation. Workers and indigenous peoples' proposal consisted in making the outcome of FPIC binding for the government, thus granting indigenous people the right to say 'no' to extractive projects and other forms of interference with their cultures and territories. For them, FPIC meant free, prior and informed *consent*.

In the end, as is so often the case in international human rights law-making, the consensus option was the least common denominator: states and employers' procedural, thin understanding of FPIC was incorporated into ILO Convention 169. This is the hegemonic approach to indigenous rights that Charlie Hale calls 'neoliberal multiculturalism': the willingness to legally recognise cultural diversity only to the extent that it does not give indigenous peoples power to make decisions regarding their territories and the resources in them.[34]

C Rodríguez-Garavito and CA Baquero Díaz, *Conflictos Socioambientales en América Latina: El Derecho, los Pueblos Indígenas y la Lucha Contra el Extractivismo y la Crisis Climática* (Argentina, Siglo Veintiuno Editores, 2020).
[33] T Simpson, 'ILO 107 – A License to Rights' (1987) 7 *Aboriginal Law Bulletin* 10.
[34] CR Hale, 'Neoliberal Multiculturalism: The Remaking of Cultural Rights and Racial Dominance in Central America' (2005) 28 *Political and Legal Anthropology Review* 10.

In addition to the outcome, what is important for present purposes, and must be highlighted, is the contested nature of the new legal regime: FPIC was, in effect, a provisional compromise between two different visions of indigenous rights, which would resurface at later episodes of the story. The same tension cut across negotiations for a comprehensive United Nations Declaration on the Rights of Indigenous Peoples (2007). Deliberations dragged on for two decades and nearly collapsed in 2005 precisely because of disagreements between states and indigenous organisations around the meaning and consequences of participation. While the neoliberal understanding of FPIC remained the rule, the language of the Declaration ceded some ground to the counter-hegemonic indigenous view centred on consent as opposed to consultation. The Declaration states that the goal of consultations is to 'obtain their free and informed consent' (Article 32) and that prior consent is specifically required in instances of forceful relocation of indigenous communities (Article 10).

The second process of vernacularization, *transnational programme transplants*, is also visible in the recent history of indigenous peoples' rights. The language of ILO Convention 169 was reproduced in myriad regulations, from constitutional provisions and new legislation throughout Latin America to World Bank operational guidelines on indigenous peoples and to corporate codes of conduct adopted by industries with the deepest impact on indigenous rights, such as mining and oil. The neoliberal version of FPIC that prevailed in ILO Convention 169 and, to a lesser extent, in the UN Declaration was palatable to a wide range of state, corporate and government actors that served as vectors of dissemination and transplantation of the new institution. However, indigenous organisations and their allies in the human rights and environmental movements continued to contest it and advance a counter-hegemonic understanding based on consent. This is evident, for instance, in the hearings and the key rulings of the Inter-American Court of Human Rights on the matter. The two positions were very much at play in cases such as *Saramaka v Suriname*[35] and *Sarayaku v Ecuador*,[36] and the Court sought to strike a balance between them by adopting an intermediate solution closer to the UN Declaration than to ILO Convention 169.

Ultimately, FPIC's practical meaning and impact are determined at the ground level, in the indigenous territories where oil or mining projects are undertaken and where legislation granting them collective rights over their territories is enforced or flaunted. This is where the *localisation of transnational knowledge* about FPIC becomes visible, as I have witnessed in numerous FPIC proceedings in Latin America. In the best case, this process takes place through highly legalistic consultation proceedings where government representatives struggle to explain the meaning of the law and the technical details of the project being proposed – a new road or dam, a timber concession, an oil drilling operation – to a nervous crowd of community elders, leaders and families. The overlap between transnational knowledge and local culture is

---

[35] See 'Saramaka People v Suriname' (Loyola Law School Inter-American Court of Human Rights Project, nd) https://iachr.lls.edu/cases/saramaka-people-v-suriname; *Saramaka People v Suriname*, Preliminary Objections, Merits, Reparations, and Costs, Inter-American Court of Human Rights Series C No 185 (28 November 2008).
[36] See 'Kichwa Indigenous People of Sarayaku v Ecuador' (Loyola Law School Inter-American Court of Human Rights Project, nd) https://iachr.lls.edu/cases/kichwa-indigenous-people-sarayaku-v-ecuador; *Kichwa Indigenous People of Sarayaku v Ecuador*, Merits and Reparations, Inter-American Court of Human Rights Series C No 245 (27 June 2012).

particularly striking when the indigenous community does not speak the majority language (Spanish in most of Latin America) and community leaders, often experienced in the terminology of FPIC, speak in their own language while switching to Spanish when they need to use legal terms that do not have an equivalent in their language, such as 'prior consultation', ILO' and 'court'. In the worst-case scenario, the localisation of transnational knowledge proceeds through shady meetings where representatives from the government and corporate entities interested in operating in indigenous territory hold rushed information sessions with a random group of community members (or with a subgroup favourable to the proposed project) in order to provide loose data about the project, without any form of genuine consultation. Sign-up sheets are almost invariably circulated in these meetings, to be used later by the conveners as proof of consultation and even agreement on the part of the community.

IV. REFRAMING HUMAN RIGHTS: THE PROCESSES OF GLOBALISATION FROM BELOW

The end product of the vernacularization cycle is thus a legal hybrid. Alongside the cultural artifacts (meetings, sign-up sheets, etc) embodying the dominant understanding of the newly transplanted international norms, local actors advance counter-hegemonic interpretations of those rights and new rights claims. In the realm of indigenous peoples' rights, counter-hegemonic understandings of FPIC and indigenous peoples' rights – based on self-determination and the inseparability of people and territory, humans and nature – are as visible at the local level as those based on neoliberal multiculturalism.

Often, the tension is a creative one and does not remain at the local level. When subaltern actors and their allies muster the requisite political power, the end point of vernacularization may be the starting point of the globalisation of human rights from below. This is also where bottom-up resistance to neoliberal understandings of rights becomes apparent, as I have witnessed in several territories and campaigns against the intrusion of extractive industries in indigenous territories. From the Brazilian Amazon, where indigenous peoples that have been displaced without consultation so as to make space for the third largest hydroelectric dam in the world (Belo Monte), to the Ecuadorian Amazon, where the Sarayaku people have successfully preserved the forest against oil drilling, and the prairies of South and North Dakota in the USA, where the Lakota people have led a multi-year campaign against the Dakota Access Pipeline, indigenous peoples have effectively argued and exercised the right to say 'no'. They have reframed FPIC as requiring consent and have gone beyond FPIC by grounding their cases on new rights framings, such as the rights of present and future generations to a liveable climate system and the rights of nature.

In terms of social movement theory, the globalisation of human rights from below takes place through framing processes.[37] Mobilisation frames are mental schemata that codify the experience of a social problem (like deforestation in indigenous territories) through legal categories (like the rights of indigenous peoples and

---

[37] R Benford and DA Snow, 'Framing Processes and Social Movements: An Overview and Assessment' (2000) 26 *Annual Review of Sociology* 611.

future generations) and offer an organised way of perceiving and responding to the problem.[38] Studies in framing theory have shown how social change depends on whether the activists who advocate for it manage to construct and reconstruct frames that give their movement an identity, so that they can resonate with their audience and connect with discourses and agendas from other movements which each have their own audiences.

Drawing on framing theory, I distinguish three processes at play in bottom-up globalisation: frame contestation, frame bridging and frame transformation (see Figure 4.2).

Figure 4.2 The human rights spiral

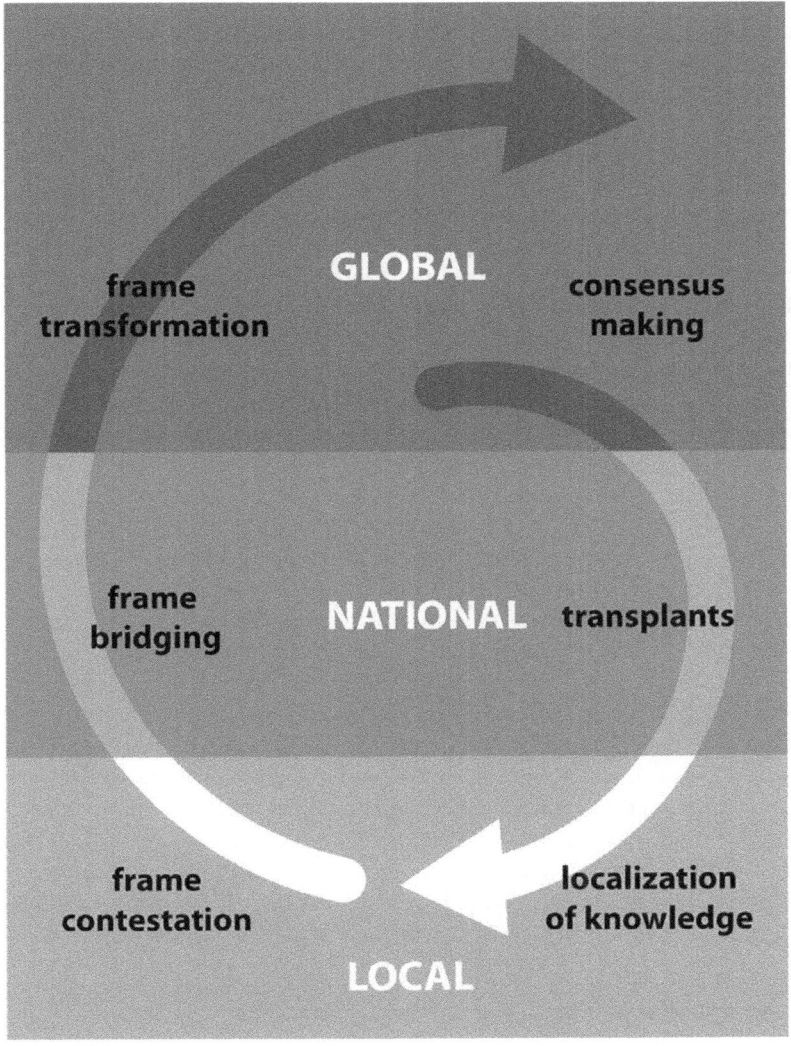

[38] DA Snow et al, 'Frame Alignment Processes, Micromobilization, and Movement Participation' (1986) 51 *American Sociological Review* 464.

Frame contestation entails active efforts to reinterpret, challenge, expand, adapt or even ignore the dominant understanding of rights in specific locales and cases. Subaltern actors and their allies engage in frame contestation through a wide range of legal and political strategies. For instance, they offer expansive interpretations of rights in lawsuits, organise protests and other forms of direct action to oppose actions justified in the name of the dominant frame and advance their alternative narrative through media campaigns.

Frame contestation is a common feature of the practice of indigenous peoples' rights. On the one hand, indigenous movements have embraced the opportunity offered by FPIC and invested heavily in acquiring the knowledge needed to mobilise its language and institutions. As the leader of the Kankuamo people, who would later become the head of the Colombian National Indigenous Peoples' Association, told me: 'that's why we indigenous leaders took to studying the law and some of us actually ended up going to law school'.[39] Although demanding compliance with the procedural requirements of FPIC has not halted the advance of extractive economies or threats to cultures and ecosystems, it has certainly slowed them down by giving indigenous peoples a concrete legal tool to put obstacles in the way of and raise awareness about the social and environmental costs of extractive capitalism.

On the other hand, even while mobilising its rules, indigenous communities challenge the procedural logic of FPIC by constantly bringing back into the conversation substantive claims based on their rights to self-determination, land and culture. In fact, this ambiguity explains the recurrent misunderstandings that mark consultation processes in practice. As I have shown elsewhere based on fieldwork on the practice of FPIC, it is common for those processes to reach dead ends, to the frustration of government and corporate representatives.[40] Just when the latter believe that a stage of consultation has been cleared and an agreement has been reached, indigenous leaders reopen the discussion by reminding their interlocutors that their claim is not about the duration or the participants of consultation mechanisms, but about indigenous prerogative to control their territories, economies and cultures. As Patricia Gualinga, leader of the Sarayaku people, told me: 'In the end, we are not interested in being consulted. They know what we will say if they asked us.'[41]

Bottom-up reframing of rights does not stop at the local level. In cases where internal organisation and external alliances are robust enough, subaltern actors scale up their struggles through *frame bridging*. The Sarayaku people, for instance, have sustained largely successful political and legal mobilisation for the preservation of the Amazon for 30 years, thanks to their ability to connect their struggle not only with the national indigenous movement, but also with the environmental and labour movements and other sectors. Indeed, they have done it so successfully that their leaders have gone on to lead the national indigenous movement, and some of their proposals that most radically challenged neoliberal multiculturalism – like recognising nature as a rights-holder– ended up making it into the national Constitution in 2008. Their

---

[39] Interview with LF Arias (2010).
[40] Rodríguez-Garavito, 'Ethnicity.gov' (n 32).
[41] Interview with P Gualinga (2017).

counter-hegemonic understanding of rights thus moved from the periphery to the centre, from local contestation to the law of the land.

Although far from being the rule, bottom-up legal mobilisation may circle back all the way to the global scale, reshaping the very frames or norms of international human rights. This is a process of *frame transformation*. The recent evolution of indigenous peoples' rights shows signals of this process. As the evidence of environmental destruction and the climate emergency became even more visible in the late 2010s, indigenous peoples' demands and frames, formerly deemed too radical or unsupported by international law, resonated with rising global mobilisation, such as the movements for urgent climate action. An icon of this convergence was the summit of Amazonian leaders and delegates of Extinction Rebellion and Fridays for Future in the middle of the Brazilian Amazon in late 2019. Indigenous groups like the Sarayaku had an active role in this convergence, as well as in highly influential documents like Pope Francis's encyclical *Laudato Si'*, released in 2015.[42] Through three decades of political and legal mobilisation, they have contributed to mainstreaming frames that are now being incorporated into new proposed forms of hard and soft law that recognise the rights of nature, limits to development and the rights of future generations.

---

[42] Interview with M Melo, Sarayaku's lawyer (2020).

5

Rites of Culture: Legal Frameworks, Indigenous Protocols, and the Circulation of Culture in Australia

FRED MYERS

I WAS A fan of Sally Merry's work long before she articulated its connection to human rights. I followed her journey from the anthropological study of disputes[1] to broader concerns with justice and the relationship between international frameworks and the messy cultural realities of local conditions.[2] I write this as a tribute to the way in which that last point in particular is explored in Sally's work.

In the early 1970s, when I was first doing fieldwork with remote-living Indigenous Australians, I remember walking in the streets of the town of Alice Springs in Central Australia. While I had become friendly with many of the Pintupi-speaking people living in distant government 'settlements' or 'outstations' such as Yayayi, Papunya and Kungkayunti, with whom I eventually worked for many years, I did not know many Indigenous people living in the town of Alice Springs – then about 10,000 in population – some 150 miles to the east.[3] Many were relatives of those further west, through marriage or relocation. I was surprised to be approached by a slight, somewhat bedraggled-looking, middle-aged Aboriginal man. He told me his name was Salomo Tjapangarti, and that he was the cousin of my friend at Yayayi, Ginger Tjakamarra. Salomo was part of an early wave of Indigenous people who had moved east from the desert; his mother was a Pintupi woman who had married an eminent Indigenous evangelist, Titus Rembaraka, from the Arrernte community identified with the Lutheran mission at Hermannsburg.

Could I help him, he asked? I was not entirely certain I understood him properly, because he assumed a familiarity I did not have. However, I came to understand that

---

[1] CB Harrington and SE Merry, 'Ideological Production: The Making of Community Mediation' (1988) 22 *Law and Society Review* 709.
[2] SE Merry, *Human Rights and Gender Violence: Translating International Law into Local Justice* (Chicago, University of Chicago Press, 2006).
[3] For an account of this situation during my fieldwork, see F Myers, *Pintupi Country, Pintupi Self: Sentiment Place and Politics among Western Desert Aborigines* (Berkeley, University of California Press, 1991); F Myers, 'We Are Not Alone: Anthropology in a World of Others' (2007) 71 *Ethnos* 233.

Tjapangarti had recorded some songs for the famous anthropologist and photographer CP Mountford, who had made several trips through Central Australia since the 1930s, making films, photographs and documenting culture.[4] These songs, he told me, were 'men's business',[5] based on important gender-exclusive initiation ceremonies. I already knew that revealing such music or ceremony to non-initiated persons, particularly women and children, was said to be punishable by death. As a man who knew their language (somewhat imperfectly) and had been given a position in their kinship system, I had been allowed to hear the songs, but I had also been warned, more than once, of this punishment, and stories about when it had been carried out. Tjapangarti looked truly miserable, incredibly anxious, even to the eyes of an inexperienced 25-year-old American. I was flustered; I had no idea what I could do. I did not know Mountford, or even whether this record existed or was simply a rumour. There were, of course, many rumours that circulated in Central Australia. The only recourse I could suggest was to go to the recently established Aboriginal Legal Aid services in Alice Springs.[6] I do not think I ever saw Salomo again, nor do I know what happened. I am not sure there was a record in the end, fortunately for him.

My encounter with Salomo is exemplary of those times – the 1970s – when concerns about the publication of Aboriginal restricted cultural material or the appropriation of sacred ritual designs were reaching into the life worlds of remote Indigenous Australians, in part due to changes in the technologies of recording and circulation. These were not the civil rights that dominated the 1960s,[7] and they represent a change that is also expressed in the Aboriginal Tent Embassy set up on Parliament House lawn in 1972[8] – namely, claims to sovereignty, land rights and refusals of Anglo-Australian legal oversight.

For this chapter, I want to tell a few stories about these matters, what material came to be formulated in terms of cultural property and how these issues came to be addressed. I regard the incidents as important in several ways, especially in the context of Sally Merry's work on the vernacularization of human rights and the subsequent developments of the UN Declaration of Indigenous Rights and later the Convention for Intangible Heritage.[9] I underscore how Indigenous concerns for control over their cultural materials came to find some redress in the Australian legal system and only later found grounding in the UN Declaration on the Rights of Indigenous Peoples,

---

[4] See below for discussion of Mountford in an important legal case that was about to happen concerning his monograph. See also CP Mountford, *Nomads of the Western Desert* (Adelaide, Rigby, 1976). Untrained as an anthropologist, he was widely known in Australia for a range of work.

[5] This is an Aboriginal English term widely used in Central Australia by Indigenous people to refer to gender-segregated ceremonies involved with male initiation.

[6] See J Faine, *Lawyers in the Alice: Aboriginals and the Whitefella's Law* (Carlton, Federation Press, 1993). For a critical Indigenous critique of Faine's account of the origins of Aboriginal Legal Aid, see G Foley, 'The Pain of Faine Goes Mainly to My Brain' (*The Koori History Website*, 31 June 1994) www.kooriweb.org/foley/essays/pdf_essays/faine.pdf.

[7] See B Attwood, *Rights for Aborigines* (Sydney, Allen & Unwin, 2003).

[8] For an Indigenous view of the Aboriginal Tent Embassy, see G Foley, A Schaap and E Howell (eds), *The Aboriginal Tent Embassy: Sovereignty, Black Power, Land Rights and the State* (Oxford, Routledge, 2014).

[9] United Nations Declaration on the Rights of Indigenous Peoples (New York, adopted 13 September 2007) GA Res 61/295, UN Doc A/RES/47/1 (UNDRIP). See also Convention for the Safeguarding of the Intangible Cultural Heritage (adopted 17 October 2003 at the General Conference of the United Nations Educational, Scientific and Cultural Organization (UNESCO) 32nd session, Paris).

passed in 2007. Article 31 of that Declaration, in particular, provides for cultural rights. It reads:

> 1. Indigenous peoples have the right to maintain, control, protect and develop their cultural heritage, traditional knowledge and traditional cultural expressions, as well as the manifestations of their sciences, technologies and cultures, including human and genetic resources, seeds, medicines, knowledge of the properties of fauna and flora, oral traditions, literatures, designs, sports and traditional games and visual and performing arts. They also have the right to maintain, control, protect and develop their intellectual property over such cultural heritage, traditional knowledge, and traditional cultural expressions.[10]

This did not exist as a platform of rights in 1970s Alice Springs, and after voting against the resolution originally, the government of Australia signed on to the Declaration only in 2009. But a sense of a moral right had emerged regarding cultural rights and wrongs for Indigenous cultural property and found its way into Australia's legal world, most notably in relation to existing intellectual property and copyright regimes. Anglo-Australian legal categories were expanded to take on the work of seeking redress for Indigenous claims of wrongdoing and harm, both inside and outside of formal legal processes. In 2006, Justice John von Doussa KC spoke on issues of Indigenous Australian cultural and intellectual property to an international conference, explaining their significance in relation to concerns over the theft and appropriation of imagery and design from Indigenous art in a lucrative and growing high art market:

> The Aboriginal art market is presently estimated to be worth about $200 millions a year. Along with the demand has grown the need to respect and protect Aboriginal cultural ownership of images and spiritual stories embedded in the works, especially against unauthorised copying and misuse. This has led to litigation which has explored the application of principles of the common law and statutory based protections in the Australian legal system.[11]

> The concepts underlying these principles are not unique to Australia. The principles of equity that protect confidential information and fiduciary obligations are well known, and widely applied. The statutory regimes for the protection and exploitation of intellectual property reflect international conventions. What is interesting is the how these principles have been applied in the novel context of Australian Indigenous traditional laws and customs.[12]

No doubt, mine was not the first suggestion to an Aboriginal complainant to seek help from 'Legal Aid', but that institution was not available before 1972. As an aside

---

[10] UNDRIP, Art 3.
[11] Important cases informing von Doussa's remarks were *Yumbulul v Reserve Bank of Australia Ltd* (1991) 21 IPR 482, 490 (French J); *Milpurrurru and Others v Indofurn Pty Ltd and Others* (1993) 130 ALR 659; *Bulun Bulun v R & T Textiles Pty Ltd* (1998) 41 IPR 513. For a summary of some of this work, see C Golvan, 'Aboriginal Art and Copyright – An Overview and Commentary Concerning Recent Development' (1996) 1 *Media and Arts Law Review* 151.
[12] J von Doussa, 'Legal Protection of Cultural Artistic Works and Folklore in Australia', paper presented to the International Association for the Protection of Intellectual Property and the Malaysia Bar Council's Intellectual Property Committee Joint Conference, Kuala Lumpur (1 September 2006) https://humanrights.gov.au/about/news/speeches/legal-protection-cultural-artistic-works-and-folklore-australia.

that perhaps explains the moment of legal evolution that existed in Central Australia, one of the early Legal Aid lawyers remembers attending a screening of a Western cowboy and Indian film at a remote Aboriginal community in which the cowboys or the cavalry were winning, when one of the Indigenous spectators stood up and shouted, 'Call in Legal Aid!'.[13]

Sally Merry's work, as she moved from the framework of legal disputing to human rights, helped me to see these interventions for Indigenous Australians as part of the post-World War II embrace of human rights that were shaping Australia's policies regarding the treatment of Indigenous people.[14] Nonetheless, while 'cultural rights' had not entered seriously into discussion, a sense of wrongs (or 'perceived injurious experiences' – as Felstiner et al phrased it[15]) were increasingly demanding response.[16] I will give, briefly, two examples of disputes that I encountered over what might be called 'cultural rights'. One prominent example, with far-reaching effects for Western Desert people, was the controversy or scandal over the archaeologist Richard Gould's book *Yiwara*, based on research around Warburton Range Mission in Western Australia, for revealing photographs of secret men's initiation.[17] Gould, a curator at the American Museum of Natural History, had taken photographs of many ceremonies with permission granted on the promise these would not be seen in Australia. Of course, despite such impossible promises, the book found its way to Australia and into the hands of a young Ngaatjatjarra woman who was at school in a nearby town. Women were forbidden access to such knowledge, and the custodians of the ceremonial knowledge threatened to spear her in punishment for looking at these photos – and to kill Gould. This scandal occurred in 1971 and, by 1973, had

---

[13] From Faine's *Lawyers* (n 6), an illuminating account of the legal situation in Alice Springs at the time.

[14] Merry wrote significantly at this very time that: 'The literature reviewed here indicates that an anthropology of law in the 1990s will increasingly need to take transnational processes into account in understanding local places. This means considering the legacy of foreign legal systems imposed along with colonial takeovers, the persistence of remnants of a previously autonomous society in a larger state, the impact of international regulations or declarations, and the effect of borrowed legal procedures (eg popular justice tribunals) and entire legal codes on local communities.' See SE Merry, 'Anthropology, Law, and Transnational Processes' (1992) 21 *Annual Review of Anthropology* 357, 371.

[15] W Felstiner, R Abel and A Sarat, 'The Emergence and Transformation of Disputes: Naming, Blaming, Claiming …' (1980) 15 *Law and Society Review* 631.

[16] In a recent important book on the translation of international human rights discourse into a local Australian language, Holcombe comments on the first cases of protecting Aboriginal secrets, seeing the foundation in the prior recognition of land rights: 'Because there are such a range of ethnographic texts where much of the material could be considered "confidential", that is; they contain gender and age grade specific forms of knowledge that are only revealed to a few in Aboriginal cultural contexts, it seems surprising that there is only one case of breach of confidentiality. Yet, the possibility for Aboriginal people to be engaged in such cases only emerged with the recognition of Aboriginal rights, notably Aboriginal land rights in this central Australian region. The *Aboriginal Land Rights Act (NT)* 1976 for the first time provided Aboriginal people with the opportunity to gain inalienable freehold title, in recognition of customary rights to land'. S Holcombe, *Remote Freedoms: Politics, Personhood and Human Rights in Aboriginal Central Australia* (Durham, Duke University Press, 2015) 7. She also remarks (30) that 'The case of *Foster v Mountford* has been described as a "landmark case" as it was the first decision in Australia to take into account Aboriginal customary rights to culturally defined notions of secrecy'.

[17] R Gould, *Yiwara: Foragers of the Australian Desert* (New York, Scribners, 1969). For a fuller and recent account of the Gould affair, see B Griffiths, *Deep Time Dreaming: Uncovering Ancient Australia* (Carlton, Black Inc Books, 2018) 99–106.

significantly affected the conditions under which I was allowed to attend ceremonies (no notes, no camera), and through these experiences I understood Salomo's predicament.

A second significant event, more visible in the legal landscape, was the litigation brought by the Pitjantjatjara[18] people against CP Mountford's classic 1976 book *Nomads of the Western Desert*.[19] Another public scandal in the revelation of restricted knowledge, the book 'contained details and pictures of secret ceremonies'[20] of Pitjantjatjara men, details provided to Mountford some 35 years earlier during a research trip. This litigation was undertaken to prevent publication of the book in the Northern Territory, where the people who are represented in the monograph lived. The case was not decided in terms of cultural rights per se, but rather in terms of 'the equitable doctrine of confidential information' – a decision rendered by Justice James Muirhead, who, interestingly, had previous considerable experience of a colonial legal administration in the Australian protectorate of Papua New Guinea. Muirhead found a remedy for trespass of restriction in cultural knowledge in terms of the unauthorised use of confidential information. As subsequent discussion by the Australian judge John von Doussa in 2006 framed the solution:

> As the disclosure would have amounted to an actionable breach of confidence, the proceedings were brought by the unincorporated council which represented all Aboriginal peoples inhabiting the Pitjantjatjara lands ... [T]he injunction was granted as the plaintiffs also sued on their own behalf as individuals threatened with damage – damage of a cultural kind. The plaintiff successfully argued that 'revelations of the secrets contained in the book to their women, children and uninitiated men may undermine the social and religious stability of their hard-pressed community.[21]

By 1972, filming was also a subject of changing protocols. To be sure, the filmic attention paid to Indigenous ceremony in the late 1960s must have provided a happy reinforcement to the Papunya people's sense of the ceremony's importance, and possibly laid the foundation for the later uptake of acrylic painting.[22] At the same time, however, the capture of the ceremony on film soon led to consternation about its circulation. As early as 1969, the anthropologist Nicolas Peterson had reported significant problems in the screening of Indigenous men's ritual for non-Indigenous audiences. In a report to the Australian Institute of Aboriginal Studies (AIAS; now Australian Institute of Aboriginal and Torres Strait Islander Studies, AIATSIS), Peterson presented the Indigenous concerns about who might see the films, even though they had consented to the filming.[23] Eventually, in consultation with source communities,

---

[18] See *Foster and Others v Mountford and Rigby Ltd* (1976) 14 ALR 71.

[19] Mountford (n 4).

[20] C Antons, '*Foster v Mountford*: Cultural Confidentiality in a Changing Australia' in AT Kenyon, M Richardson and S Ricketson (eds), *Landmarks in Australian Intellectual Property Law* (Melbourne, Cambridge University Press, 2009) 110–25.

[21] See von Doussa (n 12).

[22] See F Myers and J Long, 'In Recognition: The Gift of Painting' in H Perkins (ed), *One Sun, One Moon: Aboriginal Art in Australia* (Sydney, Art Gallery of New South Wales, 2007) 171.

[23] These events are recounted in I Bryson, *Bringing to Light: A History of Ethnographic Filmmaking at the Australian Institute of Aboriginal and Torres Strait Islander Studies* (Canberra, Aboriginal Studies Press, 2002). Bryson quotes extensively at pp 172–73 from documents in the AIAS archive: 'Peterson

AIAS withdrew from circulation all of its films that represented Indigenous secret and sacred ritual, including specifically several films of Pintupi and Warlpiri rituals that had included participants from the Papunya community, which was one of the sites of my research.[24] As the AIAS solution was an informal resolution of the dispute, one that took place without recourse to Australian law, the Pitjantjatjara case did go to court.

The question of how to recognise claims over the display, performance and circulation of culture subsequently became a more significant academic and ethical concern with Indigenous people.[25] Before these questions of cultural politics had gained academic focus, as we know, they had considerable visibility in the Indigenous communities of the English-speaking settler colonial nations: Australia, the USA, Canada and New Zealand/Aoteroa. As a result of Indigenous claims, various 'cultural protocols' have been developed, with varying legal standing.[26] The course of resolving questions of cultural custodianship can be convoluted and involve a variety of agents.[27]

From early on, however, Indigenous communities in Australia have struggled with the subordination of their own 'Law'[28] to that of the Australian nation-state. They have frequently insisted on the equality of the 'Two Laws', bewildered by the fault

---

described the agreements he had negotiated, as follows: "Whilst Research Officer for the Institute, I negotiated on its behalf nine verbal agreements with various groups of Aborigines for the filming of their secret ceremonies. On each occasion the conditions were similar: 1. The film would not be shown publicly, in cinemas or on television. 2. The film would not be shown to women or children black or white in the community, or to members of other Aboriginal tribes. 3. The film would be shown to 'business' people." There is no doubt that at face value the agreement means that the films may only be shown to adult male anthropologists. However implicitly in both the Aborigines' minds and my own, we were talking about the world as known to them. This at its maximum extent is Australia. Only a very few NT Aborigines have any understanding of Australia as a geographical unit or any conception of the vast distances which separate it from other countries of the world. Their concern, as is usual, was parochial as I interpreted it. They wanted to ensure that in the area known of to them, and that could possibly affect them directly, the films would not be shown to women or children. Beyond that region the question is academic for the Aborigines.' N Peterson, 'The Agreement Made with the Aborigines for the Filming of their Secret Ceremonies and Its Implications', Report to the Australian Institute of Aboriginal Studies, Canberra, Australia, 1969. For another discussion of the 'restrictive policy' on the distribution of ceremonial films, see Griffiths (n 17) 103.

[24] As Bryson wrote in his history of filming by the Australian Institute of Aboriginal Studies: 'This was also a time when the films of the previous phase began to haunt the Institute. In June of 1981, a committee involving Nicolas Peterson, Roger Sandall, Michael Mace (an Aboriginal man on Council) and the Principal recommended that the Institute try to buy back prints of restricted films sold to non-academic organisations or individuals outside of Australia. In addition to this, the committee recommended that the Extension Media Center in Berkley restrict its loans of films on secret and sacred ritual to university groups only. Screenings of these films in Australia had ceased and there was a ban on importing those sold overseas back into Australia.' Bryson, *Bringing to Light* (n 23) 111.

[25] Important texts include MF Brown, 'Can Culture Be Copyrighted?' (1998) 39 *Current Anthropology* 193; M Brown, *Who Owns Native Culture?* (Cambridge, MA, Harvard University Press, 2003); RJ Coombe, *The Cultural Life of Intellectual Properties* (Durham, NC, Duke University Press, 1998); B Ziff and P Rao (eds), *Borrowed Power: Essays on Cultural Appropriation* (New Brunswick, NJ, Rutgers University Press, 1992).

[26] See, eg T Janke, *Minding Culture: Case Studies on Intellectual Property and Traditional Cultural Expressions* (Geneva, World Intellectual Property Organization, 2003); J Anderson and H Geismar (eds), *The Routledge Companion to Intellectual Property* (London, Routledge, 2017).

[27] F Myers, 'Whose Story Is It? Complexities and Complicities of Using Archival Footage' in J Anderson and H Geismar (eds), *The Routledge Companion to Cultural Property* (London, Routledge, 2021).

[28] 'Law' is the term commonly applied by Indigenous Australians to the foundational frameworks of their social worlds, enshrined in myth, ceremony, song and the landscape.

lines of the Australian legal regime, which can threaten to chip away at the sovereignty of the very protocols it appears to protect. In the adjustments around cultural property in Aoteroa/New Zealand, deriving from application of the Waitangi Treaty, Māori protocols have a standing that Indigenous claims lack in Australia. In the triangulation of positions that von Doussa celebrated, there is still a gap in the articulation of cultural rights. In remote Australia, however, if the Convention on Human Rights has been difficult to translate linguistically and conceptually, the moral assertion of control over cultural property has continued unabated. Anthropologists like me are indebted to Sally Merry for offering us ways of considering how laws and rights have reached Indigenous communities.

In *Who Owns Native Culture*, the anthropologist Michael Brown moved away from a simple advocacy position to ask some difficult questions about protocols that employ the concept of 'cultural property' to regulate the circulation of culture.[29] While his considerations of the *pragmatics* of instituting a judicial regime have been regarded as a productive contribution to scholarship, there is something ultimately disturbing about taking cultural property claims just at their face value. As I have argued elsewhere,[30] the underlying logic of many Indigenous claims to 'property' is not always — or not simply — to establish a barrier to circulation, but rather to insist on the acceptance of local cultural protocols, a form of sovereignty. In Australia, frequently, I have found that people are concerned that their relationship to cultural material be acknowledged by 'asking'. And in such terms, the concern — the dispute — necessitates something other than applications of various commercial legal frameworks. Between the 1970s and the present, as the cases here indicate, the shift has been from posing the problem of Indigenous rights in terms of discrimination to insisting on cultural rights as recognition of forms of sovereignty.

While Brown and I probably share a suspicion of the legal regime's capacity to represent the fundamental conflict, the discussion of 'who owns native culture?' is problematic: it gives short shrift to the aspirations that Indigenous peoples embed in property claims. Brown treats the goal of using property-like regulations straightforwardly in legal terms as a means of controlling a resource. Based on my experience, the pursuit of control over culture is more productively viewed in terms of an underlying logic in which 'property' forms the basis of a relationship, and thereby makes claims for the recognition of another party: gaining access to cultural material would be predicated on establishing a relationship. Ownership, at least in Western Desert Indigenous social life as I have come to understand it, fundamentally involves the expectation of having one's identity-bearing rights recognised by others.[31] As the Mohawk scholar Audra Simpson[32] and others[33] are arguing more broadly, claims over

---

[29] Brown, *Who Owns Native Culture?* (n 25).
[30] F Myers, 'Showing Too Much or Too Little: Predicaments of Painting Indigenous Presence in Central Australia' in G Penny and L Graham (eds), *Performing Indigeneity* (Lincoln, NE, University of Nebraska Press, 2014) 351. I have borrowed significantly from this earlier essay in this article.
[31] See Myers, *Pintupi Country* (n 3).
[32] A Simpson, 'On the Logic of Discernment' (2006) 59 *American Quarterly* 479.
[33] GS Coulthard, *Red Skin, White Masks: Rejecting the Colonial Politics of Recognition* (Minneapolis, University of Minnesota Press, 2014).

cultural property have a link with the pursuit of 'sovereignty'.[34] One might extend this to advocate for an ethnographically informed understanding of Indigenous stakes in making property claims.

Even with my limited legal scholarship, I believe such distinctions have had a place in legal considerations of property. The view I am taking of 'property' in this regard is drawn from my own ethnographic work and the writing of those such as Marilyn Strathern; however, it is also resonant with the performative orientation in the work of the feminist legal scholars Margaret Radin and Barbara Rose, or Rosemary Coombe, who regard property as an 'identity-bearing' form.[35] Brown's careful and common-sense critique of a utopian juridicalisation is misleading by focusing so insistently on the means of these claims – some kind of propertisation – rather than considering culture as a basis of sovereignty.[36] More significantly, it may be possible to see in this appropriation of international human rights discourse (as cultural rights) a vernacularization that provides a basis for establishing relationships through the processes of negotiation and consultation that establish Indigenous parties as sovereign agents.

The questions raised here extend beyond the frameworks of legal pluralism that engaged anthropology in the 1980s and 1990s. With her considerations of the real ways in which international legal forms – such as discourses of human rights – reach into local communities, Sally Merry has pioneered the discussion and analysis of the interaction between Indigenous claims of cultural and moral injury and possible mechanisms of redress.

---

[34] Simpson (n 32). On his website, Michael Brown responded to Simpson's review of his book by claiming she had misrepresented his position: 'On balance, the book is less interested in making a romantic case for a global intellectual commons, which is what Simpson alleges, than it is in making a case against the development of multiple, dystopian anti-commonses, even when implemented in the name of Native rights'. M Brown, 'On the Protection of Indigenous Heritage: A Response to Audra Simpson' (*Who Owns Native Culture*, October 2007) https://web.archive.org/web/20100528033630/www.williams.edu/go/native/index.htm.

[35] MJ Radin, *Reinterpreting Property* (Chicago, University of Chicago Press, 1994); CM Rose, *Property and Persuasion: Essays on The History, Theory, And Rhetoric of Ownership* (Boulder, CO, Westview Press, 1994); M Strathern, 'Potential Property. Intellectual Rights and Property in Persons' (1996) 4 *Social Anthropology* 17; Coombe (n 25).

[36] I want to make it clear that I admire Brown's presentation and analysis of the varied cases of claims surrounding cultural property. In its sweep and detail, it brings the object into sustained vision. Nonetheless, it has seemed to me that the position from which he regards the prospects of cultural property is that of how this would actually be managed, of what the implications would be within existing legal regimes, and so on. These are fair questions, but the claims of *indigenous* people for cultural property may be distinctive from those of other minority groups. They have to be understood as moral claims on dominant settler societies, and these are claims that focus on reorganizing the relations between parties to the shared space of the settler nation. This is, I think, the point that Simpson (n 32) makes in distinguishing the history and claims of indigenous people from those who are members of other collectivities. While these others, in liberal societies, might expect equally to have the same claims as those of any 'different' group, this is certainly not the point of view that would emerge from those who begin with the condition of Fourth World people.

6

Vernacularization as Anthropological Ethics

MARK GOODALE

I. INTRODUCTION: AN ANTHROPOLOGIST AMONG THE PHILOSOPHERS

IN OCTOBER 2016, I was surprised to be invited to a conference organised at the University of Michigan Law School. The invitation was a surprise because the event was meant to be a gathering of the great and good from the domains of human rights philosophy, human rights law and comparative international law, brought together around the collective ambition to 'retheorize the practice of human rights'. Why, I wondered, was an anthropologist being invited to contribute to a major philosophical debate over a category like 'human rights practice'?

It is true that I had co-edited a volume in 2007 with Sally Engle Merry entitled *The Practice of Human Rights* and that this volume had, in the intervening years, become a fairly widely used text among certain constituencies. Yet, notably thin amongst this readership, as far as we could tell, were philosophers of human rights, international human rights scholars, comparative international legal scholars, political theorists who focused on human rights, political scientists and international relations specialists – in short, those working across the spectrum of disciplines and orientations that, taken together, were responsible for producing most of the concepts, critiques and frameworks that constituted human rights theory.

This sense of epistemological marginality – that is, that the anthropology of human rights did not form part of the intellectual raw materials from which orthodox human rights theory was built – was confirmed even before the meeting in Ann Arbor began. In reading the large number of pre-circulated papers in preparation for the conference, a conference, again, whose distinguished participants (unarguably, many of the leaders of the field) were planning to 'retheorize the practice of human rights', it was striking that not a single contribution made substantive reference to literature in the anthropology of human rights, including, perhaps most tellingly, our edited volume on the *practice* of human rights.

Yet the reason for the near absence of the anthropology of human rights from the regard of the human rights theorists and philosophers soon became clear: the ways in which they understood the meaning of 'practice' itself were, from an anthropological perspective, highly technical and restrictive, even unrecognisable. Or, to put it in a way that accurately reflects the hierarchy of epistemological priority (and, thus, of power): the way we anthropologists defined the 'practice of human rights' was apparently so conceptually exotic that it remained beyond the boundaries of theoretical debate in the field, unknown (and, perhaps, unknowable) to the leading citizens of the theoretical metropole.

So, with unfamiliar (to me, that is) philosophical distinctions like those between 'practice-independent' and 'practice-dependent' theories of human rights in my mind's eye, I greeted the opening of the conference with a mix of trepidation and nervous anticipation. On the one hand, I arrived as an anthropological outsider, an interloper, perhaps someone – in the bleakest of scenarios – who had been invited as something like intellectual cannon fodder for the giants seated around the imposing conference table, someone whose odd ideas about the 'practice' of human rights could easily be disposed of when the participants needed to blow off steam. But on the other hand, I was defensively eager to make sure concepts from the anthropology of human rights got a full hearing during the coming debates, less in order to try to rearrange the lines of philosophical priority – which would have been a doomed mission, in any case – than to provide an opening, however temporary, onto the vast and normatively diverse landscapes on which anthropologists had been conducting research on human rights for almost 30 years.

In the event, this opening was created not in terms of an anthropological definition of human rights practice – 'all the many ways in which social actors ... talk about, advocate for, criticize, study, [and] legally enact ... the idea of human rights'[1] – which remained, for the gathered philosophers, too far afield theoretically, too conceptually expansive, a definition that likely raised more questions than it answered. Rather, any ripples that my anthropological interventions during the event managed to produce were the result of something quite different: the insistence that the practice of human rights must not be understood first and foremost as an expression of a set of ideas, but rather as the mechanism that constitutes them, and that the complex processes through which plural conceptions of human rights emerge in practice was best described through a framework that Sally Engle Merry called 'vernacularization'.[2]

Yet, if it was the concept of vernacularization that provoked the most interest over those three days, during which the sounds of the often-heated exchanges reverberated among the impressive neo-English Gothic walls of South Hall (now called Jeffries Hall), it was an interest that bore the seeds of its own undoing. This was because, as will become clearer in the course of this chapter, the concept of vernacularization was not only a highly innovative analytical tool for parsing the subtleties of human rights practice; as it turned out, it could also be taken as an argument for radically

---

[1] M Goodale, 'Introduction: Locating Rights, Envisioning Law between the Global and the Local' in M Goodale and SE Merry (eds), *The Practice of Human Rights: Tracking Law between the Global and the Local* (Cambridge, Cambridge University Press, 2007) 24.

[2] See, eg SE Merry, 'Transnational Human Rights Activism: Mapping the Middle' (2006) 108 *American Anthropologist* 38; SE Merry, *Human Rights and Gender Violence: Translating International Law into Local Justice* (Chicago, University of Chicago Press, 2006).

reimagining the grounds of human rights theory itself, an argument, moreover, that necessarily implied a thoroughgoing critique of precisely the dominant approaches that formed the intellectual core of the Michigan conference (and the field more generally).

In contrast to the original invitation, therefore, it was not surprising that my written contribution to the conference proceedings never saw the light of day; in fact, I never heard anything from the organisers again. Multiple inquiries regarding publication plans were met with silence; even a short thank you note failed to trigger a response. Despite the initial disappointment, I eventually came to regard this post-conference exile as something of a success: the anthropological approach to the practice of human rights, and specifically the profound implications of Merry's vernacularization framework, must have touched a nerve among the arbiters of human rights scholarship. Thus, it was a delight to be able to have if not exactly the last word, then at least *another* word, on the question of how Merry's signal concept of vernacularization offers not only a pioneering approach to the practice of human rights, but, more important, a potentially transformative approach to the future of human rights itself as the basis for global justice.

* * *

The remainder of this chapter is structured in the following way. In the next section, I examine the concept of vernacularization in detail, focusing on the key places in which Merry introduces it and explains its nuances. As will be seen, some of the ways in which I eventually adapt vernacularization represent modes of argument and forms of application that are not necessarily explicit in the original source material. Nevertheless, it is important to emphasise the ways in which these extensions derive from Merry's much more grounded development of vernacularization as both an ethnographic category and conceptual device, one that has proven to be enormously influential among anthropologists and other qualitative social scientists working on questions of normative translation and what Merry herself and a colleague have more recently described as 'human rights transformation in practice'.[3]

With this anchoring in the concept of vernacularization as a point of departure, the chapter then moves to the question of implications: how does Merry's most important theory of human rights practice change the ways in which human rights themselves – as law, as politics, as moral discourse, as ideology – both can and should be understood? Rather than proposing an answer to this question in the abstract, I instead show how the far-reaching implications of vernacularization have already been revealed – even if indirectly; that is, without necessarily being formally acknowledged as such – in the work of scholars conducting anthropological research on the practice of human rights in widely divergent contexts. Here, I will focus on three compelling case studies: Shannon Speed's research with Indigenous communities in the aftermath of the Zapatista rebellion against the Mexican state; Sarah Holcombe's

---

[3] T Destrooper and SE Merry (eds), *Human Rights Transformation in Practice* (Philadelphia, University of Pennsylvania Press, 2018).

study of efforts to translate the Universal Declaration of Human Rights (UDHR) into an Australian Aboriginal language for the first time; and Lynette Chua's fascinating and difficult research among LGBT activists in Myanmar, whose commitment to human rights took shape in subtle ways that had little to do with either legal or political change.

Finally, the chapter concludes by using these expansive accounts of vernacularization to reflect more generally on the future of human rights, a subject that has become a topic of intense debate among scholars, practitioners and policy-makers alike. I will argue that Merry's concept of vernacularization offers not only a different set of potential answers to the question of the future of human rights, but, more significantly, a different approach altogether to the question: one that is grounded in the unrealised potential of human rights even in the face of profound contemporary crises such as climate change, economic inequality and the global outbreak of new infectious diseases.

II. VERNACULARIZATION BETWEEN REPLICATION AND HYBRIDITY

Between 1999 and 2004, Sally Engle Merry directed a groundbreaking research project on global efforts to make violence against women a central concern of human rights activism, implementation and monitoring. Over these five years, Merry and her research team examined the different forms that women's rights mobilisation took in five Asia-Pacific locations: Hawai'i, Fiji, China, India and Hong Kong. In addition, Merry conducted research at the centre of the international human rights system, including with UN agencies and treaty bodies in New York City and Geneva. Different sites at which women's rights were put into practice or evaluated included city-level women's shelters; NGO strategy meetings; national policy debates; and various places where the global system to monitor compliance with the Convention on the Elimination of All Forms of Discrimination against Women (CEDAW) conducted its work.

This research was novel for a number of different reasons. First, it broke new ground methodologically as a study in the anthropology of human rights that moved beyond existing ethnographic approaches, which focused on single research sites or even a limited number of research sites within a region or country. For example, during my doctoral research in Bolivia conducted just before Merry's project (1998–99), I studied the ways in which transnational human rights NGOs – working through their national partners – introduced the idea of 'derechos humanos' to peasant communities in one province in the north of Potosí Department through village workshops, support for a local legal services centre and through the diffusion of informational brochures, which often presented human rights in the simplest of terms without reference to either international or national legal documents.[4]

Although I visited almost 40 small communities to conduct research on the impact of these local human rights projects, the scope was limited to one rural province in one

---

[4] M Goodale, *Dilemmas of Modernity: Bolivian Encounters with Law and Liberalism* (Stanford, Stanford University Press, 2008).

region in one country. Yet, this ethnographic research project was relatively expansive for the time. A more typical orientation would be one like Richard Wilson's earlier anthropological study of the South African Truth and Reconciliation Commission (TRC). Although his research took account of debates and processes at the national level, the primary location for his ethnographic study was the TRC itself, where he observed sessions, interviewed participants and analysed its consequences for the forging of post-apartheid South African society.[5]

Merry's anthropological research on domestic violence as a human rights violation, however, adopted a remarkably different approach. Influenced by leading-edge anthropological theorists such as George Marcus, who was arguing at the time that scholars should reconsider traditional single-site based studies in favour of 'multisited' ethnography,[6] Merry developed an anthropological methodology for the project that she described as 'deterritorialized ethnography'.[7] As she put it, this approach allows the anthropologist to:

> study placeless phenomena in a place, to find small interstices in global processes in which critical decisions are made, to track the information flows that constitute global discourses, and to mark the points at which competing discourses intersect in the myriad links between global and local conceptions and institutions.[8]

As adapted to the anthropology of human rights, deterritorialised ethnography proved to be revolutionary. In following the deterritorialised women's rights system, the methodology allowed Merry to 'engage[ ] with the fragments of [the] larger system [while] recogniz[ing] that the system is neither coherent nor full graspable'. Instead, her research traced the women's rights system through various 'disembodied space[s] of social life', that paradoxically 'exist[ ] in various spaces but [were] not grounded in any one of them [exclusively]'.[9]

Second, the use of this innovative research methodology to examine important 'fragments' of the women's rights system across the decidedly variable contexts of Hawai'i, Fiji, China, India and Hong Kong resulted in an unprecedented comparative ethnographic dataset. Set against vast differences in political economy, political ideologies, international power, kinship structures and demographic factors, among many others, Merry's research on the practice of women's rights – understood anthropologically – documented both its social and normative particularities in a way that allowed her to make more generalisable empirical and theoretical claims about these practices.

And finally, in making these broader claims based on a five-year deterritorialised ethnography of the international women's rights system, Merry developed a theoretical framework that would prove to be enduringly illuminating. Although other human rights scholars had used the concept of vernacularization in different ways, these had been largely rhetorical; Merry was the first anthropologist to

---

[5] R Wilson, *The Politics of Truth and Reconciliation in South Africa: Legitimizing the Post-Apartheid State* (Cambridge, Cambridge University Press, 2001).
[6] See G Marcus, *Ethnography through Thick and Thin* (Princeton, Princeton University Press, 1998).
[7] Merry, *Human Rights and Gender Violence* (n 2) 28–30.
[8] ibid 29.
[9] ibid.

see the value in adapting the sociolinguistic category of vernacularization as the foundation for an anthropological theory of the practice of human rights.[10] In both her contribution to a major special issue on human rights in the journal *American Anthropologist* and in the book-length analysis of the five-year project itself, Merry proposed the concept of vernacularization as a device for making sense of the interplay between relatively abstract and globalised human rights norms and the plural forms they take in the messiness of actual political campaigns, legal struggles and even individual decisions.[11]

It is important to emphasise the fact that Merry induced the concept of vernacularization in its dual senses — as an explanatory model and as a normative theory of human rights practice — from what amounted to a profusion of ethnographic data on the women's rights system. That is, vernacularization provides a means for both explaining the complexities of human rights practices that she observed over five years in the various research sites and reflecting more generally about the normative relationship between human rights practice and the broader prospects for human rights as 'one of the key ideas of contemporary world-making'.[12] As an explanatory model, Merry found that the norms of the women's rights system — which takes both international and transnational forms at the largest scales — must be translated in different ways by different kinds of actors, but that those occupying what she called 'middle' positions play a particularly important role.[13]

For example, she describes the functioning of the *nari adalats*, or women's courts, that were established in India during the mid-1990s to give women a new resource to protect themselves against the chronic social problem of domestic violence. The staff members of the courts functioned as intermediaries between the global and national levels, which proposed the courts as a way to give practical form to women's

---

[10] For example, in an important edited volume on 'culture and rights', Rachel Sieder and Jessica Witchell (both non-anthropologists) write that 'Throughout the world, globalized political values such as human rights and multiculturalism are increasingly taken up and vernacularized in particular social contexts, often providing important leverage for opposition movements in their struggles to extract greater concessions from national states'. Later in the chapter, they add, 'the legal context is now characterized by inter-legality and the mixing of cultural codes, while global discourses become part of the local vernacular and constantly acquire new meanings'. R Sieder and J Witchell, 'Advancing Indigenous Claims through the Law: Reflections on the Guatemalan Peace Process' in JK Cowan, M-B Dembour and RA Wilson (eds), *Culture and Rights: Anthropological Perspectives* (Cambridge, Cambridge University Press, 2001) 204–07. In her own contribution to the volume, Merry does not yet use the concept of vernacularization, nor does she invoke it in one of her first efforts to analyse the results of the five-year study of the women's rights movement, an article published towards the end of the project, but before it had been completed: SE Merry, 'Rights Talk and the Experience of Law: Implementing Women's Human Rights to Protection from Violence' (2003) 25 *Human Rights Quarterly* 343. In a 2005 article analysing data from Hong Kong, by contrast, Merry (with colleague and research assistant Rachel Stern) makes the link between human rights and 'vernacular forms of globalization', but this concept had still not matured into the major theoretical framework that it would soon become: SE Merry and RE Stern, 'The Female Inheritance Movement in Hong Kong: Theorizing the Local/Global Interface' (2005) 46 *Current Anthropology* 387.

[11] Merry, 'Transnational Human Rights Activism' (n 2); Merry, *Human Rights and Gender Violence* (n 2). I was the editor of the 2006 *American Anthropologist* special issue in which 'Transnational Human Rights Activism' appears, a collection whose different articles examined 'anthropology and human rights in a new key'.

[12] U Hannerz, '"Human rights" Has Become One of the Key Ideas of Contemporary World-Making' in M Goodale and SE Merry (eds), *The Practice of Human Rights: Tracking Law between the Global and the Local* (Cambridge, Cambridge University Press, 2007).

[13] Merry, 'Transnational Human Rights Activism' (n 2).

rights norms as defined by CEDAW and Indian national legislation, and the local villagers – both women and men – who were being encouraged to make use of these new institutions. In the processes of vernacularization that marked the interface between global and national institutions and the local villagers, staff members were required to draw on work experiences, cultural expectations and human rights training in mediating the flows of understanding (and misunderstanding) between these different legal, political, cultural and moral worlds.

Moreover, in analysing these processes of vernacularization – in 'mapping the middle', as she described it – Merry found that what resulted could be placed on a spectrum based on the extent to which the act of translation changed the form and content of the norms themselves. At one end of the spectrum, 'replication', the process of vernacularization leaves the global human rights norms largely intact; the local adaptation is 'superficial and primarily decorative'.[14] At the other end of the spectrum, 'hybridity', vernacularization results in various degrees of normative change, including, at the outer limits, changes to the meaning of norms in practice that profoundly alter their received content. Nevertheless, as Merry's research also demonstrated, most effects of norm translation in practice will fall somewhere between these two poles. Even more, the same process of vernacularization, viewed historically, will vary over time in relation to its effects on the underlying human rights norms, at times involving greater degrees of replication and at times greater degrees of hybridity.

But more generally, what Merry's descriptive model suggests is that these diverse processes of vernacularization are inescapable; there is no way to envision the implementation of human rights in practice that does not imply vernacularization. This fact leads immediately to two astonishing consequences. First, at the level of policy-making, the inevitability of vernacularization in all of its actual diversity and situational particularity means that the globalisation of long-settled human rights norms, the diffusion of human rights across the world like oil spreading out across water, is impossible to achieve in practice and should therefore likely be abandoned as a goal – even an ideal one – for human rights institutions and activists.

And second, at the level of normative content, the dynamic effects of vernacularization, the constantly shifting movement along the spectrum between replication and hybridity, imply that the actual meaning of human rights norms can never be fixed in practice, that their normative content will remain open and contested, a beginning rather than an end. More theoretically, we can say that human rights norms are bound to be part of an open and porous system in which their meanings are always in a state of becoming, through negotiation, resistance and reformulation. Put another way, we can say that – perhaps contrary to the (self-)image of the international human rights system – human rights do not exist within (or themselves constitute) a closed 'autopoietic' system in which the meaning of a particular norm is established only in reference to the meaning of other norms in a kind of never-ending, self-reproducing normative feedback loop.[15] In other words, extrapolating from Merry's concept of vernacularization, we must acknowledge that, unlike biological systems,

---

[14] ibid 44.
[15] See G Teubner (ed), *Autopoietic Law: A New Approach to Law and Society* (Berlin, De Gruyter, 1987).

the international human rights system will never become an 'endless dance of internal correlations in a closed network of interacting elements'.[16]

To make this point more concretely, take Article 1 of CEDAW, the legal foundation for the international women's rights system that was at the heart of Merry's research. The Convention recognises that freedom from 'all forms of discrimination against women' is a human right to be enshrined in and enforced through law, educational reform, social change and 'all [other] appropriate measures' the state deems necessary in order to honour both the spirit and the letter of the Convention. But what, exactly, is meant by 'discrimination'? At first, the definition in Article 1 would seem to be highly specific, indeed, closed:

> [A]ny distinction, exclusion or restriction made on the basis of sex which has the effect or purpose of impairing or nullifying the recognition, enjoyment or exercise by women, irrespective of their marital status, on a basis of equality of men and women, of human rights and fundamental freedoms in the political, economic, social, cultural, civil or any other field.

Yet, as Merry's research convincingly reveals, this definition must enter the swirl of human rights practice, in which each element is subject to the discursive vicissitudes of vernacularization, the dynamic interplay of factors that ultimately gives meaning to every substantive part of the norm – 'distinction', 'sex', 'impairing or nullifying', 'enjoyment or exercise', 'marital status', etc – meanings that, moreover, remain open, contingent, even ambiguous. The result is an international human rights 'system' – if, indeed, it makes any sense to continue thinking of it as a system – in which key texts, from the UDHR to CEDAW, along with their national counterparts, at best serve as connotative normative reference points, catalysts for diverse forms of mobilisation whose outcomes will often bear little relation to the catalysts themselves. From this perspective, 'human rights implementation' or even 'human rights activism' must be understood in radically different ways.

But if the consequences of vernacularization can also be taken as a wider critique, in the way they reveal the ultimate impossibility of forging a world order based on a common global understanding of the form and content of universal human rights, they also point in a number of positive, even potentially transformative, directions. In the next section, I examine the ways in which the potentially transformative side of vernacularization has been demonstrated – even if implicitly – in the work of other ethnographers of human rights whose research likewise took place at the uncertain interfaces of human rights practice.

III. VERNACULARIZATION AS POTENTIA, ETHNO-EPISTEMOLOGY AND EMPOWERMENT

In pivoting to a more prospective discussion of vernacularization as a key component of a reformulated approach to human rights, I turn now to three noteworthy

---

[16] HR Maturana, *Erkennen: Die Organisation und Verkörperung von Wirklichkeit* (Braunschweig, Friedrich Vieweg & Sohn, 1982) 28.

case studies. Each study illustrates different ways in which the vernacularization of human rights in practice offers the possibility of envisioning new forms through which the original ambitions of the post-war human rights project might be preserved, even deepened, as an ongoing framework or logic for justice-seeking in all of its diverse senses.[17] In making the argument for vernacularization as one among several pillars of an alternative approach, it is important to underscore the extent to which this argument reflects a commitment to human rights as the normative basis for progressive action at all levels, from the development of green energy technologies as a response to climate change to the insistence on redistributive and either non-capitalist, or significantly restructured capitalist, economics as a response to pervasive global economic inequality and long-term resource depletion.[18]

The three ethnographic studies took place at different periods, both in relation to the development of the concept of vernacularization and in relation to the unfolding history of human rights. Shannon Speed conducted research in Chiapas for nearly a decade in the aftermath of the 1994 Zapatista uprising against the Mexican state. Over these nine years, Speed's work among the indigenous communities that were at the centre of the rebellion against the state began as a member of a US-based human rights observation and accompaniment organisation and ended as an activist-anthropologist committed both to the production of knowledge about human and indigenous rights within the conflict and to the protection of the communities in Chiapas that had suffered most from state repression.[19] At a broader level, Speed's research and activism took place during a time in which human and indigenous rights were becoming increasingly pervasive in both global politics and within local struggles; indeed, at the end of the first post-Cold War decade of optimistic ascendency, UN Secretary-General Kofi Annan could declare confidently that the world had entered the 'Age of Human Rights'.[20]

Yet, when Sarah Holcombe began her research with Australian Aboriginal communities as part of a long-term project to translate the UDHR into a native Australian language, the global human rights landscape had shifted dramatically from the halcyon days of the 'Age of Human Rights'.[21] Holcombe's work took place both after the attacks of 11 September 2001 had set in motion the forces of surveillance governance, neo-Realpolitik and 'forever war'[22] and after the global financial crisis of 2007–08 had given impetus to the strengthening of formations such as the G20,

---

[17] In this, the argument I make here differs from that of scholars who believe that it is precisely the ambitions of the postwar human rights project – as it has evolved through the decades – that are the problem. For example, Samuel Moyn views the trajectory of the international human rights system as one marked by increasingly 'downsized ambition' in which goals were progressively limited (notably around social and economic rights) that made it very difficult institutionally to mobilise human rights as an effective response to the devastating long-term effects of neoliberal capitalism: S Moyn, *Not Enough: Human Rights in an Unequal World* (Cambridge, MA, Belknap Press, 2018). See also this chapter's conclusion.

[18] See M Goodale, *Reinventing Human Rights* (Stanford, Stanford University Press, 2022).

[19] S Speed, *Rights in Rebellion: Indigenous Struggle and Human Rights in Chiapas* (Stanford, Stanford University Press, 2008).

[20] K Annan, 'The Age of Human Rights' *Project Syndicate* (New York, 26 September 2000) www.project-syndicate.org/commentary/the-age-of-human-rights?barrier=true.

[21] S Holcombe, *Remote Freedoms: Politics, Personhood and Human Rights in Aboriginal Central Australia* (Stanford, Stanford University Press, 2018).

[22] See D Filkins, *The Forever War* (New York, Vintage, 2008).

which came to replace as a centre of power equally – but differently – problematic institutions such as the UN Security Council.[23] In any event, Holcombe's ethnographic and linguistic study was conducted well after the post-Cold War 'Age of Human Rights' had come to a close, to be replaced by a period in which human rights apparently suffered a 'rise and fall' and then continued on in law and politics through dark and uncertain 'endtimes'.[24]

Finally, Lynette Chua's difficult and even dangerous ethnographic research among LGBT human rights activists in Myanmar took place somewhat later, when the wider backlash against human rights – especially by left-leaning intellectuals in the Global North who had felt betrayed by the failures of human rights as a replacement for socialism after the Cold War[25] – gave way to a less pessimistically critical and more reflective period in the history (and historiography) of human rights. Here, human rights scholars and practitioners alike revisited many of the basic assumptions about the origins of human rights, their relationship to cultural diversity and their effectiveness in practice, and, perhaps surprisingly, found 'evidence for hope' and a more optimistic narrative about the 'reconstruction of global values'.[26] It is this latest (and current) period of critical possibility – which I have described elsewhere as 'human rights liminality 3.0'[27] – that allows us to evaluate the three case studies, and thus reconsider the transformative potential of vernacularization, in a different light.

During her research in Chiapas, Speed studied the ways in which indigenous communities refashioned the concept of human rights as part of collective struggles with the Mexican state. Against a background in which the 'revolutionary' Mexican government had alternately abandoned the indigenous communities of Chiapas and turned the repressive forces of the state against them during periods of resistance, Speed found that indigenous people developed novel political structures based on equally novel and culturally embedded theories of human rights.

In 2003, the Zapatistas created five regional *Juntas de Buen Goberino*, or Good Governance Councils, that gave force to these regionally circulating accounts of human rights. As Speed explains, what made these alternative formulations of human rights among the communities so innovative was in the way 'human rights' were detached from their origins in international treaties, national legislation and, ultimately, the history of liberal philosophy. According to the Zapatista activists, human rights were not natural entitlements; they did not understand them as something co-extensive with a collective humanity. Instead, human rights were reformulated as a form of social and political power, a form of power, moreover,

---

[23] See Goodale, *Reinventing Human Rights* (n 18).

[24] L Allen, *The Rise and Fall of Human Rights: Cynicism and Politics in Occupied Palestine* (Stanford, Stanford University Press, 2013); S Hopgood, *The Endtimes of Human Rights* (Ithaca, NY, Cornell University Press, 2013).

[25] See M Goodale, 'Human Rights after the Post-Cold War' in M Goodale (ed), *Human Rights at the Crossroads* (New York, Oxford University Press, 2013) 1–28.

[26] K Sikkink, *Evidence for Hope: Making Human Rights Work in the 21st Century* (Princeton, Princeton University Press, 2017); SLB Jensen, *The Making of International Human Rights: The 1960s, Decolonization, and the Reconstruction of Global Values* (New York, Cambridge University Press, 2016).

[27] M Goodale, 'Liminality and Human Rights' (2020) 5 *Inference*.

that only came into being when it was being exercised by community members through social struggle.[28]

For my purposes, Speed's research contributes two elements essential to the wider argument for the transformative potential of vernacularization. First, her study shows how vernacularization can take place primarily, and most importantly, at the local level; that is, among the people and communities that Merry describes as the 'targets' for human rights implementation and activism.[29] Although various actors, including grassroots NGO workers (like Speed, during her first years in Chiapas), government officials and transnational rights institutions, did act as the kinds of intermediaries that occupied the core of Merry's research, here it was the Zapatista community members themselves who made human rights in the vernacular.[30]

And second, the refashioning of human rights as an organic theory of collective power allows us to appreciate the full creative potential of the vernacularization process. In explaining the Zapatista conception of human rights-as-power, Speed draws from the social theory of Antonio Negri, who adapted Spinoza's distinction between *potestas* (Power) and *potentia* (power) in order to guard a good, indeed vital, place for power (*potentia*) as 'creative activity or force of constitution' that can be mobilised against various forms of sovereign violence, which are expressions of Power (that is, *potestas*).[31] As Speed explains, 'This distinction [between *potestas* and *potentia*] echoed in [Subcomandante] Marco's famous statement, "We the Zapatistas want to exercise power, not take it"'.[32]

In a very different cultural and political context, Sarah Holcombe's research likewise reveals the transformative implications of vernacularization, or what she describes as its 'emancipatory potential'.[33] Holcombe's work is based in long-term engagements of different kinds – academic, activist, policy consultation – with the Anangu people, an Aboriginal population that lives in a part of Central Australia that is considered 'very remote' by the national statistics agency.[34] Holcombe's study of the Anangu's relationship with human rights activism takes place on two levels.

On one level, she examines the troubled history within which the Anangu, like all other Australian Aboriginal populations, had little to show from decades of ambivalent national mobilisation around rights as a governmental response to colonial and neocolonial violence against Australia's native peoples. As Holcombe argues, from the problematic implementation of the 1976 Aboriginal Land Rights Act to

---

[28] Speed (n 19) 156–57.
[29] Merry, *Human Rights and Gender Violence* (n 2) 134.
[30] Of the three case studies here, it is only Speed's that does not specifically invoke Merry's concept of vernacularization, which (as we have seen) had not been fully diffused in publications by the time Speed's own study was being published. However, Speed does develop a theoretical approach that is fully consistent with the concept of vernacularization. As she puts it, 'I argue that local mobilizations of the globalized discourse of human rights are products of [a] complex dialogic interaction. The appropriation by local groups of global discourses is not an acritical and mechanical process, but a dialogic and creative one, in which 'local' people participate actively, bringing in their local histories, understandings, and goals': Speed (n 19) 33.
[31] ibid 168.
[32] ibid.
[33] Holcombe (n 21) 37.
[34] ibid 26.

the conservative assault on indigenous rights by members of the Australian Human Rights Commission during the coalition government of Tony Abbott (2013–15), the use of rights — citizenship, land, human, indigenous — had manifestly failed Australia's Aboriginal peoples as a national legal or political framework.[35]

On another level, however, Holcombe's research reveals a very different orientation to what she calls 'indigenous rights as human rights' among the Anangu. In the course of her ethnographic study, Holcombe participated in an ambitious project to translate the UDHR into Pintupi-Lurijta, the language spoken by the Anangu. As part of an interdisciplinary team of researchers and translators, including native Pintupi-Lurijta speakers, Holcombe was able to explore multiple forms of vernacularization not only as translation, but as something else — what she describes as a 'dialogical process[ ] of interpretation'.[36] This was a process of deep semiotic mediation in which articles of the UDHR became categories in which colonialism, racism, cultural marginalisation and social suffering were confronted with the subversive alterity of indigenous cosmovisions, in which the UDHR was rendered into a polyvalent document that was capable of accommodating what Marisol de la Cadena and Mario Blaser have called a 'world of many worlds'.[37]

On the one hand, the team had to make decisions about how to translate passages from the UDHR in ways that resonated with the linguistic, cultural and moral understandings of native Pintupi-Lurijta speakers. For example, there was a difficulty in giving translinguistic meaning to the keyword *waltja*, which 'specifies a sense of belonging together or shared identity' for the Anangu, yet in ways that code 'decided inequalities within Anangu families, [for example,] between ages and gender'. Despite this, *waltja* was used in the translation of Article 1 of the UDHR, which holds (in part) that 'All human beings are born free and equal in dignity and rights'. The back-translated passage, in which *waltja* is used specifically to translate the 'free' in 'free and equal', reads 'All the many different people are living together well, as though they are all family'.[38]

In other words, a Pintupi-Lurijta word/concept that embeds what from an Anglosphere and liberal philosophical perspective would be considered an obstacle to freedom — structural social inequality — was found to be the best way to express what it means to be 'free' for the Anangu. This same process of discursive juxtaposition was undertaken for all the foundational concepts and phrases in the UDHR,

---

[35] For example, Australia was one of the four settler colonial countries to vote against the UN Declaration on the Rights of Indigenous Peoples (UN-DRIP) in 2007 (along with Canada, New Zealand and the USA). Although Australia later endorsed the legally non-binding declaration in 2009, the position of the country's Human Rights Commission towards indigenous rights during the Abbott government was indicative, according to Holcombe, of a much longer national orientation that ranged from ambivalent to dismissive to openly hostile. Holcombe quotes a commissioner during this period, who insisted that only the 'traditional human rights' of Western liberalism should be protected under law, since 'Australia and other Anglosphere nations were built on a liberal approach'. The indigenous rights of UN-DRIP, by contrast, should be rejected, according to the same commissioner, since they are part of an 'international treat[y] infused with the objectives of the socialist tradition': Holcombe (n 21) 19–20.

[36] ibid 35.

[37] M de la Cadena and M Blaser (eds), *A World of Many Worlds* (Durham, NC, Duke University Press, 2018).

[38] Holcombe (n 21) 48–49.

including, obviously, 'human rights' itself. Without anything approaching a concise equivalent in Pintupi-Lurijta, the translation team settled on an expansive phrasing for 'human rights' that was expository rather than definitional: 'All of us should be equal. Being peaceful, reconciled and without spite, we should be living together all as family. We should be kind to people with respect and understanding.'[39]

On the other hand, beyond the important realisation that vernacularization implies much more than simply normative translation, Holcombe discovered that the process itself was equally important. In other words, the local legitimacy of the eventual translation of the UDHR into Pintupi-Lurijta was not only a question of sociolinguistic meaning; it was also related to how the research team went about its work, that is, *how* it learned. Rather than assuming that discussion or debate about something can be measured against a universal standard (of rationality, for example), the UDHR translation project adopted an ethno-epistemological approach in which ways of knowing themselves must also be subject to the 'dialogical process of interpretation'.

As Holcombe explains, quoting the long-time anthropologist of Aboriginal Central Australia Fred Myers, 'In the [Anangu] view, the concepts "thinking," "understanding" and hearing are expressed by a single term – *kulininpa*, which means literally "to hear"'.[40] This meant that the vernacularization process was not dependent on, for example, expert intermediaries or legal or cultural specialists. Instead, it was a fundamentally social process through which knowledge was created by a particular kind of dialogic interaction, one in which interlocuters strove to hear one another, in which 'listening and talking together' (*kulirra tjungungku wangkanyi*) was the basis on which a culturally thick and discursively polyvalent account of 'human rights' might emerge.[41]

Finally, Lynette Chua's powerful ethnography of human rights activism among queer Burmese before, during and after Myanmar's post-2011 political transition offers yet another testimony to the ways in which making human rights in the vernacular points to an alternative future for human rights, a vernacular future.[42] Chua's research took place during a period of fraught liminality in Burmese history, when the country's military regime agreed to political reforms, the release of pro-democracy activist Aung San Suu Kyi from house arrest and the loosening of a number of social restrictions, including those that regulated the work of both national and foreign NGOs. In 2013 and 2014, several LGBT rights organisations, which had been running operations from exile bases in Thailand, returned to Myanmar and began a quiet, nationwide campaign of social mobilisation and human rights activism among Myanmar's largely closeted LGBT population.[43]

---

[39] The exposition (rather than definition, which was considered impossible) of 'human rights in Pintupi-Lurijta is *Tjutakulampa ngaranyi liipula nyinanytjaku mingarrtjuwiya, kalypakalypa tjungurringkula walytjarringula nyinanytjaku. Pina yalytjurarringkula kaangkurrinytjaku*: ibid 50.
[40] ibid 51.
[41] ibid.
[42] See M Goodale, 'Our Vernacular Futures' in Destrooper and Merry (n 3) 251–62.
[43] As Chua explains, during their years in exile, the Burmese LGBT organisations would sometimes ask members to smuggle human rights documents and literature back into Myanmar at great risk to the activist-couriers, who would mix the materials 'with dirty underwear to discourage customs officers from

These early years in which a nascent LGBT human rights movement took root in Myanmar were arduous and spent by activists conducting grassroots mobilisation largely at the margins of both social and political life. As Chua describes these methods:

> Working out of their headquarters in Yangon, [the LGBT activists] continued to expand the reach of their movement and practice. They boarded buses and visited new towns on advocacy trips. Ahead of their visits, they asked friends and acquaintances about informal social networks and popular hangouts for queer Burmese at their destinations. They tried to arrive one day in advance and find queer Burmese at those places to invite them to the meeting. For remote small towns where residents had little or no access to the Internet, this was an effective method of outreach and recruitment.[44]

The modesty of these initial moves was a response to the fact that LGBT Burmese confronted a triple vulnerability. First, LGBT people in Myanmar were stigmatised for religious reasons. As Chua explains, according to Burmese Buddhist beliefs – in which karma (good or bad acts in a current life) influences the form of a subsequent rebirth – LGBT sexual orientation was seen as a punishment for 'having committed sexual transgressions in past lives'. Second, Burmese society is marked by a pronounced gender hierarchy that privileges both men and heteronormativity. This means that LGBT Burmese have traditionally suffered from the full range of discrimination and social violence, including persecution by the police, bullying and harassment in schools, sexual attacks and open discrimination in employment. And third, despite the political opening in Myanmar after 2011, the longer-term prospects for civil society remained unclear. This meant that LGBT human rights activists undertook their work under the ever-present threat of a return of state repression.[45]

The result of these precarious conditions was that human rights activism among the Burmese LGBT community was not directed towards legal or political reforms by the state, or even the transformation of attitudes within Burmese society. Instead, the making of human rights in the vernacular became a project of personal empowerment, a means through which Burmese LGBT people could 'rediscover' themselves with pride and without 'self-hate, shame, and fear'.[46] Human rights became a framework that both refashioned personhood for Burmese LGBT activists and structured a new sense of collective belonging among the LGBT community.

In this way, vernacularization led to the creation of a new mode of self-orientation among LGBT people in Myanmar, one in which human rights was understood, first and foremost, as a 'way of life'. Chua's ethnographic account of these innovative shifts teaches us, among other things, that the vernacularization of human rights can have potentially far-reaching consequences that are nevertheless difficult to observe, let alone measure, since they do not involve legal processes, political

---

rummaging deeper': L Chua, *The Politics of Love in Myanmar: LGBT Mobilization and Human Rights as a Way of Life* (Stanford, Stanford University Press) 60.
[44] ibid 61–62 (the verb tense has been changed from the present to the past throughout this quotation).
[45] ibid 6–7.
[46] See R Niezen, *The Rediscovered Self: Indigenous Identity and Cultural Justice* (Montreal, McGill-Queen's University Press, 2009); Chua (n 43) 7.

campaigns or the other social and legal contexts in which human rights form the basis of formal justice-seeking.

IV. CONCLUSION: ETHICS, ANTHROPOLOGY AND THE FUTURE OF HUMAN RIGHTS

If it is true, as I have suggested above, that the future of human rights no longer looks as grim as it might have even a few years ago, then the foregoing demonstrates the ways in which vernacularization as both concept and practice can play an important, indeed fundamental, role in shaping this future. Despite key nuances, much of the debate over human rights has taken place against an explicit or implicit concern with effectiveness: do human rights actually work as the primary legal, political or social grounding for responses to the most pressing contemporary problems? It is not surprising that the answers to this question within the scholarly literature are varied, but two have proven to be particularly influential, not the least because they stand in such stark contrast to each other.

On one side, the political scientist Kathryn Sikkink has argued that human rights have proven to be remarkably effective, especially in both reducing impunity for mass violations and for bringing justice – largely through criminal trials – to victims of oppressive political regimes. Sikkink has also been a consistent and high-profile advocate for the proposition that human rights norms should be considered universal since they emerged through a process of global consensus-building in which the countries of regions like Latin America played a crucial part.[47]

But from a very different direction, the legal historian Samuel Moyn has argued that human rights – especially economic, social and cultural rights – suffer from historical and structural weaknesses that make them an ineffective tool, even in ideal circumstances, for responding to the most serious threats, especially economic inequality.[48] According to Moyn, post-war human rights underwent a devasting transformation when international policy-makers agreed to adopt them as a normative justification for global strategies to reduce poverty. The lasting consequence of this historical shift, as Moyn sees it, was that the grand scheme of human rights was reduced and eventually absorbed into programmes that worked incrementally towards the provision of minimum levels of adequate food, water, education and political participation, especially in parts of the world where these minimum 'sufficiencies' were far from assured.

The problem, according to Moyn, was that, in reconfiguring human rights as one among several rationales for guaranteeing basic minimums of provision and treatment, the international system cut human rights free from its original objectives: equality, justice, peace in the world and the other 'highest aspiration[s] of the common people', as the Preamble to the UDHR puts it.

Without taking a position with respect to these two opposing orientations, what is important for my purposes here is actually what they have in common. Both

[47] Sikkink (n 26).
[48] Moyn (n 17).

evaluate the future of human rights in relation to what, from an anthropological perspective, would be considered a narrow conception of human rights. This is partly a function of differences in disciplinary methodology. But even more, it reflects the obvious importance of human rights treaties, international monitoring bodies, transnational 'activists without borders', regional and international legal fora, and political claims and policies based on human rights.[49]

Yet, as we have seen in this chapter, there is an entirely different 'world of many worlds' in which human rights are conceptualised and mobilised in ways and in places that go far beyond the boundaries of the international human rights system. These are the worlds in which human rights are *made* in the vernacular, and this is the essential, potentially transformative point. To take these worlds seriously, not as places where human rights as such are translated or made relevant in local contexts, but as places where the human rights themselves are forged, is to reimagine radically both what human rights are and, even more, what they should be.

Whether as a form of power (Speed), a proposition for a different kind of moral learning (Holcombe) or a framework for personal empowerment (Chua), among many others that could be invoked, the extensive ethnographic record of human rights made in the vernacular demands not just an appreciation for how the practice of human rights has been fed by a seemingly endless capacity for normative creativity, especially among marginalised populations for whom such capacity remains among the most precious of resources. Even more, the realities of human rights vernacularization demand a reconsideration of where human rights are produced and who is best placed to articulate their meanings.

This, in the end, is as much an ethical as an epistemological conclusion. It is the reason vernacularization should be understood not only as an anthropological account of the practice of human rights, but as an anthropological ethics, a way of justifying – even privileging – a future for human rights animated by the values of pluralism, contingency and translocal (though not necessarily universal) solidarity.

---

[49] It should be emphasised that these dominant sites, actors and texts of human rights have also been the subject of anthropological research. See, eg R Niezen and M Sapignoli (eds), *Palaces of Hope: The Anthropology of Global Organizations* (Cambridge, Cambridge University Press, 2017).

7

The Vernacularization of Transitional Justice: Is Transitional Justice Useful in Pre-conflict Settings?

PABLO DE GREIFF

MOST OF THE contributors to this volume had the great privilege of having known Sally Engle Merry for a long time. I only met her in 2014, when I first came to New York University School of Law, but was immediately struck by her welcoming and generous attitude. Indeed, it strikes me that one of the things she is famous for, her work on vernacularization, is the product of an open and generous mind. As is well known, by 'vernacularization' Sally meant the process by which ideas from transnational sources are adapted to local institutions and meanings.[1] Luckily for the field of human rights, she decided to focus on the process by which international human rights norms are 'indigenized', 'the way new ideas are framed and presented in terms of existing cultural norms, values, and practices'.[2] As many commentators have pointed out, this is a much better view of the process of the diffusion and transmission of ideas than the more familiar spatial model of the global and the local. The spatial approach makes hierarchies difficult to avoid, since, in that model,

> the 'local' may become fixed, ahistorical, even denigrated: the language of space implies magnitude and importance, with the transnational realm regarded as more advanced in an almost evolutionary sense, the local populated by what Jonathan Friedman (2004: 195) calls 'redneck homebodies' with no greater vision beyond their own small realities. In terms of human rights, such a perspective suggests that rights language and concepts move along this linear trajectory from the global to the local, a gift that the developed North bestows upon the undeveloped, benighted South (Merry 2006b).[3]

Instead, Sally's interest in vernacularization leads her to observe closely – and therefore respectfully – the role of those 'in the middle', the 'translators': a diverse group who understand both the 'source' (of the ideas) and the 'target' (of their 'indigenized'

---

[1] See, eg SE Merry, 'Transnational Human Rights and Local Activism: Mapping the Middle' (2006) 108 *American Anthropologist* 38.
[2] ibid 39.
[3] DM Goldstein, 'Whose Vernacular? Translating Human Rights in Local Contexts' in M Goodale, *Human Rights at the Crossroads* (New York, Oxford University Press, 2014) 112.

or 'vernacularized' versions), whose situation and 'tools' she describes with great sensitivity. About the forms of vernacularization (not all of which are necessarily good), Sally writes:

> Vernacularization falls along a continuum depending on how extensively local cultural forms and practices are incorporated into imported institutions. At one end is replication, a process in which the imported institution remains largely unchanged from its transnational prototype. The adaptation is superficial and primarily decorative. At the other end is hybridization, a process that merges imported institutions and symbols with local ones, sometimes uneasily.[4]

On the ambiguous situation of the 'translators', Sally says:

> The power of the translator is her ability to set the terms of the exchange and to channel it, but her vulnerability is to persuade people with grievances to accept her definition of the problem and to extract financial and political support from states and donors ... The translator must walk a fine line between too much replication, in which case the new ideas will lose their appeal to local communities, and too much hybridity, in which case the reforms will lose the support of the global community, including its funding and publicity.[5]

I find something supple and generous in this way of seeing things that not only makes visible the contributions of many who would otherwise be ignored, but that, while avoiding the naivety that usually accompanies the romanticisation of the 'local', is equally suspicious of a type of formalistic rigorism that accompanies the glorification of the 'global'.

In this chapter, I want to examine what may be considered an atypical case of vernacularization, namely, the exploding calls for the implementation of transitional justice measures in contexts that are radically different from those in which the 'canonical' model of transitional justice took shape. That model, described, for example, in the UN Secretary General's 2004 report on transitional justice, has four main constituent pillars: truth, justice, reparation and guarantees of non-recurrence. Despite the title of the report ('The Rule of Law and Transitional Justice in Conflict and Post-conflict Societies'),[6] the model of transitional justice it refers to is the one that was shaped in the post-authoritarian transitions of the Southern Cone of Latin America, not in post-conflict (let alone ongoing conflict) societies. But recent political developments – notably, the growing influence of the Black Lives Matter movement – has led to increasing calls for transitional justice measures to be implemented outside of traditional post-conflict or post-authoritarian settings, not just in the USA, but also in countries with legacies of 'historical injustice' like colonisation.

The current global moment can be characterised, politically, in terms of two macro-level phenomena: a lurch towards populism of the left and the right on the part of many leaders (and eventually, their followers), and, simultaneously, unusually large popular mobilisations in favour of progressive causes. These seemingly dilemmatic factors arguably share a common underlying cause: namely, great lack of trust in the

---
[4] ibid 44.
[5] ibid 48.
[6] UN Secretary General, 'The Rule of Law and Transitional Justice in Conflict and Post-conflict Societies' (New York, 23 August 2004) UN Doc S/2004/616.

familiar mechanisms of political representation – a lack of trust which itself has deeper roots in increasing inequality and dysfunctional forms of the politics of recognition.[7]

The specific question that this chapter will consider is whether some of the lessons learned during the last 40 years of transitional justice practice in post-authoritarian and post-conflict settings can be of use in *pre-* or non-conflict settings.[8] The answer will be a qualified yes. Transitional justice, it has been argued, is a mechanism of social integration,[9] and to that extent, it has some valuable lessons to teach. On the other hand, transitional justice is mainly an accountability tool. Thus, in the sort of pre-conflict setting that this chapter is concerned with, *before* criminal accountability is called for, the question is not so much about the utility of each and every one of its tools. Only some of the tools of transitional justice will be needed; especially, the lessons learned in trying to repair a badly torn social fabric.

I. TRANSITIONAL JUSTICE

For the sake of clarity, let me begin with a stipulative definition. I understand transitional justice as a *comprehensive* policy implemented to cope with the legacies of massive and systematic human rights violations and abuses, and to restore or establish anew the currency of human rights. Such a policy has as its core elements truth, justice, reparations and guarantees of non-recurrence. In addition to the immediate function each element of a comprehensive transitional justice policy is supposed to serve – namely, to impart (criminal) justice, disclose truth, redress violations and prevent their recurrence – a comprehensive transitional justice also pursues two 'mediate' ends: to provide recognition to victims, not only as victims but as rights-holders, and to promote civic trust. Such a policy also pursues two 'final' goals: to strengthen the rule of law and to promote social integration or reconciliation.[10]

Whether transitional justice is of any use in contexts different from those where the model took shape (post-authoritarian transitions) or where it has been applied

---

[7] Nancy Fraser has long insisted on the importance of *both* recognition and redistribution. See her parts of N Fraser and A Honneth, *Redistribution or Recognition?* (London, Verso, 2003); see also N Fraser, *The Old Is Dying and the New Cannot Be Born* (London, Verso, 2019).

[8] If 'conflict' is itself the subject of definitional quandaries (see, eg International Committee of the Red Cross, 'How Is the Term "Armed Conflict" Defined in International Humanitarian Law?' (March 2008)), 'pre-conflict and non-conflict settings' lack any agreed upon definition. To stipulate: this chapter is interested in the utility of transitional justice measures in situations of increased polarisation, declining institutional trust, political disaffection and logjams, phenomena that are observable frequently nowadays in very diverse countries, some of which may have unredressed 'historical injustices' in their past (eg the USA), but some of them not, or at least not of the sort that are the cause of the polarisation, declining trust, etc in any mediate or immediate sense (eg Brazil, Spain, France, Sweden, Chile, etc).

[9] See, eg P de Greiff, 'Articulating the Links between Transitional Justice and Development: Justice and Social Integration' in P de Greiff and R Duthie (eds), *Transitional Justice and Development: Making Connections* (New York, Social Science Research Council, 2009).

[10] The qualifiers 'immediate', 'mediate' and 'final' above refer not to temporal proximity, but to causal sufficiency or insufficiency. Thus, the point is not that transitional justice measures, *on their own*, can produce trust or social integration, but that they are one of the factors that promote those desirable ends. See P de Greiff, 'Theorizing Transitional Justice' in M Williams, R Nagy and J Elster (eds), *Transitional Justice* (New York, NOMOS/New York University Press, 2012), which is a systematic attempt to justify the claim that transitional justice should be conceived as a comprehensive policy, that is, holistically – a claim that is already present in the UN Secretary General's 2004 Report on Transitional Justice and the Rule of Law (S/2004/616) (n 6).

with increased frequency (post-conflict countries)[11] requires further specification. For the purposes of this chapter, the main foci of concern are a few social factors that are increasingly common in pre-conflict countries, all of them related to what may be called 'failures of social integration'. Politically, polarisation has become an issue in many countries: social, xenophobic and in some cases racist tendencies have become accentuated. Furthermore, trust, both interpersonal and institutional, has plummeted. Most of these factors are also left in the wake of authoritarian terror and conflict, so the case for the utility of transitional justice in the pre-conflict contexts is prima facie arguable, even if its application appears anachronistic.

II. CHARACTERISTICS OF 'FAILURES OF SOCIAL INTEGRATION'

A. Polarisation

Even in some of the transitions of the 'third wave'[12] and those that followed in which there was a regime collapse (eg Argentina), that collapse did not automatically do away with support for the regime, nor, consequently, with political polarisation. Political preferences are not simply a function of outcomes, so even devastating political failures do not translate, especially in the short run, into a loss of support. There is always the possibility of explaining away or rationalising the failure, alleging disloyalty, conspiracies or external interventions, to cite just a few strategies. Germany's catastrophic defeat in World War I was explained by the erstwhile warmongers as a result of the backstabbing by Jewish military officers, and the Argentine Junta's shambolic military adventure in the Falklands and the consequent fall of the regime did not deprive it totally of support. Pinochet still had the support of almost half of Chileans when the Spanish request for his extradition on human rights charges was being processed in English courts (October 1998–March 2000); upon his return to Santiago, Congress approved by a huge majority a constitutional amendment creating the status of 'ex-president', granting him not only an allowance but, more importantly, legal immunity.[13] Other such examples are easily found: in 1999, Guatemalans voted down a constitutional referendum on structural changes that had been negotiated and agreed upon under the Comprehensive Peace Agreement (signed in 1994 and 1996), which had put an end to a conflict lasting almost four decades. Similarly, in 2016, Colombians voted against a referendum to ratify the Peace Agreement negotiated from 2012 to 2016 by then-President Juan Manuel Santos with the FARC in Havana, largely on account of the enduring influence of former President Uribe, a hardline conservative. Thus, neither conflict nor even *defeat* in conflict (or, alternatively, the prospect of peace)

---

[11] For some of the challenges that this transposition of the model from post-authoritarian to weakly institutionalised post-conflict contexts involves, see P de Greiff, 'Report of the Special Rapporteur on the Promotion of Truth, Justice, Reparation and Guarantees of Non-recurrence' (21 August 2017) UN Doc A/HRC/36/50.

[12] S Huntington, *The Third Wave* (Norman, University of Oklahoma Press, 1991).

[13] See, eg N Roht-Arriaza, *The Pinochet Effect* (Philadelphia, University of Pennsylvania Press, 2005). Arguably, Pinochet lost more support when it was revealed that he had bank accounts abroad whose proceeds could not be easily explained than by all the revelations of human rights abuses.

was enough to weaken support either for those who were responsible for the onset of fighting or the military defeat, or those who opposed the *end* of the conflict.

In many 'ordinary', non-conflict settings, political polarisation – in the 'classical' sense of ideological distance between parties[14] – has grown in the last few decades, especially after the Great Recession of 2007–09.[15] European parties became polarised around austerity measures, the treatment of countries in crisis within the monetary union and, more generally, the European Union itself. Within the European Union, the difference in views between those who support populist parties and those who do not can reach almost 35 percentage points, as Figure 7.1 suggests.[16]

Political polarisation, however, is not exclusively a European or even Northern phenomenon: Turkey is currently one of the most polarised countries in the world, India is following a similar path and so is Brazil.[17] In this sense, the USA is only an extreme example. Elite polarisation started in the 1970s, mass polarisation caught up in the 1980s and the trends have only worsened since then. Nor is contemporary polarisation simply a question of ideological distance between contending parties. Contemporary polarisation, as Jennifer McCoy and Murat Somer have argued in a couple of splendid articles, involves a heightened affective dimension, the deployment of identity markers in order to create in- versus out-group loyalties and antipathies, and the construction of zero-sum scenarios which hamper political collaboration and ultimately become 'pernicious' in contributing to the erosion of democratic norms.[18] The titles of some of Pew Research Center's reports illustrate McCoy and Somer's understanding of polarisation and its pitfalls: in 2006, Pew issued a report titled 'Democrats and Republicans See Different Realities';[19] in June 2012, it published 'Partisan Polarization Surges in Bush, Obama Years';[20] and in 2014, in 'Political

---

[14] See, eg G Sartori, *Party and Party System* (Cambridge, Cambridge University Press, 1976).

[15] See, eg Y Algan et al, 'The European Trust Crisis and the Rise in Populism' (Brookings Papers on Economic Activities Conference, Washington DC, 7–8 September 2017) 310–400, where the authors state: 'We document that rising voting shares for antiestablishment, especially populist, parties follow increases in unemployment. It is the change in unemployment – rather than its level – that correlates with voting for nonmainstream parties; this novel – to the best of our knowledge – result echoes the findings of the literature on the role of economic losses in self-reported well-being and happiness' (312). See also M Funke et al, 'Going to Extremes: Politics after Financial Crises, 1870–2014' (2016) 88 *European Economic Review* 227, who, studying 20 advanced economies over the years 1870–2014, document that financial crises increase political polarisation, raise fragmentation in the parliament and spur political unrest.

[16] K Devlin and M Mordecai, 'Supporters of European Populist Parties Stand Out on Key Issues, from EU to Putin' (Pew Research Center, 18 November 2019) www.pewresearch.org/short-reads/2019/11/18/supporters-of-european-populist-parties-stand-out-on-key-issues-from-eu-to-putin/.

[17] *cf* eg T Carothers and A O'Donohue (eds), *Democracies Divided: The Global Challenge of Political Polarization* (Washington DC, Brookings Institution Press, 2020); L Bernhard, 'Polarization – A Global Threat to Democracy?' (Varieties of Democracy, 2 March 2020) https://v-dem.net/weekly_graph/polarization-a-global-threat-to-democracy.

[18] See, eg J McCoy, T Rahman and M Somer, 'Polarization and the Global Crisis of Democracy: Common Patterns, Dynamics, and Pernicious Consequences for Democratic Polities' (2018) 62 *American Behavioral Scientist* 16; J McCoy and M Somer, 'Toward a Theory of Pernicious Polarization and How It Harms Democracies' (2019) 681 *Annals of the American Academy of Political Science* 234.

[19] T Rosenthal, 'Democrats and Republicans See Different Realities' (Pew Research Center, 6 November 2006) www.pewresearch.org/2006/11/06/democrats-and-republicans-see-different-realities/.

[20] Pew Research Center, 'Trends in American Values: 1987–2012: Partisan Polarization Surges in Bush, Obama Years' (4 June 2012) www.pewresearch.org/politics/2012/06/04/partisan-polarization-surges-in-bush-obama-years/.

Figure 7.1 Right-wing populists' views of the EU

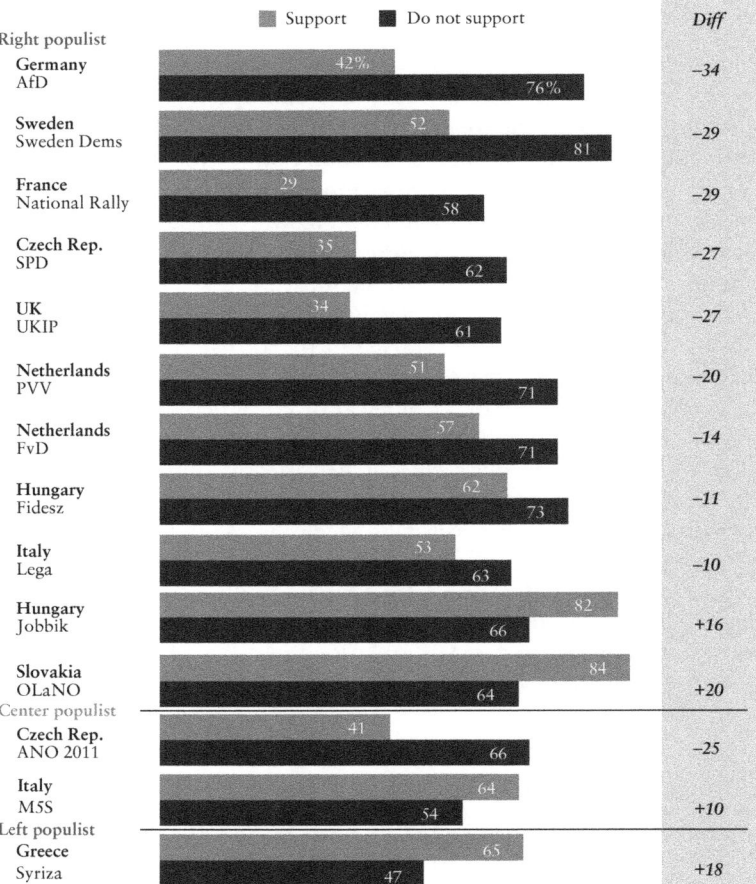

Source: Spring 2019 Global Attiudes Survey. Q8d.

Note: Only statistically significant differences shown. "Support" percentages represent respondents who have a favourable view of each party. "Do not support" percentages represent respondents who have an unfavourable view of each party. For more information on European populist parties, see "European Public Opinion Three Decades After the Fall of communism." Appendix A.

Polarization in the American Public', Pew reported that 'Republicans and Democrats are more divided along ideological lines – and partisan antipathy is deeper and more extensive – than at any point in the last two decades'.[21] On 10 November 2016, within a week of the election that led to Donald Trump's presidential victory, Pew published reports about 'A Divided and Pessimistic Electorate';[22] and in September 2021, in 'How America Changed During Donald Trump's Presidency', it stated:

---

[21] Pew Research Center, 'Political Polarization in the American Public' (12 June 2014) www.pewresearch.org/politics/2014/06/12/political-polarization-in-the-american-public/.
[22] Pew Research Center, 'A Divided and Pessimistic Electorate' (10 November 2016) www.pewresearch.org/politics/2016/11/10/a-divided-and-pessimistic-electorate/.

Even before he took office, Trump divided Republicans and Democrats more than any incoming chief executive in the prior three decades. The gap only grew more pronounced after he became president. An average of 86% of Republicans approved of Trump's handling of the job over the course of his tenure, compared with an average of just 6% of Democrats – the widest partisan gap in approval for any president in the modern era of polling.[23]

Given these trends, it is not surprising that cross-party collaboration, like many other aspects of American political, economic and cultural polarisation, is back at Gilded Age levels. Putnam makes this argument persuasively in Figure 7.2.[24]

Figure 7.2 Collaboration in Congress

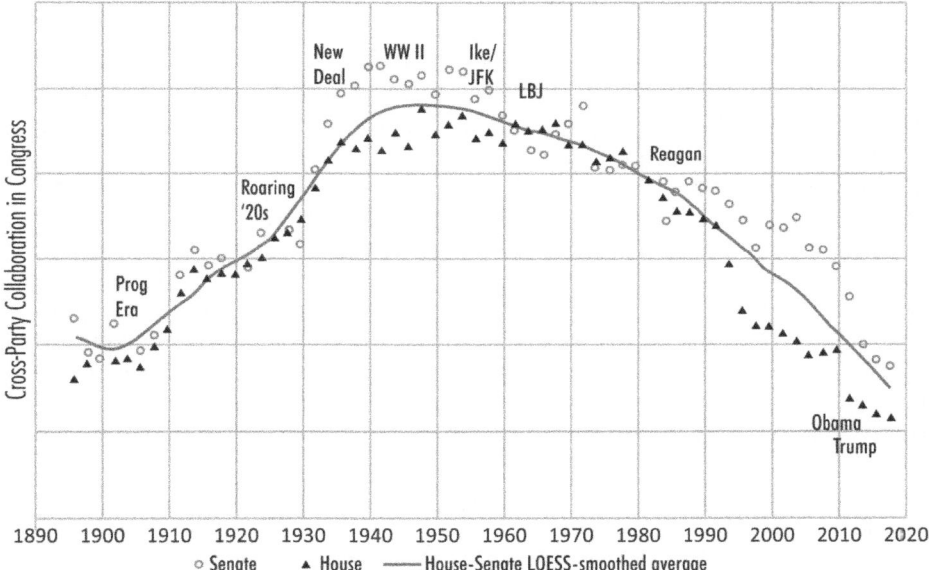

Source: Congressional Roll-Call Votes Database 2019. Data LOESS smoothed: .2.

According to Pew:

The 2020 presidential election further highlighted these deep-seated divides. Supporters of Biden and Donald Trump believe the differences between them are about more than just politics and policies. A month before the election, roughly eight-in-ten registered voters in both camps said their differences with the other side were about core American values, and roughly nine-in-ten – again in both camps – worried that a victory by the other would lead to 'lasting harm' to the United States.[25]

---

[23] Pew Research Center, 'How America Changed during Donald Trump's Presidency' (29 January 2021) www.pewresearch.org/2021/01/29/how-america-changed-during-donald-trumps-presidency/#fnref-383636-2.
[24] RD Putnam, *The Upswing. How America Came Together a Century Ago and How We Can Do It Again* (New York, Simon & Schuster, 2020) 70 (figure).
[25] M Domock and R Wike, 'America Is Exceptional in the Nature of Its Political Divide' (Pew Research Center, 13 November 2020) www.pewresearch.org/fact-tank/2020/11/13/america-is-exceptional-in-the-nature-of-its-political-divide/.

B. Xenophobia and Racism

Perhaps more worrisome than political polarisation per se (some degree of which may in fact be salutary, particularly in bipartisan political systems, since without departures from the centre there would be little party differentiation[26]) is the fact that some of the reigning political divisions concern opinions about 'others', including foreigners and peoples of different races. Increases in xenophobic and racist sentiments and incidents are in fact not so recent; some can be traced to the reactions to the European economic slowdown in the 1970s.

During the post-war boom (what the French call *les trente glorieuses*), Northern European countries actively recruited what they conceived of as temporary 'guest workers' in order to fill labour shortages.[27] This led to booming immigrant populations: West Germany recruited 95,000 workers in 1956, for example, and by the early 1970s there were 4.1 million foreign-born workers in Germany, 3.4 million in France and 1 million in Switzerland.[28] Incentives for return adopted after the slowdown had the unintended consequence of changing the composition of immigrant populations, as guest workers from Southern Europe were much more susceptible to those incentives than workers from Northern Africa. Thus, in France, for instance, 'the proportion of immigrants from the Maghreb region of western North Africa increased by 16 percentage points from 1968 to 1982'.[29] These combined trends soon manifested themselves in opinions about immigrants: whereas in 1988 only 18 per cent of respondents to Eurobarometer in European Community countries wanted the rights of immigrants restricted, by 1991 that figure had almost doubled to 33 per cent. The same percentage of French respondents thought that the members of the European Economic Community should not accept immigrants from countries south of the Mediterranean, and 56 per cent thought France already had too many immigrants. In Denmark, 25 per cent of respondents agreed with their French counterparts that no immigrants from south of the Mediterranean should be accepted at all.[30]

These were early signs of trends that would gather steam over the next three decades as several forces converged to produce increasing suspicion of

---

[26] Which can itself be exclusionary. *cf* the consequences of the 'Frente Nacional', an agreement between the two major parties in Colombia to overcome a violent confrontation leading to 200,000 deaths in the period between 1946 and 1958, a period bluntly called *La Violencia*. The agreement stipulated, among other things, turn-taking in the presidency between the two parties during four presidential periods and the splitting of the cabinet and other high-level positions – a modified consociational arrangement. The agreement did quell violence for a while. Less than 30 years later, a guerrilla group was established in order to fight the exclusion of all other views that followed this bipartisan arrangement, which predictably turned both parties mainly into bureaucratic machines, largely devoid of programmatic differences. See, eg M Palacio, *Between Legitimacy and Violence: A History of Colombia, 1875–2002* (Durham, NC, Duke University Press, 2006). For general arguments about some of the advantages of some degree of polarisation, including facilitating party building and constituency mobilisation and stabilisation, simplifying choices for voters and helping to consolidate political party systems, see, eg A LeBas, 'Can Polarization Be Positive? Conflict and Institutional Development in Africa' (2018) 62 *American Behavioral Scientist* 59; C Tilly, *Democracy* (New York, Cambridge University Press, 2007).

[27] During this period, unemployment rates were 0.6% in West Germany, 2.2% in the UK and 2.5% in France.

[28] See JB Judis, *The Politics of Our Time: Populism, Nationalism, Socialism* (New York, Columbia Global Reports, 2021) 114.

[29] ibid 120.

[30] ibid 120–21.

outsiders. One of these was the securitisation of immigration issues post-9/11.[31] Another was the increased job insecurity produced by the globalisation policies – involving deregulation, freer circulation of capital and, in the old economies, significant deindustrialisation – adopted as a reaction to the economic slowdown of the 1970s.[32]

Xenophobic tendencies were greatly strengthened after the Great Recession of 2007–09.[33] Populist politicians have fuelled these fears, aided, it must be said, by legitimate questions about dysfunctional immigration systems:[34] even the EU has been incapable of coming up with a sensible burden-sharing programme. The massive influx of refugees from conflicts in Iraq, Afghanistan and especially Syria in 2015 stressed systems even in countries like Germany, which were willing receptors. Finally, the economic and social pressures of the COVID-19 epidemic also exacerbated xenophobic and racist tendencies.[35] The political yields of 'othering' have therefore increased over time.

In both East and West Europe, anti-Jewish and anti-Muslim sentiments were already on the rise in 2005. In a survey conducted by Pew covering the period from 2005 to 2008, 'Overall, looking across the six European countries surveyed … the median percentage with a negative view of Jews … jumped from 21% to 30%, while the median percentage expressing an unfavorable opinion of Muslims … increased from 35% to 42%'.[36] In the three years covered by the survey, anti-Jewish sentiment in Spain astonishingly grew from 21 to 46 per cent, and (less surprisingly) in Russia from 26 to 34 per cent, while anti-Muslim sentiment grew in Poland from 30 to 46 per cent and in Spain from 37 to 52 per cent.[37]

Since 2008, xenophobia and racism globally have waxed and waned (arguably hand in hand with the different rhythms of economic recovery), but have remained at high levels. Racism is not easy to measure precisely, for it tends to be under-reported in surveys (people rarely self-identify as racist and few are willing to admit to racist beliefs) and, especially in Europe, for historical reasons, governments do not disaggregate data by race. However, disproportionate rates of incarceration, instances of racial profiling and lower scores on all sorts of indices of well-being (when those disaggregate by race) provide evidence of persistent racism globally.

In the USA (which lacks a single database for police violence countrywide), it is not just that police officers kill significantly more people than in other developed

---

[31] A Luedtke, 'Fortifying Fortress Europe? The Effect of September 11 on EU Immigration Policy' in TE Givens, GP Freeman and DL Leal (eds), *Immigration Policy and Security: US, European and Commonwealth Perspectives* (New York, Routledge, 2007) 130–47.

[32] Comparing the period 1950–73 with the period 1973–95, 'France's average rate of growth fell from 5.1 to 2.7 per cent, Germany's from 6.0 to 2.7 per cent; Sweden's from 4.1 to 1.5 per cent. During the 1960's unemployment in Western Europe averaged a lowly 1.6 per cent. By the end of the 1970's unemployment rose to more than 7 per cent': Judis (n 28) 115.

[33] See Algan et al (n 15) and the references therein.

[34] See, eg P Collier, *Exodus. Immigration and Multiculturalism in the 21st Century* (London, Penguin Books, 2013) esp chs 2 and 5.

[35] For an attempt to provide a global overview of the Covid-fuelled xenophobia, including a brief history of similar effects of previous pandemics, see, eg TK Noel, 'Conflating Culture with COVID-19: Xenophobic Repercussions of a Global Pandemic' (2020) 2 *Social Sciences & Humanities Open*.

[36] A Kohut and R Wike, 'Xenophobia on the Continent' *National Interest* (30 October 2008) https://nationalinterest.org/article/xenophobia-on-the-continent-2904.

[37] ibid.

countries,[38] but that they are four times more likely to use deadly force against Black people.[39] In Canada, Indigenous people form 16 per cent of the deaths by the police but only 4.21 per cent of the population (annualised over 20 years), and Black people form 8.63 per cent of deaths and only 2.92 per cent of the population.[40]

In Australia, Aboriginal and Torres Strait Islander people are significantly over-represented in prisons. About 27 per cent of Australia's prison population were Indigenous in 2017, yet Aboriginal and Torres Strait Islanders make up about 3 per cent of the population.[41] In the USA, more than a third of people in prison are Black, despite Black people making up less than 13 per cent of the overall population.[42]

The EU is not exempt from these trends. The 2018 survey administered by the European Union Agency for Fundamental Rights across all 28 EU members, 'Being Black in the EU',[43] paints a very similar picture. Finland, which has been ranked first in Freedom House's Freedom in the World Index since the 1980s,[44] recorded the highest rates of race-based harassment and violence in the EU, according to the survey. Across the Union, only 14 per cent of victims of race-based harassment reported their experiences to the police or any other authority in the belief that reporting would make no positive difference, despite awareness of anti-discrimination laws.[45]

In the USA, although the population as a whole self-reports increasingly positive views about race,[46] there is no question that race is one of the most significant factors underlying political polarisation. In 2019,

---

[38] In 2018, US police fatally shoot 31 people per 10 million, as opposed to Germany with 11 people per 10 million; Sweden with six people; Australia with three; New Zealand with two; and the UK with less than one: R Picheta and H Pettersson, 'American Police Shoot, Kill and Imprison More People than Other Developed Countries. Here's the Data' (CNN, 8 June 2020) www.cnn.com/2020/06/08/us/us-police-floyd-protests-country-comparisons-intl/index.html.

[39] Use-of-force incidents in 2016 involved Black people 273 times per 100,000 as opposed to 76 per 100,000 for white people: ibid.

[40] I Singh, '2020 Already a Particularly Deadly Year for People Killed in Police Encounters' (CBC News, 23 July 2020) https://newsinteractives.cbc.ca/features/2020/fatalpoliceencounters/.

[41] See The Conversation, 'Twelve Charts on Race and Racism in Australia' (27 November 2018) https://theconversation.com/twelve-charts-on-race-and-racism-in-australia-105961.

[42] See A Quarcoo, 'Global Democracy Supporters Must Confront Systemic Racism' (Carnegie Endowment for International Peace, 15 July 2020) https://carnegieendowment.org/2020/07/15/global-democracy-supporters-must-confront-systemic-racism-pub-82298.

[43] European Union Agency for Fundamental Rights, 'Second European Union Minorities and Discrimination Survey: Being Black in the EU' (Luxembourg, Publications Office of the European Union, 2018) Doc No EU-MIDIS II.

[44] Freedom House, 'Freedom in the World: Country and Territory Ratings and Statuses 1973–2023', https://freedomhouse.org/sites/default/files/2023-02/Country_and_Territory_Ratings_and_Statuses_FIW_1973-2023%20.xlsx.

[45] See Quarcoo (n 42).

[46] There has been a decline in people who say that a majority-minority country in the next 25–30 years will be bad for the country. In 2020, '64% of US adults say the prospect of a nation in the next 25 to 30 years in which Black Americans, Latinos and Asian Americans make up a majority of the population is neither good nor bad for the country. Nearly a quarter (24%) say this is a good thing, while fewer than half as many (11%) say it is bad … While Republicans are more likely than Democrats to say this change would be bad for the country (19% of Republicans versus 4% of Democrats), the share of Republicans who express this view has declined by 20 points since 2016': see A Budiman, 'Americans Are More Positive about the Long-Term Rise in US Racial and Ethnic Diversity than in 2016' (Pew Research Center, 1 October 2020)

about seven-in-ten Republicans and Republican-leaning independents (71%) say white people get few or no advantages in society that black people do not have. By contrast, 83% of Democrats and Democratic leaners say white people benefit a great deal or a fair amount from advantages not available to black people, while only 16% see little or no such advantages.[47]

C. Trust

The literature on trust, and on its correlate, social capital, is ample and diverse in terms of disciplinary approaches. It does, however, lack a shared definition of the term, which raises methodological and other problems.[48] Economists and political theorists, for example, do not understand the term in the same way. Surveys like the World Values Survey, which has included questions about trust since 1990, do not define the term and leave it for the respondents to interpret it. The World Values Survey uses a version of the question first introduced by Rosemberg in 1956 to measure interpersonal or generalised trust:[49] 'Generally speaking, would you say that most people can be trusted, or that you can't be too careful in dealing with people?' Possible answers include 'most people can be trusted', 'don't know' and 'can't be too careful'.[50] Eurostat's approach is only slightly more illustrative, not because the question is necessarily framed better ('would you say that most people can be trusted?'), but because it acknowledges that trust admits of different magnitudes or degrees, and therefore asks respondents to use an 11-point scale, ranging

---

www.pewresearch.org/fact-tank/2020/10/01/americans-are-more-positive-about-the-long-term-rise-in-u-s-racial-and-ethnic-diversity-than-in-2016/. Furthermore, up to two-thirds of Americans say that they support the Black Lives Matter Movement: K Parker, J Menasche Horowitz and M Anderson, 'Amid Protests, Majorities Across Racial and Ethnic Groups Express Support for the Black Lives Matter Movement' (Pew Research Center, 12 June 2020) www.pewresearch.org/social-trends/2020/06/12/amid-protests-majorities-across-racial-and-ethnic-groups-express-support-for-the-black-lives-matter-movement/). Beyond surveys, as the title of an interactive *New York Times* article puts it, 'black lives matter may be the largest movement in US history', with protests occurring in all states at more than 2000 localities, involving up to 10% of the US population (notoriously demobilised since the late 1960s and early 1970s). See L Buchanan, Q Bui and JK Patel, 'Black Lives Matter May be the Largest Movement in US History' *New York Times* (3 July 2020) www.nytimes.com/interactive/2020/07/03/us/george-floyd-protests-crowd-size.html.
[47] Pew Research Center, 'In a Politically Polarized Era, Sharp Divides in Both Partisan Coalitions' (17 December 2019) section 4, 51–62, www.pewresearch.org/politics/2019/12/17/views-on-race-and-immigration/.
[48] For some of the methodological debates, see PC Bauer and M Freitag, 'Measuring Trust' in EM Uslaner (ed), *The Oxford Handbook of Social and Political Trust* (Oxford, Oxford University Press, 2018).
[49] M Rosenberg, 'Misanthropy and Political Ideology' (1956) 21 *American Sociological Review* 690.
[50] The question has been the subject of much debate, not only for the lack of definition of the critical term 'trust', but also of the term 'most people', the referent of which can range from people in the local community to various other groups, including people in certain institutional categories, to people in the nation – or even the world at large. *cf* eg AS Miller and T Mitamura, 'Are Surveys on Trust Trustworthy?' (2003) 66 *Social Psychology Quarterly* 62; EL Glaeser et al, 'Measuring Trust' (2000) 115 *Quarterly Journal of Economics* 811. Furthermore, the 'caution rider' (italicised) – most people can be trusted, or that *you can't be too careful in dealing with people*? – has been shown to lead to lower scores, particularly by minorities and women. *cf* F Murtin et al, 'Trust and Its Determinants' (2018) OECD Statistics Working Papers No 89, 21.

from 0 to 10.⁵¹ Using these coarse methods, one still gets an intuitively correct picture of social relations in different parts of the world, as shown in Figure 7.3.

Figure 7.3 Views on people's trustworthiness

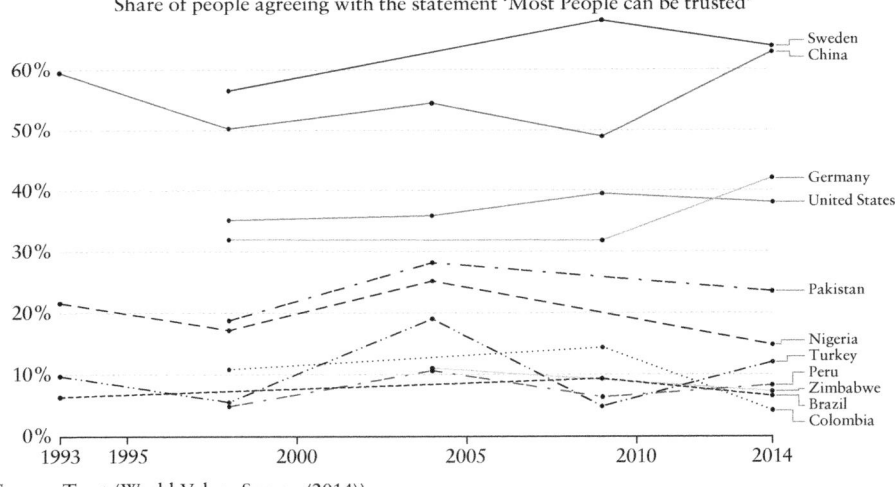

Source: Trust (World Values Survey (2014)).

Generally speaking, Northern developed countries have higher indices of interpersonal, generalised trust, with the Scandinavian countries at the top. Protestant countries are generally more trusting than Catholic countries or those with other religions; Latin American countries score towards the bottom of the pile. Asian countries generally display high levels of trust in government authorities. Levels of education correlate with levels of trust. As we saw above, economic crises usually leave in their wake not just political polarisation, but a (time lagged) decline in trust.⁵²

Institutional or political trust is measured via similarly coarse instruments. In the USA, for instance, the relevant question in the National Election Survey (NES), starting in 1958, reads: 'Trust in Government – How much of the time do you think you can trust the government in Washington to do what is right – *just about always, most of the time*, or *only some of the time*?'⁵³ The European Social Survey is slightly

---

⁵¹ See, eg Eurostat, 'The Social Situation in the European Union 2005–2006: The Balance between Generations in an Ageing Europe' (Luxembourg, Office for Official Publications of the European Communities, 2007).

⁵² See, eg reflections on cultural change from Ronald Inglehart, the longest-running director of the World Values Survey, in R Inglehart, *Cultural Evolution* (Cambridge, Cambridge University Press, 2018).

⁵³ The question is part of a set that also includes: 'Government Attention – Over the years, how much attention do you feel the government pays to what people think when it decides what to do – *a good deal, some*, or *not much*? Faith in Parties – How much do you feel that political parties help to make the government pay attention to what the people think – *a good deal, some*, or *not much*? Faith in Elections – How much do you feel that having elections makes the government pay attention to what the people think – *a good deal, some*, or *not much*? Government Waste – Do you think that people in government waste *a lot* of the money we pay in taxes, waste *some* of it, or *don't waste very much of it*? Big Interests – Would you say the government is pretty much run by a *few big interests* looking out for themselves or that it is run *for the benefit of all* the people? Crooked Politicians – Do you think that *quite a few* of the people running the government are crooked, *not very many* are, or do you think *hardly any* of them are crooked?'

more differentiated, both in asking about trust in different institutions (police, judiciary, political system) and in using the familiar 0–10 scale, but again leaves 'trust' undefined.

Regardless of the coarseness of the measuring instruments, the picture that time series suggest for the last few decades is one of variable degrees of trust, but with a generally descending slope (Figure 7.4).[54]

Figure 7.4 OECD average trust in Governments

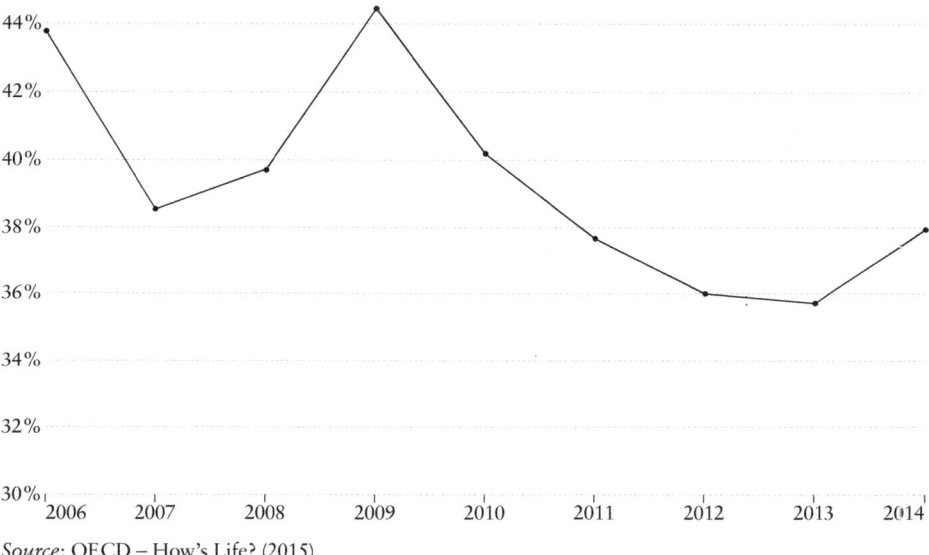

Source: OECD – How's Life? (2015).

The two generally observable shifts are the post-Great Recession dip in trust in most countries[55] and the increase in trust in 2020 provoked by the pandemic (alas, a short-lived increase, as other surveys demonstrate).[56] But more than shifts, what is noteworthy are the generally low levels of trust in government. This is true even in the countries of the OECD, an organisation of largely wealthy states with a mandate for good governance. Even before the pandemic, the organisation itself declared (in common irony-free bureaucratese):

> *Less than half of the population* in the average OECD country (43%) trust their national government. But this represents a slight improvement from the level (40%) recorded in the aftermath of the financial crisis in 2010–12 ... Indeed, after a general deterioration post-2008, trust in government has now rebounded to just below 2006 pre-crisis values *in a quarter* of OECD countries. The largest increases compared to 2010–12, of more than 15 percentage points, occurred in the Czech Republic, Ireland and Japan. Meanwhile, falls of more than 10 percentage points were seen in Chile, and 20 percentage points

---

[54] E Ortiz-Ospina and M Roser, 'Trust' (Our World in Data, 2016) https://ourworldindata.org/trust.
[55] See also, eg Y Lee, 'The Great Recession, Government Performance, and Citizen Trust' (2018) 25 *Journal of International and Area Studies* 55.
[56] See, eg Edelman, '2021 Edelman Trust Barometer' (16 March 2020) www.edelman.com/trust/2021-trust-barometer.

in Colombia. Overall, trust in the national government is highest (at 65% or more) in Luxembourg, Norway and Switzerland, and lowest (at 25% or less) in Colombia, Italy, Greece and Slovenia.[57]

The US, perhaps not surprisingly, is again in a class of its own with the clearest descending curve and low records of trust. According to Pew:

> When the National Election Study began asking about trust in government in 1958, about three-quarters of Americans trusted the federal government to do the right thing almost always or most of the time. Trust in government began eroding during the 1960s, amid the escalation of the Vietnam War, and the decline continued in the 1970s with the Watergate scandal and worsening economic struggles. Confidence in government recovered in the mid-1980s before falling again in the mid-1990s. But as the economy grew in the late 1990s so too did confidence in government. Public trust reached a three-decade high shortly after the 9/11 terrorist attacks, but declined quickly thereafter. Since 2007, the share saying they can trust the government always or most of the time has not surpassed 30%. (emphasis added)[58]

Only about one-quarter of Americans say they can trust the government in Washington to do what is right 'just about always' (2 per cent) or 'most of the time' (22 per cent) (Figure 7.5).[59]

Figure 7.5 Trust in government in the USA

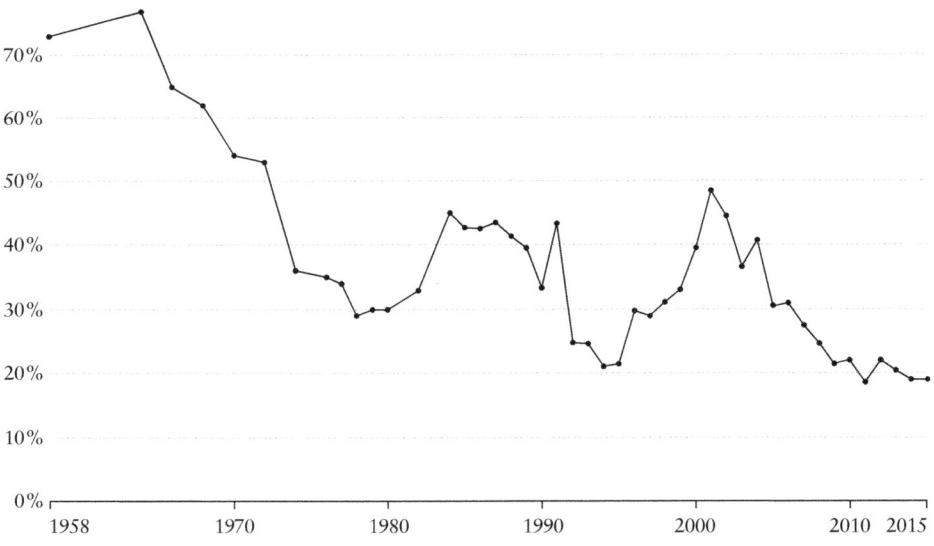

Source: Trust – PEW Research Center (2017).

---

[57] OECD, *How's Life? 2020: Measuring Well-being* (Paris, OECD Publishing, 2020).
[58] Pew Research Center, 'Public Trust in Government: 1958–2022' (6 June 2022) www.pewresearch.org/politics/2022/06/06/public-trust-in-government-1958-2022/.
[59] Our World in Data, 'Public Trust in Government in the United States' (2022) ourworldindata.org/grapher/public-trust-in-government.

Before considering whether some of the lessons learned in the practice of transitional justice can help at all in pre-conflict but highly polarised societies, it is worth returning to the general account of pernicious polarisation offered by McCoy and Somer. In their view, as stated before, contemporary polarisation is not simply a matter of ideological distance. A succinct formulation of their view states:

> [W]e maintain that the constitutive trait of severe polarization is its inherently *relational* and *political* nature: it suppresses 'within-group' differences and collapses otherwise multiple and cross-cutting intergroup differences into one single difference that becomes negatively charged and used to define the 'Other'. We therefore define polarization as a process whereby the normal multiplicity of differences in a society increasingly align along a single dimension, cross-cutting differences become instead reinforcing, and people increasingly perceive and describe politics and society in terms of 'Us' versus 'Them'.[60]

Their summary of the causal chain leading from polarisation to democratic erosion is illuminating and worth a lengthy quotation:[61]

- A polarizing society, or one that is open to polarization, whether from demographic change and political realignment, state or economic crises, or deep grievance and perceived injustice causing resentment, may be politicized by a leader or movement to mobilize political action from above or below.
- Polarizing political rhetoric centered on Us versus Them aligns group interests around one social cleavage, while suppressing and reducing the importance of other cross-cutting cleavages.
- Rhetorical focus on intergroup competition reinforces resentments and contributes to rising mass negative partisanship (dislike of out-party is greater than like of in-party) and affective polarization (sympathy toward in-group and antipathy toward the out-group).
- Deepening affective polarization, in turn, strengthens tribal tendencies of loyalty to in-group and conflict with out-party, enhances zero-sum perceptions, increases social distance, and decreases willingness to cooperate and compromise with the political out-group.
- Perceptions of the policies and political project of the 'Other' as an existential threat to the nation lead both government and opposition groups to consider undemocratic actions.
  - Government supporters condone democratic norm violations and erosions, and tolerate illiberal practices by the incumbent in the interest of keeping power and reducing threats.
  - Opposition groups are motivated to contest power outside the electoral arena if necessary. If they win, it indicates a change of power has occurred outside democratic rules (thus, democratic breakdown). If they lose, it facilitates greater erosion by the incumbent.

A simplified graphic representation of the causal chain is presented in Figure 7.6.

---

[60] McCoy et al, 'Polarization and the Global Crisis of Democracy' (n 18).
[61] ibid 26.

Figure 7.6 Causal chain from polarisation to democratic erosion

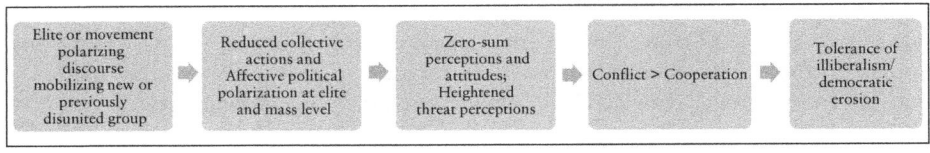

III. HOW TRANSITIONAL JUSTICE CAN HELP

The exercise of assessing whether a policy or practice designed mainly for redress purposes may be useful preventively in entirely different contexts than those in which the model took shape hinges, in my opinion, on three considerations. First, the current context is one in which truth-telling measures may be important, including as vehicles of recognition, which turns out to also be closely related to the very possibility of redistribution.[62] Second, transitional justice frameworks have developed consultative and participatory methods that may be of some use in contexts characterised by different forms of fragmentation and exclusion. And third, the development of the notion that transitional justice measures are trust-inducing and socially integrative may offer some lessons worth keeping in mind at this juncture.

A. Truth-Telling

Truth commissions, the main vehicle for truth-seeking and truth-telling in the transitional justice field, have accomplished some goals that are relevant to the current context: first and foremost, and even beyond the narratives they have produced, truth commissions have made victims visible and have given them voices.[63] This counters the tendency of the elite in conflict/post-conflict countries – who retain the possibility of transforming some of their assets and power into security or, *in extremis*, leaving areas where violence is occurring – to consider conflicts as victimless, threats merely to economic interests and infrastructure. This was evident in the Colombian conflict, but there is nothing peculiar to the Colombian case. Wherever conflict can be kept at bay – for example, contained in rural or marginal areas – urban elites are prone to think mainly about the economic costs of the conflict. Truth commissions, especially those with public hearings and effective dissemination strategies, can bring the impact of the conflict on individuals and communities to the awareness of those that have 'normalised' it. The South African Truth and Reconciliation Commission (SATRC) arguably succeeded

---

[62] I do not mean to elide the difficulties that truth-telling mechanisms will now face in an environment rife with social media-spread disinformation, a challenge that former truth commissions, for example, were spared.

[63] See, eg P de Greiff, 'On Making the Invisible Visible: The Role of Cultural Interventions in Transitional Justice Processes' in C Ramírez Barat (ed), *Transitional Justice, Culture, and Society: Beyond Outreach* (New York, SSRC, 2014).

in this regard: the television summaries of its work, which garnered huge audiences in the country, removed a wilfully self-imposed veil of ignorance from the eyes of the white community about the realities of apartheid.[64] Without public hearings, Argentina's Commission on the Disappeared produced a report, *Nunca Más! (Never Again!)*, which was a bestseller in the country, excerpted in newspapers and reprinted severally. Even before the Truth Commission in Colombia finishes its work, the victims' movement has gained a place in the public sphere in the country, from which it is difficult to think it will be dislodged.

This sort of recognition, for all the hardship and the frictions it may produce, is an essential part of recognising the humanity of the other. It establishes the status of victims as rights-holders and fellow citizens, and is consequently an integrative measure. It is a precondition of giving those whose rights have been violated a reason to think that they are members in equal standing of a *shared* political project.[65]

One of the worst pitfalls of great inequality is that it allows members of different groups – classes, races, religious and other groups – to live in different realities. Over time, it is difficult for the privileged to understand the indignities to which others are subjected on an everyday basis.[66] The privileged lose all notion of their privilege and 'deaths of despair', and the intergenerational effects of hopelessness become nothing more than an abstraction to them.[67] In contexts where such

---

[64] See, eg CM Cole, 'Reverberations of Testimony: South Africa's Truth and Reconciliation Commission in Art and Media' in Ramírez Barat (n 63).

[65] Here it is worth quoting Nancy Fraser again: 'To view recognition as a matter of justice is to treat it as an issue of *social status*. This means examining institutionalised patterns of cultural value for their effects on the *relative standing* of social actors. If and when such patterns constitute actors as *peers*, capable of participating on a par with one another in social life, then we can speak of *reciprocal recognition* and *status equality*. When, in contrast, institutionalised patterns of cultural value constitute some actors as inferior, excluded, wholly other, or simply invisible, hence as less than full partners in social interaction, then we should speak of *misrecognition* and *status subordination*.' Fraser and Honneth (n 7) 29.

[66] See, eg R Sennet and J Cobb, *The Hidden Injuries of Class* (New York, Norton, 1972), which follows the life of a unionised janitor; see also the follow-up, R Sennet, *The Erosion of Character. The Personal Consequences of Work in the New Capitalism* (New York, Norton, 2000), which follows the life of the janitor's son, part of the 'precariat'. Even though the latter book is 'dated' – the son had all the uncertainties that accompany jobs in the new economy, but he was still earning more than his father, something that, especially after 2008, is the exception, rather than the rule – the two books still offer deep insights into class differences. See also JC Williams, 'What So Many People Don't Get About the US Working Class' *Harvard Business Review* (12 November 2016) https://hbr.org/2016/11/what-so-many-people-dont-get-about-the-u-s-working-class.

[67] Poverty, for instance, is taken by the World Bank in its 2006 World Development Report to be a developmental blockage, at least in part, because it leads to diminished expectations, one of the intergenerational effects of hopelessness and fear: The World Bank, *World Development Report 2006: Equity and Development* (Washington, DC, World Bank, 2006) ch 2, esp 48ff. People adjust their preferences in light of considerations of feasibility in order to avoid suffering permanently defeated expectations, leading to what Arjun Appadurai, in talking about deep poverty, calls the stunting of 'the capacity to aspire'. This mechanism operates even in economically prosperous countries, particularly among those affected by structural, 'horizontal inequalities', which play such a central role in the UN–World Bank *Pathways to Peace*. See A Appadurai, 'The Capacity to Aspire: Culture and the Terms of Recognition' in V Rao and M Walton (eds), *Culture and Public Action* (Stanford, Stanford University Press, 2004) 68. See also A Sen, 'How Does Culture Matter?' in the same collection. On shifting preferences, see, eg R Goodin, 'Laundering Preferences' in J Elster and A Hylland (eds), *Foundations of Social Choice Theory* (Cambridge, Cambridge University Press, 1986); C Sunstein, 'Democracy and Shifting Preferences' in A Hamlin and P Pettit (eds), *The Good Polity: Normative Analysis of the State* (Oxford, Polity Press, 1989). For the notion of horizontal inequalities, see F Stewart (ed), *Horizontal Inequalities and Conflict: Understanding Group Violence in*

inequalities exist, measures to give voice to those left behind would be an important first step in creating a more equal society. In some ways, the socialisation of *their* reality, the reality of the underclass, is a precondition for the creation of the demand for change.[68]

This double process – giving victims a voice and holding a mirror to the privileged – may help undo the simplifying narratives which McCoy and Somer argue are at the heart of pernicious forms of polarisation: narratives that force cross-cutting differences between groups and generate an 'Us versus Them' dynamic. In a sense, truth humanises by complexifying, and it is in part this liberating process of complexification that allows for a more respectful and consensual form of social integration.

One important dimension of a truth-telling process is understanding the deception in the expression 'left behind'. The passive voice makes it seem that the fate of those that have been excluded and marginalised is something that simply befell them (or worse, for which they themselves are responsible). Truth-telling measures in such contexts can explain some of the decisions that led to particular patterns of distribution of wealth, opportunities and power. These are not 'facts of nature', but the result of policy decisions.[69] Think, for example, of processes of deindustrialisation or the (related) adoption of Friedman's notion of 'shareholder value maximization',[70] both of which have arguably been so influential in the rise of the new populism and in generating polarisation more generally. For the sake of healthy, transparent politics, it would be helpful for a citizenry to gain an understanding of the deliberate nature of this process. For example, much remains to be understood regarding the US Federal Government's management of the COVID-19 pandemic: in particular, how decision-makers from the president down exercised their powers in ways that may have aggravated the crisis and led to notoriously inequitable burdens.

Truth-telling, I want to emphasise, can not only create a demand for change, but also provide direction to those changes. In examining patterns of exclusion and institutional weaknesses, truth-telling can provide clues about which institutions have been captured, by whom and for what purpose. This type of analysis can lead to reforms to strengthen the so-called 'guarantor institutions', and inform the creation

---

Multiethnic Societies (Basingstoke, Palgrave, 2008). For the intergenerational effects of different types of trauma in general, see Y Danieli (ed), *International Handbook of Multigenerational Legacies of Trauma* (New York, Springer, 2010).

[68] For a revealing expression of the type of lack of awareness of privilege, see the following headline in the *Financial Times* of 27 May 2021: 'Worker shortages raise fears of higher wage costs in developed economies'. Clearly neither the author nor the editor asked the basic question, higher wages raise fears in whom? Obviously, not the workers ... This article has now been erased from the newspaper's website and is not archived. However, it is referenced in D Brown, 'Letter: Give Dickensian Headline a Gig Economy Refresh' *Financial Times* (30 May 2021) www.ft.com/content/7b2f9a50-b642-4e16-8517-447359a408a8.

[69] See, eg S Holmes and C Sunstein, *The Cost of Rights: Why Liberty Depends on Taxes* (New York, Norton, 2000); M Sandel, *The Tyranny of Merit: What Became of the Common Good?* (New York, Farrar, Straus & Giroux, 2020); P Collier, *The Future of Capitalism* (New York, Harper, 2018).

[70] M Friedman, 'The Social Responsibility of Business Is to Increase Its Profits' New York Times (13 September 1970) www.nytimes.com/1970/09/13/archives/a-friedman-doctrine-the-social-responsibility-of-business-is-to.html. For an example of the connection between Friedman and current populism, see, eg M Wolf, 'There Is a Direct Line from Milton Friedman to Donald Trump's Assault on Democracy' in L Zingales (ed), *Milton Friedman 50 Years Later* (Chicago, Stiegler Center, 2020).

of oversight mechanisms and independent institutions that help keep constitutional promises and therefore prevent conflict.[71]

Of course, in order to avoid naivety, it is important to mention three caveats stemming from lessons that have also been learned in the transitional justice field. First, it is a mistake to engage in what some economists and organisational sociologists call 'isomorphic mimicry', the tendency to think that the very same institutional formation will work equally well regardless of circumstances.[72] So the point here is one on behalf of truth-telling, but not necessarily of truth commissions. Other mechanisms may be more adequate to the task in the contexts we are concerned about in this chapter. Thus, for example, there are truth-telling mechanisms within institutions, such as the work done by particular German companies to interrogate their own role in the Holocaust[73] or the growing number of US universities that are examining their own involvement with slavery.[74] There are also local, official and unofficial truth commissions established in different parts of the world. In Brazil, for instance, the Federal Truth Commission established under the presidency of Dilma Rouseff was preceded by or coexisted with more than 20 different local commissions of different types, some of them established by states, others by cities or even universities. In 2005, a local, unofficial truth commission was established in Greensboro, North Carolina, to examine white supremacist murders that took place in collusion with local authorities in 1979.[75] Motivated by the Black Lives Matter movement, more than 50 US cities are currently considering similar mechanisms.[76]

Second, the operation of a truth-telling mechanism does not, on its own, lead to a narrative that will be immediately accepted and shared by all. Rather than aiming at this as the proximate goal of truth-telling, it is better to think, with Michael Ignatieff, in terms of 'limiting the range of permissible lies'.[77] In other words, truth-telling can establish some basic facts that any attempt to understand the prevailing situation in a particular national or social context would have to take into account and, perhaps more importantly, a set of factors which cannot be ignored by any serious effort to explain a conflict or the risk of conflict.

---

[71] See T Khaitan, 'Guarantor Institutions' (2021) 16 *Asian Journal of Comparative Law* S40, prepared for the prevention project directed by the present author and hosted by the Center for Human Rights and Global Justice at NYU.

[72] See, eg L Pritchett and F de Weijer, 'Fragile States: Stuck in a Capability Trap?' *World Development Report 2011* background paper (Washington DC, World Bank, 2010).

[73] See, eg L Bilsky, *The Holocaust, Corporations, and the Law: Unfinished Business* (Ann Arbor, University of Michigan Press, 2017) ch 8.

[74] LM Harris et al (eds), *Slavery and the University* (Athens, University of Georgia Press, 2019).

[75] See Greensboro Truth & Reconciliation Commission, https://greensborotrc.org/. On the USA reckoning with its past, see S Neiman, *Learning from the Germans. Race and the Memory of Evil* (New York, Farrar, Straus & Giroux, 2019).

[76] In the opposite direction, ie towards not the local but the transnational, it is worth following the commission established by the Belgian Parliament in 2020 to examine Belgium's historical relations with the DRC, Rwanda and Burundi. The commission is off to a slow start. See, eg C Dikiefu Banona and J-S Sépulchre, 'Belgium – Moving from Regrets to Reparations' (Human Rights Watch, 30 June 2020) www.hrw.org/news/2020/06/30/belgium-moving-regrets-reparations#.

[77] M Ignatieff, 'Articles of Faith' (1996) 25 *Index on Censorship* 110.

Finally, we have learned the obvious lesson that truth is not the same as transformation. Unfortunately, contrary to the lemma of the SATRC, truth on its own does not set us free. It is unlikely that truth, in the absence of other initiatives to redress the very real problems that polarising figures latch on to (eg deindustrialisation, unplanned patterns of migration, high levels of inequality, dysfunctional systems of political representation, captured institutions, various forms of marginalisation), would be sufficient to provoke transformation.

Yet, causal insufficiency is not the same thing as causal impotence or irrelevance. For the reasons stated above, truth-telling may make some contributions in contexts other than their 'natural home', the post-transitional, post-conflict ones. In fact, various forms of parliamentary commissions of inquiry in non-conflict contexts illustrate the importance of truth for governance in general.[78] The discussion here merely extends both the range of topics and the range of tools that can be employed in pre-conflict contexts. One can imagine truth-telling exercises contributing to (eventual) depolarisation regarding some of the events – such as Brexit, the unprecedented levels of inequality in some countries, the opiate crisis, deaths of black people at the hands of the police or the 6 January attack on the Capitol in Washington DC – that have heightened social divisions in the recent past in non-conflict countries. This is provided, of course, that best practices concerning 'nuts and bolts issues', from the selection of commissioners to methodology to impartiality, are followed.[79]

B. Memorialisation

Different forms of memorialisation are closely associated with truth-telling and are, in fact, a crucial tool for the socialisation of truth. Examples include the establishment of museums, monuments and days of remembrance. These kinds of initiatives can supplement truth commissions and commissions of inquiry reports, which are rarely the best vehicles for the dissemination and internalisation of truths.

In a political context characterised by culture wars, history itself – as well as manifestations of various interpretations of historical events – has become a major object of contestation. The world, as a recent report in *The Economist* put it, 'is fixated' on the past, having 'an orgy of reminiscence'.[80] That both socially integrative and socially divisive examples of this fixation on the past can be given raises questions about whether memorialisation can be of help under the current circumstances and for the purposes of this chapter, which are to a large extent integrative and preventive.

---

[78] For a beautiful general reflection about the importance of truth in the constitutional state, see P Häberle, *Wahrheitsprobleme im Verfassungsstaat* (Baden-Baden, Nomos, 1995).

[79] I address some of these issues in my report on truth commissions to the Human Rights Council: P de Greiff, 'Report of the Special Rapporteur on the Promotion of Truth, Justice, Reparation and Guarantees of Non-recurrence' (28 August 2013) UN Doc A/HRC/24/42.

[80] The Economist, 'The World Is Fixated on the Past' (22 December 2018) www.economist.com/leaders/2018/12/22/the-world-is-fixated-on-the-past. See also, eg M Gessen, *The Future Is History* (New York, Riverhead Books, 2017); S Boym, *The Future of Nostalgia* (New York, Basic Books, 2002).

The history of the manipulation of history through different means is long and continues into the present. Nazism and communism deployed the past for the sake of political ends. In the Balkans, the 'memory' of the losses to the Ottoman Empire (itself long gone and without any present-day 'successor state' in the region) were used to fan 'retaliatory' attitudes that laid the ground for war. Extremist violence in the Muslim world appeals to 'memories' of the Crusades put to instrumental ends. Israel and Palestine are rife with pasts to suit political expedience. The list does not end there. Putin has constructed part of his political appeal around the idea of recovering for Russia the respect the Soviet Union had as a superpower; China uses the memory of the 'century of humiliation' as a unifying narrative; and most recently, in the USA, former President Trump appointed the 1776 Commission (without a single historian) as a response to the 1619 project, which looked at American history through the prism of slavery.[81] In this sense, it is not surprising that even seasoned war correspondents like David Rieff end up writing books like *Against Remembrance*[82] and *In Praise of Forgetting*.[83]

There is therefore no question that 'historical memory' (an oxymoronic expression that should not be used in serious discussions[84]) can be instrumentalised and used both to stoke divisions and, as is happening in the USA and elsewhere, often to 'help to distract from questions of material distribution', turning this part of the 'culture wars' into what Jan-Werner Müller calls an 'elite device' for those who want to continue pursuing a neoliberal economic agenda.[85]

Yet, there is something substantive about memorialisation. This explains why a country like Spain, for example, is currently debating what it calls a 'democratic memory' law,[86] which includes dispositions about street names and monuments. Importantly, it also makes provisions regarding the Valle de los Caídos, the cavernous monument to 'reconciliation' designed by Franco and constructed with forced labour, where 30,000 victims of the civil war were buried (in the case of the Republican victims, without consulting their families).[87] More than 80 years after

---

[81] See 'The 1619 Project' *New York Times Magazine* (14 August 2019) www.nytimes.com/interactive/2019/08/14/magazine/1619-america-slavery.html; The President's Advisory 1776 Commission, *The 1776 Report* (January 2021) https://trumpwhitehouse.archives.gov/wp-content/uploads/2021/01/The-Presidents-Advisory-1776-Commission-Final-Report.pdf.

[82] D Reiss, *Against Remembrance* (Melbourne, Melbourne University Press, 2011).

[83] D Reiss, *In Praise of Forgetting* (New Haven, CT, Yale University Press, 2017). For an exchange with Rieff, see ICTJ, 'Does Collective Remembrance of a Troubled Past Impede Reconciliation?' (4 May 2016) https://web.archive.org/web/20210414061643/www.ictj.org/debate/remembrance/opening-remarks.

[84] References to 'memory' and 'remembrance' are undifferentiated and insufficiently defined. Appeals to these terms can refer to acts of recollection that have undergone no 'filtering', 'processing' or effort to check for veracity or comprehensiveness. Conversely, it can also refer to those acts of recollection that have already gone through the sort of examination, contestation, contextualisation and verification characteristic of both historical methodologies and the work of eg truth commissions, whose reports are much more than mere records of the memories of those who provided testimonies to them.

[85] J-W Müller, 'Why Culture Wars Are an Elite Device. Plutocratic Populists Reduce Economic Conflicts to Questions of Belonging' *New Statesman* (6 September 2021) www.newstatesman.com/long-read/2021/09/beyond-the-culture-wars.

[86] For the draft Bill, see Congreso de los Diputados, Proyecto de Ley de Memoria Democrática (30 August 2021) No 64-1, www.congreso.es/public_oficiales/L14/CONG/BOCG/A/BOCG-14-A-64-1.pdf.

[87] The Bill under discussion in parliament would replace the so-called 'historical memory law' of 2007 (Ley 52/2007, www.boe.es/eli/es/l/2007/12/26/52/con), widely seen to have been insufficient in many respects.

the civil war finished and more than 45 since the transition to democracy, family members of Republican victims continue a struggle for recognition in the broadest sense: recognition of the fact that those who fought the war or were convicted during the dictatorship were not criminals; of the fact that they deserve the same reparations as were offered to nationalist soldiers and their families; of the illegitimacy of their sentences and convictions; and of the various harms they suffered, including expropriations, fines, and loss of employment and pensions. Some of these aims are more tangible than others. In a country with more unrecovered remains than any other in Europe (including the nations of the Balkans), people want remains to be exhumed and given proper burial; but they also want the stories of their family members not to be forgotten. And they particularly resent the fact that, despite the 2007 law, there are still street names and symbols in public spaces that glorify the victors. They resent, moreover, the way the history of the war has been taught for decades: as if it had been everywhere a 'fratricidal struggle' between two rival factions who shared responsibility (an obvious distortion of a conflict that started with a military insurrection against a legally constituted government, and in which many provinces saw massacres and executions without any organised opposition). This Nationalist effort to reframe the war was, not surprisingly, extraordinarily effective, and so is still the dominant view.[88]

There is, of course, nothing peculiar about Spain's interest in memorialisation. Following the murder of George Floyd, a large number of monuments associated with racism, slavery and colonialism have been either toppled by crowds or ordered removed by local governments or institutional (eg university) authorities. Remarkably, this trend was not limited to the USA (as unlikely as this was in places such as Louisiana, South Carolina and Virginia): statues were also toppled in the UK, South Africa, Peru and Colombia, and removed in Belgium, among many other countries.[89] The trend continues to this day, both in the USA and elsewhere. By February 2021, more than 100 confederate statues had been removed in the USA;[90] and as I write this, Mexico City is planning to replace a statute of Columbus in one of the city's major thoroughfares with a statute of an indigenous woman.[91]

See my report on Spain to the Human Rights Council: P de Greiff, 'Report of the Special Rapporteur on the Promotion of Truth, Justice, Reparation and Guarantees of Non-recurrence' (22 July 2014) UN Doc A/HRC/27/56/Add.1.

[88] Although the curriculum has changed, politicians still engage in this type of historical revisionism to this day. In July 2022, a former minister, at an event chaired by the leader of the Popular Party, denied that there had been a coup in 1936. See, eg E Tasca and E García de Blas, 'Críticas al PP por el acto que organizó en el que un exministro negó que Franco diese un golpe de Estado' *El País* (20 July 2021) https://elpais.com/espana/2021-07-20/criticas-al-pp-por-el-acto-que-organizo-donde-un-exministro-nego-que-franco-diese-un-golpe-de-estado.html.

[89] See, eg 'Activists Target Removal of Statues Including Columbus and King Leopold II' *The Guardian* (10 June 2020) www.theguardian.com/us-news/2020/jun/10/columbus-king-leopold-ii-statues-could-be-next-to-fall-black-lives-matter-protests. See also A Ebrahamjli et al, 'Confederate Statues Are Coming Down Following George Floyd's Death. Here's What We Know' (*CNN*, 1 July 2020) www.cnn.com/2020/06/09/us/confederate-statues-removed-george-floyd-trnd/index.html.

[90] See, eg R Treisman, 'Nearly 100 Confederate Monuments Removed in 2020, Report Says; More Than 700 Remain' (*NPR*, 23 February 2021) www.npr.org/2021/02/23/970610428/nearly-100-confederate-monuments-removed-in-2020-report-says-more-than-700-remai.

[91] J Díaz, 'Mexico City to Replace Columbus Statue With Indigenous Woman Monument' *New York Times* (7 September 2021) www.nytimes.com/2021/09/07/world/americas/mexico-city-columbus-statue.

Despite the manipulation, opportunism and lack of reflexivity rife in 'memory work', including memorialisation, it continues to be important. Susan Neiman articulates the reason why persuasively in relating it to values. 'Monuments', she says,

> are values made visible ... They embody the ideals we choose to honor, in the hopes of reminding ourselves and our children that these ideals were actually embodied by brave men and women. What is at stake is not the past, but the present and future. When we choose to memorialize a historical moment, we are choosing the values we want to defend, and pass on.[92]

This is why, she argues, there are no Nazi monuments in Germany: 'A hypothetical Germany still valorizing soldiers who served a murderous cause would have failed to reject the cause itself.'[93] This is essentially the same argument made by Mitch Landrieu, mayor of New Orleans from 2010 to 2018, in his speech explaining the removal of the four confederate statues in the city. First, he affirms, 'These statues are not just stone and metal. They're not just innocent remembrances of a benign history. These monuments celebrate a fictional, sanitized Confederacy: ignoring the death, ignoring the enslavement, ignoring the terror that it actually stood for'. Then he asks his audience to

> consider these four monuments from the perspective of an African American mother or father trying to explain to their fifth grade daughter why Robert E. Lee sat atop our city. Can you do it? Can you do it? Can you look into the eyes of this young girl and convince her that Robert E. Lee is there to encourage her? Do you think she feels inspired and hopeful by that story? Do these monuments help her see her future with limitless potential? Have you ever thought that if her potential is limited, yours and my potential [is limited] as well?[94]

So, memorialisation can be preventive precisely because it is not mainly concerned about the past, but about the values that we expect to be relevant in the present and the future. The antidote to the claimed unreliability of acts of remembrance, to the fact that memory can be used for divisive purposes, is not to do away with the concern for the past – as if that were possible – but to make sure that the accounts of the past that are taken to be authoritative are both veridical and comprehensive, and that the disposition of memorials also obey some form of 'distributive justice in recognition'.[95] It goes without saying that there is no *complete* account of the

---

html. Resistance to celebrations of Columbus have a longer history. See, eg C Caron, 'Why Some Italian-Americans Still Fiercely Defend Columbus Day' *New York Times* (5 October 2018) www.nytimes.com/2018/10/05/us/columbus-day-italians-indigenous-peoples-day.html.

[92] Neiman (n 75) 263. A virtual industry on questions of memorialisation has grown over the years. In between, say, S Levinson, *Written in Stone: Public Monuments in Changing Societies* (Durham, NC, Duke University Press, 1998) and LA Macaluso, *Monument Culture: International Perspectives on the Future of Monuments in a Changing World* (Lanham, MD, Rowman & Littlefield, 2019), thousands of articles and hundreds of books have been published on this topic.

[93] Neiman (n 75) 264.

[94] M Landrieu, 'On the Removal of Four Confederate Monuments in New Orleans', speech delivered 19 May 2017, Gallier Hall, New Orleans LA, www.americanrhetoric.com/speeches/mitchlandrieuconfederatemonuments.htm, 4–5.

[95] The 'Victory Monuments' established by the Sinhala majority government in Sri Lanka in the Tamil and Muslim majority provinces in the North and the East, having razed Tamil and Muslim shrines and

past, one that embodies *all* and *only* true facts. And in terms of monuments, there is, of course, no public space that can bear setting in stone each and every past misdeed. What is called for are accounts of the past that are sufficient to set inquiry in directions that have been previously kept hidden and memorials that offer sufficient recognition to previously unrecognised groups. Recalling that what is at stake here is not memory but the *public acknowledgment* of great violations of rights – or, in the pre-conflict contexts, the public acknowledgement of great harms – a refusal to acknowledge them, to give them a place in our public space, involves a value judgement that there is no way to spin without demeaning the value of the victims or the importance of rights – not just the rights of victims, but rights in general, for the value of the notion these days rests to a large extent on their generalisability. To the extent that we expect others to be part of a shared political community, we owe them sufficient recognition for them to take the project to be truly shared. This is very clear in the case of our fellow citizens.

'Fellow citizens', however, does not refer to our compatriots only, or to those with whom we share a nationality; today, we are fellow citizens of a community of rights. To the extent that we expect others to trust us in that capacity, we have the duty to remember everything that we cannot reasonably expect our fellow citizens to forget.

Countries that have succeeded in using memorialisation as an instrument of social integration have succeeded to the extent that the memorialisation activities are not simply the representation of the memory of the victors. Memorials will more often foster integration where they promote democratic values (in contrast to the classical model, which concentrates almost exclusively on 'great' military men), and where they are conceived not merely as static but designed as 'living' objects. The lessons that have been learned about how to achieve such aims highlight the importance of participatory methods in the design and implementation of memorialisation activities; the importance of diversifying media, going well beyond stone and steel only; and the importance of linking the memorialisation activities to other policy interventions that address the relevant grievances directly. Memorialisation cannot replace policy initiatives, although it can motivate, support and even provide some guidance to them.[96]

---

cemeteries to erect such monuments, are a perfect example of how *not* to engage in memorialisation activities. See, eg PEARL, 'Erasing the Past. Repression of Memorialization in North-East Sri Lanka' (Washington DC, PEARL, 2016) https://pearlaction.org/wp-content/uploads/2016/11/pearl-erasing-the-past-nov-1-2016-report-b-1.pdf. Contrast this with the numbers published by the German Federal Office of Political Education, which show that in 1989 Berlin alone had more than 423 monuments to the victims of National Socialism. See Neiman (n 75) 110. The USA, of course, has problems of its own. According to the National Register of Historical Places kept by the National Park Service, of 95,214 properties listed, only 2% are related to African American History, 0.14% to Latino heritage and 0.1% to 'Asian' history. Data from E Akcan, 'Right to Heal: Architecture in Post-Conflict and Post Disaster Societies' (unpublished manuscript) 29.

[96] While, in the recent past, memorialisation discussions and activities have emphasised toppling of statues, alternatives to removals should be kept in mind. Removals are easy and replacements feasible, but not necessarily the most effective option, especially in the long run. Reinterpretation, contextualisation and other pedagogically more sophisticated reactions should be kept in mind.

C. Apologies

Another kind of initiative that often accompanies the implementation of transitional justice policies and which is worth considering in the present context is an official apology. The study of official apologies has grown significantly since the late 1990s, despite the fact that official apologies have a long history indeed.[97] One can study apologies as speech acts and argue that, leaving conditions of success aside, something is an apology if and only if it accepts responsibility and expresses regret.[98] This minimalist understanding of the semantics of apologies can be elaborated in detail (for example, Nick Smith's account of 'categorical apologies' includes, among other factors, a corroborated factual record, the identification of each harm and of the moral principles underlying each harm, acceptance of blame and categorical regret with the attendant emotions[99]). If one is concerned not just with the semantics of apologies but with their conditions of success, it is undeniable that such an expression is more likely to be accepted if accompanied by other apologetic elements. These may include, for example, the 'performance of penance',[100] the 'express[ion] of concern for future good relations'[101] and, most of all, the offer of repair.[102]

---

[97] The non-exhaustive list of 'political apologies' compiled by GG Dodds ('Political Apologies: Chronological List', www.angelfire.com/un/just1/apologies.htm) starts with the apology offered in 1077 by Holy Roman Emperor Henry IV to Pope Gregory VII for church–state conflicts, which included standing barefoot in the snow for three days, but clearly this is not the first one. Other lists of apologies appear in E Yamamoto, 'Race Apologies' (1997) 1 *Journal of Gender, Race, and Justice* 47; M Cunningham, 'Saying Sorry: The Politics of Apology' (1999) 70 *Political Quarterly* 285; D Stoltz and B Van Schaack, 'It's Never Too Late to Say "I'm Sorry"; Sovereign Apologies over the Years' (Just Security, 16 March 2021) www.justsecurity.org/75340/its-never-too-late-to-say-im-sorry-sovereign-apologies-over-the-years/. We now have a database of official apologies: Political Apologies across Cultures, 'The Political Apology Database', www.politicalapologies.com/.

[98] As I do in P de Greiff, 'The Role of Apologies in National Reconciliation Processes: On Making Trustworthy Institutions Trusted' in M Gibney et al (eds), *The Age of Apology. Facing Up the Past* (Philadelphia, University of Pennsylvania Press, 2007) 120–36. Other authors who follow this tack are N Tavuchis, *Mea Culpa: A Sociology of Apology and Reconciliation* (Stanford, Stanford University Press, 1991) 36; L Taft, 'Apology Subverted: The Commodification of Apology' (2000) 109 *Yale Law Journal*, 1135, 1154; DL Levi, 'The Role of Apology in Mediation' 72 *NYU Law Review* 1165, 1174–75.

[99] N Smith, *I Was Wrong: The Meanings of Apologies* (New York, Cambridge University Press, 2008).

[100] See E Goffman, *Relations in Public: Microstudies of the Public Order* (New York, Basic Books, 1971) 113.

[101] A Orenstein, 'Apology Excepted: Incorporating a Feminist Analysis into Evidence Policy Where You Would Least Expect It' (1999) 28 *Southwestern University Law Review* 221, 239.

[102] In addition to Goffman and Orenstein, the following authors include the offer to repair as an essential component of apologies: H Wagatsuma and A Rosett, 'The Implications of Apology: Law and Culture in Japan and the United States' (1986) 20 *Law & Society Review* 461, 469–70; EA O'Hara and D Yarn, 'On Apology and Consilience' (2002) 77 *Washington Law Review* 1121, 1133; S Alter, 'Apologising for Serious Wrongdoing: Social, Psychological and Legal Considerations' (Law Commission of Canada, May 1999). Nick Smith in *I Was Wrong* seems to conflate the essential characteristics of the speech act with its conditions of success as well, except that, as he has come to argue, 'Apologies are a process requiring time for policies to develop and patterns of behavior to emerge. They are treatments, not cures': N Smith, 'Should Biden Apologize for Trump? National Remorse and the 2020 US Presidential Election' (2020) 57 *Society* 698, 702. A process-based analysis of apologies would need to examine conditions of acceptability or success. Under those conditions, I would agree that what he calls 'Reform and Redress' are essential parts of an apology conceived as a process. See N Smith, 'An Overview of Challenges Facing Collective Apologies' in D Cuypers et al (eds), *Public Apologies between Ritual and Regret* (Amsterdam, Rodopi, 2013) 31.

There can be no doubt that some apologies, even public, collective ones, can have profound effects. Perhaps a good illustration is one that is not even verbal: Willy Brandt kneeling in front of Warsaw's Monument to the Ghetto Heroes in 1970 during the first visit by a German Chancellor to Poland since the countries suspended diplomatic relations at the end of World War II. The gesture was on most accounts spontaneous, and conveyed unconditional regret and acceptance of responsibility. It also signalled to the international community an image of a peace-seeking Germany.[103]

When Australian Prime Minister Kevin Rudd apologised for the mistreatment of Aboriginal and Torres Strait Islander peoples in 2008,[104] several members of these communities experienced this moment as a real breakthrough. A member of the 'stolen generation' – aboriginal children who were removed from their families and raised in white homes and missions – expressed exactly what makes the current exercise, examining whether transitional justice may have anything to offer in pre- or non-conflict contexts, worthwhile: 'It gave me peace.'[105]

The interesting question for us is whether an account of such an effect, not so much at the individual, micro-level, but at the societal, macro-level, can be offered. The literature on apologies centres around two leading views. The first one concentrates on the fact that apologies involve an exchange of power. Aaron Lazare gives a succinct expression of this view:[106]

> [W]hat makes an apology work is the exchange of shame and power between the offender and the offended. By apologizing, you take the shame of your offense and redirect it to yourself. You admit of hurting or diminishing someone, and, in effect, say that you are really the one who is diminished – I'm the one who was wrong, mistaken, insensitive, or stupid. In acknowledging your shame you give the offender the power to forgive. The exchange is at the heart of the healing process.[107]

---

[103] Germans themselves were not so keen on the gesture. In polls at the time, 48% disagreed with what the Chancellor did and only 41% approved. The international community was much more positive: *Time Magazine* made Brandt Man of the Year, and he was awarded the Nobel Peace Prize the next year. In his memoirs, Brandt says of his silent gesture: 'At the abyss of German history and burdened by millions of murdered humans, I acted in the way of those whom language fails.' For a succinct account of the event, see Deutsches Historisches Museum, 'The Warsaw Genuflection: Willy Brandt's Historic Gesture' (7 December 2016) www.dhm.de/blog/2016/12/07/392/.

[104] Available at Parliament of Australia, 'Apology to Australia's Indigenous Peoples', www.aph.gov.au/Visit_Parliament/Art/Exhibitions/Custom_Media/Apology_to_Australias_Indigenous_Peoples.

[105] F Mao, 'Australia's Apology to Stolen Generation: "It Gave Me Peace"' (BBC News, 13 February 2008) www.bbc.com/news/world-australia-43039522.

[106] I am using Lazare's formulation of this view, but his own position is actually more complex. Lazare starts his analysis of successful apologies by examining the psychological needs of the 'offended party', arguing that success must mean that the apology must have met one of those needs. The needs he identifies are: 'restoration of self-respect and dignity, assurance that both parties have shared values, assurance that the offenses were not their fault, assurance of safety in their relationships, seeing the offender suffer, reparation for the harm caused by the offense, having meaningful dialogues with the offenders': A Lazare, *On Apology* (Oxford, Oxford University Press, 2004) 44. However, Lazare acknowledges that there is a difference between identifying a need that an apology might satisfy and understanding *how* an apology might satisfy that need. Even in his later work the most categorical statements about how apologies work reaffirm the exchange relationship described below. See, eg ibid 52. Independently of where Lazare finally stands on this issue, the exchange relationship account has taken hold. See, eg M Minow, *Between Vengeance and Forgiveness* (Boston, MA, Beacon Press, 1998) 115.

[107] A Lazare, 'Go Ahead, Say You're Sorry' (1995) 23 *Psychology Today*, 42. Lazare elaborates this position in *On Apology* (n 106) 52.

On this view, what is important is not only the redirection of shame in its own terms, but the fact that it puts the offender in a position of vulnerability and therefore redraws the balance of power. The person or community offended is now in a position to either grant or withhold something the offender wants, the release that comes through forgiveness:

> Originally having had the power to hurt, the offender now gives the power to forgive or not to forgive to the offended party. This exchange of humiliation and power between the offender and the offended may be the clearest way of explaining how some apologies heal by restoring dignity and self-respect.[108]

While I do not doubt that there are some circumstances – especially face-to-face apologies – which are fittingly described in these terms, to make an exchange of *power* the cornerstone of an explanatory account of how apologies work seems to me to stretch credibility a bit. Although it is difficult to be certain of what a successful apology is, I am not sure that Queen Elizabeth's apology to the Māori in New Zealand,[109] President Clinton's apologies to the victims of the Tuskegee experiments[110] or – to include non-state apologies – Texaco's chairman's apology for racial slurs,[111] to mention just a few instances, are best described in terms of a redrawing of the balance of power between the offender and the offended.[112] I think this account overestimates the significance of a power shift between the parties for two reasons. First, it is not clear that an apology actually has as its end result the redrawing, to any important degree, of the balance of power between the relevant parties. This is particularly important in the case of institutional, official apologies, where the relationship between offender and offended is frequently asymmetrical (as in the three examples mentioned above). Second, even if one sets aside the question of the effects of the apology and concentrates on what the account considers to be the relevant exchange – an apology for release – many of these instances may constitute examples of an offer one cannot refuse, if for no other reason that the apologies might be the only gesture on offer. If this is so, there are reasons to question the moral significance of the exchange.

The second account of how apologies work, rather than concentrating on the exchange of power, focuses on the fact that apologies are unthinkable in the absence of norms and values whose validity – despite the transgression – is reaffirmed in the act of apologising. This is a view that can be constructed on the basis of Tavuchis's sociological approach to apologies in his *Mea Culpa* (although he does not offer an explanatory account of their effectiveness). Tavuchis argues in the introduction

---

[108] Lazare, *On Apology* (n 106) 52.
[109] Available at Ngāi Tahu, 'The Crown's Apology', https://ngaitahu.iwi.nz/ngai-tahu/the-settlement/settlement-offer/the-crowns-apology/.
[110] Available at Clinton Digital Library, 'Apology to Survivors of the Tuskegee Syphilis Experiment', https://clinton.presidentiallibraries.us/items/show/16076.
[111] See, eg C Milloy, 'Texaco Taps a Deep Well of Racism' *Washington Post* (10 November 1996) www.washingtonpost.com/archive/local/1996/11/10/texaco-taps-a-deep-well-of-racism/e5767eb2-4918-4070-adbe-053be672804d/.
[112] Now that we have a database of official apologies, as mentioned before, it would be a revealing exercise to go through these lists considering how many of the examples fit the description of an exchange of power; in my view, not many, at least not in any strong sense.

to his book that, in examining a wide variety of apologies, the common theme he found was 'the violation of an unstated but consequential, moral rule'.[113] I find the reference to specifically moral rules unduly constraining, and Tavuchis himself eventually broadens the scope of his attention; but, in my view, focusing on the fact that apologies reaffirm norms and values is fundamentally correct. In the most elaborate statement of this point in his book, Tavuchis writes:

> Genuine apologies ... may be taken as the symbolic foci of secular remedial rituals that serve to recall and reaffirm allegiance to codes of behavior and belief whose integrity has been tested and challenged by transgression, whether knowingly or unwittingly. An apology thus speaks to an act that cannot be undone but that cannot go unnoticed without compromising the current and future relationship of the parties, the legitimacy of the violated rule, and the wider social web in which the participants are enmeshed.[114]

The point that I want to make is not only that, conceptually speaking, an apology is unthinkable in the absence of a norm that the offender considers to be binding – and that is typically, although not always, shared with the offended – but that the reason why an apology may be thought to 'work' is that it involves the affirmation of the validity of the norm. Here again, one must avoid naivety: the affirmation of a norm is never simply a matter of words or gestures. Chancellor Brandt's genuflection had the effect it did in the context of a trip designed to restore diplomatic relations with Poland (including, for example, German recognition of the Oder-Neisse Line as the border with Poland) and within the framework of Brandt's promotion of his *Ostpolitik*, a policy of engagement with the Soviet Union and the countries in Eastern Europe. Prime Minister Rudd's apology to the Aboriginal and Torres Strait Islander peoples was received so positively in part because it was accompanied by the adoption of the 'Closing the Gap' programme, which was supposed to redress the inequalities suffered, especially by members of the 'stolen generation'.[115] But, as Stoltz and Van Shaack put it, after 10 years,

> the lack of concrete policy changes following Rudd's apology, especially the failure to meet so many imperative Closing-the-Gap goals, leaves many with the impression that the apology was more of a political stunt to provide artificial closure than a *bona fide* process to usher in transformative change.[116]

Norms, and the recovery of their *validity* or currency as the 'guardrails' of social relations, are critical for trust, and all the measures being considered in this chapter (truth-telling, memorialisation, apologies, consultations, etc) work, to the extent they do, in virtue of their norm-affirming character. Social integration, from this point of view, is an achievement that depends on the ability of a group to live by norms that all can accept.[117]

---

[113] Tavuchis, *Mea Culpa* (n 98) 3.
[114] ibid 13.
[115] See 'Closing the Gap', www.closingthegap.gov.au/.
[116] Stoltz and Van Shaack (n 97).
[117] This is the sociological 'translation' of a basic Kantian insight. No one has developed it more than Jürgen Habermas. See, eg J Habermas *Between Facts and Norms* (Cambridge, MIT Press, 1998).

D. Consultation and Participation

National consultation processes are not necessarily a transitional justice measure, though many transitional countries have engaged in various modalities of such processes with varying degrees of success. Some of these processes are explicitly designed to lead to a new or reformed constitution, while others have vague, undefined goals:

> National Dialogues are nationally owned political processes aimed at generating consensus among a broad range of national stakeholders in times of deep political crisis, in post-war situations or during far-reaching political transitions. Depending on the context, National Dialogues can be employed as mechanisms for (a) *crisis prevention and management*, a shorter-term endeavour, undertaken strategically as a means to resolve or prevent the outbreak of armed violence, breaking political deadlocks and re-establishing minimal political consensus ... or (b) *fundamental change, with a longer-term trajectory*, envisioned as a means to redefine state-society relations, or establish a new 'social contract' through institutional and constitutional changes ...[118]

There is a much longer tradition of national dialogues (especially in the francophone world) than one would guess from the meagre literature on the topic. National dialogues have acquired more visibility of late, in large part thanks to the Nobel Peace Prize awarded in 2015 to the Tunisian *quartet du dialogue national* in virtue of its contribution to that country's constitution-making process.[119] In the West, Emmanuel Macron's 2019 'grand national dialogue' as a response to the demonstrations by the *gilets jaunes* ('yellow vests') also brought attention to national dialogues, although the results of this exercise were significantly more ambiguous than the Tunisian example.

Here again I think it is important to avoid naivety. As one of the very few comparative analyses of national dialogues points out, 'While most National Dialogues reached an agreement, only half of these agreements were implemented'. The same study acknowledges that 'National Dialogues have often been used by national elites as a tool to gain or reclaim political legitimacy, which has limited their potential for transformative change'.[120] So national dialogues are far from a panacea.

Having said that, in my opinion, it is a mistake to judge the success or failure of national dialogues or consultation processes on the basis of short-term transformations. The comparative study cited above, for example, also mentions that 'In the

---

[118] Berghof Foundation, *National Dialogue Handbook: A Guide for Practitioners* (Berlin, Berghof Foundation Operations, 2017) 1.

[119] The quartet was a group of four civil society organizations: UGTT, Union Générale Tunisienne du Travail [The Tunisian General Labour Union]; UTICA, Union Tunisienne de l'Industrie, du Commerce et de l'Artisanat [The Tunisian Confederation of Industry, Trade, and Crafts]; LTDH, La Ligue Tunisienne pour la Défense des Droits de l'Homme [The Tunisian Human Rights League]; and Ordre National des Avocats de Tunisie [The Tunisian Order of Lawyers], that is, a labour union, a trade group (representing the interests of Tunisia's businesses), a network of human rights NGO and an association of lawyers. This group of strange bedfellows helped the deadlocked constituent assembly, which was badly divided between secularists and religious forces, with the latter in the majority, adopt a constitution that all Tunisians could accept.

[120] T Paffenholz, A Zachariassen and C Helfer, *What Makes or Breaks National Dialogues?* (Geneva, Inclusive Peace and Transitions Initiative, 2017) 8.

short term, and most notably in cases of mass protests, National Dialogues have been able to reduce violence by transferring grievances from the streets into formalized processes'.[121]

Participatory methods are usually defended in terms of two types of argument. The first, 'epistemic' argument refers to the type of knowledge or insight consulting people may produce, and on the positive consequences that improvements in understanding may have. On this account, consultations can increase the likelihood that reform proposals capture the sense of justice of victims and other beneficiaries, and their judgements of what would constitute effective redress; help ensure a close fit between the to-be-designed measures and the expressed needs of victims on the one hand, and cultural, historical and political realities on the other; and broaden the range of adequate alternatives by putting more ideas for effective redress on the table.

The second type of argument made in defence of participation generally and consultations more specifically are 'legitimacy' arguments. On this account, consultations are important not just because of the specific contributions that canvassing opinions may have, measured in terms of 'proposals', but also because the process of consulting is itself a measure of recognising and empowering victims, helping them gain a place in the public sphere which they may have been denied before. Similarly, consultation processes may widen the circle of stakeholders in justice processes, pulling in both official and unofficial groups who were previously excluded from the discussions, but on whose consent and participation the success and sustainability of reform proposals may depend to some extent. Finally, consultations may facilitate the identification of commonalities of experiences, values and principles between different groups, which are important in building coalitions and consensus, and are crucial in the adoption of policies about contentious issues.[122]

Once again, the common theme is the contribution of these methods to a sense of social integration. I would like to stress the point that, beyond the immediate results of national consultations, the very exercise of identifying constituencies that have traditionally been excluded from conversations about an inevitably shared destiny is both a means of recognition and a contribution to raising effective claims for transformation, including redistribution. The national consultation process in Colombia during the peace negotiation, for example, identified 18 categories of groups whose participation they tried to secure (in addition to victims). These included peasants' movements, indigenous populations, afro-descendant populations, labour and business organisations, trade unions, political parties, human rights organisations, development and peace programmes, churches, academia, children and adolescents, youth organisations, LGBTI organisations, minority communities (Palenqueros, Raizales and Roma), environmental organisations and the media. Gender and regional considerations were also applied across the different categories, aiming for 50 per cent female representation and significant participation by people from

---

[121] Continuing with the doubly ambiguous statement, 'In cases with ongoing violence, National Dialogue outcomes were sometimes constrained, but no clear pattern was found in the analysis': ibid.
[122] See my report to the General Assembly on National Consultation Processes, P de Greiff, 'Promotion of Truth, Justice, Reparation and Guarantees of Non-recurrence' (25 October 2016) UN Doc A/71/567.

different regions (an aim also served by the decision concerning the location of the consultations). Similarly, for the 2009–10 consultations in Burundi, efforts were made to promote the participation of groups, including public officials, government representatives, parliamentarians, political representatives, civil society organisations, women's groups, academics, journalists, elderly and youth organisations, persons with disabilities, churches and religious communities, displaced persons, demobilised persons, former child soldiers, and widows and orphans. Sampling methods were used to equalise the chances of participation of members of different ethnic groups. In other words, these consultations were a far cry from the typical convenings in notoriously centralised, stratified and exclusionary societies.[123]

In a context characterised by increasing fragmentation, by the autonomisation of the political class from their supposed constituencies and, therefore, by deep distrust in familiar methods of representation, inclusive consultations like this may contribute to, at the very least, establishing a forum where people can recognise each other. So, while there is nothing that can guarantee that their promise will be fulfilled, national dialogues and consultation processes offer a forum uniquely suited to historical moments, like the present, that require modes of reconnection:

> National Dialogues are typically convened at times when the fundamental nature or survival of a government is in question. Thus, they are usually intended as a means of redefining the relationship between the state, political actors, and society through the negotiation of a new social contract.[124]

Opportunities to 'de-naturalise' the status quo come only seldomly. It would be wise to take those opportunities and exploit whatever potential they have.

E. Enhancing Trust

Trust – or, more exactly, the erosion of trust – was central in characterising this chapter's domain of concern. It is therefore fitting to close with some considerations about the notion, stemming from lessons learned in the field of transitional justice. Post-authoritarian and post-conflict societies are left with profound deficits of trust, and the theoretical reconstruction of the aims of transitional justice argues that, to some extent, all the elements of a comprehensive transitional justice policy share as a (mediate) aim strengthening civic trust.[125]

In the preceding sections, I made much of the fact that the burgeoning literature on trust, particularly that which is survey-based, does not offer a definition of trust at all. Here, I want to address that issue head-on, for it seems to me that without a clear idea of what we are seeking to accomplish, our interventions will be nothing more than shots in the dark.

---

[123] ibid and the literature therein.
[124] Paffenholz et al (n 120) 9.
[125] See P de Greiff, 'Theorizing Transitional Justice' (n 10); P de Greiff, 'Some Thoughts on the Development and Present State of Transitional Justice' (2011) 5 *Zeitschrift für Menschenrechte /Journal for Human Rights* 2.

The argument concerning the trust-inducing potential of any transitional justice measure must start with what again can only be a stipulation: namely, that trust should not be reduced to mere empirical predictability. That reliability is not the same as trustworthiness can be seen in our reluctance to say that we *trust* someone about whose behaviour we feel a great deal of certainty, but only because we both monitor and control it (eg through enforcing the terms of a contract), or because we take defensive or pre-emptive action.[126] Trust, far from resembling a sort of 'mechanical reliability', involves an expectation of a shared *normative* commitment. I trust someone when I have reasons to expect a certain pattern of behaviour from them, and those reasons include not just their consistent past behaviour, but also, crucially, the expectation that among their reasons for action is the commitment to the norms and values we share.

Trusting an institution, the case that is particularly relevant here, amounts to assuming that its constitutive rules, values and norms are shared by its members or participants and are regarded by them as binding. As Claus Offe puts it:

> 'trusting institutions' means something entirely different from 'trusting my neighbor': it means *knowing* and recognizing as valid the values and the form of life incorporated in an institution and deriving from this recognition the assumption that this idea makes sufficient sense to a sufficient number of people to motivate their ongoing active support for the institution and the compliance with its rules. Successful institutions generate a positive feedback loop: they make sense to actors so that actors will support them and comply with what the institutionally defined order prescribes.[127]

How do transitional justice measures promote this sense of civic trust? Prosecutions can be thought to promote civic trust by reaffirming the relevance of the norms that perpetrators violated, norms that precisely turn natural persons into rights-bearers. Judicial institutions, particularly in contexts in which they have traditionally been essentially instruments of power, show their trustworthiness if they can establish that no one is above the law. An institutionalised effort to confront the past through truth-telling exercises might be seen by those who were formerly on the receiving end of violence as a good-faith effort to come clean, to understand long-term patterns of socialisation and, in this sense, to initiate a new political project around norms and values that this time around are truly shared. Reparations can foster civic trust by demonstrating the seriousness with which institutions now take the violation of their rights, a seriousness that is manifested, to put it bluntly, by the fact that 'money talks'. Symbolic reparation measures signal that, even under conditions of scarcity and competition for resources, the state responds

---

[126] See LM Thomas, 'Power, Trust, and Evil' in L Bell and D Blumenfeld (eds), *Overcoming Racism and Sexism* (Lanham, Rowman & Littlefield, 1995) 160. Annette Baier argues that trust in general, as a disposition that mediates social interactions, 'is an alternative to vigilance and reliance on the threat of sanctions, [and] trustworthiness ... an alternative to constant watching to see what one can and cannot get away with, to recurrent recalculations of costs and benefits'. See AC Baier, *Moral Prejudices* (Cambridge, MA, Harvard University Press, 1994) 133.

[127] C Offe, 'How Can We Trust Our Fellow Citizens?' in M Warren (ed), *Democracy and Trust* (Cambridge, Cambridge University Press, 1999) 70–71.

to the obligation to fund programmes that benefit those who were formerly not only marginalised but abused. Finally, vetting can induce trust, and not just by 're-peopling' institutions with new faces, but by thereby demonstrating a commitment to systemic norms governing employee hiring and retention, disciplinary oversight, prevention of cronyism and so on.

Much more important for the purposes of this chapter than the details of how transitional justice measures promote civic trust is the core idea that trust is a *normative* conception, that in the end it involves the possibility of *shared* normative commitments.[128] This helps, in my view, for it clarifies both the challenges and the opportunities: on the one hand, if trust cannot be reduced to predictability but involves normative commitments, there are no quick fixes, no technocratic solutions to trust deficits. This is not something that can be resolved by fiat. Consider the old adage, 'trust takes ages to construct, a second to shatter'. The underlying reasons should be apparent: a state or institution's commitment to norms is something that we cannot observe directly, but only read off long patterns of consistent behaviour (hence also its brittleness: a norm-breaking act on its part makes us question at the very least the strength of that commitment). On the other hand, keeping in mind that *civic* trust is not the same as trust between intimates, but that the relevant *shared* norms are abstract and general (for example, constitutional principles, human rights), makes the challenge one that can actually be met. Complying with norms of this level of generality is presumably less demanding than meeting the far more fine-grained norms that govern the expectations between intimates. With more than a little irony, one can say the task is easy: we just need to make sure that we establish conditions for the achievement of 'participatory parity', which (as Fraser argues) involves *both* recognition and redistribution.[129]

Sally's notion of vernacularization was not intended as an analytical tool to assess the quality or appropriateness of particular transformations of norms or practices (despite the fact that she was very clear that not all such transformations are equally successful).[130] If the application of transitional justice lessons is going to be successful in pre-conflict settings, it will have to be more an instance of hybridisation than of replication, to use the categories that I mentioned in the introduction

---

[128] This was always an unarticulated part of questions about trust in surveys reviewed above. Recall the NES question: 'How much of the time do you think you can trust the government in Washington to do what is right?' Interestingly, in 2020, Richard Edelman (CEO of the eponymous company) announced a shift in the way the barometer will understand the notion of trust, paying more attention to its normative dimensions: 'We have always known that people grant their trust based on two distinct considerations: competence and ethical behavior; for two decades we have asked people if they trust institutions "to do what is right". Now, based on new societal expectations, we are probing deeper into 'what is right', measuring purpose, vision, honesty and fairness as the dimensions of ethical behavior.' R Edelman, 'The Evolution of Trust' (Edelman, 19 January 2020) www.edelman.com/insights/evolution-trust.

[129] 'the structure of modern society is such that neither class subordination nor status subordination can be adequately understood in isolation from the other. On the contrary, misrecognition and maldistribution are so complexly intertwined today that each must be grasped from a larger, integrated perspective that also encompasses the other. Only when status and class are considered in tandem, in sum, can our current political dissociations be overcome': Fraser (n 7) 69.

[130] See, eg ch 5 of SE Merry, *Human Rights and Gender Violence* (Chicago, University of Chicago Press, 2006).

to this chapter. Replication is, in my mind, almost guaranteed to fail, for reasons I tried to articulate above. 'Hybrid' models, in the loosest sense of 'models' – referring more to lessons than to mechanisms – have the potential of making a contribution to current challenges, so long as they are not taken as substitutes for the real work involved in trying to solve our dual (but related) crises of distribution and representation.

Part II

Quantification and Human Rights

8

Beyond the Vanishing Point: Quantification as Rhetoric in Today's Anti-slavery Campaigns

SAMUEL MARTÍNEZ

SALLY MERRY'S WORK on indicators, indices and quantification explores a seeming paradox, in which less information can yield more power in global governance: information can become more persuasive if it is condensed into easily sharable and understandable symbols, numbers or rankings. When information of highly varied certainty and quality about something in the world – say, labour ethics – is gathered together and reduced to a classification or a ranking, the resulting icon or numerical value may make it possible for the level of compliance of a country, a business corporation, an industry or a supply chain to be assessed at a glance, possibly eventuating efforts to prescribe corrective measures or punish noncompliance. Yet 'synopsising' information[1] in these ways can achieve even more. When qualitative and heterogeneous global governance information is bundled and distilled into a sign or a ranking, it does not just permit the viewer to quickly assess and mentally classify a corresponding, complex whole: it also creates a new form of value, information as a currency that, like money, is an abstract, standard equivalent of other forms of value.[2] Once messy bundles of heterogeneous information get encapsulated in such ways – be it as positive or negative, a number from one to 100 or a place in a ranking of all the world's countries – this information derivative becomes like money or a share of stock: it can easily be compared with other, similarly bundled and standardised symbols or quantities; it is primed to travel and be used in institutional contexts other than that of its origin; and it is made fungible, capable of taking new forms, which may eventuate their own unanticipated effects. These ways of quantifying the world are so generative – and, indeed, seductive – that it is not surprising to see Merry's foundational work itself spreading virally among other scholars.

---

[1] S Martínez, 'From Commoditizing to Commodifying Human Rights: Research on Forced Labor in Dominican Sugar Production' (2015) 6 *Humanity* 387.
[2] SE Merry, 'Measuring the World: Indicators, Human Rights, and Global Governance' (2011) 52 *Current Anthropology* S83, S84.

In my practice as a university professor and human rights anthropologist, reading Merry's agenda-setting article, 'Measuring the World',[3] led me later to consult two contributory volumes that she and a multi-disciplinary group of scholars produced on indicators,[4] which then set me up to greet her 2016 work, *The Seductions of Quantification*,[5] as a must-read and must-assign book.

In this chapter, I examine one aspect of a larger research project, which might seem at first glance to coincide only tangentially with Merry's work on quantification but which actually responds immediately to her call to go beyond simply approving of quantification or rejecting it, to consider also quantification's 'knowledge effects and governance effects'.[6] I am currently writing a book, titled *Trafficking in Possibilities*, on the visual and verbal rhetoric of the 'new abolitionism', the activism of non-profit groups combating all manifestations of modern slavery, including human trafficking. In this chapter, based on a section of that book, I build on Merry's observation that estimates of the prevalence of trafficking typically emerge 'alongside personal stories, photographs of particular people or generic victims, and color-coded map'.[7] I examine the representational contexts in which prevalence estimates appear on the websites of some of the world's leading anti-trafficking and anti-slavery NGOs.[8] My interest lay not in the numbers per se so much as the ways in which numbers, images and text coincide. Does the juxtaposition of numbers with photographs and stories enable knowledge effects distinct from what numbers could achieve on their own?

In many instances, words or pictures work differently in combination than they ever could alone. Images and texts in new abolitionist websites most often arrive on the computer and smartphone screens of social justice consumers as composites of what WJT Mitchell calls 'imagetext'.[9] Text and photography, when paired, boost each other's power to evoke modern slavery's hiddenness and menace. Consider, for example, Figure 8.1, in which a story headline is supplemented by a photograph showing the foggy figure of a slender young woman. It is impossible to describe her precisely from the photograph. Her image is murky, because she stands on the other side of a fogged-over glass partition. The one part of her that can be seen clearly is her left hand, which is raised to touch the glass, palm outward, as if beckoning for our attention while at the same time warning us to come no closer. The visually spectral character of the photograph complements the article's headline ('Slavery continues to

---

[3] ibid.
[4] K Davis, A Fisher, B Kingsbury et al (eds), *Governance by Indicators: Global Power through Classification and Rankings* (Oxford, Oxford University Press, 2012); SE Merry, K Davis and B Kingsbury (eds), *The Quiet Power of Indicators: Measuring Governance, Corruption, and Rule of Law* (Cambridge, Cambridge University Press, 2015).
[5] SE Merry, *The Seductions of Quantification: Measuring Human Rights, Gender Violence, and Sex Trafficking* (Chicago, University of Chicago Press 2016).
[6] ibid 113.
[7] SE Merry, 'Counting the Uncountable: Constructing Trafficking through Measurement' in P Kotiswaran (ed), *Revisiting the Law and Governance of Trafficking, Forced Labor and Modern Slavery* (New York, Cambridge University Press, 2017) 278.
[8] The organisations whose websites I studied are the Polaris Project, Free the Slaves, Anti-Slavery International, End Slavery Now, the International Justice Mission, Love146, Not for Sale, the Coalition Against Trafficking in Women, Stop the Traffik and ECPAT-USA.
[9] WJT Mitchell, *Picture Theory: Essays on Verbal and Visual Representation* (Chicago, University of Chicago Press, 1994).

haunt the modern world'), while also adding a noir visual accent to the article's nightmarish survivor account of being duped into sex slavery. Hence, a keyword for my project is *imagetext*, and the natural habitat of my inquiry is the World Wide Web. To be clear, there is nothing new about activating readers' imaginations through photographs – in Figure 8.1, a photograph that seems to have been drawn from a mystery film – yet the World Wide Web is nevertheless a promised land of imagetext, in the unprecedented ease with which it permits words and photographs to be bundled.

Figure 8.1 Spectralising the unfree worker

Slavery continues to haunt the modern world, but efforts to eradicate it are growing

BY STEVEN SEIDENBERG

APRIL 27, 2013, 12:58 PM CDT

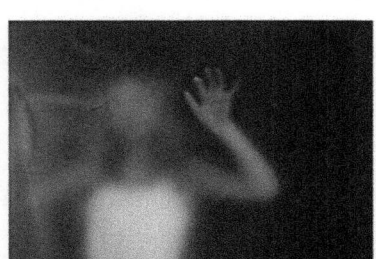

Photo by *Winky Lewis*

Maria watched the expensive car roll into her small town in Honduras. Two well-dressed men stepped out of the vehicle. They walked toward Maria, 15, and two friends who were with her. The men said they were recruiting people to work in a textile factory in the United States.

It sounded like a terrific opportunity—a chance for Maria to earn enough money to help her family while supporting herself. Most of all, it meant she would be able to send money to her mother, who was struggling to raise six other children on her own.

Source: S Seidenberg, 'Slavery Continues to Haunt the Modern World, but Efforts to Eradicate It Are Growing' *ABA Journal* (1 April 2013) www.abajournal.com/magazine/article/slavery_continues_to_haunt_the_modern_world.
Photo credit: Winky Lewis, reproduced with the copyright holder's permission.

Looking back at a decade's worth of web-based representations of modern slavery, between 2008 and 2019, I focus on those pages where new abolitionist activists explain what counts as trafficking and slavery and what does not, and then examine how prevalence estimates and other forms of quantifying slavery and trafficking – whether at a local, provincial, national or global level – enter into these didactic expositions of what captive exploitation is today. I find that quantification's effects cannot be disentangled from its surrounding texts and imagery. For this reason, my chapter is at key points a visual essay: QR codes in the text will permit you to see the webpages that provide necessary visual evidence for what I write.

More specifically, quantification enters into and contributes to a larger pattern of 'have-it-both-ways', 'now-slavery-is-one-thing-then-it's-the-opposite' flip-flopping, which I call *strategic equivocation*.[10] One message of the book from which I draw material for this chapter is that the new abolitionism is a progenitor or early example of post-truth politics, a diagnostic feature of which is seeking always to occupy both sides of any debatable point. By 'post-truth', I mean circumstances in which facts are less influential in shaping public opinion than appeals to emotion and personal belief.[11] The new abolitionism is post-truth because it seeks to win minds, not through facts and contextualised descriptions of systems of exploitation, but through the evocation of fears that slaves may lay hidden all around. Doubt and faith, rather than scepticism and evidence, are what post-truth politics is all about. Doubt is both foe and friend of the new abolitionism. Seeing that it impossible to banish doubt, new abolitionists equivocally negate doubt at times, only to honour it soon after, by implying that it is morally virtuous to take a stand even when you can neither find today's slaves nor know what form their captivity and exploitation may take. In the new abolitionist world, faith thus converts doubt from a reason to hesitate into a reason to act. At one moment new abolitionists project certainty – asserting unequivocally that slavery today is a global epidemic – only to say at the next moment that slavery today is hidden and hence its prevalence is unknowable. I identify in this approach the following hallmarks of post-truth politics: equivocating about the facts; equating political positions with moral stances; appealing to intuitions and emotions; and defining truth as a matter of belief, not evidence. If slavery's existence is both indubitable and unknowable, then the resulting contradiction is resolvable only by deciding in your heart what is true. Through this and other instances of strategic equivocation, a first object of new abolitionist representation is not truth per se, but a new, faith-based ground for truth.

It is important to note at the outset that multiple trafficking researchers have rejected anti-slavery activists' practice of extrapolating an epidemic of trafficking of giant proportions from relatively few survivors' testimonies and legal prosecutions of traffickers. A vocal counter-tide of anti-anti-trafficking critics have voiced scepticism

---

[10] New abolitionists consistently position modern slavery as either or both of two opposites. Slavery is hidden but takes place in plain sight; it is an ancient survival but differs in kind from the chattel slavery of old; its invariant core is one person stealing another's freedom (K Bales and Z Trodd (eds), *To Plead Our Own Cause: Personal Stories by Today's Slaves* (Ithaca, NY, Cornell University Press, 2008) 10), but it takes myriad forms worldwide, hence 'there is no magic bullet that will stop slavery in every country or village' (ibid 13).

[11] Post-truth politics is not the same thing as 'fake news'. It may involve fake news – such as the 'Pizzagate' rumour, according to which Hillary Clinton advisor John Podesta ran a child sex trafficking ring out of a Washington pizzeria (C Kang and S Frenkel, '"PizzaGate" Conspiracy Theory Thrives Anew in the TikTok Era' *New York Times* (28 June 2020) www.nytimes.com/2020/06/27/technology/pizzagate-justin-bieber-qanon-tiktok.html) – or be based on false suppositions – such as when British journalists jumped to the conclusion that 20 trafficking victims had been freed by a police raid on a massage parlour sex shop in the West Midlands, only for it later to emerge that none of the women had been held against her will (A Hill, 'How to Stage a Raid: Police, Media and the Master Narrative of Trafficking' (2016) 7 *Anti-Trafficking Review* 39). Even So, outright fabrications are exceptional in new abolitionist reporting. New abolitionists more often take a small and contradictory fact base – of a relative few, scattered prosecutions and survivor narratives – and on the basis of this anecdotal and narrative evidence extrapolate a major crisis of trafficking and other forms of slavery, in which tens or hundreds of thousands of desperate migrants or innocent or abused girls are lured into captive exploitation by bad men and women. Where fake news presents pure fabrications, then, post-truth merely spins the facts as far as they can go, matching scattered evidence with global accounts of wrongdoing in ways that confirm consumers' pre-existing beliefs, fears and anxieties.

about the shaky evidence behind estimates of slavery's prevalence, and questioned the law enforcement priorities sustained by the idea that slavery today is a 'hidden wrong'.[12] As anthropologist Annemarie Samuels summarises, '"human trafficking" has been constructed as a global concern in the face of a lack of verifiable data, with far reaching consequences for, among others, labor migration and sex workers' rights'.[13] 'The elephant in the room', writes Kay Warren, is that 'there are really no reliable or credible statistics on the number of people who are internationally trafficked'.[14] In spite of the promise that more reliable estimates are forthcoming, Warren's conclusion holds as true today as it did 10 years ago. Yet, even though I agree with anti-anti-trafficking experts about the unreliability of new abolitionist prevalence estimates, I fear they may be pursuing a political labour of Sisyphus when they point to facts to counter appeals that are not based on facts but on fears and intuitions. And the sceptics have missed a scholarly opportunity to try to figure out what, in spite of a shaky fact base, makes new abolitionist representations appealing. In their haste to wreak political destruction on their adversaries, anti-anti-trafficking sceptics have skipped an important effort of analytic deconstruction, failing to ask how a sense of urgency has rhetorically been built around modern slavery's alleged omnipresence, in spite of a lack of verifiable data.

Samuels contributes an insight of fundamental importance to my effort to explain why anti-trafficking has succeeded in gaining millions of believers in spite of questionable evidence. In seeking to explain why child trafficking rumours persisted in post-tsunami Aceh, Indonesia, in spite of such rumours being extremely rarely proven true, Samuels points to 'affective force': 'rather than being convictions or beliefs,

---

[12] DA Feingold, 'Trafficking in Numbers: The Social Construction of Trafficking Data' in P Andreas and KM Greenhill (eds), *Sex, Drugs, and Body Counts: The Politics of Numbers in Global Crime and Conflict* (Ithaca, NY, Cornell University Press, 2010); KB Warren, 'The Illusiveness of Counting "Victims" and the Concreteness of Ranking Countries: Trafficking in Persons from Colombia to Japan' in P Andreas and KM Greenhill (eds), *Sex, Drugs, and Body Counts: The Politics of Numbers in Global Crime and Conflict* (Ithaca, NY, Cornell University Press, 2010); R Weitzer, 'New Directions in Research on Human Trafficking' (2014) 653 *Annals of the American Academy of Political and Social Science* 6; S Yea, 'Editorial: The Politics of Evidence, Data and Research in Anti-trafficking Work' (2017) 8 *Anti-Trafficking Review* 1. Gender studies scholar Sallie Yea questions 'the growing potential for unsubstantiated claims to fulfil the place of rigorous evidence to inform anti-trafficking work' (ibid 1). Independent researcher, Alison Bass, writes 'As many researchers note with chagrin, there has yet to be a trustworthy count of victims trafficked to the United States or globally': A Bass, *Getting Screwed: Sex Workers and the Law* (Lebanon, ForeEdge, 2015) 90. She quotes criminologist Jay Albanese in saying 'When it comes to this crime, never has there been so much written on such little data … There is no good count. A worthy estimate is based on an underlying actual count and there has been no such count done for human trafficking' (90–91). Qualitatively distorting the trafficking picture, law enforcers and non-governmental activists are still said to give sex trafficking attention disproportionate to its prevalence: D Brennan, *Life Interrupted: Trafficking into Forced Labor in the United States* (Durham, NC, Duke University Press, 2014) 60–66; also, reporters are criticised for falsely equating all sex workers with trafficking victims: A Bloch, 'Discourses on Danger and Dreams of Prosperity: Confounding US Government Positions on "Trafficking" from the Former Soviet Union' in S Martínez (ed), *International Migration and Human Rights: The Global Repercussions of US Policy* (Berkeley, University of California Press, Global, Area, and International Archive, 2009) 11; J Doezema, *Sex Slaves and Discourse Masters: The Construction of Trafficking* (London, Zed Books, 2010); C Vance, 'Innocence and Experience: Melodramatic Narratives of Sex Trafficking and Their Consequences for Law and Policy' (2012) 2 *History of the Present* 200.

[13] A Samuels, 'Narratives of Uncertainty: The Affective Force of Child Trafficking Rumors in Postdisaster Aceh, Indonesia' (2015) 117 *American Anthropologist* 229, 233.

[14] Warren (n 12).

the child trafficking rumors resulted in haunting possibilities'.[15] Samuels calls this constellation of intuition, imagination and affect anti-trafficking's 'subjunctive mode', rooted in the logic that trafficking is never definitively 'untrue' but only ever 'unsubstantiated'.[16] 'To be in the subjunctive mode is', according to psychologist Jerome Bruner, 'to be trafficking in human possibilities rather than in settled certainties'.[17] I argue that Samuels's insight is true of the new abolitionism generally: in the new abolitionism's subjunctive ways of knowing, the claim that slaves are hidden all around us is believed or not on the basis of its affective force, rather than through rational, evidence-based arguments.

It helps heuristically, then, to distinguish two modes of exposition which are reflected in new abolitionist representation. One mode triggers emotions and builds empathy. Its favoured genres and media are testimonial and visual. Survivor narratives or investigators' stories evoke imaginings of what it might feel like to undergo captive exploitation or help trafficked people escape from captivity. Photographs and video – frequently involving staged poses and expressive blurring and cropping of the subject – enable website visitors to see authentic faux scenes of subjection while also simulating the hiddenness of these scenes. These narrative and visual representational devices add up to a *subjunctive mode of exposition*, which aims to activate fears of unseen danger and promote feelings of personal identification with sufferers and rescuers. The second mode of exposition is *didactic* – presenting definitions of slavery, historical overviews and sociological generalisations – and *evidentiary* – consisting of maps and prevalence estimates. Its aim is to persuade the public and policy-makers alike that there are instances of exploitation today that are coercive enough to be called 'slavery', and that these cases may in fact be very common. 'May in fact' is all that need be established. New abolitionists do not have to prove their case beyond doubt. All they need to do is persuade the public and policy-makers that slavery today is real and that it *may in fact* be widespread. Even if its prevalence is tiny, few people could in good conscience feel indifferent to a crime so heinous, much less if 'reliable estimates' indicate that the problem may be large.

In the actual minds of social justice consumers, then, as opposed to the sceptical minds of social researchers, a scarcity of evidence may give momentary pause. For many, however, those doubts last only long enough for them to feel it even more deeply when they reach the epiphany of believing that slaves may in fact be hidden all around. Sex worker rights advocates deride the stories that anti-trafficking activists tell as primary colour fables of the rescue of innocents.[18] Yet these critics of anti-trafficking may have generally underestimated the complexity of the emotions triggered by new abolitionist appeals. It is not just the mix of emotions – of indignation about coerced exploitation, of suspense about how the story will turn out and of identification with the enslaved as a blameless person in whose shoes audience members can imagine themselves to stand. Overtopping the pile-up of emotional states is

---

[15] Samuels (n 13) 236.
[16] ibid 234.
[17] J Bruner, *Actual Minds, Possible Worlds* (Cambridge, MA, Harvard University Press, 1986) 26.
[18] W Chapkis, 'Trafficking, Migration, and the Law: Protecting Innocents, Punishing Immigrants' (2003) 17 *Gender and Society* 923; Vance (n 12).

the literary/dramatic allure of deciphering the unknowable, of grappling mentally with the simultaneous possibility, impossibility and necessity of visualising unfree labour today. New abolitionist reporting draws the mind's eye to the *possibility* of seeing coerced exploitation. Stories of the hunt for today's slaves evoke the purported extreme difficulty, verging on *impossibility*, of actually finding today's slaves. And, more compellingly than libraries full of social research, the intuition that the global economy has broken dangerously free from any moral strictures confirms the *necessity* of trying to find hidden sufferers.

I. THE VANISHING POINT

The common practice of juxtaposing prevalence estimates with personal narratives tacitly positions the survivor's story as one instance of a much larger problem. For example, the International Justice Mission (IJM) website recounts the story 'of a brave girl named Kim' (Figure 8.2).[19] This story of the rescue of an underage Filipina sex worker begins with a narrative of entrapment. A kind neighbour, AJ, inveigles himself into Kim's life, paying for her schooling out of seeming benevolence, until he betrays Kim's trust through an act of sexual exploitation. AJ's abuse escalates as he poses Kim naked in front of a webcam and subjects her to sexual abuse. This very brief narrative culminates with Kim's rescue and AJ's arrest.

Figure 8.2 International Justice Mission, 'Nothing Seemed Wrong at First. But Everything Was About to Change'

The story of Kim is representative of the larger domain of anti-trafficking representation not just because it is a morally simple narrative, pitting innocence against evil,[20] but also because suspense tales like it serve as the launchpad for persuading the website

---

[19] International Justice Mission, 'Nothing Seemed Wrong at First. But Everything Was About to Change', https://web.archive.org/web/20190301171953/https://www.ijm.org/stories/kim.
[20] Vance (n 12).

visitor that modern slavery is real, horrible and hidden all around them. Almost always, depictions of the crime of modern slavery start with survivor narratives or rescue stories, rather than with definitions of slavery or estimates of its prevalence. The very structure of new abolitionist reporting thus evinces the primacy of subjunctive evocation over didactic/evidentiary exposition. Whether written by activists or journalists, reports on trafficking and slavery never begin with a distanced, didactic view, grounded in statistics, global histories and typologies of modern slavery; they open instead by 'recruiting the reader's imagination'[21] into the sufferer's world through the story of one person's entrapment and escape. At the heart of the personal narrative's appeal is suspense and uncertainty, not closure and knowledge. Personal narratives touch readers' hearts not just because these concern individuals about whom we can care, but because they are stories. 'Concern about how the story might turn out'[22] grabs readers' interest better than evidence-based arguments. Starting with survivor narratives before segueing into numerical estimates, expositions of the reality of modern slavery and human trafficking appeal first to the 'night mind'[23] of the imagination – attuned to what dangers might be out there 'in the dark' – and only later speak to the 'day mind' of evidence-based arguments – seeking to establish that the wrongs are real and prevalent, and fit the paradigm of modern slavery.

A prevalence estimate enters near the end as denouement to Kim's story: 'Kim is one of thousands of children being exploited online today in the Philippines because people like AJ have absolutely no fear of being held accountable for their crimes.'[24] 'Thousands': whether the geographic scale is national or global, personal narratives often appear side by side with 'view from 30,000 feet' offered by imprecise estimates of this kind. The prevalence estimate is not a thing known with any certainty; it is unknown or at best not yet substantiated, a quantity that can only be guessed at and is quite possibly unknowable. Knowing for sure how many Filipina children are being exploited matters less than knowing that thousands *might possibly* be being exploited like Kim. 'Thousands' might therefore be called a 'subjunctive number', a figure that stands in plausibly for the value we would be likely to find if we could know.

Subjunctive ways of knowing are rooted in fears of what might be, while didactic/evidentiary ways of knowing speak to what is happening and where, and what must be done about it. Numbers in this scheme lead a seemingly paradoxical double rhetorical life: they must look like facts, but must also bolster the idea that we must act even though we cannot know how prevalent slavery is. Placement is key: entering at the point in the text where subjunctive evocation segues into didactic/evidentiary exposition, prevalence estimates bear an almost palpable structural weight, as textual hinges that open and close the door between the potential visibility and knowability of slavery today and the purported actual invisibility and unknowability of the crime. Some time ago, Warren observed that new abolitionist prevalence estimates might

---

[21] Bruner (n 17) 25.
[22] BJ Good, *Medicine, Rationality, and Experience: An Anthropological Perspective* (Cambridge, Cambridge University Press, 1994) 153.
[23] J Haidt, *The Righteous Mind: Why Good People Are Divided by Politics and Religion* (New York, Pantheon Books, 2012).
[24] International Justice Mission (n 19).

be ambiguous,²⁵ capable of either aggravating doubt or relieving it. She remarked on the juxtaposition of ranking – 'a rigorous evidence-based process' – with victim stories and images – 'designed to stir up moral outrage' – and how, ironically, 'the often demeaned subjective and anecdotal evidence is, in effect, shoring up a numerical edifice with uncertain foundations'. These numbers both look like evidence and permit plausible deniability of their accuracy, as is confirmed by new abolitionists' frequent disclaimer that better prevalence estimates are needed and will soon be available. Quantification in new abolitionist representation keeps the door open for doubt while also looking like fact.

In unpacking this problem of quantification as rhetoric through literary and imagetextual techniques of close reading, I take help from an unexpected quarter: Karl Ove Knausgaard's essay, 'Vanishing Point', published in 2015 in *The New Yorker*.²⁶ Knausgaard ruminates on the feelings triggered globally by the now iconic photograph of the body of Alan Kurdi, a tiny Syrian refugee boy found washed up dead on a Turkish beach. He identifies this photograph's emergence into global awareness as a rare occasion in which media coverage of the Syria crisis shed its emotional remoteness in favour of something particular, singular and unique. The photograph forced upon its viewers the realisation that not just masses, but *people*, were dying. 'While this insight may be banal', says Knausgaard, 'its repercussions are not'. He adds:

> In our humanity, there is a vanishing point. We step in and out of it; it's a kind of zone in which we shift each other's perspective from definite to indefinite, and vice versa. The vanishing point has to do with remoteness and is inevitable. The indefinite human, faceless and devoid of character, the mass human lives its life in patterns by which it is bound and is the material of statistics. But this point is also the locus for the opposite movement, in which the other goes from indefinite to definite – and if there is an ethics of the novel, then it is here, in the zone that lies between the *one* and the *all*, that it comes into force and takes its basis. The instant a novel is opened and a reader begins to read, the remoteness between writer and reader dissolves.²⁷

The relationship between fiction and social justice mobilisation, to which Knausgaard points, is not the direction I want to go. What fascinates me rather is the concept of the vanishing point itself – the zone that lies between the *one* and the *all*. Vanishing points include (but, as I explain, are not limited to) the textual hinge points where the individual gives way to the mass, narrative yields to statistics, and subjunctive ways of knowing segue into didactic/evidentiary exposition. I disagree with Knausgaard that the novel uniquely possesses the power to allow readers to cross such boundaries. On the contrary, vanishing points are crossed and re-crossed so often in journalistic reporting and social justice appeals that they constitute a standard, if generally unnoticed, device within the expository toolkit used by non-fiction writers and filmmakers. The concept of the vanishing point is of interest to me, then, not because Knausgaard has pinpointed something distinctive about fiction, but because he has

---

²⁵ Warren (n 12) 112.
²⁶ KO Knausgaard, 'Vanishing Point', speech delivered for the Welt Literaturpreis at the Axel-Springer-Haus on 6 November 2015) *The New Yorker* (Berlin, 17 November 2015) www.newyorker.com/books/page-turner/vanishing-point.
²⁷ ibid.

given us a term with which to talk about something that is much more widely prevalent and yet mysterious. Do we know what effects are triggered when we cross textual frontiers between feeling and knowing, even when we fail to notice it when we cross them? And why, in the anti-trafficking literature specifically, does quantification often enter just at the point where subjunctive ways of knowing – such as the personal narrative of a survivor or a rescuer – segue into a didactic/evidentiary mode of exposition?

The prevalence estimate is made not just informative, but expressive, when it comes directly after a story like Kim's. Some of the affective force of the survivor's nightmarish account lingers; the empathy it arouses and the mystery it conjures cling to the number. Read in context, then, the prevalence estimate is not just a best guess at the problem's dimensions; it is also a plea that we *need to know more*. The conclusion – that all the children who are suffering as Kim suffered must be found and rescued – fits perfectly with the IJM's preferred method of fighting trafficking through rescue missions carried out in coordination with local law enforcers. The transition from one human (Kim) to vaguely defined humanity ('thousands') is a vanishing point, through which 'we shift each other's perspective from definite to indefinite'.[28] Upon this vanishing point, the IJM stakes the credibility and persuasiveness of its appeal to the public for support. To achieve that aim, there is no need to say exactly how many Filipina girls are being trafficked online. It only matters that there may in fact be many.

In chapters five and six of *The Seductions of Quantification*, Sally Merry anticipates how the impersonal number often intertwines with personal narratives.[29] She describes, for example, how, in 2000, the Trafficking Victims Protection Act was pitched to members of the US Congress through 'horror stories about the treatment of victims … combined with huge estimates of the number of victims'.[30] In like manner, Merry writes about the distortions inherent in making the face of trafficking 'a young girl, usually poor and brown, who has been kidnapped and passed from hand to hand until she ends up in a brothel in a large city'.[31] Merry was not the first to draw attention to the frequent juxtaposition of personal narratives with prevalence estimates in the anti-trafficking literature. She does plot new analytic ground, however, when she adds that we need to go beyond questioning the reliability of the numbers to consider also the knowledge effects of quantification. It matters whether the numbers are reliable or not, but it may matter even more whether the numbers are *believed* or not. How is it that unbelievable numbers get believed by some, and may recruit even people who do not believe to support government action against trafficking and slavery?

II. ADD PICTURES AND STIR

Where do icons, indexes and prevalence estimates go, once they come to life? After shedding their wordy chrysalises of origin, how do they move about and shift shape? Often, they become pictures. When levels of compliance with human rights norms are

---

[28] ibid.
[29] Merry, *The Seductions of Quantification* (n 5).
[30] ibid 120.
[31] ibid 115.

turned into a global ranking, for example, it enables the creation of a colour-coded world map, such as that through which the Walk Free Foundation shows the country-by-country prevalence of modern slavery around the world (Figure 8.3).³²

Figure 8.3 Walk Free Foundation, *Global Slavery Index 2018*

Based on the Foundation's *Global Slavery Index* (*GSI*), a worst-to-best ranking of the world's countries according to the estimated prevalence of modern slavery in each, this global map executes multiple transformations and shifts in audience and meaning. Information that had been sequestered in wordy reports becomes the basis for a striking image. Matters previously understandable only to regional area experts are now opened for discussion by policy-makers with no special knowledge of particular crises of, say, child labour in Haiti or sex trafficking in Thailand. A 'sociological shortcut' is created by the pretence that the darkest ochre 'hot spots' of modern slavery on the *GSI* map may be targeted for intervention of special intensity, without it being necessary for policy-makers to learn the particular aetiologies of unfreedom in those places.³³ The map also congeals features of today's anti-slavery ideology in ways that make these seem like matters of fact: for example, slavery happens particularly often in those lesser-developed countries, like Haiti or Thailand, where unfree workers are born, but not very much in those places, like France or the USA, to which they may travel.³⁴ The map shows this. Above all else, however, the colour-coded world map conveys the meta-message that the consumer of new abolitionist reporting

---

³² Walk Free Foundation, *Global Slavery Index 2018*, www.walkfree.org/global-slavery-index/map/.
³³ Cultural anthropologist Ann Stoler coins the term 'sociological shorthands' to describe how the Dutch colonial overlords of Indonesia reduced the cognitive expense of governing by lessening 'how much of certain kinds of information one need[s] to operate and how much one need[s] to know': AL Stoler, *Carnal Knowledge and Imperial Power: Race and the Intimate in Colonial Rule* (Berkeley, University of California Press, 2002) 207. Classifying colonial subjects as discrete human types – slave, proletarian or yeoman – enabled colonial governors to govern with less effort and greater self-assurance. Classifying humanity thus enabled weighty tasks of governance to be done more lightly, by making disciplinary or pastoral intervention seem reasonable on the basis of little more than categorising what kind of humans those others were.
³⁴ Built into the map thus is the dominant narrative that blames trafficking not on Western government policies, but on the tragic meeting up of ruthless traffickers with gullible migrants. The *Global Slavery*

must accept a mixed message: slavery is mostly invisible, but it can nevertheless be estimated reliably enough to be projected onto a world map.

Much the same can be said of all-new abolitionist image-making: slavery winks in and out of visibility in a dramatically alluring play of the ostensibly known and the purportedly unknowable. Photographs on the websites of the leading new abolitionist organisations do this, too. On one hand, these organisations, varied in tone and approach as they are, all sustain an overt commitment to factual reality. They are *not* peddling sensationalist fables, or at least not overtly so. The action-suspense thriller *Taken* or the second season of the television police drama *The Wire* have no doubt had a greater public impact than the Polaris Project's website, but these entertainment products were not made to portray reality. New abolitionist organisations assert that the information on their websites contrasts with Hollywood fiction through their fundamental commitment to 'the real'.[35] Yet even this commitment is tacitly subject to strategic equivocation. While maintaining that the things they represent are real, new abolitionists are not too picky about the techniques through which they create illusions of the real. When compared to other human rights issue leaders, it is remarkable how frequently and prominently the world's leading anti-slavery organisations feature obviously staged photographs on their websites (with the notable exception of Free the Slaves, which seems to use no obvious re-enactments on its website).

Worries about the 'pornification' of the movement's public imagery – as voiced, for example, by Mariah Long, Program Manager of End Slavery Now[36] – seem to have had an effect. Voyeuristic images of scantily clad women, sitting in cheap motel rooms or bent over in conversation with unseen motorists on the street, are less often displayed on new abolitionist websites than they once were. Yet, particularly often in campaigns against sex slavery, depictions of scenes of subjection gain ocular magnetism through photographs evoking fantasies of violated innocence. A staged photograph[37] in Anti-Slavery International's 'Protect, Not Neglect' campaign of early 2019 shows a slender young woman in tight jeans sitting in a foetal tuck in the corner of a room, next to a rumpled bed (Figure 8.4).

Index counts any particular country's nationals against its estimates of slavery's presence in that country, regardless of where it is they actually experience coerced exploitation: S McGrath and S Watson 'Anti-slavery as Development: A Global Politics of Rescue' (2018) 93 *Geoforum* 22, 26. Similarly, the US Department of State's *Trafficking in Persons Report* conceptualises trafficking as a 'risk' within global supply chains for corporations and consumers but avoids saying any Western actors are responsible for it. Rather, it includes only traffickers, pimps and brothel owners, armed rebel groups and the corrupt governments of Tier 3 states among those who are to be blamed for profiting from trafficking (ibid 28).

[35] On its 'Human Trafficking Myths and Facts' page, the Polaris Project distances its vision of trafficking from sensationalist media, warning that 'Human trafficking Hollywood-style looks a lot like kidnapping. The reality is much more complicated': Polaris, 'Human Trafficking Myths and Facts', https://web.archive.org/web/20191008164527/https://polarisproject.org/human-trafficking-myths-and-facts..

[36] M Long, 'Visual Stereotypes for Human Trafficking' (End Slavery Now, 22 October 2015) https://web.archive.org/web/20180721050116/www.endslaverynow.org/blog/articles/visual-stereotypes-for-human-trafficking.

[37] Anti-Slavery International, 'Protect, Not Neglect', https://web.archive.org/web/20190226120912/www.anti-slavery.org/take-action/campaigns/protect-not-neglect/.

Figure 8.4 Anti-Slavery International, 'Protect, Not Neglect Campaign' homepage

This abject portrait places emphasis on the moral purity of its subject: face hidden, cowering in shame or fear, she is seemingly powerless to resist. The photograph also triggers the imagination by freezing time at a moment of maximum dramatic impact: the young woman appears to be having an emotional breakdown, perhaps after being raped or following the realisation that she has been entrapped.

Staging photographs permits new abolitionist organisations to deploy noir visual aesthetics to show what slavery looks like today whilst simulating its hiddenness. The conceit seems to be that, because modern slavery is incontestably real, it is OK to fake it visually. That angle is consistent with the new abolitionism's thoroughgoing pattern of have-it-both-ways representation. Through staging scenes of subjection, new abolitionists are saying 'this is what it would look like if you could see it'. The first and surest thing that the use of re-enactment establishes, then, is that the wrongs are seeable but hidden, thus positioning adherence to the anti-slavery cause as a matter of belief, not evidence. The staged photograph is evidence of things not seen, the sole indicator of whose truth is what the public is ready to believe.

The same thing holds true of the knowledge effects of quantification for the new abolitionism: the numbers establish that the truth is to be determined by faith, not facts. Where the photographs say 'this is what it might look like if you could see it', the numbers say 'this is how big it might be if you could count it'. Into the expository slot where evidence should go are inserted estimates, often so obviously uncertain that some will think these actually *undercut* the case for a global slavery epidemic. Even new abolitionists vary in the level of confidence they claim for prevalence estimates. Some signal tacit recognition that these are numbers to be doubted, by saying that better enumeration methods are needed or that new and better estimates are on their way. Others say that prevalence estimates almost surely underestimate the prevalence of slavery, being based on incomplete case data, which is logically analogous to their contention that a lack of evidence is evidence of the hiddenness of the crime.

Along with the segue from a personal story into a prevalence estimate, then, a second kind of vanishing point is created through the overlap of text and staged photography. At moments, the vanishing point is crossed not by moving through a text, but by plumbing the layers of a single imagetext. Figure 8.5 is a link to the banner image on the Polaris Project's 2019 Webpage on 'human trafficking'.[38] This image and its accompanying text convey a mixed message. The words and numbers speak with certainty – they declare, describe and quantify what human trafficking is:

> *What human trafficking is … and isn't*
>
> Human trafficking is the business of stealing freedom for profit. In some cases, traffickers trick, defraud or physically force victims into providing commercial sex. In others, victims are lied to, assaulted, threatened or manipulated into working under inhumane, illegal or otherwise unacceptable conditions. It is a multi-billion dollar criminal industry that denies freedom to 24.9 million people around the world.

Nothing about this text is ambiguous or equivocal. It provides a succinct paradigm: trafficking is the business of stealing people's freedom. It says how trafficking most often happens: through force or fraud. And it quantifies the problem with no hint of uncertainty, in both monetary and demographic terms, albeit through estimates that carry long tails of zeros.

Figure 8.5 Polaris Project, 'Human Trafficking'

But look at the photograph upon which this text is superimposed: subliminally, it evokes a different story. It shows the head and shoulders of an attractive, young white woman with long, wind-tousled straight hair, seen as if through an opaque screen. A vanishing point is traversed here not processually, by moving through a text, but through the superposition of a text, which constructs a mass of humanity, onto a photograph, which tacitly situates the particular human as the site of salvific intervention. The partially obstructed visibility of the figure contrasts with the words' clarity, evoking the shadows in which trafficking is said to thrive. Text and image together confirm that while human trafficking is widely prevalent, it is also a hidden

---

[38] Polaris, 'Human Trafficking', https://web.archive.org/web/20190218143605/https:/polarisproject.org/human-trafficking.

wrong, which will likely go unperceived and unreported. The text bids us to act even as the picture tacitly warns that we might not be able to recognise trafficked persons or know where they are to be found. By merging a voice of clarity and certainty with an image of occlusion and uncertainty, this webpage from one of the world's oldest and best networked anti-trafficking organisations conveys something fundamental about the new abolitionism: its pervasive have-it-both-ways approach to knowledge. Seeing that it is impossible to banish doubt, new abolitionists at times artfully highlight it. New abolitionist websites periodically evoke uncertainty through words and images foregrounding the unknown and perhaps unknowable dimensions of slavery today, only to cajole readers to ignore their doubts and act in spite of not knowing where, how or against what.

III. BEYOND THE VANISHING POINT

Particular analytic significance attaches to the hinges in the text. Persuasive work takes place not just through imagetext – compelling conjunctures of words and pictures – but through vanishing points, the points at which the definite, singular human, endowed with a story that matters and about whom we can care, gives way to the 'mass human' of patterns and statistics.[39] Vanishing points are far from being the special concern of authors of serious artistic intent. They are, rather, so ubiquitous a feature of social justice reporting that few consumers probably notice them any longer when they pass through them, and fewer still pause to wonder why they are there. To me, it is not at all obvious that vanishing points are necessary, at least not as they are conventionally constructed, as shifts from singular narratives to mass statistics. Are there expository alternatives to these familiar yet abrupt transitions in perspective? And, if alternative ways might be found of assessing the contours and causes of unfree labour, then why do new abolitionists seem to prefer vanishing points over other forms of evidence and analysis?

Familiar as they may be, it bears remembering that vanishing points are expository constructs and not the products of unavoidable gaps in knowledge. A choice has to be made to superimpose definitions and enumerations of modern slavery on to the image of a beautiful young woman's face, and to screen that face from clear view through creative photographic treatment. A decision has to be taken to follow a survivor's story with the information that thousands are being exploited in the same intolerable way. A photo shoot has to be organised once it is decided that a staged photograph will illustrate the sexual exploitation of unknown numbers of minors. It is not *ipso facto* wrong or deceptive to aestheticise coerced exploitation or spike the effectiveness of a text through photography. I am arguing not against pictures, but in favour of being attentive to the visual contexts in which rankings, icons and prevalence estimates often make their entry. Quantification is already seductive in its simplicity, but it may be made doubly seductive when paired with verbal and visual devices of storytelling and photography.

---

[39] Knausgaard, 'Vanishing point' (n 26).

In another possible world, information of other kinds might go where new abolitionists now provide prevalence estimates. Detailed qualitative studies, to quote Merry, would be 'essential for understanding trafficking in all its variation and complexity'.[40] Outside the exceptional case of actual captive exploitation, qualitative case studies could provide deeper understanding of trafficking and modern slavery. Unlike prevalence estimates, which say nothing other than that the problem is big, qualitative studies can inform policy-makers and concerned global citizens in what ways workers' freedoms are being constrained and how workers are resisting these constraints. On the basis of case-specific information, clearer indicators of unfreedom could be identified, surer information could be shared with concerned global citizens about their complicity and policy-makers could take into consideration priorities defined by workers themselves. The new abolitionism could clearly do more to promote context-specific methods for generating policy-relevant information.

Instead, new abolitionists are not just sticking with prevalence estimates, but doubling down on their importance, committing ever increasing investigative resources to the search for the epistemological unicorn of the reliable estimate. It is said, for example, that the creation of the *GSI* was the product of advice that Bill Gates gave to fellow billionaire philanthropist Andrew Forrest: 'if you can't measure it, it doesn't exist'.[41] After more than a decade of pointed criticism of the failure of gross quantification and country-ranking efforts, it may seem surprising that ranking countries on the basis of slavery's estimated prevalence should have been chosen as the focus for one of the major anti-slavery interventions of the last decade. Forrest can hardly be blamed, however, if new abolitionists doggedly hold out hope that better estimates are forthcoming and that these will place anti-slavery efforts at last on a solid evidentiary footing. Every time it is repeated that more reliable estimates will soon make anti-slavery breakthroughs possible, an implicit message is sent that other forms of information-gathering are impossible. Giving pride of place to prevalence estimates makes it appear that they are our only guide for action. If quantification is productive, then the first thing it produces for the new abolition may not be false certainty so much as ignorance and its jaundiced acceptance. In the now-it's-one-thing-then-it's-the-opposite world view of new abolitionist representation, the big round numbers of prevalence estimates will soon prove slavery is a ubiquitous presence in our world; until then, trusting untrustworthy estimates will be the inevitable, natural basis of anti-slavery activism. Providing ersatz evidence in a subjunctive but 'truthy' style, prevalence estimates are a numerical sideshow to the shadow plays staged by new abolitionists when they ask us to imagine the realities of coerced exploitation through dimly lit photographs of partially occluded, abject sufferers. The estimates and the photographs both ask us to accept that the truth of modern slavery is both evident and unknown – and, possibly, unknowable.

Paradoxically, the referential emptiness of numbers, whether reliable or not, may increase rather than diminish the confidence with which new abolitionists can act.

---

[40] Merry, *The Seductions of Quantification* (n 5) 116.
[41] E Behrmann, 'Gates Helps Australia's Richest Man in Bid to End Slavery' (*Bloomberg*, 14 April 2013) www.bloomberg.com/news/articles/2013-04-10/gates-helps-australia-s-richest-man-in-bid-to-end-slavery.

By sticking to prevalence estimates, activists avoid the messiness and ambiguity that ethnographic evidence might introduce into discussions of what modern slavery is and how to counteract it. Ignorance permits action in ways that knowledge might hinder. If you give no systematically gathered and sociologically valid information about how labour discipline is exacted in any particular kind of workplace, for example, then you give sceptical outsiders no basis on which to question whether the survivor narrative you chose to lead with is a common scenario. Sticking with simple estimates above all minimises the chance of making the inconvenient finding that captive exploitation is rare in any particular community or workplace. Far fewer workers may be held captive than are entrapped within the complex intersections of multiple oppressions. Being empty and being uncertain are thus paradoxically both forms of ignorance that yield the political dividend of confirming simple narratives – slavery today is captivity, anti-slavery is rescue – and affirming straightforward and invariant salvific interventions. And stories and images that say slavery is a hidden wrong confirm tacitly that it is to be combated by anti-trafficking organisations and the police – outsiders, for whom oppression is hard to see – rather than by members of the afflicted communities – insiders, for whom exploitation is impossible to ignore.

Sticking to simple narratives and empty numbers, then, avoids sticky questions about who is best positioned to lead the anti-slavery struggle. Does the very idea that modern slavery is 'hard to see' not assume an external (white? Bourgeois?) change agent, who has the privilege of either seeing unfreedom or ignoring it? The movement's dependence on speculation and equivocation and the bourgeois position of its presumptive agents of change are two points on the same representational clock face, at the centre of which stands a pro-policing bias. A central place for law enforcement must be locked in, for without it, new abolitionists' long-time alliance with prostitution abolitionists would fall apart.[42] The entire movement arose from anti-prostitution roots in the 1990s, and the legal suppression of sex work through policing and prosecution has remained non-negotiable ever since. Without it, both the Evangelical right and anti-prostitution feminists would be lost to the movement. Seeing the police as the solution, rather than the problem, has been called 'carceral feminism',[43] 'carceral protectionism'[44] and 'governance feminism'[45] by long-term scholars/critics. In the abolition-through-law-enforcement scheme, unauthorised migrants, Blacks, sex workers and anyone else who cannot easily look to the police as saviours are welcome

---

[42] The story of the conflicts exposed in the drafting of the Palermo Protocol is well known: M Ditmore and M Wijers 'The Negotiations on the UN Protocol on Trafficking in Persons' (2003) 4 *Nemesis* 79. So, too, is that of the coalition forged between Evangelical Christians and anti-porn feminists around the aim of making the suppression of sexual commerce the main focus of anti-trafficking: G Soderlund 'Running from the Rescuers: New US Crusades against Sex Trafficking and the Rhetoric of Abolition' (2005) 17 *NWSA Journal* 64. Anti-trafficking started as prostitution abolitionism, broadened to encompass labour trafficking, then grew broader still by fusing with anti-slavery activism to become the new abolitionism.

[43] E Bernstein, *Brokered Subjects: Sex, Trafficking and the Politics of Freedom* (Chicago, University of Chicago Press, 2018).

[44] J Musto, *Control and Protect: Collaboration, Carceral Protection, and Domestic Sex Trafficking in the United States* (Berkeley, University of California Press, 2016).

[45] SE Merry and V Rachmachandran, 'The Limits of Consent: Sex Trafficking and the Problem of International Paternalism' in MN Barnett (ed), *Paternalism beyond Borders* (Cambridge, Cambridge University Press, 2016).

to conform to established rescue-and-rehabilitation scripts but are not welcome to add their own, decriminalisation and police-abolitionist perspectives. It bears emphasising here that critical race theorists are asking whether ramping up punishments and policing explains racial disparities in trafficking arrests and imprisonment similar to those produced by the war on drugs.[46] Seen in this light, the new abolitionism not only battens on deeply ingrained paternalist and imperialist habits of thought; it also enforces what legal scholar Jonathan Todres[47] calls an 'intersectional othering', operating across dimensions of race, gender, class, culture and nationality, which gives poor women of colour 'little or no voice in shaping the dominant understanding of human trafficking or appropriate remedies to the problem'.

IV. CONCLUSION

At issue, then, are not just dubious numbers and the dubious methods by which they are made, but also the rhetorical devices through which dubious numbers are made believable or, at least, believed enough to warrant action. A first, especially important, point is that the seduction of quantification in the new abolitionist field happens not just through numbers' false concreteness and specious certainty, but through image-textual amalgamations of prevalence estimates with personal narratives, didactic text and evocative photography. Prevalence estimates gain in persuasive power when they are juxtaposed with photographs and personal narratives. In more general terms, then, 'imagetext' is a key concept for researchers who seek to move beyond positioning themselves as either for or against anti-trafficking and go on to consider also the verbal and visual rhetorics through which new abolitionists seek to persuade people that human trafficking is a widely prevalent but hidden crime.

The knowledge effect that interests me most is how estimates create not just false certainty, but also a mood in which not knowing looks like a reason to act rather than a reason to hesitate. Rather than always and only seeking to impose an illusion of certainty onto things unknown, new abolitionists frequently refer to or allude to doubt, or conjure slavery's hiddenness and unknowability through creatively staged photographs and emotive narratives. Doubt about slavery's existence and prevalence is not simply suppressed, then, but is evoked in order to be suppressed, and then incited and suppressed again, doubt surfacing and submerging repeatedly in a never-ending discursive cycle. The objective seems to be to prepare the consumer of social justice reporting to tolerate doubt while also concluding that decisive action is necessary. One diagnostic of post-truth politics is the resulting motivated determination to have it both ways, not just equivocating on the reliability of estimates, but sustaining opposing ideas, at times even simultaneously, on every debatable point. New slavery is thus old yet new, hidden yet plainly visible, invariant yet diverse and enforced through

---

[46] LP Beutin, 'Black Suffering for/from Anti-trafficking Advocacy' (2017) 9 *Anti-Trafficking Review*, 14; J Phillips 'Black Girls and the (Im)possibilities of a Victim Trope: The Intersectional Failures of Legal and Advocacy Interventions in the Commercial Sexual Exploitation of Minors in the United States' (2015) 62 *UCLA Law Review* 1642.

[47] J Todres 'Law, Otherness, and Human Trafficking' (2009) 49 *Santa Clara Law Review*, 605, 609.

violence yet filled with willing recruits. New abolitionists say they combat all forms of coerced exploitation today while also, in practice, remaining obsessed with sex trafficking. Above all, slavery today is irrefutably real yet also an object of mystery, the whos, whys, hows and wheres of it being hidden and, hence, possibly unknowable. New abolitionists thus do not just tacitly concede that doubts are inevitable; they actually build their expositions around doubt, at times through beguiling techniques of simulated realness and visible hiddenness.

Hand in glove with this is a second diagnostic feature of post-truth politics: the basis of the appeal is not evidentiary but intuitive, moral and affective – you either believe it or you do not, which is the same as saying you either *feel* it or you do not. Once the ground of politics has been established as faith rather than fact, demonstrating the truth through facts becomes merely demonstrative: new abolitionist reporting and public appeals still have parts that look evidentiary, but this is a false front. Conventional rhetorical expectations – that you supply the public and policy-makers with definitions, numbers, mappings and other information – are thus satisfied, even as the need for evidence is sidestepped. There is no demand for accuracy if the fundamental condition, established through the repeated evocation and suppression of doubt, is that the decision to respond or not is a matter of faith and not evidence.

On the surface, this idea contradicts what Merry calls the 'magic' of numbers: 'their ability to create certainty in spaces of great ambiguity'.[48] One sign of the magic of numbers is that they can break free of their original source or data collection method and gain credibility through a kind of textual laundering, in which estimates are scrubbed of the uncertainty with which they were hedged about by their authors in their original source texts and then take on an aura of authoritative expert knowledge after being cited as fact in other reports. Most famously, Kevin Bales framed his estimate of 27 million slaves worldwide in *Disposable People* as an inexact first guess, but this number has since travelled the world and become not just 'fact', but almost an icon of the global movement to fight all intolerable deprivations of human freedom worldwide as 'slavery'.[49] I have seen evidence of the magic of numbers in my own teaching. I once asked students in my 'Migration' class at the University of Connecticut to identify the one thing that came to their minds first after watching a television documentary on human trafficking: the thing my students most often remembered was not the wrenching details of entrapment, threats and humiliation told by survivors, but the film's estimate that human trafficking was a $6 billion annual industry. These numbers seem to have a well-nigh magical, autonomous power to persuade. Maybe the question is whether numbers can be not only strong and autonomous, but also weak and needy, dependent on stories, maps and photographs to win credibility. My sense of it is that prevalence estimates can be both: they can look like facts while also confirming that the truth is elusive, thereby throwing resolution of what is truth or falsehood onto the audience rather than the activist, and affirming that truth is a matter better resolved through intuition rather than research.

---

[48] Merry, *The Seductions of Quantification* (n 5) 127.
[49] K Bales, *Disposable People: New Slavery in the Global Economy*, revised edn (Berkeley, University of California Press, 2004).

This argument that trafficking prevalence estimates can function as either evidence or 'subjunctive numbers' – which you either believe or do not believe – or can even be both, cannot make sense from the standpoint of evidence-based reasoning. It can look plausible only if the analyst adopts a critical vocabulary of feeling, rooted in literary and visual culture studies. Even as experts in human rights studies have welcomed humanities scholarship, some may balk at applying techniques of deconstruction to human rights reporting as well as to literature or cinema. Some also will find it hard to accept that claims that are neither proven nor disproven but merely unsubstantiated may be as persuasive in human rights as objective facts. But if you accept the possibility that new abolitionist reporting persuades through pictures and stories as much as through numbers and other forms of evidence, then other, humanities-based analytic methods may be called for to understand the workings of these subliminal persuaders. Specifically, my view that today's anti-slavery is discursively at war against itself will look like nonsense from the standpoint of social research standards of evidence. Yet, if you analyse activist websites through the style of close reading that a student of literature or cinema might apply to canonical texts or movies, then different and more permissive conclusions might emerge. If new abolitionists favour shadows over light, put conjecture over facts and more generally sustain a series of mutually contradictory characterisations of modern slavery, might that not, from a literary critical standpoint, seem more like a plausibly lifelike complexity than a disabling logical flaw? Is it not often through sloppy thinking and cognitive shortcuts that humans come to terms with and seek to uncover how the world holds its secrets? And is the unravelling of mysteries not the very stuff of drama and literature?

Whether or not a reader finds my approach convincing, Sally Merry has helped me get here, by prompting us all not just to question the reliability of numbers, but also to examine their knowledge effects. This chapter signals in its broadest sense that these effects may be more complex than even Merry has yet found terms for. Intuitions and emotions, photography, personal stories and vanishing-point devices may amplify the seductions of quantification. In addition to assertions of certainty, tacit appeals to accept not knowing may also be in play as the public and policy-makers are asked to support legal measures aimed at abolishing trafficking and slavery. More unexpected twists may yet lay in wait as more scholars seek to untangle the ways in which quantification seduces. Yet it will always stand beyond doubt that this road doubles back to Sally Merry's fundamental analyses of the seductions of quantification.

9

The Competitive Pressures of Rankings: Experimental Evidence of Rankings' Influence on Domestic Priorities

RUSH DOSHI, JUDITH KELLEY AND BETH A SIMMONS

The use of indicators in global governance has the potential to alter the forms, the exercise, and perhaps even the distributions of power in certain spheres of governance.[1]

I. INTRODUCTION

INDICATORS HAVE BECOME an important part of the international information landscape. Numbers are used to measure every aspect of political output and economic performance. Sally Engle Merry's groundbreaking research emphasised the political character of such indicators: 'The production of indicators is itself a political process, shaped by the power to categorize, count, [and] analyze'. Most importantly, her work showed that indicators 'promote a system of knowledge that has effects beyond the producers'. This insight has given rise to a robust inquiry into the pervasiveness of the move to make everything from human rights practices to sustainable cities indicators.

In this essay, we argue that quantitative indicators have a particularly important role when they are deployed as Global Performance Indicators (GPIs). We define GPIs as regularised public assessments that rate, rank and categorise state policies, qualities and/or performance.[2] GPIs are increasingly deployed to influence state behaviour and shape policy agendas as 'technologies of power'.[3] Indeed, almost half of the GPIs in a recently published database include ranking systems designed to pressure, shame or provoke competition among states.[4] Increasingly, numbers are not only used to

---

[1] KE Davis et al (eds), *Governance by Indicators: Global Power through Classification and Rankings* (Oxford, Oxford University Press, 2012).
[2] JG Kelley and BA Simmons, 'Introduction: The Power of Global Performance Indicators' (2019) 73 *International Organization* 491, 491.
[3] HK Hansen, 'The Power of Performance Indices in the Global Politics of Anti-corruption'. (2012) 15 *Journal of International Relations and Development* 506.
[4] J Kelley and BA Simmons (eds), *The Power of Global Performance Indicators* (Cambridge, Cambridge University Press, 2020).

count and measure 'objective' outputs, but are used by a range of actors to intentionally nudge public policy in desired directions.

The World Bank was an early adopter and is a particularly powerful wielder of GPIs. Aware of the power of numbers, and especially the power to rank and rate the policies of their own members, organisations like the World Bank intentionally exert competitive social pressure on states to deregulate. The Bank has been delighted with the results, especially those relating to its Ease of Doing Business (EDB) indicators.[5]

In fact, many countries perceived the EDB to be so influential that the rankings became vulnerable to political pressure. In 2021 the EDB was terminated after an internal investigation of such matters. Calls to revive a version of the index were strong, however, and the Bank is launching a successor, Business Ready (B-READY), which incorporates more checks on external pressures, but adopts on the same intention to use quantitative assessments to promote policy reforms.[6] In this essay, we deploy original experimental evidence to elucidate one major reason for the EDB's success: business rankings stimulate latent competitive dynamics within polities for their country to outperform competitors. In addition to competitive dynamics documented elsewhere,[7] we demonstrate that rankings plausibly stimulate domestic political demands for governments to implement policies that would boost their competitive standing – at least, according to the agenda of the ranker. By so doing, GPIs contribute to a form of global governance that replaces more overtly coercive exercises of power with social pressures, competitive dynamics and performative nudges that can nonetheless be highly influential.

II. THEORY: INDICATORS, INTERNATIONAL COMPETITION AND THE POTENTIAL FOR POLITICAL PRESSURE

Competition is a prime motivator for human behaviour. People compete for 'social rank' for several reasons, including to attract attention, admiration and the social or material investment of others.[8] Studies have found that competition is especially keen when people are struggling among the top tier of competitors and to avoid 'being last'.[9] Competition is stimulated, social psychology studies find, when the competition is with a 'commensurable' reference person[10] along a dimension that is important to the competitors.[11]

---

[5] World Bank, 'Doing Business: About Us', www.doingbusiness.org/about-us.

[6] Curtis S Chin and Abhinav Seetharaman, Op-ed: 'It's time for the World Bank to get back to the business of doing business', published Monday 2 May 2022, https://www.cnbc.com/2022/05/03/op-ed-world-bank-must-bring-back-ease-of-doing-business-report.html and Business Ready (B-READY) https://www.worldbank.org/en/businessready.

[7] R Doshi, JG Kelley and BA Simmons, 'The Power of Ranking: The Ease of Doing Business Indicator and Global Regulatory Behavior' (2019) 73 *International Organization* 611.

[8] P Gilbert, 'Evolution and Depression: Issues and Implications' (2006) 36 *Psychological Medicine* 287.

[9] SM Garcia, A Tor and R Gonzalez, 'Ranks and Rivals: A Theory of Competition' (2006) 32 *Personality and Social Psychology Bulletin* 970.

[10] J Suls and L Wheeler, 'A Selective History of Classic and Neo-social Comparison Theory' in J Suls and L Wheeler (eds), *Handbook of Social Comparison: Theory and Research* (New York, Springer, 2000).

[11] SRH Beach and A Tesser, 'Self-Evaluation Maintenance and Evolution' in Suls and Wheeler, *Handbook of Social Comparison* (n 9).

The Competitive Pressures of Rankings 175

These are precisely the dynamics of which GPIs take advantage. Following the lead of many well-established rating systems, from US News and World Report's Best Colleges and Universities rankings to product assessments in consumer reports, competitive prompts are clear in the publicity messages of many GPIs. For example, when Transparency International first released its Corruption Perceptions Index in 1995, the headline of its press release read 'Indonesia Worst in World Poll of International Corruption'.[12] Similarly, GPI raters like to spark competitive juices in their year rating announcements. When the United Nations announced its 2019 ranking of the World's Happiest Countries, the headlines blared 'Finland Comes Top Ahead of Nordic Neighbours'.[13] Comparisons are rife among GPIs. Almost all such assessments place countries in a rank ordering or clearly distinct normative categories, or both.[14]

In the early 2000s, the World Bank decided to rank states in the EDB report deliberately to impact policy. The EDB Index was computed using expert assessments of local laws in place that present hurdles to establishing or maintaining businesses with a national jurisdiction. The Index comprised information on the time and costs involved in securing construction permits, registering a business, accessing credit, making tax payments and more.[15] EDB's 'lively communication style' was designed to establish benchmarks and promote interstate competition in support of the World Bank's private sector-led development agenda.[16] To promote its 'flagship knowledge product',[17] the Bank staff carried out a massive media campaign every year when the ratings are released.

Despite questions about their singular deregulatory emphasis and validity,[18] the EDB rankings became a focal point of state policy. Indeed, within the first year of publicising the rankings, leaders from many countries, including Algeria, Burkina Faso, Malawi, Mali, and São Tomé and Príncipe, had reportedly requested specific advice on how to improve their standings. According to a 2005 staff report, 'This illustrates the main advantage of showing a single rank: it is easily understood by politicians, journalists, and development experts and therefore created pressure to reform. As in sports, once you start keeping score everyone wants to win.'[19] The World Bank itself has succinctly summarised our theory: decision-makers view the EDB Index as a way to compare performance, engage reputations and incite competition. The Bank explicitly and intentionally designed an assessment system calculated

---

[12] Transparency International, 'New Zealand Best, Indonesia Worst in World Poll of International Corruption', press release (15 June 1995) www.transparency.ca/9-Files/Older/Reports- Older/CPI-OtherReports/cpi1995.pdf.
[13] C Adams, 'World's Happiest Countries 2019: Finland Comes Top Ahead of Nordic Neighbours' *The Independent* (20 March 2019) www.independent.co.uk/travel/news-and-advice/happiest-countries-world-2019-winner-finland-bhutan-denmark-norway-iceland-a8831576.html.
[14] Kelley and Simmons, *The Power of Global Performance Indicators* (n 4).
[15] See World Bank, 'Doing Business: Ease of Doing Business Rankings', www.doingbusiness.org/en/rankings.
[16] Independent Evaluation Group, *Doing Business: An Independent Evaluation – Taking the Measure of the World Bank-IFC Doing Business Indicators* (Washington DC, The World Bank, 2008) xxvi.
[17] ibid xv.
[18] The ILO has understood this point very well, and has been a strong proponent of keeping the labour flexibility measures out of the Bank's overall EDB Index, while countries like Saudi Arabia have balked at the recent addition of gender components. See Doshi et al (n 6) 640.
[19] From 2001 to 2005, the Bank did not rank. Data that would eventually form the basis of the rankings were first published on the Bank's website in autumn 2001. See S Djankov et al, 'Doing Business Indicators: Why Aggregate and How To Do It' (World Bank, 2005) 1, http://web.archive.org/web/20020806155832/http://rru.worldbank.org/DoingBusiness/AboutDoingBusiness.aspx.

to draw attention to a few very simple criteria that the Bank associates with a 'better' business environment.[20] Comparative judgements are crucial in this process.[21] The Bank's overall rankings and sub-index made it easy to sort all states by their total number of reforms or a specific reform category.[22] Such comparative information is more likely to influence opinions and drive decisions than raw data alone. Indeed, actors may not even quite know what to make of the Bank's raw data unless it is put in comparative context.[23]

Because of its simple comparative format, the EDB Index engaged the reputations and status concerns of relevant bureaucrats and politicians, in some cases fuelled by national pride of domestic audiences more generally.[24] When King Abdullah of Saudi Arabia declared in 2006 that 'I want Saudi Arabia to be among the top 10 countries in Doing Business in 2010. No Middle Eastern country should have a better investment climate by 2007',[25] he was displaying a status motivation that has no other metric than his kingdom's relative performance on the World Bank's narrowly defined, but highly focal scale. The Bank amplified such peer comparisons through its website. Selecting a given country produced a tailored graphic, with that country's ranking situated amidst relevant comparisons (China and Mexico for India; the USA and Hong Kong for China). We suggest that these carefully orchestrated comparisons were intended precisely to constitute 'commensurate references', which theory suggests stimulates competition for status.

We believe competitive dynamics often work through domestic political pressures, both actual and anticipated. Coverage of the EDB ranking in domestic media perpetuated its significance and created new 'information' about how citizens' own governments compare with those of other states.[26] For domestic constituencies in countries with lower scores, the rankings were a unique representation of how much more heavy-handed their government's approach to regulation is than its peers. Thus, World Bank assessments in effect recalibrated the expectations of domestic constituents and legitimate their demands for reducing regulatory barriers to conducting business. Figure 9.1 illustrates a cycle of how the rankings framed the informational environment, creating social pressure on governments to implement reforms.

---

[20] S Schueth, 'Assembling International Competitiveness: The Republic of Georgia, USAID, and the Doing Business Project' (2011) 87 *Economic Geography* 51.

[21] TJ Sinclair, *The New Masters of Capital: American Bond Rating Agencies and the Politics of Creditworthiness* (Ithaca, NY, Cornell University Press, 2008).

[22] See World Bank, 'Doing Business: Reforms since Doing Business 2005', https://archive.doingbusiness.org/en/reforms/reforms-count.

[23] K Robson, 'Accounting Numbers as "Inscription": Action at a Distance and the Development of Accounting' (1992) 17 *Accounting, Organizations and Society* 685; HK Hansen and A Mühlen-Schulte, 'The Power of Numbers in Global Governance' (2012) 15 *Journal of International Relations and Development* 455, 457.

[24] J Kelley and BA Simmons, 'Politics by Number: Indicators as Social Pressure in International Relations' (2015) 59 *American Journal of Political Science* 1146; J Kelley, *Scorecard Diplomacy: Grading States to Influence Their Reputation and Behavior* (New York, Cambridge University Press, 2017).

[25] PJ Brook et al, *Celebrating Reform 2008 – Doing Business Case Studies* (Washington DC, World Bank, 2008) 17.

[26] X Dai, *International Institutions and National Policies* (Cambridge, Cambridge University Press, 2007).

Figure 9.1 The cycle of GPI pressure. Adapted from Kelley, *Scorecard Diplomacy* (n 23); Doshi et al, 'The Power of Ranking' (n 6)

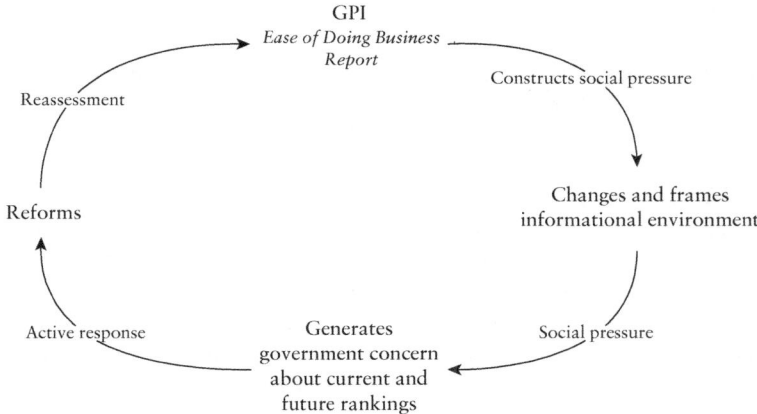

Depending on their own policy preferences and political power, political leaders may choose to ignore the international and domestic pressure, respond to the status pressure reluctantly or even use it to their advantage. Indeed, we posit that such status motivations – and the ability to signal high performance – can be useful for political elites aligned with the deregulatory goals of the EDB. That is, in Figure 9.1, the government action may not be purely reactive, but can also be a proactive link in the cycle. In a form of inverted boomerang effect,[27] elites may use the rankings as a tool to stoke domestic political pressure in order to overcome political opposition to regulatory reforms. In the traditional boomerang theory, domestic actors who lack access to pressure their own governments for reform engage international actors to exert such pressure on the government. In this case, however, domestic elites who wish to obtain international status and force through their preferred policies influence domestic audiences by using the international status concern and the power of the GPI to change the information environment, thus creating domestic social pressure for reform.

While prior evidence has demonstrated the link between rankings and reforms,[28] little evidence exists about the direct influence of EDB rankings on domestic constituencies and whether this translates into a preference for reforms. In this chapter, we provide evidence on these micro-foundations of EDB influence. We posit that if rankings work partly through domestic constituent pressure, then poor rankings *relative to peer countries* should elicit increased domestic demand for government reform. Thus, we expect to observe some evidence that the public respond to the competitive prompts of the EDB Index. We therefore posit that domestic constituents should be more likely to favour government reform which lowers barriers to business

---

[27] ME Keck and K Sikkink, *Activists beyond Borders: Advocacy Networks in International Politics* (Ithaca, NY, Cornell University Press, 1998).
[28] Doshi et al (n 6).

operations *when their country's EDB ranking is unfavourably presented against that of peer country.*

In sum, in this chapter, we explore the domestic political mechanisms of GPIs in greater depth. First, we argue that the EDB Index changes the information environment for both domestic elites and constituents. As a result, domestic constituents will demand greater reforms when they perceive their country to be at a competitive disadvantage relative to peers, as indicated by the EDB. We present experimental evidence that suggests the plausibility of this 'bottom-up' claim. Second, we argue on the basis of qualitative analysis that – in a form of inverted boomerang – domestic elites can and do use this mechanism to create their own pressures for regulatory reforms. In making these two claims, we focus on the case study of India. As the world's second-largest emerging market economy, India is an important test of EDB influence. Relevantly for our purposes, when the experiment was conducted, India was engaged in a multi-year inter-agency effort, led by Prime Minister Modi, to improve its EDB ranking from 130 to 30.

III. EXPERIMENTAL EVIDENCE: RANKINGS AND DOMESTIC SOURCES OF COMPETITION

To test the proposition that 'domestic constituents will demand greater reforms when they perceive their country to be at a competitive disadvantage relative to peers as indicated by the EDB', in 2016 we conducted an online survey experiment of 217 Indian participants to determine what effect India's EDB rank and the rank of a useful status comparison – in this case, China – has on Indian preferences for (i) improving India's business climate and (ii) improving India's EDB ranking. The experiment varied China's EDB rank relative to India's EDB rank and measured Indian support for economic reforms, hypothesising that a higher Chinese rank would lead Indians to be more supportive of an improved business climate and a higher EDB ranking, holding India's own ranking constant.

China is perhaps the most important status comparison for the Indian public on economic matters. Comparisons with China are salient for Indians because India shares a variety of key traits with China: both countries have populations of over one billion, post-colonial legacies and civilisations that date back millennia. Both gained independence at roughly the same time and initially had similar levels of development, though China's success has now left many Indians anxious and concerned for their country's own future. As the *New York Times* notes, 'it seems to be a national obsession in India' to measure 'the country's economic development against China's yardstick … Indian newspapers are filled with articles comparing the two countries. Indian executives refer to China as a template for development.'[29] It is for this reason that we chose to manipulate China's ranking

---

[29] V Bajaj, 'India Measures Itself against a China that Doesn't Notice' *New York Times* (31 August 2011) www.nytimes.com/2011/09/01/business/global/india-looks-to-china-as-an-economic-model.html?_r=0.

on the EDB relative to India's to see what effect it had on the Indian public's policy preferences.

The respondents were gathered through Amazon Mechanical Turk, which has a significant Indian user base. We screened for Indian workers and offered a modest incentive for their participation. The sample came from 15 Indian states, was roughly 70 per cent male and had a median household income of between 180,000 and 200,000 rupees (approximately US$2900). Respondent age ranged from 22 to 69 years, with a median of 32. Roughly 90 per cent possessed a college degree or higher. Participants supported 10 different political parties, with roughly half supporting the ruling Bharatiya Janata Party (BJP) and the other half supporting parties opposed to the BJP and/or outside its ruling coalition. As a caveat, we do not claim that our sample is representative, nor that our findings extend to India's population; we claim only that the experiment illustrates that rankings can trigger status concerns that change policy preferences in an important (educated, somewhat well-off, technologically savvy, predominantly male) segment of the Indian population.

Respondents were randomly assigned to one of five groups. Group 1 (No Rank) received no information on India's rank or the EDB indicator. The other four groups were all given India's true ranking of 130, were told that this ranking was out of 189 countries and were clearly informed that 1 was the best ranking and 189 the worst. Of these four groups, the only variation was China's rank. Group 2 (India's Rank Only) received information on India's rank but no information on China's rank (which is 78). Group 3 (China Higher) was told China's rank was 30 and India's 130. Group 4 (Equal Ranks) was told that China and India had equal ranks of 130. Finally, Group 5 (India Higher) received information that India's rank was 130 and China's 180.

Respondents were then asked how important it was to them to improve India's business climate and EDB ranking, respectively. Their answers were scored on a five-point Likert scale and then converted into a numeric, with 5 serving as the highest measure of importance and 1 the lowest. Thus, higher means and positive coefficients reflect an *increase* in importance.

The results in Table 9.1 suggest that the EDB shapes domestic policy preferences by facilitating status comparisons. First, and most conclusively, those Indians who were told that China is ranked 100 places ahead of India on the EDB indicator rated an improved business climate and an improved EDB ranking as more important to them (by 0.46 and 0.45 points on a five-point scale, or roughly 10 per cent more important) than respondents who were told China is ranked 50 places behind India. Because India's ranking was held constant at 130 in these comparison groups, the results suggest that the manipulation of China's rank *alone* significantly affected the policy preferences of some Indian respondents. These results are consistent with a hypothesis that status concerns play a role in framing Indian policy views, and that relative EDB rankings successfully stimulate status concerns. The results are robust across a variety of statistical models, including ordinary least squares (OLS), a bootstrapped Welch's *T*-Test and a Wilcoxon Rank Sum Test.

Table 9.1 Experimental results: status comparisons on importance of EDB and business climate improvements

	OLS	Bootstrapped Welch's T-Test	Wilcoxon Rank Sum Test
China higher versus India	0.462***	0.4603***	W = 672***
Higher:	(0.1292)	(0.1322)	p = 0.0007
Business climate importance	p = 0.0006	p = 0.0005	
China higher versus India	0.4515***	0.4513***	W = 707.5***
Higher: EDB importance	(0.1628)	(0.1623)	p = 0.003
	p = 0.007	p = 0.005	
India rank only	0.2884	0.2893	W = 674*
Rank: EDB importance	(0.1746)	(0.1772)	p = 0.0615
	p = 0.102	p = 0.17	

Second, India's ranking was influential even when it was not explicitly compared with other countries and when the comparative element of the ranking was left implicit by situating India among all countries. Respondents who were provided only India's ranking of 130 out of 189 rated both an improved business climate and an improved ranking as more important to them than those who received no information on the EDB ranking.

Finally, across our five comparison groups, the average importance respondents attached to improving India's business climate and EDB ranking varied systematically and as expected with the information provided about China's rank. Figure 9.2 shows that respondents rated these goals as most important when China's rank was higher than India's, less important when their ranks were equal and least important when India ranked above China. This suggests that the sample population displayed a discernible competitive causal effect, consistent with claims that the EDB Index draws attention to policies on which the public believe a competitor outperforms their own country. Relative rankings, in this survey experiment, caused respondents to reprioritise their policy preferences consistent with the policies rated as positive by the World Bank.

Figure 9.2 Assessments of importance of improving India's BUSINESS CLIMATE and EDB rankings, by exposure to EDB information

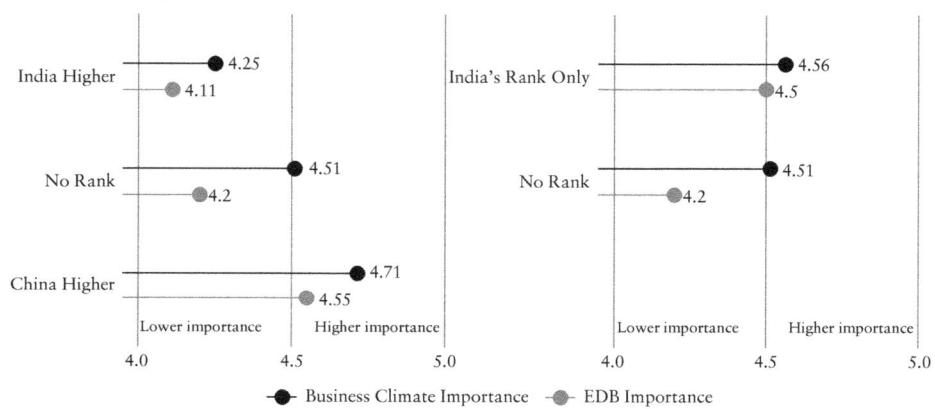

IV. QUALITATIVE ANALYSIS OF INDIAN POLITICAL STRATEGY

Next, we examine our second proposition: that 'domestic elites can and do use EDB competition to create their own pressures for regulatory reforms'. We explore India's engagement with EDB for evidence of how the ranking implicates domestic political mechanisms; in particular, how politicians of both major Indian political parties have acted on the assumption that the Indian public cares about status as reflected in the EDB Index. The analysis which draws on Doshi et al (2019), relies exclusively on independent (non-World Bank) evidence, including Indian English and Hindi-language media and primary sources.

A. EDB and the 2014 Election

Narendra Modi's focus on the EDB indicator began in the late stages of his campaign for Prime Minister in 2013.[30] At the time, India's poor rating could have been blamed on India's ruling Congress Party, and a promise to improve it was useful criticism of the preceding government as well as a way for Modi to make economic reform the centre of his campaign.

Moreover, a message of good governance and economic progress was important not only in its own right, but also as a way of rebranding his political party, the BJP, as a business-friendly party rather than one better known for outbreaks of communal violence and its support for Hindu nationalism. When the BJP released its party platform in 2014, it made an indirect reference to the EDB indicator in a section on bolstering manufacturing: 'we will ensure that a conducive, enabling environment is created making "doing business" in India easy'.[31] In the early stages of his initial national campaign, Modi already reached for the country's poor EDB rating to berate his predecessors and compete for Indian voters.

B. EDB and Modi's Major Initiatives

After winning the election, Modi entered office and immediately made India's economy, employment and manufacturing base a priority. Shortly thereafter, he announced his signature 'Make in India' programme, intended to transform the country into a manufacturing powerhouse. Manufacturing was politically salient because it offered the possibility of employment in an economy struggling to produce enough jobs to keep pace with India's surging numbers of young workers. And, just as the EDB was linked to manufacturing and investment within the BJP policy platform, so too was it given pride of place in Modi's 'Make in India' branding effort. Indeed, Modi

---

[30] 'Don't Run from Big Retail, Face Them, Modi Tells Traders' *The Indian Express* (New Delhi, 27 February 2014) http://indianexpress.com/article/india/india-others/dont-run-from-big-retail-face-them-modi-tells-traders/; A Ayres, 'How Modi Can Bring US Businesses Back to India' (*Fortune*, 21 May 2014) http://fortune.com/2014/05/21/how-modi-can-bring-u-s-businesses-back-to-india/.
[31] Bhatatiya Janata Party, 'Election Manifesto 2014: Ek Bharat Shreshthah Bharat' (2014) https://library.bjp.org/jspui/bitstream/123456789/252/1/bjp_lection_manifesto_english_2014.pdf.

first formally announced his EDB initiative in the same major national speech that launched his 'Make in India' campaign, and it was the second enumerated priority for his government. Modi's language on the EDB was colloquial, but nonetheless clearly linked to his priority, as the excerpt below demonstrates:

> What else does [an investor] want? These days there is a ranking for ease of doing business. Recently I met with the World Bank Chairman and he was also worrying about [what investors want]. Probably we were 135th in the world at that time. What hinders ease of doing business? If we have to come to 50 from 135 then the Government alone can do this. If the Government brings transparency in its decisions and rules, if they can easily move things forward, then today we could move to 50 from 135 in ease of doing business. I have sensitized my entire team [on ease of doing business] and asked, whether in the name of scrutiny and perfection, are we not hindering ourselves? On the basis of my three months' experience, I can say today that my entire team in the Government, my entire bureaucracy, is moving two steps ahead of me in this positive thinking.[32]

The effort to improve India's EDB ranking was thus an important part of the country's most visible political programme and a defining Modi initiative. Over the course of the next year, Modi established a robust interagency process tasked with improving India's EDB ranking. The rankings proved useful for Modi as a means to provoke bureaucrats to focus and compete over business deregulation.

C. Subnational EDB Rankings as Political Tools

Even though the EDB rating primarily focused on India's efforts in Mumbai and New Delhi, two of India's largest cities, the ruling government nonetheless sought to improve India's ease of doing business in its various states as well. Accordingly, the government took a number of steps to influence or compel localities to make reforms in service of the overall effort. In December 2014, it sponsored a meeting of central and local governments where state leaders committed to a 98-point action plan intended to improve EDB at the local level.[33] In addition, the Department of Industrial and Policy Planning (DIPP) itself created a list of 344 recommendations for state-level governments intended to improve the local business climate.[34] With the

---

[32] Prime Minister's Office, 'PM Launches "Make in India" Global Initiative' (*PMIndia*, 25 September 2014) www.pmindia.gov.in/en/news_updates/pm-launches-make-in-india-global-initiative/]; 'Text of Prime Minister Shri Narendra Modi's Address at the Launch of "Make in India" Global Initiative' (*Narendra Modi*, 25 September 2014) www.narendramodi.in/text-of-prime-minister-shri-narendra-modis-address-at-the-launch-of-make-in-india-global-initiative-2867; Government of India, Ministry of External Affairs, 'English Rendering of Prime Minister Shri Narendra Modi's Address at the Launch of "Make in India" Global Initiative' (26 September 2014) www.mea.gov.in/Speeches-Statements.htm?dtl/24033/English+rendering+of+Prime+Minister+Shri+Narendra+Modis+address+at+the+launch+of+Make+in+India+global+initiative.

[33] S Nidhi, 'Ease of Doing Business: Here's All You Need to Know About the Top 10 States' *Daily News and Analysis* (16 September 2015) www.dnaindia.com/money/report-ease-of-doing-business-here-s-all-you-need- to-know-about-the-top-10-states-2125690.

[34] Government of India, Department of Industrial Policy and Promotion: Ministry of Commerce and Industry, 'Business Reform Action Plan 2016 for States/UTs' (2015) http://dipp.nic.in/English/Investor/Ease_DoingBusiness/StateRecommendations_26102015.pdf.

support of India's powerful Cabinet Secretary, DIPP also organised meetings through which states could share their best practices.[35]

Despite these steps, the central government had long been aware that local governments would prove recalcitrant – especially those controlled by the government's political rival, the Congress Party, as well as other parties in opposition to the BJP. For that reason, the central government sought to leverage the legitimacy of the World Bank to create its own domestic, state-level EDB indicator – in concert with the World Bank – that would be used to gather data and score states on their compliance with the various action plans developed by the annual reform action plan put together by DIPP. Importantly, the EDB state-level rankings are created using entirely different criteria from the international rankings: a higher score is given to those who are in compliance with the government's reform action plans. In effect, the subnational EDB ranking is in part a measure of the degree to which states are compliant with central government policy. Using rankings in a top-down fashion, the central government essentially forced local jurisdictions to compete on criteria of its own choosing.

It is plausible that the government saw these rankings as a political tool, particularly because the vast majority of state-level rankings do not affect India's national EDB ranking, the main focus of Modi's government. Indeed, states led by BJP governments have generally done best on the rankings. The very first batch of rankings released in 2015 found that Gujarat, the state that Prime Minister Modi led for a decade and whose success formed the basis of his campaign, topped the EDB rankings and was given the highest rating of all Indian states. Seven states led by his party made the top 10, which suggests either party-line cooperation or efforts to reward political allies through the ranking system.[36]

Importantly, the rankings were then deployed by Prime Minister Modi in domestic political rhetoric, and effectively became proxies for bureaucratic competence. During a visit to BJP-governed Jharkhand, Modi praised its leaders for working hard to improve their EDB ranking.[37] In advance of critical elections in Bihar that would determine the balance of power in India's upper house of parliament, Modi's finance minister attacked Nitish Kumar, the chief minister of Bihar, for his state's low EDB ranking in 2015:

> Nitish says let us debate the development issue. What is there to debate? This debate is over. Gujarat [the state Modi previously managed] is number one and Bihar stands at twenty-one [on EDB]. The economy speaks through statistics and not through debate.[38]

---

[35] R Chitravanshi, 'States Share Best Ideas to Lift India's Global Ease-of-Doing Business Ranking' *The Economic Times* (New Delhi, 19 October 2015) http://economictimes.indiatimes.com/news/economy/policy/states-share-best-ideas-to-lift-indias-global-ease-of-doing-business-ranking/articleshow/49446000.cms.
[36] 'Ease of Doing Business: Seven of Top 10 States Ruled by BJP, Allies; Gujarat on Top' *The Indian Express* (New Delhi, 15 September 2015) http://indianexpress.com/article/business/business-others/ease-of-doing-business-seven-of-top-10-states-ruled-by-bjp-allies-gujarat-on-top/.
[37] 'Through Mudra Yojana We Want to Accelerate Development Process in India: PM at Inauguration of Mega Credit Camp in Jharkhand' (*Narendra Modi*, 2 October 2015) www.narendramodi.in/text-of-pm-s-address-at-the-inauguration-of-mega-credit-camp-under-pradhan-mantri-mudra-yojana-at-dumka-362451.
[38] 'Arun Jaitley Mocks Nitish Kumar on Development; Says Gujarat Number One, Bihar at Twenty-one' *The Economic Times* (New Delhi, 17 September 2015) https://economictimes.indiatimes.com/news/politics-and-nation/arun-jaitley-mocks-nitish-kumar-on-development-says-gujarat-number-1-bihar-at-21/articleshow/48998967.cms.

In 2018, roughly one year before parliamentary elections, the government released a second batch of state-level EDB rankings. Although BJP states generally did better than states governed by other parties, compliance with the ranking criteria was in general much higher. In 2015, only seven states implemented at least half of the suggested recommendations; in 2018, that number had grown to 21 states, with many perhaps motivated by the headlines generated from the first batch of rankings.[39]

D. EDB in National Politics

In India's national political contests, EDB only became more salient after the BJP's initial elevation of the issue in 2013. Modi's efforts to centre the EDB in Indian politics was even been recognised by the World Bank, which offered an unusual public explanation for why India's ranking ascended so little in Modi's first year that absolved him of responsibility. The Bank also praised him regularly for his cooperation, even sending its CEO to attend Modi's celebratory address on India's 30-place climb and first-ever entry into the top 100 ranks.[40]

India's EDB ranking eventually moved from a political liability for the BJP into a significant political asset. For example, even as India's growth slowed to a three-year low ahead of its 2019 national elections, Modi leaned on India's 30-place climb in EDB rankings to demonstrate that he had improved the country's status and economy.[41] To accentuate that argument, he gave a major address dedicated to India's climb in the rankings and trumpeted its success relative to other countries: 'This year, India's jump in ranking is the highest [of all countries]. India has been identified as one of the top reformers … [and] may become an example for many other nations.' To make EDB even more politically salient, Modi linked it to the 'life of a common man' by recasting it as the 'Ease of Living Life' indicator.[42] He also leveraged the rating to shame his opposition:

> Had these kinds of reforms … been carried out during [the opposition's] tenure, then our ranking would have improved much earlier. And the credit for improvement in ranking would have gone to them … they did nothing and have had been raising questions about someone who has been doing something. It's just a coincidence that the World Bank

---

[39] S Chakraborty, 'Jharkhand Set to Top the Ease of Doing Business Ranking for States' (*Business Standard*, 10 July 2018) www.business-standard.com/article/economy-policy/jharkhand-set-to-top-the-ease-of-doing-business-ranking-for-states-118071000319_1.html.
[40] 'World Bank "Ease of Doing Business" Report Doesn't Factor in Modi Government's Reforms: BJP' *The Economic Times* (New Delhi, 30 October 2014) http://articles.economictimes.indiatimes./com/2014-10-30/news/55595538_1_modi-government-doing-business-report-world-bank. These actions attest to the bank's willingness not only to engage in social pressure through rankings, but also to engage in related strategies of back-patting for favourite pupils as well.
[41] 'PM Modi Attends Programme on "Ease of Doing Business"' (*Narendra Modi*, 4 November 2017) www.narendramodi.in/pm-modi-attends-programme-on-ease-of-doing-business-537653.
[42] ibid.

started the process of releasing the ease of doing business ranking in 2004. It's an important year. And all of you know who was in the government [the Congress Party] since then till 2014.[43]

One of India's major newspapers, *The Indian Express*, wrote that India's 30-rank increase 'comes as a shot in the arm for the Narendra Modi government amid dissenting voices in certain quarters about implementation of the Goods and Services Tax (GST) as well as demonetization', two policies that had called into question Modi's economic credentials.[44]

If the EDB were truly salient in Indian politics, then one would expect to see the opposition party attack Modi's efforts. This is indeed precisely what occurred during the 2019 election. Modi's chief political opponent, Rahul Gandhi, even made attacking Modi's EDB gains a part of his stump speech, stating that Modi's team 'listens to outsiders' and should instead ask the Indian people 'whether ease of doing business has improved for them … What is spoken abroad is truth for this government but what the poor say in India is farce'.[45]

In short, the India case clearly demonstrates that Indian politicians believed that the Indian public would be sensitive to India's EDB rank as well as its status implications. The ranking appeared in party platforms, national- and state-level campaigns, and was even implemented at the subnational level, in part for political reasons. Together, the evidence illustrates an important mechanism through which GPIs shape state behaviour. The ranking has been a key part of national political debates. It has been used to distract from the ruling government's various setbacks, been acknowledged by the World Bank as relevant in Indian politics and even been implemented at a subnational level to stimulate competition, embarrass political opponents and reward supporters. Together, the Indian evidence strongly suggests the ranking's salience in domestic politics and the ability of political elites to employ an inverse boomerang strategy to engage international pressure to stoke domestic support for government-preferred reforms.

Indicators 'not only make sense of the messy social world, but also help to manage and govern it'.[46] Sally Merry and her collaborators opened our eyes to the 'quiet' power of indicators. This chapter has aimed to focus our attention on their intentional use for specific policy agendas as well. Merry's seminal work pointed to the importance of numbers for organising 'the messy social world'. We have sought to develop her insights to see how simplifying reality with numerical indicators could render it perceptible, but also, for better or for worse, *governable*.

---

[43] ibid.
[44] 'This Is What Helped India Go Up in World Bank Rankings in "Ease of Doing Business"' *The Indian Express* (New Delhi, 31 October 2017) http://indianexpress.com/article/business/economy/world-bank-ease-of-doing-business-india-rank-100-arun-jaitley-gst-demonetisation-narendra-modi-4916051/.
[45] 'Ease of Doing Business: Rahul Gandhi, Arun Jaitley Take Potshots at Each Other Over India's Ranking' *Hindustan Times* (New Delhi, 1 November 2017) www.hindustantimes.com/assem-bly-elections/gst-and-note-ban-have-ruined-ease-of-doing-business-rahul-gandhi-takes-on-govt-day-after-world-bank-report/story-68LlcqSuLmiyTDvfrS7qcP.html.
[46] KE Davis, SE Merry and B Kingsbury, *The Quiet Power of Indicators: Measuring Governance, Corruption, and the Rule of Law* (Cambridge, Cambridge University Press, 2015).

V. CONCLUSIONS

GPIs take the logic of governing by indicators to a higher level. It is one thing to attempt to measure GPIs, and much follows from whether and how to do so. But the lust for measurement has encouraged a range of actors – from international organisations and institutions to state and non-state actors – to devise measurements specifically for a melange of purposes: from holding states accountable to highlighting 'best practices' and to creating not-so-subtle forms of social pressure to alter policies and priorities through comparative systems of rating and ranking.

Many of these systems, which we referred to as GPIs, are explicitly comparative, designed to provoke states to strive for social recognition in the form of higher rankings. But why should states be influenced by these rankings? Both experimental and qualitative analysis demonstrates just how powerful comparative rankings can be. The experimental evidence drawn from the responses of everyday people demonstrates the potential bottom-up power of rankings to affect their policy preferences and priorities.

Interestingly, without varying reality, or even one's own country's ranking, it is possible to provoke competitive concerns about business regulations merely by manipulating the ranking of a salient competitor. For Indians, this competitor is China. The business climate becomes notably more urgent among Indian respondents when they believe China has outperformed their own country, even if conditions in India are held constant. Conversely, the Indian public may conclude their government is doing 'well enough' – so long as they rank above China.

GPIs are useful for top-down manipulation within countries as well. Modi's agenda for India illustrates the way that *global* indicators have been repurposed for *domestic* political and policy advantage. Not only has Modi berated opponents and rebranded the BJP using the EDB; he has also replicated the index's competitive aspects among the states of India.

This research illustrates new ways actors capture governance spaces and exert influence, using GPIs as strategic communication. GPIs can be used to define problems and offer solutions using extreme forms of simplification. As such, they are an international counterpart to 'nudge' tactics much touted by behavioural economists and psychologists as ways to shift human behaviour in desired ways. Actors that try to create competitive dynamics or even social shame through ranking systems know that they oversimplify reality, strip concepts of their context and history, conceal their underlying theoretical origins and offer a false sense of precision and certainty.[47] But the point of ranking systems, we have argued, is to influence behaviour, not to faithfully render reality. The evidence presented in this chapter shows that in the case of the EDB indicators, rankings have clearly provoked policy priorities and reforms in the deregulatory direction desired by the World Bank.

---

[47] SE Merry, 'Measuring the World: Indicators, Human Rights, and Global Governance: With CA Comment by John M. Conley' (2011) 52 *Current Anthropology* 83.

10

Between Conduct and Counter-conduct: Human Rights Translation at the Universal Periodic Review

JULIE BILLAUD

WHEN JANE COWAN and I entered the Palais des Nations in Geneva in 2010–11 to study the Universal Periodic Review (UPR), a United Nations mechanism of human rights monitoring, both of us had read the seminal work of Sally Engle Merry extensively. The research methods she had used in her study of human rights and gender violence,[1] notably her experience of working with a team, observing UN diplomatic negotiations in New York and Geneva as well the translation of human rights law in local contexts (in Hawai'i, Beijing, Delhi, Fiji and Hong Kong), had been an important source of inspiration. The team Jane had constituted when she had initially conceived this research project was nevertheless smaller: we were only three researchers, including one, Basak Cali, who only worked intermittently with us. We were therefore not able to travel as extensively beyond Geneva as Sally did with her team, even though we aimed to document some aspects of the social life of the UPR in two national contexts – Belgium and Greece – where we spent a few weeks each. Finally, Sally's reflections on how activists operate as intermediaries seeking to translate human rights both downward (to meet local cultural and social realities) and upward (to meet international standards and norms) offered important insights on the vibrant social dynamics within which human rights are embedded. It is therefore with many of her reflections in mind that we entered our new fieldsite.

In this chapter, I discuss these important themes present in Sally's writings in relation to the knowledge practices of drafters working within the UPR secretariat, an actor that is often overlooked in studies of UN human rights mechanisms. Indeed, the secretariat maintains a rather low profile in the UPR process even though it plays an essential role in mediating relations between NGOs and states and maintaining a space where criticisms can be expressed. By collecting and summarising NGOs'

---

[1] SE Merry, *Human Rights and Gender Violence: Translating International Law into Local Justice* (Chicago, University of Chicago Press 2005).

written contributions, the secretariat acts as a guarantor of civil society participation in a mechanism where the presence of NGOs has been a subject of intense debate from the start. UPR drafters therefore operate backstage, without drawing too much attention to themselves. Their relative absence of public visibility, together with their command of bureaucratic rules, they believe, enables them to more effectively shape the content of discussions. By using 'creative expedients to open up new administrative possibilities within the scope of accepted rules',[2] the UPR drafters aim to implement their belief in the possibility of making the world a better place through human rights.

UN civil servants often admit their 'activist' inclinations in private conversations, even though they prefer to be seen as human rights experts – or 'keepers of the truth'[3] – endowed with the responsibility of maintaining the reputation and legitimacy of the Office of the High Commissioner for Human Rights (OHCHR). The drafters' work is therefore marked by a constant attention to keeping a balance between their commitment to make documents speak the truth and the necessity to preserve states' sensitivity by embracing the principle of 'neutrality' that guides the activities of the OHCHR. Interestingly, since the first UPR cycle, and in spite of procedural limitations, the participation of NGOs has increased exponentially, not only in terms of the number of contributions submitted to the UPR secretariat, but also qualitatively, as they have familiarised themselves with the various institutional channels via which they can express their concerns.

In this chapter, I situate the knowledge practices of UPR drafters in between 'conduct' and 'counter-conducts',[4] ie covert forms of resistance marked by persistent and relentless efforts to make 'subjugated and disqualified knowledges'[5] audible within the UPR process. I examine the extent to which 'counter-conducts' – 'those efforts whose aim is to invoke new directions, priorities or objectives, and to chart ways of escaping direction by the subjects of power themselves'[6] – create the conditions of possibility for an 'insurrection of knowledges'.[7] The many administrative procedures drafters have to follow to authorise information provided by NGOs turn participation into an exercise of epistemic capture that imbeds NGOs' human rights claims within the dominant agenda,[8] while simultaneously offering possibilities for

---

[2] C Bortolotto et al, 'Proving Participation: Vocational Bureaucrats and Bureaucratic Creativity in the Implementation of the UNESCO Convention for the Safeguarding of the Intangible Cultural Heritage' (2020) 28 *Social Anthropology* 66, 68.

[3] J Billaud, 'Keepers of the Truth: Producing "Transparent" Documents for the Universal Periodic Review' in H Charlesworth and E Larking (eds), *Human Rights and the Universal Periodic Review: Rituals and Ritualism* (Cambridge, Cambridge University Press, 2015).

[4] M Foucault, *Security, Territory, Population: Lectures at the Collège de France 1977–1978* (New York, St Martins Press, 2009) ch 8.

[5] M Foucault, *Power/Knowledge: Selected Interviews and Other Writings, 1972–1977* (New York, Pantheon Books, 1980) 82.

[6] L Odysseos, 'Human Rights, Self-Formation and Resistance in Struggles against Disposability: Grounding Foucault's "Theorizing Practice" of Counter-conduct in Bhopal' (2016) 30 *Global Society* 179, 183.

[7] Foucault, *Power/Knowledge* (n 5) 87.

[8] O Nay, 'La « captation épistémique » : les institutions internationales et la digestion de la critique sociale' (Thematic Session 79 at Congrès de l'Association Française de Sciences Politiques, Sciences-Po Bordeaux, 2019) www.afsp.info/congres/congres-2019/sections-thematiques/st-79/.

'confronting governments'.[9] I underline the contradictory effects of documentation practices, forms of expertise and bureaucratic procedures on the articulation and understanding of social criticism. I examine the forms of discipline and subjectivation generated by the bureaucratic modalities of civil society participation as well as expressions of resistance or 'counter-conducts' that such constraints nevertheless enable. Building on critical scholarship that aims to simultaneously capture the enabling and constraining potentials of human rights,[10] I pay specific attention to the parrhesiastic contract[11] that OHCHR drafters struggle to maintain with states as they take ownership of contentious information provided by NGOs. While such processes give this information legitimacy and value within the official discourse, they also tend to distort ideas in a way that reduces their critical content. However, by making NGOs' claims compliant with the dominant paradigm, such techniques paradoxically seek to achieve politically significant forms of 'co-governing'.[12]

The analysis presented here is informed by a one-year ethnographic fieldwork at the UN Human Rights Council in Geneva carried out in 2010–11 in collaboration with Jane Cowan, which included three months of participant observation at the UPR secretariat in the context of an internship at the OHCHR. The information collected during this first fieldwork was complemented with interviews with UPR drafters conducted in 2019 in the context of a consultancy commissioned by the OHCHR. During my 2011 internship, I became embedded in the everyday bureaucratic work of the secretariat. Like other UPR drafters, I was tasked with preparing documents for the reviews of several states to be examined during the last session of the first UPR cycle. This involved attending meetings, reading guidelines and databases, and selecting, organising and summarising information. It is through this – rather daunting – personal experience of putting documents together that I eventually gained insights into the working methods and ethos of international bureaucrats, who, in spite of the tediousness of their tasks, were passionately committed to preserving the ideal of NGOs' participation.

In the same spirit as Sally's efforts to conceptualise human rights not as abstract normative categories but as dynamic social processes, I emphasise the intense social dynamics and affects at play in the production of official and authoritative United Nations documents. Like her, I believe that a great part of the story of human rights, notably their enormous expansion since World War II and their continuous utopian appeal, cannot be fully grasped by accounts that focus solely on the written content of documents. Overlooking the everyday bureaucratic labour of international bureaucrats and dismissing it as mere routine, mundane and repetitive practices fails to understand how sociality in international governance processes is

---

[9] M Foucault, 'Human Rights: Confronting Governments' in *Power: Essential Works of Foucault* (New York, New Press, 2000).

[10] L Odysseos, C Death and H Malmvig, 'Interrogating Michel Foucault's Counter-conduct: Theorising the Subjects and Practices of Resistance in Global Politics' (2016) 30 *Global Society* 151; J Cowan and J Billaud, 'Between Learning and Schooling: The Politics of Human Rights Monitoring at the Universal Periodic Review' (2015) 36 *Third World Quarterly* 1175.

[11] M Foucault, *Fearless Speech* (J Pearson ed, Semiotext(e)/Foreign Agents, 2001).

[12] Odysseos (n 6).

primarily organised and structured around forms.[13] Paying attention to how 'graphic artefacts'[14] are collectively crafted and to the technicalities that regulate their production offers fertile methodological avenues for opening the administrative black boxes of human rights processes and gaining insights into the politics of knowledge production they foster.

I. WHAT IS THE UNIVERSAL PERIODIC REVIEW?

Before discussing the technicalities of the documentation process at the UPR, some information on the origins and guiding principles that gave shape to this complex and unique mechanism is necessary. The original impetus for the reform process of the UN human rights system which started in 2005 was a widely held view according to which the Human Rights Commission had become 'politicised'. The Commission was accused of adopting 'double standards' whereby a few states (mostly from the African continent) were systematically singled out for evaluation and criticism while others were left unscrutinised. The UPR was specifically designed to address these limitations: the mechanism, as its name makes explicit, was meant to achieve 'universality' by providing a systematic state-led peer scrutiny of the human rights record of the 193 UN member states. Universality was also to be achieved through the inclusion of all human rights: civil and political rights, as well as economic, social and cultural rights. Finally, even though the mechanism was designed as a 'peer review' with states occupying the centre stage, it encouraged everyone to participate, including NGOs, civil society, the media and national human rights institutions (NHRIs).

Reviews are carried out on a regular cycle of four and a half years and comprise three key stages. The first stage is the examination of the human rights situation of the State under Review (SuR), also called the 'Working Group meeting' or 'interactive dialogue'. This three-and-a-half-hour-long session takes place in the magnificent Room XX in the Palais des Nations in Geneva. During the review, the SuR presents its national report and Working Group members (also called 'recommending states') ask questions and make recommendations that the SuR is free to accept or to simply note. The second stage, which takes place a few days after the review, consists in the adoption of the draft report – containing all the recommendations accepted and noted by the SuR, as well as voluntary pledges and commitments – before the Working Group. During the third stage, the SuR implements the recommendations it has accepted and prepares its national report for the next review. It is also during this stage that the OHCHR collects information and prepares documents and NGOs follow up on states' implementations and write their contributions to the 'summary'.

The UPR can therefore be conceived as an iterative process via which states learn to comment on their own and others' human rights performance. The UPR functions

---

[13] A Riles, 'Infinity within the Brackets' (1998) 25 *American Ethnologist* 378.
[14] MS Hull, *Government of Paper: The Materiality of Bureaucracy in Urban Pakistan* (California, University of California Press, 2012).

as a 'public audit ritual'[15] which nurtures 'a cultural system whose coin is admission into the international community of human-rights-compliant states'.[16] The friendly language of the Institution Building Package (2007 Human Rights Council Resolution 5.1), which emphasises 'cooperation' and the 'sharing of best practices' as guiding principles, makes states responsible for providing an account of themselves and others.[17]

The review is based on three key documents: (i) a 'national report' written by the SuR, in which information is provided on progress achieved since the previous review; (ii) 'the compilation of UN documents' prepared by the OHCHR and containing information from independent human rights experts and groups, such as the Special Procedures, human rights treaty bodies and other UN entities; and (iii) 'the summary of other stakeholders' information', also prepared by the secretariat and including information provided by NGOs and NHRIs.

This last document is the main channel via which NGOs can voice their claims by offering a counter-narrative to the 'national report' written by the SuR. With a strict 10-page limit, the summary represents a condensed version of their grievances and offers very limited room for contextualisation. Such restrictions force drafters to be strategic in the information they select so as to preserve the essence of the NGOs' claims and concerns.

The public reviews which take place in Room XXI of the Palais des Nations only represent the 'front stage' of the UPR. The most significant moments of the process take place 'backstage': in the Serpentine Bar, where diplomats negotiate the recommendations they will give to each other; in the pre-sessions organised by UPR Info, at which NGOs present their concerns to state representatives; and in the OHCHR, where drafters devise narrative strategies so as to increase the impact of the documents they are in charge of drafting.

NGOs' participation also occurs backstage: if they cannot take the floor during the 'interactive dialogue', they can intervene in a number of other ways. Specifically, they can lobby states to take their recommendations on board; organise side events in parallel to each review; participate in national consultations organised by the SuR during the drafting of its national report; follow up on accepted recommendations; and submit information to the UPR secretariat at the OHCHR. Their room for intervention is peripheral, but has nevertheless increased, notably via the lobbying opportunities opened up by the establishment of UPR Info's pre-sessions in 2012 and the greater availability of in-country trainings specifically designed to enhance their advocacy capacities.

In the next section, I focus on the knowledge practices of international servants working within the UPR secretariat. I study how drafters interpret the principles of 'impartiality', 'neutrality' and 'universality' that are supposed to guide the UPR

---

[15] J Cowan, 'The Universal Periodic Review as a Public Audit Ritual: An Anthropological Perspective on Emerging Practices in the Global Governance of Human Rights' in Charlesworth and Larking (n 3) 42.
[16] Merry (n 1).
[17] J Butler 'Giving an Account of Oneself' (2001) 31 *Diacritics* 22; Cowan and Billaud, 'Between Learning and Schooling' (n 10).

process. I follow Nikolas Rose's suggestion to conceive 'governmentality' beyond a clear-cut dichotomy between forces of reaction and those of progression embedded in fixed identities. In so doing, I examine 'the ways in which creativity arises out of the situation of human beings engaged in particular relations of force and meaning, and what is made out of the possibilities of that location'.[18] I argue that, in spite of the many administrative procedures that limit their room to manoeuvre, UPR drafters' awareness of bureaucratic restrictions, expressed in sentiments of disappointment and frustration, triggers creative efforts to meet the utopian principles of human rights and civil society participation. By using the cracks in the system, UPR drafters seek to reconcile their own convictions with the political realities they face in their work.[19]

II. ETHICS, AFFECTS AND POLITICS IN DOCUMENTS PRODUCTION

Anyone reading UPR documents for the first time is immediately puzzled by their opacity. Providing very few cues to the contexts they are supposed to depict, all UPR documents appear oddly similar, except for the names of the countries present on their cover page. The unacquainted reader finds themself easily lost in the obscure diplomatic jargon, the repetitive phrasings ('X recommends', 'Y urges', 'Z is concerned') and the abundance of acronyms and footnotes. Only an investigation of their 'psychic',[20] 'affective'[21] aspects can shed some light on their inner meaning.

I came to this realisation after interviewing Manuela, an international civil servant working at the OHCHR who later became my internship supervisor. The purpose of this interview was to put some faces to the documents I had collected since the beginning of my fieldwork. Unable to fully comprehend their content, I thought a discussion with the persons in charge of crafting them would provide me with information on the secretariat's role in the UPR and its working methods. Surprised that someone could be interested in her work, Manuela pulled folders and binders from her shelves with great excitement, running her fingers through paragraphs of UN resolutions and organisation charts as she struggled to describe the complex routes documents followed before their public release. Because her efforts did little to clarify the documentation process, I offered to intern for her, a proposal she immediately accepted. As I later discovered, the burden of paperwork at the OHCHR is largely borne by an army of unpaid workers without whom the Office could simply not function: namely, the interns!

---

[18] N Rose, *Powers of Freedom: Reframing Political Thought* (Cambridge, Cambridge University Press, 1999) 279.

[19] J Cowan and J Billaud, 'The Bureaucratisation of Utopia: Ethics, Affects and Subjectivities in International Governance Processes' (2020) 28 *Social Anthropology* 6.

[20] B Kafka, *The Demon of Writing: Powers and Failures of Paperwork* (New York, Zone Books, 2012).

[21] Y Navaro-Yashin, 'Affect in the Civil Service: A Study of a Modern State-System' (2006) 9 *Postcolonial Studies* 281; Y Navaro-Yashin, 'Make-Believe Papers, Legal Forms and the Counterfeit Affective Interactions between Documents and People in Britain and Cyprus' (2007) 7 *Anthropological Theory* 79; M Laszczkowski and M Reeves, *Affective States: Entanglements, Suspensions, Suspicions* (New York, Berghahn, 2015).

Since UPR modalities restrict their capacity to speak, NGOs' recommendations are primarily voiced by others, ie 'recommending states' and the OHCHR, notably via the Summary it is tasked with producing. Because NGOs' voices are always mediated, civil society actors have to tutor themselves to master the art of ventriloquism. Their relevance within the mechanism is ensured through their capacity to find a friendly mouth able and willing to speak their words.

The role of UPR drafters can therefore be compared to that of the 'intermediaries' Sally Merry observed in her study of human rights and gender violence, in the sense that the Summaries they produce are acts of translation of local rights claims for an international audience. However, as international civil servants, drafters occupy a somewhat different position from NGO representatives or social movement activists. Indeed, their role consists in translating up communities' claims reflected in NGOs' contributions. In other words, their work aims to remake human rights claims in the vernacular 'culture of transnational modernity'[22] that the United Nations embody. The documentation process at the UPR is therefore an act of 'transnational consensus building'.[23] In their struggle to produce consensual documents that nevertheless reflect 'collective patterns of intention',[24] UPR drafters aim to bridge the divide between transnational actors and local activists.

However, the tension between the moral duty of protecting the 'voices from the field' and the necessity to preserve the credibility of the process implies that drafters have to engage in a myriad of bureaucratic procedures whose repetitive performance serves to maintain the principles of neutrality, objectivity and transparency. Such procedures entail classifying NGOs according to their United Nations Economic and Social Council status, verifying the compliance of their contributions with the OHCHR's internal guidelines or verifying NGOs' acronyms in official databases, to name just a few. If such practices may at first sight be interpreted as paradigmatic manifestations of the 'iron cage of bureaucracy',[25] they also reflect the 'mediating' function of documents. As Mathew Hull rightly argues in his ethnography of bureaucracy in Pakistan, documentation is not simply about record keeping. Documents also have a deeper social function. They act as 'mediators', ie things that 'shape the significance of the signs inscribed on them and their relations with the objects they refer to'.[26]

Indeed, in spite of the tedious administrative procedures that the production of documents entails, their drafting involves intense discussions which are not deprived of affects and even, at times, passion.[27] This observation contrasts with the tenor of the 'interactive dialogue', which, despite its promising title, does not provide much room for genuine interaction or debate. Such negotiations, I realised during my three-month internship, take place elsewhere: notably, in the offices of the OHCHR, where

---

[22] Merry (n 1) 16.
[23] ibid 19.
[24] Riles, 'Infinity within the Brackets' (n 13).
[25] M Weber, *Economy and Society: An Outline of Interpretive Sociology* (California, University of California Press, 1968).
[26] MS Hull, *Government of Paper: The Materiality of Bureaucracy in Urban Pakistan* (California, University of California Press, 2012) 253.
[27] Billaud (n 3).

drafters engage in vigorous debates over the content of a paragraph and take strategic decisions on which issues to prioritise.

The 'bureaucratic stamina'[28] that was noticeable in such discussions was proportional to the level of procedural restrictions that regimented the drafting of the Summary. Indeed, in order to preserve an aura of professional impartiality, drafters had to be cautious in the way they presented information. During meetings, for example, drafters often devised arguments to justify why they had decided to incorporate the contribution of an NGO that was unregistered in its country of origin or why they had placed an issue in a specific paragraph. These arguments were essential to counter the potential critiques of states and preserve the reputation of the OHCHR. By contrast with the *libido sciendi* – the fervent desire to know, which, according to Bruno Latour,[29] animates the research of scientists – UPR drafters cannot publicly exhibit the same degree of passionate interest. Rather, like for the lawyers of the French Conseil d'Etat that Latour studied,[30] they have to adopt an attitudinal posture of detachment reflecting the absence of belief or judgement in their work: what Latour calls '*libido judicandi*'. Such a posture is maintained by making documents appear as 'legal things' following the singular aesthetics of legal texts that serve to neutralise the intense affects noticeable in internal discussions.

According to the general guidelines of the Human Rights Council, the Summary cannot alter the original texts written by NGOs. Such a modality was devised to make sure Summaries do not contain any opinions, views or suggestions on the part of the OHCHR and to guarantee 'impartiality'. In practice, this means that Summaries are a collection of 'best quotes' extracted from NGOs' contributions, organised according to a standard template of paragraphs and sub-paragraphs, fostering the impression of a strong anchorage in the 'sphere of legal knowledge'.[31] The imposition of the copy/paste technique renders their reading arduous, making them resemble an assortment of soundbites without any distinct unifying melody. These limitations force drafters to be particularly creative and tactical in the selection and formal arrangement of quotes. Such strategies were collectively discussed during our weekly team meetings, during which we raised the dilemmas we faced with specific reports: we deliberated on how to handle contributions defending a conservative agenda, and what to do with the submissions of GONGOs (governmental non-governmental organisations) or those of civil society organisations banned in their home countries. Drafters shared their worries with regard to authoritarian states whose representatives insidiously tried to intimidate them. The commonly shared conviction that issues raised in documents were automatically reflected in the interactive dialogue provided drafters with a deep sense of moral responsibility. This sense of purpose contrasted with the feelings of irritation and boredom they often experienced otherwise – notably, when

---

[28] B Latour, 'Scientific Objects and Legal Objectivity' in A Pottage and M Mundy (eds), *Law, Anthropology, and the Constitution of the Social: Making Persons and Things* (Cambridge, Cambridge University Press 2004).
[29] ibid.
[30] B Latour, *The Making of Law: An Ethnography of the Conseil d'Etat* (Cambridge, Polity, 2010).
[31] A Riles, 'Anthropology, Human Rights, and Legal Knowledge: Culture in the Iron Cage' (2006) 108 *American Anthropologist* 52, 54.

they had to produce the report of the Working Group after each review, a task which involved rushing to type up the recorded statements of states so as to meet the impossible 48-hour deadline. As one drafter located in the Human Right Council branch once told me: 'We [drafters] write the play and they [states] act [with the texts we produce]'. If, in reality, states' recommendations were informed by various rationalities, including their own human rights priorities, bilateral relations and information received from their diplomatic delegations, the possibility of imagining themselves as the playwriters of the UPR intensified their commitment to get the script right.

This theatrical metaphor poignantly illustrates the ritualistic dimension of the UPR.[32] Indeed, beyond the extremely coded format and tightly timed verbal exchanges taking place during the public reviews, the documentation process also follows a series of 'rituals of verification',[33] whose purpose is to achieve both conformity and transformation ('making human rights real in the world'). Drafting procedures and rules serve to ensure consistency and to produce a communal artefact (the document) that can be considered authoritative. Contrary to treaty bodies' monitoring mechanisms, in which experts occupy a central role in the evaluation process,[34] the UPR relies on a decentralised form of authority whereby states' representatives, human rights activists and OHCHR drafters are responsible for presenting valid and trustworthy information. Drafters' attention to rules and procedures should therefore not be interpreted as a mere reflection of the 'banality of evil',[35] but rather as an illustration of their awareness of the ritual power of rules for achieving international legitimacy.[36] In this sense, documentation at the UPR reflects the culture of transnational consensus-building embedded in international governance processes. Drafters mobilise 'a distinctive cultural repertoire of procedures for dealing with difference, conceptions of how change takes place, and strategies for implementing change. They spend considerable effort drafting and editing documents that express the norms of this culture.'[37]

At the time of my fieldwork in 2011, the drafting process followed an inter-divisional methodology that mobilised the knowledge and expertise of civil servants working in the four divisions of the OHCHR: namely, the Field Office and Technical Cooperation Division (FOTCD), the Human Rights Treaties Division (HRTD), the Research and Right to Development Division (RRDD) and the Human Rights Council and Special Procedures Division (HRC-SPD). In each of these divisions, drafters called 'UPR focal points', under the supervision of a single coordinator, were in charge of gathering the information that was required for the division's 'input to the compilation and summary'. These teams of focal points worked in close collaboration with a team of 'drafters-coordinators' located within the Human Rights Council branch (under the HRC-SPD), who were responsible for collecting all the drafts and finalising the documents. This inter-divisional method had been put in place in order to avoid

---

[32] Charlesworth and Larking (n 3); Cowan, 'The Universal Periodic Review' (n 15).
[33] M Power, *The Audit Society: Rituals of Verification* (Oxford, Oxford University Press, 1999).
[34] Merry (n 1) 83.
[35] H Arendt, *Eichmann in Jerusalem: A Report on the Banality of Evil* (New York, Penguin Books, 2006).
[36] Merry (n 1) 90.
[37] ibid 100.

the personalisation of documents and to prevent the association of a document with a single author. This strategy, I was told, protected anonymity, guaranteed objectivity and enhanced the bureaucratic legitimacy of the material produced.

Because of their direct access to geographic desk officers who were in regular contact with OHCHR staffs in the field, FOTCD drafters were responsible for the first draft of the 'Summary of other stakeholders' information'. However, the inter-divisional methodology enabled them to share responsibility for authorship with their colleagues located in other divisions. The feeling of safety that came with anonymity and collective responsibility enabled drafters to occasionally bend the rules so as to avoid the exclusion of NGOs' contributions they found important. For example, internal policies (unknown to NGOs) stipulated that contributions written by members of parliament or political parties would be automatically excluded. Contributions using 'abusive language' (such as direct accusations of government officials) or 'second-hand information', or written in a non-official UN language, also had to be rejected. However, all these rules were not written in stone and were constantly negotiated and reinterpreted by drafters, notably during their weekly team meetings. When, on some occasions, drafters came across a problematic joint contribution, which was signed by political opposition leaders but included content considered important, they would call human rights activists to inquire about their methodology. Through these conversations, drafters would evaluate the extent to which the political parties were trying to use the UPR to get official recognition. If they estimated NGOs' responses were genuine, they would ask the heads of the coalition whether they would consider removing the signatures of political parties so as to facilitate the incorporation of their contribution in the summary. Their capacity to put faces to documents and build relationships with people located elsewhere in the world brought a feeling of satisfaction which was otherwise lacking in their everyday routine work. The social connections produced through documentation strengthened their consciousness of belonging to a community with the power to choose and shape, and their more profound 'feeling of pursuing an ideal'.[38]

This sentiment was particularly noticeable in the last phase of the documentation process, when the content of UPR documents was collectively assessed during the meeting of the Country Consultative Group (CCG). This meeting, which used to take place about 10 weeks before the review, gathered together the drafters from the different divisions who had been involved in the production of the documents. The presence of the geographic desk officers was important to validate the accuracy of the information provided. The objectives of the meeting were to highlight contentious issues for the selected reader (head of division) to decide upon, maintain a balance in the types of issues presented (civil and political rights versus economic, social and cultural rights), ensure complementarity and consistency between the Summary and the compilation, and select the information that should be given priority in the documents. The meeting of the CCG was a strategic moment during which drafters decided which issues needed to be emphasised. Individual drafters brought their

---

[38] J Cowan, '"The Feeling of Pursuing an Ideal": A League of Nations Civil Servant Reflects on His Work' (2020) 28 *Social Anthropology* 17.

own opinions and sought to find a consensus with their colleagues on the best strategy to adopt to make the documents speak. For example, during one CCG meeting, drafters discussed the opportunity of placing the contentious issue of LGBTQI rights under the 'right to privacy' section of the Summary, so as to avoid the criticisms of a state whose legislation criminalised homosexuality. Far from cultivating an ethos of professional detachment, such meetings functioned as 'chatterscapes' (in French, *caquetoir*),[39] where personal ideas were articulated through vigorous intellectual frictions with the collective. They involved intense emotions as drafters confronted their views and struggled over the content or the wording of a specific paragraph.

Here, Foucault's reflections on the Greek concept of 'parrhesia' as a form of 'free-spokenness', derived from a work on the self that involves a commitment to tell the truth, embrace specific virtues (a readiness to take a risk and be exposed to danger) and master bureaucratic techniques (adjustment to pre-defined rules and textual templates), captures the governmentality at play in the production of UPR documents quite well. Indeed, if drafters' political subjectivities were the product of a certain cultural capital shaped by their professional experience, knowledge practices and working conditions necessitating a constant discipline of the self, their compliance was never total and absolute. Foucault's notion of 'counter-conduct' as 'a category for capturing resistances to conduct that do not simply refuse or reject power, but resist by enacting counter-conducts'[40] is particularly apt at apprehending the productive relationship between ethics and politics and the mechanisms of power via which individuals' actions are structured. As Foucault argues in *Security, Territory, Population*:

> The relationship between power and freedom's refusal to submit [*insoumission*] cannot, therefore, be separated. The crucial problem of power is not that of voluntary servitude (how could we seek to be slaves?): at the very heart of the power relationship, and constantly provoking it, are the recalcitrance [*rétivité*] of the will and the intransigence [*intransitivité*] of freedom.[41]

Drafters' agency has therefore to be placed within the larger field of power determined by the parrhesiastic contract that binds them to the 'rulers' (ie states). Indeed, in a series of lectures delivered in Berkeley in 1983 and published under the title *Fearless Speech* in 2001,[42] Foucault offers a genealogy of the tradition of critique in Western philosophy. Reflecting on the Greek concept of parrhesia – a verbal activity that consists in speaking frankly and, by doing so, exposing one's life to potential danger – Foucault explains how the principles, techniques, norms and values governing truth-telling changed over time when Athenian democracy started to be challenged. As 'truth' became identified as a problem requiring philosophical inquiry, the reasoning process of this activity (ie what rationale must be followed in order to ensure a statement is true) gradually took prominence over the critical attitude (ie the concern with the importance of telling the truth). Foucault also highlights how the parrhesiastic contract between the ruler and those qualified to 'tell the truth' shifted from

---

[39] M de Certeau, 'Qu'est-Ce Qu'un Séminaire?' (1978) No 22/23 (11/12) *Esprit* 176.
[40] S Binkley and B Cruikshank, 'Introduction: Counter-Conduct' (2016) 21 *Foucault Studies* 3, 5.
[41] Foucault, *Security, Territory, Population* (n 4) 201.
[42] Foucault, *Fearless Speech* (n 11).

a relationship based on courage and frankness to a more complex one that required education and personal training. In the following section, I describe the transformations of parrhesiastic activities at the UPR resulting from increasing concerns over economic efficiency and rationalisation. I show how drafters' capacity to 'tell the truth' is constantly shaped and disciplined by the growing exigencies of power.

III. DISCIPLINING CONDUCT BY STREAMLINING MODALITIES

Since the beginning of the UPR, the drafting methodology has been the object of heated internal debate, especially between managers, who shared the view that it mobilised too many internal resources and was not cost-effective as a result, and drafters, who defended the idea that the methodology guaranteed the quality of the information produced and strengthened the links between the different UN human rights mechanisms. In a meeting held with their superiors during which drafters vigorously defended their point of view, a drafter working in the Treaty Bodies division explained that the methodology also served another equally important purpose: to mainstream the UPR in the OHCHR so as ensure its complementarity with other existing human rights monitoring mechanisms. For many drafters, the drafting of UPR documents was an opportunity to increase the visibility and relevance of treaty bodies and Special Procedures, by making the recommendations and analyses they produced appear in the compilation.

Furthermore, the inter-divisional drafting methodology had been initially conceived as a means to bring together the distinctive expertise and knowledge of each division. During the meeting, drafters insisted on the fact that the identification of the most up-to-date information required institutional knowledge as well as personal connections. One drafter within the Special Procedures division explained her superiors during the meeting that

> UPR focal points within Special Procedures have the power to put pressure on special rapporteurs' assistants to get the most up-to-date information simply because of the relationship of trust they have been able to develop with them over the years.

She argued that the selection of information for the Compilation was a delicate task, since public documents were often buried in the complex architecture of the OHCHR's website. In her view, personal relations were essential to retrieve reliable material on the most pressing human rights issues. Only such an intimate institutional knowledge could protect the UPR secretariat against the criticisms of states. She insisted:

> [State] Delegations frequently ask questions regarding the Compilation and it is the role of [Special Procedures] to find answers. Providing coherent answers on how we select our sources necessitates a good knowledge of the work and functioning of [Special Procedures].

Other drafters explained the importance of having serious discussions among colleagues on whose 'voice' would be the most influential – that of the High Commissioner, a Special Rapporteur or a less personalised UN report – to address certain states whose sensitivity had to be more carefully managed than others in the Compilation. 'We don't pick and choose our sources! We debate!', one of them argued. Her remark echoed a pattern Jane had already identified in her work on the Minority section at the League of Nations: namely, that states' anxieties about honour, sovereignty and legitimacy often crystallise around issues of language.[43] The choice of documents to quote in the compilation was therefore a diplomatic exercise that required an insider knowledge of the relationships between Special Rapporteurs, UN Envoys and the states engaged in international discussions around pressing human rights issues.

In spite of all their efforts, drafters did not succeed in convincing their hierarchy. The production of documents now follows a different methodology, whereby each drafter is in charge of the entire production of documents for two reviews per UPR session. The CCG meetings no longer take place, and focal points have been removed. Instead, each drafter is responsible for obtaining information from the other divisions. The advantage of this new methodology, according to a drafter I interviewed in 2019, is that it enables drafters to develop in-depth knowledge of the human rights situation in specific countries.

The possibility for drafters to be in full command of the content of documents provides them with a different sense of expert knowledge, less embedded in the intricacies of UN institutional mechanisms than in the human rights situation of the countries whose documents fall under their responsibility. For example, a drafter now working with the new methodology explained to me during an interview that she was assigned the documentations of countries that belonged to her geographic area of expertise, being herself from the same region. She enjoyed the possibility of carrying out in-depth research rather than the more scattered examination of countries' situations that the previous methodology promoted.

However, the centralisation of the drafting process also means that OHCHR divisions have lost ownership of UPR documentation and that individual drafters are personally accountable for the integrity of the information presented in each report. Furthermore, as discussed earlier, CCG meetings were important strategic moments when drafters collectively endorsed the content of documents and took decisions on which issues to prioritise. In this sense, CCG meetings had the ritual power of producing a community of international civil servants bound together by the principles of impartiality and transparency. They represented a 'venue for the alignment of various forms of expert knowledge and in particular for techniques of [human rights] assessment objectivity'.[44] One effect of the individualisation of documents is that the UPR secretariat is now deprived of the technical means to 'engage as a community': a feature of its everyday work that gave meaning to drafters' otherwise highly tedious and burdensome bureaucratic tasks. As Iver Neumann argues in his study of speech writing processes in the Norwegian Ministry of Foreign Affairs, 'speech writing is an identity-building project with the resulting text serving as an instantiation of the

---

[43] J Cowan, 'Who's Afraid of Violent Language?' (2003) 3 *Anthropological Theory* 271.
[44] H Brown, A Reed and T Yarrow, 'Introduction: Towards an Ethnography of Meeting' (2017) 23 *Journal of the Royal Anthropological Institute* 10, 16.

Ministry itself'.[45] The crafting of a speech, like the drafting of a UPR document, requires establishing a rapport between various divisions and departments, receiving their input and establishing a feeling of consensus among them. Although such face-to-face interactions are still possible under the new methodology, the absence of formal meetings where drafts can be discussed and compared leaves individual drafters with the responsibility for taking the hard final decisions mostly by themselves.

To compensate for the possible association of reports with individual drafters, internal rules have been consolidated. The personal relationships that drafters were able to develop with NGOs' representatives under the previous drafting methodology can no longer be maintained. NGOs' contributions that do not follow established standards and formats or that are submitted after the deadline are automatically dismissed. As UPR drafters have to carry the burden of responsibility for the documents they produce alone and are more directly exposed to states' pressures as a result, the flexibility with which they used to interpret rules is gradually disappearing. A stricter compliance with bureaucratic procedures is now the only strategy left at their disposal to demonstrate their commitment to 'impartiality' and to shield themselves against the potential attacks of states. The 'fuzzy logic'[46] that prevailed during the first cycle has partly disappeared, making it harder for drafters to short-circuit rules.

The social dimension of their work has therefore been partially eliminated in favour of efficiency and productivity criteria. From 'keepers of the truth' in a Foucauldian sense[47] – ie knowledge authorities bound to the ruler through a 'parrhesiastic contract' which authorises them to speak freely – drafters have been turned into more diligent bureaucrats, able to produce documents on time and according to specific administrative rules and standards. If the streamlining of modalities did not necessarily reduce drafters' commitment to speak the truth, it has nevertheless reconfigured the boundaries within which criticisms can be expressed. By removing the bureaucratic ambiguities that had been willingly left open,[48] the rationalisation and standardisation of procedures has eliminated the possibility of collective labour, compelling drafters to further squeeze their texts into existing boxes.

IV. CONCLUSION

As a truth-telling mechanism, the UPR involves a certain discipline of speech and the mobilisation of specific forms of knowledge. However, the power that it unleashes is never unidirectional or absolute. Instead of forming docile subjects, the UPR forms creative agents who constantly push the confines of established rules. The power of the UPR is therefore 'capillary' and circular, shaping actors' behaviours, ethical

---

[45] IB Neumann, '"A Speech That the Entire Ministry May Stand For," or: Why Diplomats Never Produce Anything New' (2007) 1 *International Political Sociology* 183, 186.

[46] M Halme-Tuomisaari, 'Methodologically Blonde at the UN in a Tactical Quest for Inclusion' (2018) 26 *Social Anthropology* 456.

[47] Billaud (n 3); Foucault, *Fearless Speech* (n 11).

[48] J Best, 'Bureaucratic Ambiguity' (2012) 41 *Economy and Society* 84.

inclinations and subjectivities, but also triggering 'counter-conducts' which contribute to its constant transformation. The seemingly neutral drafting techniques employed by drafters are not means to refuse conduct, but rather technologies deployed so as to promote NGOs as credible government partners. As Odysseos explains in her work on campaigns for justice following the Bhopal gas disaster, 'attempts to co-govern, that is, to reflexively participate in, redirect and modify our own conduct, are inextricably tied to "etho-poetic" practices of self-formation'.[49] In other words, the apparently impartial bureaucratic interventions of UPR drafters should be simultaneously interpreted as powerful manifestations of their ethical commitment to human rights as well as the product of human rights' governing effects.

Foucault defines 'government' as the attempt to shape human conduct by calculated means. Power is therefore the 'conduct of conduct' (of others and oneself): it operates by educating desires and configuring habits, aspirations and beliefs. In the UPR, such goals are achieved through a *dispositif* that combines 'forms of practical knowledge, with modes of perception, practices of calculation, vocabularies, types of authority, forms of judgement, architectural forms, human capacities, non-human objects and devices, inscriptions, techniques and so forth'.[50] The administrative practices it sets in motion powerfully contribute to the modelling of actors' subjectivities, encouraging them to adopt the bureaucratic mindset of templates and to express their criticisms according to predetermined formats and standards. Yet such practices demonstrate that, if drafters are instrumental in producing and reproducing 'conduct', they also maintain a critical attitude[51] which enables certain forms of insubordination[52] to emerge and a constant search for ways to conduct and be conducted *differently*. The rationalisation and streamlining of procedures have reduced the scope of possibilities for short-circuiting rules, since these rules also serve as a shield against the potential accusations of states.

---

[49] Odysseos (n 6) 190.
[50] Rose (n 18) 52.
[51] M Foucault, *The Politics of Truth* (S Lotringer ed, Semiotext(e)/Foreign Agents, 1997) 44.
[52] Foucault, *Security, Territory, Population* (n 4) 201.

11

Recommendations in Words and Numbers: Thinking with Sally Engle Merry at the Universal Periodic Review

JANE K COWAN[*]

IN THIS CHAPTER, I explore practices of language and enumeration within and around the relatively new and still evolving United Nations human rights mechanism, the Universal Periodic Review (UPR), which Julie Billaud and I began to investigate ethnographically in autumn 2010, during the final year of its first cycle. The UPR is a periodically held, intergovernmental and state-led peer evaluation scrutinising a state's human rights situation.[1] A product of a wide-ranging institutional reform of the UN human rights system initiated in 2005 in response to accusations of selectivity and politicisation against the Commission on Human Rights, the UPR was designed 'to shine a light equally on the human rights practices of all countries'.[2] The UPR is universal in its aim to review all UN member states and to include in the review's scope all of a state's human rights commitments. It works as a 'soft' global governance mechanism in which states are asked to provide accounts of their own human rights situation (presenting their 'achievements' and 'challenges') in the context of a public review to which all 193 UN member states are invited to participate. Reframing human rights monitoring from an exercise in 'naming and shaming' to

---

[*] I am grateful to Philip Alston, Julie Billaud, Marie Bénédicte Dembour, Mark Goodale, Charles Gore, Andrew Graan, Miia Halme-Tuomisaari, Agathe Mora and participants in the Allegra Lab webinar series in honour of Sally Engle Merry (April 2021) for stimulating questions and helpful feedback on earlier versions of this chapter.
[1] F Gaer, 'A Voice, Not an Echo: Universal Periodic Review and the UN Treaty Body System' (2007) 7 *Human Rights Law Review* 109; E Domínguez-Redondo, 'The Universal Periodic Review: Is There Life beyond Naming and Shaming in Human Rights Implementation?' (2008) 4 *New Zealand Law Review* 673; R Freedman, *The United Nations Human Rights Council: A Critique and Early Assessment* (Abingdon, Routledge, 2013); H Charlesworth and E Larking (eds), *Human Rights and the Universal Periodic Review: Rituals and Ritualism* (Cambridge, Cambridge University Press, 2014); JK Cowan and J Billaud, 'Between Learning and Schooling: The Politics of Human Rights Monitoring at the Universal Periodic Review' (2015) 36 *Third World Quarterly* 1175; S Gujadhur and M Limon, *Towards the Third Cycle of the UPR: Stick or Twist? Lessons Learnt from the First Ten Years of the Universal Periodic Review* (Versoix, Universal Rights Group, 2016).
[2] Charlesworth and Larking, *Human Rights and the Universal Periodic Review* (n 1) 2.

one of 'learning', the collectively agreed institution-building (IB) document instructs that the UPR 'should be conducted in an objective, transparent, non-selective, constructive, non-confrontational and non-politicised manner',[3] with states sharing best practice and collaborating in the joint project of improving human rights.

I approach the UPR as an example of 'audit culture',[4] one that has created a new political field in which actors are engaging in novel ways.[5] A major innovation of the mechanism is that all states are called upon to take the role of reviewer: to engage in constructive criticism and offer recommendations on how the state could improve. Thus, the UPR places upon fellow UN member states, rather than experts or, alternatively, affluent Western countries which have hitherto seen themselves as guardians of international human rights, the responsibility to hold the state to account and suggest improvements. This shift from expert review to peer review, and the enlistment of *all* states in the project of persuasion, dramatically alters the dynamics of human rights supervision.

I describe this exploration as 'thinking with Sally Engle Merry' to acknowledge multiple conversations since 2006 – in person, over email and through comments on draft papers – where we puzzled together over the intriguing, and sometimes perplexing, operation of human rights mechanisms at the UN. I frame my discussion using the broad categories of words and numbers, informed and stimulated by Merry's attention to a variety of linguistic and enumerative processes of translation, reformulation, measurement, ranking, counting and accounting in her studies of human rights practices. I begin with an overview of the UPR institutional design and evolving modalities, explaining how the mechanism works. As the chapter will focus on recommendations, I elaborate on a few aspects of emergent practices of recommending that constitute important background information for my unfolding argument.

Having established how the UPR works, with an emphasis on its implications for UN member states within this state-led mechanism, I shift my analytical attention to the intermediaries that fascinated Merry: the people 'in the middle' who act as 'knowledge brokers between culturally distinct social worlds'.[6] I follow how civil society activists use both language practices and enumeration practices in efforts to insert their agendas into state-dominated UPR proceedings. As they do in other UN human rights mechanisms,[7] civil society activists continue a long-standing practice

---

[3] United Nations Human Rights Council, 'Institution-Building of the United Nations Human Rights Council' (18 June 2007) UN Doc A/HRC/RES 5/1, Annex.

[4] M Strathern, (ed) *Audit Cultures: Anthropological Studies in Accountability, Ethics and the Academy* (London, Routledge, 2000).

[5] JK Cowan, 'The Universal Periodic Review as a Public Audit Ritual: An Anthropological Perspective on Emerging Practices in the Global Governance of Human Rights' in Charlesworth and Larking, (eds) *Human Rights and the Universal Periodic Review* (n 1) 42; Cowan and Billaud, 'Between Learning and Schooling (n 1); JK Cowan and J Billaud, 'The "Public" Character of the Universal Periodic Review: Contested Concept and Methodological Challenge' in R Niezen and M Sapignoli (eds), *Palaces of Hope: The Anthropology of Global Organizations* (Cambridge, Cambridge University Press, 2017) 106.

[6] SE Merry, 'Transnational Human Rights and Local Activism: Mapping the Middle' (2006) 108 *American Anthropologist* 38, 38.

[7] See, eg SE Merry, *Human Rights and Gender Violence: Translating International Law into Local Justice* (Chicago, University of Chicago Press, 2006); T Kelly, 'The UN Committee against Torture: Human Rights Monitoring and the Legal Recognition of Cruelty' (2009) 31 *Human Rights Quarterly* 777; M Halme-Tuomisaari, 'Meeting "The World" at the Palais Wilson: Embodied Universalism at the

of monitoring their own government's actions and policies. What is distinctive in the UPR, however, is that they now also 'monitor the monitors', assessing how diligently, and how effectively, UN member states carry out their still novel role of holding their fellow states to account. These linguistic and enumerative efforts focus on, and converge in, a political technology familiar in international human rights contexts: the recommendation. Civil society groups strive to ensure that their issues are 'taken up' by sympathetic states as recommendations, and that those recommendations are efficacious in producing improvements 'on the ground'.

I. UPR INSTITUTIONAL DESIGN AND MODALITIES

The UPR process, as I have described it elsewhere, is 'an untidy and unruly assemblage of people, objects, texts and utterances that extend across time and space'.[8] The new political field it has generated extends transnationally and enables existing categories of actors to speak and act in new ways.[9] In this chapter, I focus on the Geneva moment, and set out in this section, schematically and with selective details, the logic and working methods (in UN parlance, 'modalities') of the review. This apparently simple task is complicated by the fact that the mechanism is an evolving one: a comprehensive, and contentious, 'review of the work and functioning of the Human Rights Council' after its first five years led in 2010–11 to a number of significant changes in the UPR instituted at the start of the second cycle.[10] But the UPR continues to be debated, amended and altered, not only through formal decision-making, but also through informal practices that have arisen in and around it.

Launched in 2008, the UPR is the newest mechanism within a system of complementary human rights monitoring mechanisms in Geneva.[11] As set out in the IB document, its objectives are:

a) The improvement of the human rights situation on the ground;
b) The fulfilment of the States' human rights obligations and commitments and assessment of positive developments and challenges faced by the State;
c) The enhancement of the State's capacity and of technical assistance, in consultation with, and with the consent of, the State concerned;
d) The sharing of best practice among States and other stakeholders;

UN Human Rights Committee' in Niezen and Sapignoli (n 5); M Halme-Tuomisaari, 'Guarding Utopia: Law, Vulnerability and Frustration at the UN Human Rights Committee' (2020) 28 *Social Anthropology/Anthropologie Sociale* 35.

[8] Cowan, 'The Universal Periodic Review as a Public Audit Ritual' (n 5) 45.

[9] Cowan and Billaud, 'Between Learning and Schooling' (n 1); Cowan and Billaud, 'The "Public" Character of the Universal Periodic Review' (n 5).

[10] United Nations Human Rights Council, 'Report of the Working Group on the Universal Periodic Review: United States of America' (18 March 2011) UN Doc A/HRC/16/DEC/115, Agenda item 6; Cowan and Billaud, 'Between Learning and Schooling' (n 1) 1183–86.

[11] H Charlesworth and E Larking, 'Introduction: The Regulatory Power of the Universal Periodic Review' in Charlesworth and Larking, (eds) *Human Rights and the Universal Periodic Review* (n 1) give a more detailed yet concise description, whereas the other chapters in that book give views from the perspectives of a wide range of UPR actors and scholars. See also Freedman, *The United Nations Human Rights Council* (n 1) 253–82.

e) Support for cooperation in the promotion and protection of human rights; and
f) The encouragement and full cooperation and engagement with the Council, other human rights bodies and the Office of the United Nations High Commissioner for Human Rights.[12]

The UPR is unique in its universality. All (currently 193) UN member states can participate in two capacities: once per cycle as a 'State under Review' (SuR) and at all other reviews as a member of the UPR Working Group, also known as a 'Participating Government', 'Reviewing State' or, informally though increasingly, a 'Recommending State' (RS).[13] The UPR is also unique in its holistic character: each SuR is reviewed in light of the UN Charter, the Universal Declaration of Human Rights, any human rights instruments to which it is a party, any voluntary pledges or commitments it has made and any applicable humanitarian law. Although universal, the review 'should take into account the level of development and specificities of countries'.[14] Unlike the treaty body committees or the system of Special Rapporteurs, the UPR has no experts. Rather, states constitute a Working Group of peers who comment on the human rights situation and offer suggestions for improvement. A 'troika' of three member states, from different regions and chosen by lot, 'facilitates' the review, especially the preparation of the Working Group report (also called the 'outcome report'), while the Office of the High Commissioner of Human Rights (OHCHR) acts as the secretariat, offering assistance and expertise and producing the documents.[15] Non-governmental organisations and national human rights institutions are recognised as relevant stakeholders.

Organised as an ongoing review process with each cycle lasting several years,[16] the UPR cycle has three phases. In the first phase, 'objective and reliable' information is gathered and the three reports on which the review is based are prepared: the SuR writes its national report and the OHCHR drafts the Compilation (relevant extracts of reports by UN bodies such as treaty bodies) and the Stakeholder Summary (compiled from submissions by civil society, the country's national human rights institution and other multilateral bodies such as the UN High Commission for Refugees, the European Union and the International Organization for Migration).

---

[12] United Nations Human Rights Council (n 3).

[13] In the IB document, Human Rights Council, Resolution 5/1, Annex, only the term 'member of the Working Group' appears. During the first cycle, the terms 'Participating Government', 'Reviewing State' or simply 'delegation' were used. The designation 'Recommending State', proposed originally during the first cycle as an informative shorthand by the academic Edward McMahon and taken up energetically by the NGO UPR-Info, is increasingly used. I adopt the term Reviewing State, abbreviated here to RS, as descriptively more accurate as well as less partisan. Throughout the text, I retain the UN usage of denoting categories of actor, UN bodies and types of document in capital letters.

[14] United Nations Human Rights Council (n 3).

[15] J Billaud, 'Keepers of the Truth: Producing "Transparent" Documents for the Universal Periodic Review' in Charlesworth and Larking, (eds) *Human Rights and the Universal Periodic Review* (n 1).

[16] Originally, a UPR cycle lasted four years. Since the second cycle, the cycle has been extended to four and a half years. A break added between the second and third cycles means that reviews are effectively taking place in a five-year cycle.

The second phase is a series of three events that I theorise as 'public audit rituals'.[17] The most important of these is the review,[18] officially called the UPR Working Group, held in the magnificent Room XX of the Palais des Nations complex. Although the Working Group is chaired by the Human Rights Council president and composed of the 47 elected Council members, all other UN member states, called observers, may in fact participate fully in any or all reviews; in effect, the review is conducted by the collectivity of UN member states. Depending on the significance of the SuR in the international system, the numbers of UN member state delegations participating may range from a few dozen to close to a full house.[19] During this public and webcast session, in which all speech recognised by the chair is simultaneously translated into the UN's six official languages (English, French, Spanish, Chinese, Arabic and Russian), the chair opens the proceedings and invites the head of the SuR's delegation to present its national report, noting its 'achievements' and 'challenges', and answering any advance questions. This is followed by what is called the 'interactive dialogue'.[20] RSs, according to a prescribed order and one state following immediately after another, read out short, pre-drafted statements.[21] The statements include greetings, congratulations, condemnations, observations, concerns, questions and recommendations for improving the SuR's human rights practices. As the session unfolds, the SuR can request the chair to pause the flow of RSs' statements so that it can answer questions and present new information, and then does a final summing up.

When this session finishes, the delegation of the SuR and the troika, with the burden of work carried by OHCHR staff, prepare the Draft Report. This report summarises the SuR's presentation as well as the interactive dialogue and the SuR's responses. Following this are sections on 'Conclusions and/or recommendations', and, where relevant, 'Voluntary pledges and commitments' made by the SuR. The Draft Report is presented at 'The Adoption' (ie the adoption of the Draft Report of the UPR Working Group), a public meeting of the same constituents convened

---

[17] Cowan, 'The Universal Periodic Review as a Public Audit Ritual' (n 5).

[18] The UPR Working Group review originally lasted three hours, but from the second cycle onwards, from May 2012, the time has been increased to three and a half hours. The original allocation of 60 minutes to the SuR and 120 minutes to all other states has been increased to 70 and 140 minutes, respectively.

[19] As elicited by the reviews of the USA, for instance.

[20] The apparent plain-speaking of UN terminology can be deceptive. A UN interactive dialogue is neither 'interactive' nor a 'dialogue' in the ordinary sense of continuous turn-taking and immediate, improvised response to one's interlocutor. In the UPR Working Group, RSs read out statements prepared in advance and the SuR also presents the national report from a written summary. When the SuR requests pauses in the flow of statements to answer questions that have been raised, in many cases it hands over to representatives of relevant government departments that, in the preparation phase, have spent time anticipating likely questions and drafting written responses.

[21] The order of speaking for RSs was not specified in the institutional building document, and in the first cycle was handled by requiring individual diplomats or interns physically to queue to register on the list of speakers. As behaviour in the queue was marked by continuous contravention of diplomatic fair play, the original speakers' list procedure became highly contentious and was replaced, in the second cycle, by a procedure where the president chose the first speaker by lot, followed by all states requesting speaking time in alphabetical order according to the English name of the state.

about 48 hours later, in which any 'technical issues' arising can be raised.[22] The final version, called 'Report of the Working Group on the Universal Periodic Review: [country name]', is presented and adopted several months later, at the plenary of the next Human Rights Council under Item 6 of the agenda, 'Consideration of UPR outcomes'. It is allocated an hour, divided equally between the SuR, other RSs and civil society, this being the first and last opportunity for members of civil society to speak publicly within the UPR's formal space.[23]

The third phase, the moment during which the UPR is meant to lead to change 'on the ground', is a roughly four-year period of implementation for the SuR to act upon accepted recommendations. The SuR is strongly encouraged, though not required, to submit a mid-term report on progress made in implementing each recommendation. Civil society organisations monitor implementation of recommendations in their watchdog role, but also, often, as partners, collaborating with the state and other stakeholders. In the final year, the various stakeholders prepare for the next review: raising awareness of the review and new human rights 'challenges', gathering information and drafting reports.

Finally, the cycle culminates in the next review: this is the end point of the ongoing cycle, in which the Working Group, in principle, focuses on the SuR's implementation of accepted recommendations. It is also the starting point for the new cycle: the Working Group is informed of current human rights situation, including developments arising since the last review, on the basis of which RSs offer new recommendations.

II. THE EMERGENCE OF THE RECOMMENDATION IN THE UPR

As recommendations are this chapter's focus, it is important to set out some additional historical and procedural detail. First, the currently overwhelming focus on the UPR recommendation, observable among all categories of UPR stakeholders, is something that has emerged over time; it was not there from the start. RSs are not obliged to make recommendations. Indeed, in early reviews, the majority of states made detailed interventions without formulating recommendations.[24] Recall that the UPR is unprecedented in creating a public, international forum where every UN member state is invited to comment, question and make suggestions regarding another state's human rights situation. Diplomats have appreciated, and sometimes feared, the opportunity this offers to speak to multiple audiences. Statements are

---

[22] As we shall see, technical and procedural disagreement is very often about political disagreement.

[23] A revision in the modalities decided at the 2011 review provides that from the second cycle onwards, the national human rights institution may speak directly after the SuR at the plenary adoption.

[24] For instance, in the first session of the first cycle, 38 RSs participated in the UK's review on 10 April 2008, with 17 RSs (less than half) contributing 28 recommendations: United Nations Human Rights Council, 'Universal Periodic Review: Report of the Working Group on the Universal Periodic Review – United Kingdom of Great Britain and Northern Ireland' (23 May 2008) UN Doc A/HRC/8/25. A total of 45 RSs participated in the interactive dialogue of South Africa's review on 15 April 2008, with 18 RSs (just over a third) contributing a total of 22 recommendations: United Nations Human Rights Council, 'Universal Periodic Review: Report of the Working Group on the Universal Periodic Review – South Africa' (23 May 2008) UN Doc A/HRC/8/32.

always scripted in advance, and diplomatic delegations spend considerable time and thought crafting these richly layered public communications, addressed to the SuR but witnessed by the entire collectivity of states and, through the webcast, by the world.[25] In the first cycle, when time slots were two or three minutes, a statement normally contained greetings, thanks, some combination of congratulations, condemnations, observations, concerns, questions ... and only then (and not always) recommendations. Remarkably, since the second cycle, when time slots were reduced, often to less than a minute, diplomats have generally resisted pressures to cut out diplomatic niceties and get down to business: their statements still articulate these varied elements, just more concisely. Recommendations have gradually become de rigueur, however.

My second point: phrases formulated as recommendations have always been treated differently in the Working Group report compared to other textual elements of the RS's statements, as if in implicit recognition of their potential illocutionary force. When composing the draft report, OHCHR staff have discretion on what points from each RS's statement in the interactive dialogue to include in their summaries (each RS receiving a separate number); demands for brevity mean important interventions do get lost.[26] By contrast, all recommendations, as well as the voluntary pledges the SuR has made, receive a separate number and are included in their entirety, though dropping the preliminary '[RS] recommends that [SuR] ...'. Thus, in the Draft Report for Ireland's October 2011 review, we find recommendations from France and Uruguay:

106.14 Develop and adopt a gender parity law (France);

106.21 Enact laws setting principles on law, rights and obligations that govern family reunification (Uruguay);[27]

UPR Working Group reports have, from the beginning, represented recommendations in this way, indicating the recommender(s). But a decision taken in August 2008, only a few months after UPR had been launched, has given this textual form additional significance (my third point): UN member states agreed that recommendations would be recognised *not* as endorsed by the Working Group as a collectivity, but rather as inputs by the states who proposed them.[28] This arose when Egypt, on behalf of the African Group, objected that creating an impression that the entire Working Group endorsed every recommendation presented by a UN member state was a violation of the sovereign rights of states. This decision was hailed by Ethiopian diplomat Allehone Mulugeta Abebe as 'a "brilliant" solution to handling some quite sensitive

---

[25] For an analysis of the semiotic, political and ethical dimensions of country statements at the UPR, see JK Cowan, 'Modes of Acting Virtuously in the Universal Periodic Review' in GV Vilaça and M Varaki (eds), *Ethical Leadership in International Organizations: Concepts, Narratives, Judgment and Assessment* (Cambridge, Cambridge University Press, 2021).

[26] Cowan, 'Modes of Acting Virtuously' (n 25) 192–201.

[27] United Nations Human Rights Council, 'Draft Report of the Working Group on the Universal Periodic Review: Ireland' (10 October 2011) UN Doc A/HRC/WG.6/12/L.7, 18.

[28] AM Abebe, 'Of Shaming and Bargaining: African states and the Universal Periodic Review of the Human Rights Council' (2009) 9 *Human Rights Law Review* 1, 15–16; S Bertotti, 'Separate or Inseparable? How Discourse Interpreting Law and Politics as Separable Categories Shaped the Formation of the UN Human Rights Council's Universal Periodic Review' (2019) 23 *International Journal of Human Rights* 1140.

recommendations' on which delegations did not agree,[29] for instance, on the issue of sexual orientation. Recommendations thus became understood as bilateral agreements between the RS(s)[30] and the SuR.

Fourth, recommendations are distinguished by, and placed in the report document according to, the SuR's response to them, the terminology for which has evolved over time. Originally, an SuR was required to declare its position on all recommendations made – to 'accept' or 'reject' them – though it has always been possible for the SuR to postpone decision on some or all recommendations, normally with a promise to provide responses no later than the next session of the Human Rights Council.[31] When we began our fieldwork in autumn 2010, almost everyone spoke of recommendations as either 'accepted' or 'rejected' (in the reports, the phrasing is: 'recommendations that enjoy [the state's] support' or '... did not enjoy its support'). By autumn 2011, OHCHR staff, as well as the staff of UPR Info, an NGO central to the UPR process that I describe in the next section, were emphasising at meetings that, according to the original IB document,[32] a recommendation could be only 'accepted' or 'noted' (not 'rejected') and urging everyone to use the correct terminology. They argued that a 'noted' recommendation remained in the record and could be returned to at a future date. The seemingly technical discussion around terminology expressed a struggle between those who, on grounds of a state's sovereign rights, hold that 'no means no' and those who see human rights as a long-term project of persuasion, such that 'no' should be treated as 'not now, but maybe later'. Such is the intensity of advocacy around 'noted' recommendations that the 2011 'Review of the Work and Functioning of the Human Rights Council' was compelled explicitly to spell out that 'the second and subsequent cycles of the review should focus on, inter alia, the implementation of the accepted recommendations and the developments of the human rights situation in the State under Review'.[33]

This leads to my final point, regarding monitoring the implementation of accepted recommendations in the SuR's subsequent review. The situation is, in fact, complex. The UPR 'was created without any systematic way to keep track of improvement'.[34] This was a result not only of reluctance on the part of some states (eg the Non-Aligned Movement) to set up a follow-up mechanism, but, according to Sara Bertotti's analysis, a reluctance also on the part of some UN independent experts who wished to preserve their authority as arbiters of a state's fulfilment of its human rights obligations and were unwilling to hand this task over to states.[35] In the absence of such a

---

[29] Abebe (n 28) 16.

[30] Some issues received duplicate or similar recommendations from multiple RSs and these might be grouped as a single recommendation. Thus, Ireland's report lists the following, accepted recommendation: '105.2. Become a party (Estonia), consider accession (Brazil), ratification (Chile), ratify the Optional Protocol to the Convention Against Torture (OP-CAT) (France, Greece, Slovenia, UK) and set up a national prevention mechanism that meets the criteria and guarantees under this instrument (Switzerland)'. United Nations Human Rights Council, 'Draft Report: Ireland' (n 27) 14.

[31] Abebe (n 28) 15.

[32] United Nations Human Rights Council, 'Institution-Building' (n 3) para 32.

[33] United Nations Human Rights Council, 'Review of the Work and Functioning of the Human Rights Council' (12 April 2011) UN Doc A/HRC/RES/16/21, para 6.

[34] Bertotti (n 28) 1140–41.

[35] ibid.

follow-up mechanism, monitoring implementation relies, to a large extent, on the SuR's self-reporting on implementation (in optional mid-term reports as well as in the subsequent national report) and on civil society shadow reporting. However, once states decided to treat recommendations as bilateral, many UPR stakeholders viewed this as conferring responsibility for following up the implementation of an accepted recommendation during the subsequent Working Group to the RS that had made the recommendation.

Has this happened? A study looking at RS follow-up, undertaken by the NGO UPR Info on the first 70 reviews (out of 193) in the second cycle found, surprisingly, that 'only 18.8% of 1st cycle recommendations were linked to recommendations made at the 2nd cycle (930 out of 4935)'.[36] Factors that UPR Info thought could explain this low level of follow-up by the RS included:

> lack of comprehension of the cyclic nature of the UPR and the importance to refer back to previous recommendations; lack of knowledge of the previous recommendations made; lack of political will to confront the state under review for a second time on the same issue; commitment to only make two recommendations to each State under Review; the emergence of new priorities in the country under review or in the foreign policy of the Recommending State.[37]

Although limited follow-up by RSs on the recommendations they have made is indisputable, the authors themselves admit that the alarmingly small figure of 18.8 per cent may reflect in part their methodology, which only tracked recommendations: 'If a state made comments, objections or concerns about the implementation of previous recommendations, but did not turn these comments, objections or concerns into new recommendations, this effort by the RS is not reflected in our study.'[38] Their acknowledgement of this and seven other potential 'contributing factors' to low numbers of linkages notwithstanding, the methodology of this study reflects and reinforces a view that recommendations are the only words that count in the UPR.[39] In such circumstances, civil society, along with OHCHR staff, labour to influence recommendations, to keep track of them and to remind RSs of their responsibilities to recommend effectively, as well as to monitor their peers' implementation of those recommendations.

III. RECOMMENDING WORDS

As one of the first generation of anthropologists grappling with the ways that social and indigenous movements drew on human rights in their struggles for justice, Sally

---

[36] UPR Info, *Starting All Over Again? An Analysis of the Links between 1st and 2nd Cycle Recommendations* (Geneva, UPR Info, 2015) 3.
[37] ibid 4.
[38] ibid 14. A Universal Rights Group study analysed the second cycle Working Group statements (rather than only the recommendations) of 74 RSs. Discounting any fully implemented recommendations, they found that '38% of partially implemented, not implemented, or not indicated recommendations from the first cycle saw effective follow up during the second': Gujadhur and Limon (n 1) 39.
[39] In other contexts, including the pre-sessions, UPR Info staff stressed the importance of the UPR in creating opportunities for dialogue, so the narrow focus here on recommendations is unfortunate.

Engle Merry saw human rights not as 'simply the imposition of Western cultural forms and legalities', but rather as 'an open text, capable of appropriation and redefinition'.[40] She took up the concept of vernacularization and developed it as a tool for theorising the many ways this global set of standards was being received and reformulated 'on the ground' in various communities. Having observed such reformulations in local sites from Hawai'i and Hong Kong to India and New York City, Merry recognised the critical role played by 'intermediaries such as community leaders, nongovernmental organization participants and social movement activists'[41] in translating human rights ideas between and across spaces. The examples in her landmark article on theorising human rights vernacularization[42] mostly concerned how human rights concepts disseminated 'downwards' or 'outwards' from international meetings, conferences and UN monitoring processes, and it is striking that the many scholars she inspired to investigate vernacularization in new sites have similarly found the movement to flow mostly in one direction. Examples of local formulations of human rights *percolating upwards* to international human rights committees and expert meetings continue to be rare. Merry was not surprised by this. Indeed, her analytical exploration of 'the middle' – of the intermediary's interstitial, often ambiguous, position between two or more discourses, and two or more communities – is strongly informed by her awareness of the unequal prestige of languages and the asymmetries of translation.[43]

I am concerned here with that translation upwards: when intermediaries like those that Merry described – representatives of civil society organisations, both grassroots and international, from around the world – speak publicly about human rights at home in the context of the UPR process in Geneva. Civil society organisations are recognised as legitimate stakeholders in the UPR and are active in various ways: they may participate in consultations for their government's national report, submit written reports, approach and lobby embassy personnel in their own country and/or diplomatic missions in Geneva, and organise information sessions (called 'side events') during UPR sessions. Nonetheless, by design, civil society activists are excluded from speaking in the UPR's formal public proceedings until the Human Rights Council plenary, item 6 'Consideration of UPR reports' – the very last moment of the public review. Most view this invitation to participate as ritualistic, since by that time it is far too late to influence anything in the collective report of the state review.

It is in response to this exclusion that the UPR pre-session was initiated in April 2012, a month before the UPR's thirteenth session in May 2012, which kicked off the second cycle; it has now become a regular event. It was devised by an NGO that

---

[40] SE Merry, 'Legal Pluralism and Transnational Culture: The Ka Ho'okolokolonui Kanaka Maoli Tribunal, Hawai'i, 1993' in RA Wilson (ed), *Human Rights, Culture and Context: Anthropological Perspectives* (London, Pluto Press, 1997) 30; SE Merry, 'Changing Rights, Changing Culture' in JK Cowan, M-B Dembour and RA Wilson (eds), *Culture and Rights: Anthropological Perspectives* (Cambridge, Cambridge University Press, 2001); Merry, *Human Rights and Gender Violence* (n 7).
[41] Merry, 'Transnational Human Rights and Local Activism' (n 6) 38.
[42] ibid (n 6).
[43] ibid.

has become central to the UPR process: UPR Info.[44] Founded in 2008 in the first year of the UPR's first cycle, this innovative and entrepreneurial Geneva-based non-profit NGO undertakes a set of activities that can be glossed as 'monitoring the monitors': its staff, including interns, provide a continuously updated overview of the engagement in the UPR of UN member states who are meant to be monitoring each other. UPR Info staff do this by gathering, collating and analysing information related to the reviews and making this available on their database, which I will discuss shortly. They have also developed ambitious capacity-building programmes and workshops for all UPR actors, and host information sessions and social events.

The pre-session of a country is held about a month before the UPR session in which that country will be reviewed. Individuals representing diplomatic delegations – often interns, sometimes ambassadors, depending on the member state's diplomatic capacity and the 'importance' of the review – attend the country's one-hour slot if they wish to hear civil society perspectives on their country's human rights issues. At the pre-sessions I attended in 2013 and 2014, held in a large, rented meeting room of an international conference hall about 10 or 12 minutes' walk from the Palais des Nations, 20–37 diplomatic delegations attended (about 10–20 per cent of UN member states). By 2019, once pre-sessions had been moved into the Palais des Nations, the percentages had become much higher. UPR Info's founding director, the French political scientist Roland Chauville, would normally be present and would open the one-hour slot allocated to each country by reminding those assembled of the relevant facts: that (taking as an example one of the three countries addressed on an October morning in 2014) The Gambia was reviewed in February 2010 and received 153 recommendations, of which 68 were accepted and 85 were noted. He would then introduce the first panel member, keep time and chair the session.

In important ways, the pre-sessions 'mimic' the state reviews, except that civil society speaks and states – often including the prospective SuR – listen. Thus, in an all-morning pre-session I attended in early October 2014, 50-minute slots (each followed by a 10-minute break) were given to 'The Gambia', 'Angola' and 'Italy', following UPR practice in naming the session after the SuR, but allocating time not to states, but rather, to 'civil society', a category that in this context includes the country's national human rights institution. The individuals speaking were, in the majority, representatives of organisations based in the country being reviewed; however, on that day (and not atypically), several Geneva-based international NGOs spoke on behalf of colleagues who could not travel to Geneva.[45] Individuals were given slots

---

[44] UPR Info, *Pre-Sessions: Empowering Human Rights Voices from the Ground* (Geneva, UPR Info, 2016).

[45] They included Amnesty International, International Service for Human Rights, International Lesbian, Gay, Bisexual, Trans and Intersex Alliance, and Women's International League for Peace and Freedom. For insightful discussions of benefits and tensions in collaborations between international and national (grassroots) NGOs at the UPR, see N Baird, 'The Role of International Non-governmental Organisations in the Universal Periodic Review of Pacific Island States: Can "Doing Good" Be Done Better?' (2015) 16 *Melbourne Journal of International Law* 1; F McGaughey, 'The Role and Influence of Non-governmental Organisations in the Universal Periodic Review: International Context and Australian Case Study' (2017) 17 *Human Rights Law Review* 421; M Roesdahl, 'Universal Periodic Review and Its Limited Change Potential: Tracking the Complexity of Multiple Actors and Approaches to Human Rights Change through the Lens of the UPR Process of Nepal' (2017) 9 *Journal of Human Rights Practice* 401.

of 8–10 minutes; they spoke on behalf of a single NGO, or a coalition, network or alliance, and each addressed a limited range of topics. A few minutes at the end were saved for questions and discussion; in the sessions I observed, it was rare for delegates of more than one or two states to ask a question. Civil society activists then used the coffee break between country slots to network and to lobby the representatives of specific states individually.

How, then, do civil society activists speak in these newly invented public spaces of dialogue? In what linguistic forms must their claims be squeezed to be heard? First, it is important to acknowledge the diversity of speakers, the vast variation in their cultural capital and what, in Geneva's international organisation milieu, would be called their 'capacities'. Visiting Geneva for the first time, an Angolan speaking on behalf of a domestic violence NGO struggled with English and appeared generally unconfident in this still unfamiliar setting. By contrast, a British staffer for the Geneva-based International Service for Human Rights had the luxury of operating in her native language in a setting she knew well, while also benefiting from the prestige of her organisation, which hosted and assisted visiting civil society activists. Standing in for a representative of a Gambian NGO coalition whose fears of reprisal had prevented him from travelling to Geneva, she presented fluently and authoritatively the threats faced by journalists and human rights defenders.

These variations were noticeable, reflecting the speakers' different positions within the linguistic and cultural hierarchies of the UN's everyday practices and their vastly different levels of experience with the UN system. Along with nearly all their NGO colleagues, these two speakers nonetheless shared a common language of description and analysis, one that anglophones and francophones from the Global North could slip into with relative ease, whereas for Global South speakers it required a more complex labour of linguistic, conceptual and cultural translation.[46] Speaking about situations in the country to be reviewed in their allotted 8–10 minutes, they rarely talked about cultural or social specificities. They discussed issues using categories of international human rights, development and security discourses such as 'violence', 'discrimination', 'inadequate housing' and 'vulnerable minorities', as well as the ubiquitous acronyms (VAW, GBV, MDGs, SDGs). They referred to conventions and agreements that the state had accepted, as well as its voluntary commitments to ongoing campaigns and strategies (eg the UN Foundation's 'Every Woman, Every Child' health initiative, launched in 2010 as part of the Millennium Development Goals (MDGs)); sometimes they cited a recommendation made by another UN body, such as the Committee on the Elimination of All Forms of Discrimination against Women (CEDAW) or the Human Rights Committee. Civil society activists regularly talked about distressing situations, yet rarely showed anger. Even when clearly frustrated or cynical, they worked hard to adopt a 'constructive' tone. They employed a vocabulary of 'removing obstacles', 'seeking buy-in', 'progress made' and 'remaining challenges', and of wishing to persuade governments to see them as 'partners', rather than 'adversaries'.

---

[46] SE Merry and S Wood, 'Quantification and the Paradox of Measurement: Translating Children's Rights in Tanzania' (2015) 56 *Current Anthropology* 205.

Every presentation included a set of recommendations – note, not 'demands'. NGOs formulated these in the hope that one (or more) of the diplomatic missions present would 'take up' a recommendation they had suggested and include it in its own short statement in the upcoming interactive dialogue of that state's UPR. For less experienced NGOs (including those national NGOs generally unfamiliar with how things work in Geneva and whose representatives flew in especially for this event), recommendations could be long and unwieldy. Many recommendations contained two or three clauses that, in fact, recommended several different things. More experienced NGOs, or those who had been coached by colleagues from Geneva-based international NGOs (notably, Amnesty International), had learned to articulate recommendations that contained a single request and were extremely concrete, making them easy for a state to use. Many NGOs provided one- to two-page fact sheets which included three to six (and sometimes more) recommendations.

Occasionally, an NGO-composed recommendation, verbally presented at a pre-session or submitted as text and included in the Stakeholders' Summary, would indeed be 'taken up' and uttered, word for word, by a diplomat as part of her country's statement during the interactive dialogue. More frequently, that original NGO recommendation would be reframed in more general terms to include the human rights priorities of the state enunciating it and leaving room for manoeuvre for the state receiving it; yet, when uttered, it remained recognisable to the NGOs concerned as 'their issue'. In either case, staff of the NGO(s) involved claimed authorship of the recommendation, presented it as evidence of their influence on the UPR process and used this 'success story' in their subsequent advocacy.

In fact, verifying the 'origin' of recommendations pronounced during the UPR Working Group is extremely difficult.[47] Practices of drafting recommendations vary. Diplomats may cut and paste from the Stakeholders Summary and the Compilation, inserting an authoritative text – for instance, a previously received treaty body recommendation – whose own sources of influence may not be acknowledged, then reframe and rework that text.[48] The country statement itself, at least among the better resourced diplomatic missions, is likely to have been collectively authored, passed back and forth between the Geneva diplomatic mission of the 'State under Review' (SuR) and state agents in the 'capital', in a process of drafting and redrafting taking several months. In light of these dense processes of negotiating texts by multiple agents from different branches of the state and the intertextuality of documents that involve citation across human rights mechanisms and across time, we might join the linguist Mikhail Bakhtin[49] in asking 'Who is speaking?' when the diplomat reads their statement.

---

[47] ER McMahon et al, *The Universal Periodic Review: Do Civil Society Organization-Suggested Recommendations Matter?* (Friedrich-Ebert-Stiftung Dialogue on Globalization, November 2013).
[48] McGaughey (n 45) 444 identifies a recommendation by Poland at Australia's 2015 UPR concerning birth registration for indigenous children. Poland had picked up this issue from the Compilation report for Australia's review that included a Committee on the Rights of the Child (CRC) recommendation that closely correlated with the Polish recommendation and which itself was probably influenced by a shadow report to the CRC from the Castan Centre for Human Rights Law at University of Melbourne.
[49] MM Bakhtin, *The Dialogic Imagination: Four Essays* (M Holquist ed, C Emerson and M Holquist trans, Austin, University of Texas Press, 1984).

Bringing their concerns to Geneva, civil society activists may influence perceptions and may even succeed in persuading a state delegation to adopt their recommendations, in whole or as a starting point for editing.[50] Through such engagements, these activists are inducted into what Kamari Clarke calls an 'international justice assemblage' composed of 'technocratic practices, psycho-social embodied performances and emotional regimes'.[51] Back home, they may be noisily and creatively making rights claims.[52] In Geneva, their interventions require feats of linguistic, conceptual and cultural translation: they must learn how to articulate local concerns in the normative linguistic and conceptual categories of UN language, in the appropriate emotional registers and conforming to the precisely designated technical parameters of speaking time and space on the page. Significantly, they must reformulate local claims, grievances and experiences of suffering into a technocratic language of recommendation.

IV. NUMBERS, BUT NOT INDICATORS

Since her earliest fieldwork in the use of the courts by urban residents in the northeast USA, Merry's research included numbers.[53] As she moved deeper into research on gender violence, as well as the documenting of incidents by police and courts, she became interested in questions of how violent acts were named, described and measured: questions that were already preoccupying activists as well as staff in international organisations such as the World Health Organization and the OHCHR. Her ethnographic work in the 1990s, talking to Hawai'ian women about experiences of being hit by male partners, sharpened her sense that counting incidents of violence against women depended on *what counted as violence*, and that this was culturally defined and changed over time.[54] Violence was not a self-evident event, but an interpretation which required women to see the hitting as something more serious than the natural course of things: 'just what men do'. She brought this awareness to her work following the UN Statistical Commission's attempt to facilitate the measuring of violence against women through developing a set of indicators and guidelines that could be used by countries across the world.[55] This was one strand of the investigation by Merry and her colleagues of the 'turn to numbers' in global governance.[56]

---

[50] McGaughey (n 45); McMahon et al (n 47).

[51] KM Clarke, 'Affective Justice: The Racialised Imaginaries of International Justice' (2019) 42 *Political and Legal Anthropology Review* 244, 244. See also J Billaud, 'Between Conduct and Counter-conduct: Human Rights Translation at the Universal Periodic Review', ch 10 in this volume.

[52] K Zivi, *Making Rights Claims: A Practice of Democratic Citizenship* (Oxford, Oxford University Press, 2012); S Madhok, *Vernacular Rights Cultures: The Politics of Origins, Human Rights, and Gendered Struggles for Justice* (New York, Cambridge University Press, 2021).

[53] SE Merry, 'Going to Court: Strategies of Dispute Management in an American Urban Neighborhood' (1979) 13 *Law and Society Review* 891; SE Merry, *Getting Justice and Getting Even: Legal Consciousness among Working-Class Americans* (Chicago, University of Chicago Press, 1990).

[54] SE Merry, *Gender Violence: A Cultural Perspective* (Chichester, Wiley-Blackwell, 2009) 110–16.

[55] SE Merry, *The Seductions of Quantification: Measuring Human Rights, Gender Violence and Sex Trafficking* (Chicago, University of Chicago Press, 2016) 44.

[56] SE Merry, 'Measuring the World: Indicators, Human Rights and Global Governance' (2011) 52 Current Anthropology S83; KE Davis et al (eds), *Governance by Indicators: Global Power through Quantification*

Situating this turn in a longer history of the use of statistics in colonial and modern state governance, Merry and her colleagues were particularly interested in the rise of indicators.

From late autumn 2008, Merry and I had been corresponding about new research each of us was developing to carry out at the UN. I intended to apply the lens of audit culture to the new 'cooperative' human rights mechanism, the UPR. Merry was hoping to extend her work on indicators: 'I see a lot of concern about their adequacy, but not so much about whether they should be used at all. I think they are unstoppable, at this point', she wrote in an email in April 2010. We met several times in Geneva during 2010 and 2011, and compared notes on our respective projects. Indicators were a central topic of discussion in the contexts Merry was investigating. Since the 1980s and 1990s, UN treaty bodies had encouraged states to set their own standards and develop indicators and benchmarks. From the late 1990s, treaty bodies began to move towards a more universal system, while the OHCHR indicators project got underway in 2005.[57] Interestingly, the treaty body committee that Merry had followed closely for many years, CEDAW, was one of the most receptive to the development of indicators. Merry's research was still in progress and her comprehensive analysis was still to come; she would later acknowledge the ultimately lukewarm response of many treaty body experts to indicators, their uneven uptake by countries submitting reports and the broad resistance of the human rights community to using indicators for ranking.[58] At the time, though, Merry was diligently following 'indicator culture' and puzzling over the problems of commensuration that it raised.

What therefore surprised me as I began to spend time with actors involved in the UPR was how seldom I ever heard anyone mention indicators. It was true that indicators or references to them might occasionally be included in any of the three reports on which the review was based: in the national report submitted by the SuR, in a submission sent in by a civil society organisation and included in the Stakeholders Summary or as an element derived from a treaty body report on that state and included in the Compilation of UN Information.[59] Nonetheless, in contrast to its growing use by certain treaty bodies, the very minor presence of indicators and the rarity of discussion about them during the UPR's first cycle struck me as remarkable.

There were undoubtedly several reasons why indicators were not prominent in UPR sessions. Anxieties that indicators within the broader UN human rights system could be used to create country rankings in respect of a particular right, and that such data could be used to reward or punish, were already being voiced by some human rights experts in 2009;[60] this would have been even more unacceptable to diplomats in a mechanism like the UPR, which emphasised equality and cooperation. Probably

---

and Rankings (Oxford, Oxford University Press, 2012); KE Davis, B Kingsbury and SE Merry, 'Indicators as a Technology of Global Governance' (2012) 46 *Law and Society Review* 71; Merry, *The Seductions of Quantification* (n 55).

[57] Merry, *The Seductions of Quantification* (n 55) 176–77.
[58] ibid 200–05.
[59] United Nations Human Rights Office of the High Commissioner, *Human Rights Indicators: A Guide to Measurement and Implementation* (United Nations, 2012) UN Doc HR/PUB/12/5, 26.
[60] Merry, *The Seductions of Quantification* (n 55) 201–02.

the most important reason was a practical one: the UPR is a holistic review covering the entire array of a state's human rights obligations within a relatively short Working Group session. Its very large UPR Working Group (potentially – though, in practice, rarely – including all 193 UN member states) with its holistic remit does not undertake the kind of detailed examination that is possible in treaty body sessions. In those, a committee of up to 25 independent human rights experts, focusing on a single convention and examining state compliance on the basis of periodic reports sent by state parties in advance, spends around six hours querying a state on its compliance in one specific area of human rights (eg regarding women, children or people with disabilities). In such sessions, commonly characterised as 'constructive dialogue', the experts do not hesitate to probe intensely the data provided and press forthrightly into issues of concern.

While indicators played a very minor role in UPR proceedings in the first cycle, numbers were and are important in the UPR. But what numbers? What was being counted, measured or ranked, and how? Merry's quest to understand how indicators were made and used in other parts of the UN system, especially the treaty bodies, stimulated me to notice the drive to count and quantify in the UPR, and to wonder what work numbers were doing there. I noticed that, for civil society actors in particular, the recommendation was the thing that counted – and was counted.

V. WHAT IS A RECOMMENDATION?

But what exactly *is* a recommendation? Our interlocutors at the UPR rarely thought it necessary to explain the term, treating it as self-evident. Yet, when asked to define it, various meanings emerged. During early discussions on the Human Rights Council reform, Andrew Clapham, a professor of international law, described a recommendation as 'a political request from one state to another'. His description anticipated the important decision taken by states in August 2008 and examined above: that the act of recommending simply initiated a bilateral encounter between two states. Specifically, the Report of the Working Group would be a factual record of the interactive dialogue, including all the recommendations made, but did not constitute an endorsement by the whole Working Group of those recommendations.[61] Roland Chauville, the founding director of UPR Info, in an interview with me in October 2014, defined a recommendation slightly differently, as 'a political reminder of a state's existing obligations': a mere nudge to fulfil conscientiously what the state had already agreed to. In practice, a recommendation might be aimed at existing commitments, but might, equally, ask a state to take on a new commitment or otherwise change its practices.

Recommendations are used throughout the UN system and beyond. Peter Bille Larsen[62] identified recommendations as one of a number of techniques within an

---

[61] Abebe (n 28) 16; H Collister, 'Rituals and Implementation in the Universal Periodic Review and the Human Rights Treaty Bodies' in Charlesworth and Larking, (eds) *Human Rights and the Universal Periodic Review* (n 1) 115.

[62] PB Larsen, 'The Politics of Technicality: Guidance Culture in Environmental Governance and the International Sphere' in B Müller (ed), *The Gloss of Harmony: The Politics of Policy-Making in Multilateral Organisations* (London, Pluto Press, 2013).

'international guidance culture' that guides rather than dictates. They are a familiar form in what Christina Garsten and Kerstin Jacobsson call 'post-political forms of regulation and governance',[63] drawing on Chantal Mouffe's notion of the 'post-political'.[64] These forms, now pervasive and widely studied, tend to be associated with the rise of neoliberalism since the 1970s. Yet the recommendation is not a new technique: it has a long history in international organisations that, since their founding after the First World War, have faced the tricky task of attempting to establish, and even more, to see realised in practice, internationally agreed standards in a context of state sovereignty.[65]

Analysing efforts of the International Labour Organization (ILO) to improve labour standards in the first half of the twentieth century, Ernst Haas noted that 'the technique of Recommendations tends to be used as a political compromise or delaying tactic, when the adoption of more rigorous standards runs into opposition'.[66] This seems an unsurprising conclusion, but it is contradicted by Haas's own comprehensive studies on the ILO, as well as work by subsequent scholars, which reveals a more complicated history in the ways emergent practices and shifting relations between the various actors affected perceived distinctions between ratified and non-ratified and binding and non-binding agreements. That history is provocative for reflecting on current recommending practices. The case study examined by legal historian Laurence Helfer is instructive. Helfer points out that, already in 1921, in the face of unwillingness by ILO member states to interpret their own labour conventions and make them known to ILO's membership, ILO 'officials' (the term for international civil servants in this period) began to provide unofficial interpretations of the treaties to their members. Furthermore, in order 'to improve the legal and technical assistance they provided to their membership', they began to collect and publish information on ILO member states' compliance with unratified conventions and non-binding recommendations.[67] Taking on such tasks, ILO officials 'expanded their own authority'; over time, their information-gathering exercise – a nascent form of monitoring – 'blurred the distinction between ratified and unratified treaties'.[68] In other words, shifts in who monitored (from diplomats to bureaucrats), and how (through information gathering) and what they monitored (agreements, whether ratified or unratified), emerged quietly and rather organically, transgressing norms that only sovereign states could make such decisions. Remarkably, for a variety of contingent reasons, this appropriation of authority by ILO officials – to oversee, to monitor – was not contested by the majority of states, as it suited their purposes.

---

[63] C Garsten and K Jacobsson, 'Post-political Regulation: Soft Power and Post-political Visions in Global Governance' (2011) 39 *Critical Sociology* 421.
[64] C Mouffe, *On the Political* (London, Taylor & Francis, 2005).
[65] See, eg JE Alvarez, *International Organizations as Law-Makers* (Oxford, Oxford University Press, 2005); LR Helfer, 'Monitoring Compliance with Unratified Treaties: The ILO Experience' (2008) 71 *Law and Contemporary Problems* 193.
[66] EB Haas, *Beyond the Nation-State: Functionalism and International Organisation* (Stanford, Stanford University Press, 1964) 249.
[67] Helfer (n 65) 198.
[68] ibid.

In light of cases like this one, legal scholars have emphasised the importance of looking at the varieties of actual practice within international organisations: tracing the shifting configurations of stakeholders who become involved in monitoring a state's agreements, and the ways in which they do so. Surveying 'the varied forms of international institutional law', José Alvarez finds a 'purposeful ambiguity' that blurs distinctions between binding standards and non-binding recommendations to be a characteristic feature of technocratic regulation in many contexts of international governance.[69] The UN is the primary site where such an ambiguity can be observed: without the power to enforce decisions or impose sanctions, a whole range of UN bodies – from the General Assembly to treaty body committees to commissions of inquiry – constantly make recommendations, although with varying effects. The question becomes: what is it that enables recommendations in some contexts to be transformed into significant expectations and gain purchase, while those in others remain little more than pious wishes? It is this wider dynamic that helps explain the stakes involved at the UPR. The arduous efforts of civil society activists, in particular, to influence, shape, disseminate, count, assess and analyse recommendations 'might be seen as ways to transform "mere" recommendations into something that has considerably more significance or importance'.[70]

For civil society activists, UPR recommendations are seen to 'determine the actions to be taken to improve human rights'.[71] Recommendations are also the hook for their own involvement. A recommendation that a state has received and is considering might prompt government ministries to conduct human rights workshops with civil society and other stakeholders in order to develop a response, as happened in Indonesia.[72] A recommendation that is accepted can be a basis for civil society's dialogue with the state on how to implement it. Once accepted, a recommendation becomes a commitment whose fulfilment civil society can monitor. A recommendation that is not accepted becomes noted, and thus remains legible in the public record and can be returned to and lobbied for in subsequent advocacy.[73]

VI. COUNTING RECOMMENDATIONS

Yet, as the first cycle unfolded, just keeping track of recommendations quickly became an enormous challenge. The fact that any UN member state can potentially make one or more recommendations within any review expanded the activity of recommending beyond anything seen in other human rights bodies. The sheer numbers are astonishing. In the first four-year cycle, 21,353 recommendations were made, with

---

[69] Alvarez (n 65) 223.
[70] P Alston, personal communication.
[71] R Chauville, 'The Universal Periodic Review's First Cycle: Successes and Failures' in Charlesworth and Larking, (eds) *Human Rights and the Universal Periodic Review* (n 1) 97.
[72] Y Wahyuningrum, 'Indonesia and the Universal Periodic Review' in Charlesworth and Larking, (eds) *Human Rights and the Universal Periodic Review* (n 1) 273.
[73] B Schokman and P Lynch, 'Effective NGO Engagement with the Universal Periodic Review' in Charlesworth and Larking, (eds) *Human Rights and the Universal Periodic Review* (n 1).

the numbers per SuR starting small and rising dramatically. A state being reviewed in 2008 received an average of 27 recommendations, while for states reviewed in 2012, this had increased more than fivefold, to 147.[74] In the second cycle (May 2012–May 2016), states made 36,338 recommendations. At the time of writing, UPR is towards the end of the third cycle and the numbers remain high.

Counting recommendations and reporting on the counts are frequent rhetorical elements in talk about the UPR, as we saw in the UPR pre-sessions, but there has been debate about the significance and desirability of high numbers. Initially, certain states – including Algeria, France and the USA – committed to modelling 'best practice' by offering recommendations at every review. The emphasis was on encouraging states reluctant to engage in this unfamiliar activity of constructive criticism to become more 'active'.[75] As the numbers of recommendations started rising, this was seen positively as indicating participation by more and more states. Although, as Gujadhur and Limon observed, state delegations regularly complain of 'being overwhelmed' or 'lost in a jungle' of recommendations',[76] not all diplomats found this to be a problem. 'In my country, people liked having a lot of recommendations', a diplomat representing a small island state told me in May 2011. 'It means other countries have engaged with you and have taken the time to read the documents.'

By the end of the first cycle, nonetheless, many UPR participants recognised that very high numbers of recommendations were counter-productive: too many for the SuR to work out how to implement, too many for those involved in monitoring – which included the states making recommendations, the country's civil society and the OHCHR – to keep track of. There was some recognition of state capacity issues: Chauville noted that 'small island states can genuinely claim the impossibility of implementing 111 recommendations in only four and a half years' and acknowledged the danger that such high numbers might discourage them for appearing for a second review.[77] Many civil society actors were also sceptical of states' motives, suspecting that they would exploit the high numbers to 'act on the least challenging recommendations first and claim lack of time to implement the hardest'.[78] The fact that developing countries have since the 1980s been dealing with multiple sets of conditionalities, programmes, recommendations and targets from Global North donors and international financial institutions, constraining their room for manoeuvre and rendering them 'choiceless democracies',[79] did not receive much comment in the UPR discussions that we witnessed. Nonetheless, early in the second cycle, some diplomats agreed to limit themselves to two recommendations. Even so, as mentioned above,

---

[74] Chauville (n 71) 97.
[75] Cowan, 'The Universal Periodic Review as a Public Audit Ritual' (n 5); ER McMahon, 'The Universal Periodic Review: A Work in Progress – An Evaluation of the First Cycle of the New UPR Mechanism of the United Nations Human Rights Counci'l (Friedrich-Ebert-Stiftung Dialogue on Globalization, September 2012).
[76] Gujadhur and Limon (n 1) 4.
[77] Chauville (n 71) 97.
[78] ibid.
[79] T Mkandawire, 'Crisis Management and the Making of "Choiceless Democracies" in Africa' in R Joseph (ed), *The State, Conflict and Democracy in Africa* (Boulder, CO, Lynee Rienner, 1999).

recommendations in the second cycle increased, totalling 36,388, an average of 188 received by each SuR.

While the OHCHR reports of the Working Group are the official record of recommendations, civil society activists wishing to identify patterns of recommending across reviews – which states recommended what to who, in what words – found it cumbersome to do so from paper or even electronic documents. To facilitate this advocacy-related civil society research, the NGO UPR Info began in 2008 to develop its 'Database of Recommendations', collating recommendations, organising knowledge about them and making them visible, accessible and usable. Each recommendation was painstakingly copied and inputted manually by UPR Info staff, and its various components coded, allowing them to be broken down and recombined electronically to create various statistics. The database showed raw numbers of recommendations and voluntary pledges submitted per review, per session, per cycle and per thematic issue. It also allowed the user to use various filters to access and search all UPR recommendations and voluntary pledges across several categories: SuR, Recommending State, Regional Group, Organization of States, Response, Thematic Issues and Type of Action. Finally, UPR Info's database included 'a tool to produce statistics, a unique engine' that could create tables and charts and other statistics that

> allow the user to quickly access information such as which are the most active States or which issues are most frequently raised, in addition to a lot of other information that is useful for a better participation in the UPR.[80]

Using various filters on the database, the user can see who is recommending what to whom. A researcher from a charity like Save the Children can search the database to see how many and what kinds of recommendations pertaining to children and their rights were submitted in past reviews, which states consistently submitted such recommendations (ie which ones championed this issue), what type of action they involved (ie how specific, how demanding) and how the SuR had responded to those recommendations in the previous review (whether they were 'supported' or 'noted').

VII. RANKING RECOMMENDATIONS

The categorisation of action, a 'key value-added element'[81] of the database, is particularly significant to this discussion. Early in the first cycle, the political scientist Edward McMahon, in collaboration with UPR Info, developed the 'type of action' category. It focuses on the key action verbs contained in the recommendation, disaggregating them into five types and ranking them, creating a scale of 1–5, which 'reflect[s] increasing levels of effort, including political and financial resource allocation, on the

---

[80] UPR Info 2015, 8–9. The organisation launched a new, more 'robust' website in May 2020, using 'Uwazi', a flexible database application designed for human rights defenders with similar, though not identical, functions. Interestingly, the previously included search engine allowing statistics to be produced from the database has been dropped from the updated website.
[81] McMahon, 'The Universal Periodic Review: A Work in Progress' (n 75) 15.

part of the state to implement'.⁸² The five types of action and their criteria, with UPR Info's ranking of five recommendations from The Gambia's 2010 review provided as examples, are as follows:

1 – 'Minimal action' is for recommendations directed at states not being reviewed, or calling upon the SuR to request technical assistance, or share information, all of which require in general no or limited allocation of resources from the SuR (verbs include call on, seek, share).

Example: 'Seek the assistance of the international community in its efforts to combat poverty and to provide the necessary social services to its population based on the national priorities determined by the Government of Gambia' (Egypt to The Gambia – Supported)

2 – 'Continuing action' is for recommendations to continue or maintain existing efforts (verbs include continue, persevere, maintain).

Example: 'Continue to fight resolutely against the practice of arbitrary or summary executions and against impunity' (Cote d'Ivoire to The Gambia – Supported)

3 – 'Considering action' is for recommendations to consider change (verbs include consider, reflect upon, review, envision, analyze).

Example: 'Consider establishing a moratorium on executions with a view to abolishing the death penalty' (Brazil to The Gambia – Noted)

4 – 'General Action' is for recommendations of general action (verbs include take measures or steps toward, encourage, promote, intensify, engage with, respect, enhance, strengthen).

Example: 'Intensify measures to effectively combat child sexual abuse and exploitation' (Azerbaijan to The Gambia – Supported)

5 – 'Specific action' denotes recommendations calling for specific, tangible and verifiable actions (verbs include conduct, develop, eliminate, establish, investigate and undertake, as well as legal verbs such as abolish, accede, adopt, amend, implement, enforce, ratify)

Example: 'Repeal all provisions of law criminalizing sexual activity between consenting adults' (United States to The Gambia – Noted).⁸³

The categorisation and ranking are presented as neutral and objective, in that they do not assess the recommendation's content. Nonetheless, as Merry stressed, quantification always involves unspoken assumptions and power relations.⁸⁴ This scale is informed by values of liberalism, progress and autonomous individualism.⁸⁵ It explicitly values new action over continuing action, specific over general action, and action requiring the state to take responsibility over assistive action by others. It ranks effort according to a calculus of financial expenditure, in a context where many poor countries struggle to find such resources,⁸⁶ or political expenditure when these same countries have limited policy space.⁸⁷ The correlation of types of action with levels

---

⁸² ER McMahon, 'Framing the Picture: UPR Info Database Action Category' (UPR Info, 26 May 2020) www.upr-info.org/en/news/framing-the-picture-upr-info-database-action-category.
⁸³ Synthesised from McMahon, 'The Universal Periodic Review: A Work in Progress' (n 75); McMahon, 'Framing the Picture' (n 82); UPR Info, *Pre-Sessions* (n 44).
⁸⁴ Merry, *The Seductions of Quantification* (n 55).
⁸⁵ Cowan, 'The Universal Periodic Review as a Public Audit Ritual' (n 5); Cowan, 'Modes of Acting Virtuously' (n 25).
⁸⁶ Abebe (n 28); Baird, 'The Role of International Non-governmental Organisations' (n 45).
⁸⁷ Mkandawire (n 79).

of effort or cost involves some disputable judgements: why is sharing good practice assumed to involve minimal effort? Why would 'continuing' an initiative necessarily be less costly than starting a 'new' one? Do increasing specificity, effort, cost and value always line up so neatly?

The five categories distinguish 'levels of effort' required from the SuR to fulfil the recommendation. Yet the scale is applied to the verbs of the recommender, not the recipient. Moreover, it is applied with an eye to the recommender's intent. As McMahon explains:

> The way in which recommendations are phrased can be extremely revealing in terms of the intent of the recommending state. Are recommendations phrased in a 'soft' way, which can make it easy for the SuR to accept the recommendation and later claim compliance? Or are they posed in more rigorous language, which requires specificity of action and accountability?[88]

Such an explanation makes clear that the action category has several purposes. It helps civil society activists identify potential allies supportive of 'their' issues, and to distinguish among them as more and less rigorous recommenders. It also reminds the recommenders of their obligations, urging them through numbers to push harder for human rights improvement.

Unsurprisingly, civil society and the OHCHR alike favour verbs that convey 'specific actions'. Adopting a tool borrowed from management practices, they advocate SMART (specific, measurable, attainable, relevant and time-bound) recommendations. UPR Info has held trainings for diplomats to help them improve their phrasing of recommendations, including making them more specific. At an online launch in September 2021 of a study on 'emerging good practices' at the UPR[89] that focused on the 'implementation agenda', an OHCHR official noted approvingly that reviews now saw an average of 100 states making two or three recommendations, and that recommendations were becoming 'sharper, more time bound, more actionable'.

Phrasing a recommendation in a SMART way makes clearer what is being recommended and thus easier to monitor its implementation. But is a top-ranked specific (thus, 'strong' or 'tough') recommendation necessarily a 'good' recommendation? The action category was devised explicitly to steer clear of potentially controversial assessments of content and thus to be neutral, but is it possible to ascertain a recommendation's value in isolation from its content and context appropriateness?

The UPR experiences[90] of 12 Pacific Small Island Developing States (SIDS), analysed by Natalie Baird,[91] are an illuminating case in point. SIDS are less active in Geneva processes due to geographical distance, limited governmental capacity and

---

[88] McMahon, 'Framing the Picture' (n 82).
[89] M Kothari, *Study on Emerging Practices from the Universal Periodic Review* (United Nations Human Rights, Office of the High Commissioner, 2021).
[90] Baird analysed the 18 reviews to date of the 12 states; thus, all had undergone their first review and six had also undergone their second, the most recent being in May 2015. The states are, in order of their reviews: Tonga, Tuvalu, Vanuatu, Fiji, Kiribati, Marshall Islands, Federated States of Micronesia, Nauru, Palau, Solomon Islands, Samoa and Papua New Guinea.
[91] Baird, 'The Role of International Non-governmental Organisations' (n 45); see also N Baird, 'To Ratify or Not to Ratify? An Assessment of the Case for Ratification of Human Rights Treaties in the Pacific' (2011) 12 *Melbourne Journal of International Law* 249.

resource constraints. They are therefore less known to UN colleagues, and frequently receive recommendations that fail to appreciate their realities; notably, the fact that their biggest human rights challenge is the climate crisis. Baird reports 'oft-repeated recommendations ... that Pacific states "ratify all outstanding [human rights] treaties" in the face of clear statements by the Pacific SuR that it has limited resources and capacity to do so'.[92] Recommendations to ratify treaties were, in fact, routine: as UPR Info's database shows, 'international instruments' was the most common recommendation issue across the first and second cycles for the totality of countries, expressing the widely held view that being part of a universal human rights system requires signing up to its international legal framework. UPR Info coded and, effectively, endorsed these very specific and substantively straightforward recommendations as action category '5'.

While there is nothing wrong with such recommendations in the abstract, the problem is their appropriateness 'here' and 'now' in a Pacific island context, where the desirability of ratifying these international human rights treaties is being intensely debated, where ratification of some, rather than all, might be a medium- or long-term goal rather than short-term one, and where other, less costly, more creative and more locally appropriate ways of ensuring human rights are being explored.[93] Given Pacific island leaders' explicit appeals regarding their priorities and material constraints, routine recommendations like these seem remarkably insensitive. Pacific island states were being guided by their peers *towards* devoting scarce resources to ratifying treaties and complying with reporting obligations and *away* from human rights policies more appropriate to their size, specificities, capacities and priorities, including developing urgent human rights-sensitive responses to the existential climate crisis now facing them.

Subhas Gujadhur and Marc Limon, similarly, find McMahon's focus on actionability as the key to a recommendation's quality, to the exclusion of other considerations, overly narrow.[94] Former UN diplomats representing Mauritius and the Maldives, with extensive experience at the Human Rights Council and the UPR, they criticise his analysis for being 'based on a restrictive understanding of what ... "UPR ideals" are'. They advise being mindful of the UPR's collectively agreed terms of reference and argue for a criterion of 'usefulness':

> [A] given recommendation may well be action-oriented, according to Professor McMahon's categorization, but if the proposed action does not take into account the specific situation and characteristics of the country concerned, if the proposed action is unachievable considering a country's capacity constraints, or if the proposed action is unrealistic in terms of the ability of the State to bring about such a change within the specified time-frame, can we really say such a recommendation is 'useful' to the SuR, or that it has a high qualitative value?[95]

---

[92] Baird, 'The Role of International Non-governmental Organisations' (n 45) 8. Detail is provided in Baird, 'To Ratify or Not to Ratify?' (n 91) 23–24.
[93] Baird, 'To Ratify or Not to Ratify?' (n 91).
[94] Gujadhur and Limon (n 1).
[95] ibid 29.

Merry was attentive not only to the seductions of quantification, but also to their paradoxical effects. Two paradoxes stand out from this discussion. First, the rising number of recommendations since the UPR began in 2008 are a consequence of the rising numbers of states participating and, as such, index success. Yet, as more states participate, each making two, three, four or even more recommendations, and the numbers of recommendations grow, the SuR's response is necessarily diluted; it cannot implement all of them. Second, in a context where a powerful narrative exists that certain states will try to evade their human rights responsibilities, a database tool has been created to differentiate and rank a recommendation according to its rigour and specificity, but without regard to its content or contextual relevance. In this tool, monitorability trumps content, appropriateness and usefulness.

VIII. CONCLUSION

This chapter has examined how a range of UPR actors, as individuals and collectivities, do things with words and numbers in a context where the SuR is asked to give an account of itself with respect to its human rights situation. I have looked particularly at how civil society activists, operating between culturally distinct social worlds, have attempted to insert their words and agendas into state-led conversations about human rights at the UPR. I paid attention to the human rights talk of civil society activists in UPR pre-sessions that mimic the codes of the UPR Working Group, while inverting its roles: in the pre-session, civil society speaks and states listen. Whatever translations and reformulations of human rights they have made in their own communities, civil society activists do not bring them to this table in Geneva. Rather, translating 'upwards', they adopt the language of the UN human rights milieu, a version of what people in Geneva call 'UN language', a hybrid that combines discourses of diplomacy, law, management and development. They adopt this way of speaking – what we might think of as the 'high-church Latin' of the UN universal human rights system – in an effort to persuade state diplomatic delegations to take up their proposed recommendations.

My discussion of numbers, similarly, owes much to Merry's tracking of the growing importance of quantification in the UN, especially of indicators within the treaty body system. In the UPR, by contrast, recommendations were the 'principal currency'[96] and had become objects of intense quantitative attention. Delving briefly into the history of the recommendation in the context of international organisations, I drew attention to this technology's indeterminacy: hovering between suggestion and directive, its significance is contextually defined, negotiable and historically changing. This alerted us to the stakes involved, as civil society actors have responded energetically to the proliferation of non-binding UPR recommendations in efforts to influence their content and enhance their quality and effects. Having described in the previous section efforts to influence the content and phrasing of recommendations through

---

[96] ibid.

language, here I traced how they do this through enumeration. Creating a database of recommendations that is both a repository and a calculating machine, UPR Info staff have taken charge of collating, counting, parsing, coding and, generally, organising recommendations, making data as well as additional calculative tools available for analysis, advocacy and monitoring. I examined, in particular, a tool created to differentiate and rank recommendations neutrally and objectively, and considered its effects.

Within a public audit ritual whose modalities promise equal treatment through a quantitatively guaranteed 'level playing field', the SuR reports its achievements and challenges; in tiny, equally apportioned speaking slots, its fellow states thank, commend, worry and query, perhaps checking on implementation of previously accepted recommendations, before offering the SuR new ones. To this monitoring of a state by other states, civil society activists add another layer of scrutiny. They monitor the monitors using numbers: counting, analysing and ranking recommendations to assess how diligently RS A monitors the SuR, compared to RSs B, C or D. Then, having identified potential allies among the RSs, the activists offer their words, hoping to influence the recommendation's content and hoping their government, in turn, will accept the recommendation. Yet, an accepted recommendation cannot speak for itself. Transported home in a laptop, presented, say, to a Working Group creating an action plan for implementation, the recommendation triggers new translations. It generates new debates on what it means, what it requires and what it takes to make it real.

12

Visualising the 'Women, Peace and Security Agenda'

HILARY CHARLESWORTH*

I. INTRODUCTION

I FIRST ENCOUNTERED Sally Engle Merry through her wonderful book, *Human Rights and Gender Justice: Translating International Law into Local Justice*,[1] published in 2006. This is an investigation of how the United Nations came to define violence against women as a human rights violation. The book studies how global human rights norms are translated at local levels through the operation of the 1979 UN Convention on the Elimination of all Forms of Discrimination against Women.

Human Rights and Gender Justice was a revelation to me. As an international lawyer, I tend to measure progress in terms of jurisprudential clarity and expansive accounts of legal norms, but Sally emphasises the way that communities actually use international instruments. She shows how groups, rather than being passive recipients of international legal norms, can shape them to respond to their local agendas. Sally also explores how the gendered subjectivity of a woman survivor of violence can be altered through engagement with law—'through acting as a legally entitled subject in the context of these injuries'.[2] This process, she suggests, detaches the individual from the family structure and creates a new relationship to the state, thus reducing 'the patriarchal privileges of males within the domain of the family'.[3]

At a more general level, Sally's work describes the 'vernacularization' of international standards, a term that has become associated with her. She identifies the way that human rights are translated into local languages and contexts, and how they can gain novel meanings. In turn, she argues, local meanings can affect the international.

---

* Thanks to Philip Alston and Stephanie Guest for their comments on this chapter, and Michael MacArdle, Emma Macfarlane, Nikiforos Panagis and Elif Sekercioglu for their research assistance.
[1] SE Merry, *Human Rights and Gender Violence; Translating International Law into Local Justice* (Chicago, University of Chicago Press, 2006).
[2] ibid 186.
[3] ibid 187.

Sally has pointed to

the genius of ethnography: its ability to look closely at a small social space, to listen to the language, to pay attention to the social linkages and information exchanges, to notice the power relationships, and to pay attention to the cultural constructions of social life at play in everyday interactions.[4]

She has been a pioneer in bringing an ethnographical eye to international institutions. While international lawyers are drawn to the written word—treaties, UN resolutions, general comments and recommendations, court decisions—Sally has investigated the social life of these institutions, exposing the intricacies of and tensions in their operation. She has illuminated the way that norms are designed at the international level and how they are received and deployed at the local level.

Looking back over Sally's scholarship, I was reminded how innovative her work has been in the transnational sphere. In 1992, Sally wrote an article on 'Anthropology, Law, and Transnational Processes' in the *Annual Review of Anthropology*, where she argued that 'transnational processes are becoming increasingly important in theorizing about the nature of local legal phenomena'.[5] Scholars in both the fields of international relations and international law often measure the efficacy of the international legal system using the lens of coercion on and compliance by states. Sally, however, draws attention to the more complex forms of influence that international institutions exercised over local legal orders.

It is important to record that Sally's intellectual influence is not only a product of her rich academic writing. My Australian National University (ANU) colleague, anthropologist Margaret Jolly, and I invited Sally to visit Canberra in 2011. Neither of us had met her in person and wondered whether she would be a prima donna academic celebrity, requiring kid-glove treatment. Our concerns were misplaced. We made the most of Sally's visit, filling her days with workshops, public lectures, master classes and student consultations, and we were amazed at her good humour, kindness and energy. Over the past decade, she made further visits to the ANU, and later to Melbourne Law School, always encouraging and stimulating students and colleagues.[6]

Sally is widely known as a superb colleague and collaborator. I had the good fortune to teach with her and also to work with her as co-editor on a section of the report of the International Panel on Social Progress.[7] Sally's hard work, generosity and mischievous sense of humour made the task of wrangling 13 international co-authors enjoyable. While I would sometimes despair about getting our disparate group to the finish line, Sally's hardwired diplomacy and optimism kept the project on foot.

---

[4] ibid 29.

[5] SE Merry, 'Anthropology, Law, and Transnational Processes' (1992) 21 *Annual Review of Anthropology* 357.

[6] One of the fruits of Sally's Canberra visits is a special issue of the journal *Intersections: Gender and Sexuality in Asia and the Pacific* (issue 33, December 2013) http://intersections.anu.edu.au/issue33_contents.htm.

[7] International Panel on Social Progress, 2 *Rethinking Society for the 21st Century* (2018).

Inspired by Sally's intrepid scholarship to venture beyond the legal texts of international institutions, in this chapter I look at the way that these institutions use visual images of women, using the UN Security Council's (UNSC's) 'Women, Peace and Security' agenda as a case study. Images lend a semblance of immediacy and authenticity that is unmatched by text. The global range and speed of the dissemination of images further increase the political power of visuality, as does its 'democratisation'—the capacity of any person with a smartphone to circulate images.[8] Images, then, are an important way of understanding the culture of international institutions. Indeed, visuality forms a critical aspect of the global politics of gender by shaping the ways in which the idea of gender is understood and transmitted.[9]

II. THE 'WOMEN, PEACE AND SECURITY AGENDA'

After introducing the UNSC's 'Women, Peace and Security' agenda, often abbreviated to WPS, I will consider the role of images within it. The violence women and girls had encountered in armed conflicts during the 1990s and their absence in international peace processes prompted women's organisations to lobby the Security Council to take action. The United Nations Development Fund for Women (UNIFEM, now part of UN Women) and certain governments, notably Bangladesh and Namibia, supported this activism.[10] This resolution marked the first time that the Security Council had specifically addressed women's experience in conflict and post-conflict. It has been supplemented by nine further resolutions, the most recent adopted in 2019.[11]

Security Council Resolution 1325, adopted in 2000,[12] established four themes that characterise the women, peace and security agenda: women's representation in the prevention, management and resolution of conflict;[13] the need to protect women and girls from conflict-related violence, 'particularly rape and other forms of sexual abuse';[14] the integration of a 'gender perspective' (defined as taking account of the 'special needs of women and girls') throughout the UN system;[15] and the accountability of perpetrators of sexual violence, or ending impunity.[16] Men were referred

---

[8] R Bleiker, 'Mapping Visual Global Politics' in R Bleiker (ed), *Visual Global Politics* (Abingdon, Routledge, 2018) 5.
[9] L Åhäll, 'Gender' in Bleiker, *Visual Global Politics* (n 8) 150.
[10] NF Hudson, *Gender, Human Security and the United Nations: Security Language as a Political Framework for Women* (Abingdon, Routledge, 2009) 11–14; F Hill, M Aboitiz and S Poehlman-Doumbouya, 'Nongovernmental Organizations' Role in the Buildup and Implementation of Security Council Resolution 1325' (2003) 28 *Signs: Journal of Women in Culture and Society* 1255. See also D Otto, 'The Security Council's Alliance of Gender Legitimacy' in H Charlesworth and J Coicaud (eds), *Fault Lines of International Legitimacy* (Cambridge, Cambridge University Press, 2010) 256–58.
[11] UNSC Res 1325 (31 October 2000); UNSC Res 1820 (19 June 2008); UNSC Res 1888 (30 September 2009); UNSC Res 1889 (5 October 2009); UNSC Res 1960 (16 December 2010); UNSC Res 2106 (24 June 2013); UNSC Res 2122 (18 October 2013); UNSC Res 2242 (13 October 2015); UNSC Res 2467 (23 April 2019); UNSC Res 2493 (29 October 2019).
[12] UNSC Res 1325 (31 October 2000).
[13] UNSC Res 1325 (31 October 2000), paras 1–4.
[14] ibid para 10.
[15] ibid paras 5, 7, 8, 15.
[16] ibid para 11.

to only in the context of disarmament, demobilisation and reintegration, where 'all those involved' were encouraged 'to consider the different needs of female and male ex-combatants'.[17] The Resolution also called for compliance with existing international humanitarian and human rights law.[18]

Resolution 1325 addressed the Security Council, UN member states and the United Nations system as a whole. While it placed the issue of women's security within the Security Council's primary responsibility for the maintenance of international peace and security,[19] Resolution 1325 was not adopted under Chapter VII of the UN Charter and thus does not formally bind UN member states.[20] It has nevertheless prompted extensive institutional activity: the UN and other international organisations have launched training programmes on the agenda and developed a plethora of policies, action plans and guidelines.[21] The Security Council has held annual open debates and 'Arria formula' meetings on women and peace and security. Since 2010, the UN Secretary-General has provided annual reports to the Security Council on the implementation of Resolution 1325.[22] Over half the UN's member states have adopted national action plans on women, peace and security.[23] Civil society, in particular women's organisations and groups, have used the resolution in conflict areas to formulate demands for political and disarmament processes.[24]

Despite all this hum of institutional and normative activity, the UN Secretary-General regularly acknowledges that 'aspirations fall short of reality',[25] and that there is a 'lack of progress across the most fundamental commitments to peace and security, human rights and gender equality'.[26] The resolutions themselves refer to 'persistent implementation deficits in the women, peace and security agenda'.[27]

---

[17] ibid para 13.
[18] ibid para 9.
[19] Charter of the United Nations, UNCIO XV, 335; amendments by General Assembly Resolution in UNTS 557, 143/638, 308/892, 119, Art 24.
[20] The Charter of the United Nations states that UN member states 'agree to accept and carry out the decisions of the Security Council'. Ibid Art 25.
[21] United Nations, 'Women and Peace and Security: Report of the Secretary-General' (28 September 2010) UN Doc S/2010/498, para 122.
[22] United Nations, 'Statement by the President of the Security Council on Women, Peace and Security' (25 October 2010) UN Doc S/PRST/2010/22.
[23] In 2022, there were 98 national action plans: PeaceWomen, 'WPS Implementation: National Level Implementation', www.peacewomen.org/member-states.
[24] The development of normative standards and institutional practices is discussed in the UN Secretary-General's Annual Reports on Women and Peace and Security. See, eg UN Security Council, 'Report of the Secretary-General on Women and Peace and Security' (23 September 2014) UN Doc S/2014/693.
[25] ibid para 76. See also UN Security Council, 'Report of the Secretary-General on Women and Peace and Security' (9 October 2019) UN Doc S/2019/800, para 74.
[26] UN Security Council, 'Report of the Secretary-General on Women and Peace and Security' (9 October 2018) UN Doc S/2018/900. See also R Coomaraswamy, *Preventing Conflict, Transforming Justice, Securing the Peace* (UN Women, 2015) www.peacewomen.org/sites/default/files/UNW-GLOBAL-STUDY-1325-2015%20(1).pdf.
[27] UN Security Council, 'Report of the Secretary-General on Women and Peace and Security' (23 September 2014) UN Doc S/2014/693, para 76.

A favoured statistic in discussion of the WPS agenda is that, when women are involved in peace negotiations, the peace agreement is 35 per cent more likely to last at least 15 years.[28] Between 1992 and 2019, however, only six per cent of mediators, 13 per cent of negotiators and six per cent of witnesses and signatories in peace processes were women.[29] Since 2019, there has been little improvement. For example, in negotiations that took place in 2020 in Afghanistan, Libya and Yemen, women represented 10 per cent, 20 per cent and zero per cent of the negotiators, respectively.[30] In the same year, only 28.6 per cent of peace agreements contained 'gender-related' provisions, compared to a high of 37.1 per cent in 2015.[31] As of February 2021, women comprised 48 per cent of all heads and deputy heads of UN peacekeeping and special political missions, but the numbers of women among military troops in UN peace operations remained low, at five per cent.[32] With respect to Resolution 1325's call for the technique of 'gender mainstreaming' in peacekeeping, UN peacekeeping mandates invoke the language of gender mainstreaming principally when sexual violence has been prevalent during a conflict but not otherwise.[33]

The lack of progress in the WPS agenda is typically met with general rallying calls. The Security Council has offered an institutional *mea culpa* for this situation, recognising 'the need for more systematic attention to the implementation of women, peace and security commitments in its own work, particularly to ensure the enhancement of women's engagement in conflict prevention, resolution and peacebuilding'.[34] It has promised to 'focus more attention on women's leadership and participation in conflict resolution and peacebuilding'.[35] The Security Council's proposed tools are primarily technocratic. It calls for the improved collection of information and timely analysis;[36] regular briefings from UN officials on women,

---

[28] See, eg Council on Foreign Relations, 'Women's Participation in Peace Processes', www.cfr.org/interactive/womens-participation-in-peace-processes.

[29] See UN Women, 'Facts and Figures: Women, Peace and Security', www.unwomen.org/en/what-we-do/peace-and-security/facts-and-figures.

[30] Council on Foreign Relations (n 28).

[31] UN Women, 'Facts and Figures' (n 29). Even when countries commit to implementing gender-based approaches to peace agreements, follow-through is not assured. For example, as of July 2020, 32% of the 130 gender-related provisions in Colombia's 2016 peace accord had not been initiated. An additional 45% of the provisions had achieved only the 'minimum' level of implementation: Barometer Initiative, Peace Accords Matrix and Kroc Institute for International Peace Studies, 'Towards Implementation of Women's Rights in the Colombian Final Peace Accord: Progress, Opportunities and Challenges' (Notre Dame, University of Notre Dame, 2020) https://peaceaccords.nd.edu/wp-content/uploads/2020/11/Towards-Implementation-of-Womens-Rights-in-the-Colombian-Final-Peace-Accord-2.pdf.

[32] UN Women, 'Facts and Figures' (n 29); UN Security Council, 'Report of the Secretary-General on Women and Peace and Security' (27 September 2021) UN Doc S/2021/827, para 33.

[33] A-K Kreft, 'The Gender Mainstreaming Gap: Security Council Resolution 1325 and UN Peacekeeping Mandates' (2017) 24 *International Peacekeeping* 132, 155–56.

[34] UN Security Council, 'Statement by the President of the Security Council on Women, Peace and Security' (31 October 2012) UN Doc S/PRST/2012/23, para 12.

[35] ibid para 1.

[36] ibid para 2.

peace and security;[37] increasing information and recommendations from the UN Secretariat to the Council;[38] monitoring progress in implementation;[39] and integration ('mainstreaming') of women, peace and security as an issue throughout all UN activities, including peacekeeping and peacebuilding missions,[40] commissions of inquiry[41] and the work of special envoys and special representatives.[42]

The faltering of the WPS agenda may be due in part to the inadequacy of the resources devoted to it, and the limited institutional commitment.[43] There is, however, an important question of the design of the WPS project itself: does it identify the root causes of violence and insecurity, and does it offer methods to deal with these causes? The WPS agenda is built on contradictory and impoverished images of women and men and of gender roles.[44] On the one hand, it depicts women as agents of political change through preventing and resolving conflicts and engaging in peacebuilding, typecasting women as 'peacemakers'.[45] The assumption of women's essentially peaceable nature explains why there should be more women involved in dealing with conflict. On the other hand, the resolutions present women, girls and children as a group with 'special needs', requiring protection by a strong (male) authority to determine the proper measures for their security.[46]

The elision of the terms 'women and girls' and 'gender' in the WPS agenda is also significant. There is no suggestion that these terms have a distinct meaning or that gender might encompass expectations of masculinity as well as of femininity. Resolution 1325 defines 'a gender perspective' as giving attention to the 'special needs' of women and girls in conflict, during repatriation, resettlement and reconstruction, supporting local women's peace initiatives and protecting the human rights of women and girls in any new legal order.[47] Despite references in the WPS resolutions to gender-based violence, gender advisers and experts, the resolutions focus 'in particular' on sexual violence against women and children, largely sidestepping the

---

[37] ibid paras 2(a) (b) (c).
[38] ibid para 2(d).
[39] ibid para 1.
[40] ibid paras 4, 5.
[41] ibid para 2(e).
[42] ibid para 7.
[43] For example, just 33% of the WPS National Action Plans adopted by 2019 included a budget for implementation. See PeaceWomen (n 23).
[44] For the context of these resolutions, see D Otto, 'Power and Danger: Feminist Engagement with International Law through the UN Security Council' (2010) 32 *Australian Feminist Law Journal* 97, 100–03.
[45] eg UNSC Res 1325 (31 October 2000) Preamble, '*Reaffirming* the important role of women in the prevention and resolution of conflicts and in peace-building'; UNSC Res 1889 (5 October 2009) Preamble, 'given their vital role in the prevention and resolution of conflict and peacebuilding'.
[46] See IM Young, 'The Logic of Masculinist Protection: Reflections on the Current Security State' (2003) 29 *Signs: Journal of Women in Culture and Society* 1.
[47] UNSC Res 1325 (31 October 2000), para 8.

issue of sexual violence against men and boys, a significant phenomenon in armed conflict.[48] Indeed, the implication is that men and boys are only involved as perpetrators of sexual violence and as protectors against the commission of such acts by other men.[49]

The WPS agenda does not draw links between violence against women in armed conflict and structural elements such as militarisation, the political economy of conflict or the struggle for control of economic resources.[50] Unlike the 1995 Beijing Platform for Action, the resolutions do not make recommendations with respect to the reduction of military expenditures and the availability of armaments.[51] Resolution 2122, adopted in 2013, acknowledges the adoption of the Arms Trade Treaty in March 2013[52] and looks forward to its contribution to reducing violence against women and girls in times of conflict. Beyond this, however, broader feminist proposals of disarmament, reduction of military expenditure or restrictions on arms production as responses to conflict and insecurity appear to have had no impact on the WPS agenda.[53]

III. VISUAL IMAGES OF WOMEN IN THE WPS AGENDA

Images often used to support the Security Council's WPS agenda illustrate some of its tensions and shortcomings. The 'visual economy'[54] of the agenda, and its broad acceptance at a rhetorical level, depends on presenting women in recognisable categories. Particular modes of thought are evoked in our engagement with these representations.[55] To identify these, we need to observe what is highlighted; what is hidden within the frame; what perspectives are represented; and what views

---

[48] S Sivakumaran, 'Sexual Violence against Men in Armed Conflict' (2007) 18 *European Journal of International Law* 253. See also C Lewis, 'Systematic Silencing: Addressing Sexual Violence against Men and Boys in Armed Conflict and Its Aftermath' in G Heathcote and D Otto (eds), *Rethinking Peacekeeping, Gender Equality and Collective Security* (London, Palgrave Macmillan, 2014) 203.

[49] See, however, UNSC Res 2106 (24 June 2013). It references the Declaration on Preventing Sexual Violence in Conflict adopted by G8 foreign ministers in London, 11 April 2013, which recognises 'the importance of responding to the needs of men and boys who are victims of sexual violence in armed conflict' and notes that sexual violence in armed conflict also affects men and boys. See Foreign and Commonwealth Office, Declaration on Preventing Sexual Violence in Conflict, adopted 11 April 2013, para 3, www.gov.uk/government/publications/g8-declaration-on-preventing-sexual-violence-in-conflict.

[50] See, eg Yakin Ertürk, 'Report of the Special Rapporteur on Violence against Women, Its Causes and Consequences: Political Economy and Violence against Women' (18 May 2009) UN Doc A/HRC/11/6, para 62.

[51] United Nations, 'Report of the Fourth World Conference on Women' (4–15 September 1996) UN Doc A/CONF.177/20/Rev.1, ch I, annex, II, para 143.

[52] Arms Trade Treaty (2013) 3013 UNTS 269, Art 7(4).

[53] Heathcote and Otto (n 48) 255.

[54] WS Hesford, *Spectacular Rhetorics: Human Rights Visions, Recognitions, Feminisms* (Durham, NC, Duke University Press, 2011) 39.

[55] See S Sliwinski, 'Human Rights' in Bleiker, *Visual Global Politics* (n 8) 173.

are obscured.[56] Attention to the visual illustrates an ambivalence in the UN about women's roles in conflict.

Scholars have pointed out that women and children are the quintessential victims in all humanitarian imagery: they signal passivity, innocence and non-violence. Images of groups of men are likely to be read in a quite different way.[57] The imagery of the WPS agenda does, however, offer some variations on the 'women as victims' image as shown in NATO's version of the agenda. NATO would not give permission for inclusion of the logo in this chapter, but it is available at https://www.smashstrategies.com/category/peace/.

This image is found on many official and unofficial websites dealing with WPS. The number 1325 dominates the image, displayed in UN blue—the colour of the UN flag and of the blue berets of UN peacekeepers. The staccato words 'women', 'peace' and 'security', separated by vertical lines, provide a foundation for the numerals. The abstract compass points of NATO's logo suggest the universality of the remit of Resolution 1325. It takes a second look to discern the white silhouette of a woman standing between the two middle numerals, woven into the text. The image is computer-generated, a cartoon, and there are no facial features evident. The woman is slender, clearly young and dressed in Western style, with a dress nipped in at the waist and the hemline above her knee. She wears her long, wavy hair loose and it is blown to one side by a gust of wind or toss of the head. The woman's arms, neatly contained within the frame of the blue numerals, stretch upwards to suggest a dance movement, or perhaps simply *joie de vivre*. It is reminiscent of advertisements for hair shampoo.

The image implies that this female figure is the archetype of a truly peaceful and secure woman. The message seems to be that the goal of the UNSC's WPS agenda is to enable women to realise the exuberance, prosperity and perhaps even the glamour of this figure. Women become exotic and playful actors on the international stage.

The national action plans (NAPs) of states to implement the WPS agenda are rich repositories of visual images. The two photographs of Australian soldiers in Afghanistan presented in Figures 12.1 and 12.2, taken by official army photographers, provide the covers of Australia's National Action Plan 2012–2018 and the 2014 Progress Report on the Plan.[58] Presumably, the images are designed to reassure that Australia is delivering on its commitments under Resolution 1325. In Figure 12.1, we

---

[56] In her study of images in UK national action plans, Columba Achilleos-Sarll employs a spectrum of categories – 'hypervisibility', 'visibility' and 'invisibility'. See C Achilleos-Sarll, '"Seeing" the Women, Peace and Security Agenda: Visual (Re)productions of WPS in UK Government National Action Plans' (2020) 96 *International Affairs* 1643, 1648–49.

[57] See, eg R Bleiker et al, 'The Visual Dehumanisation of Refugees' (2013) 48 *Australian Journal of Political Science* 408.

[58] A second Australian National Action Plan on Women, Peace and Security was adopted in 2021. See Australian Government, *Australian National Action Plan on Women, Peace and Security 2021–2031*, www.dfat.gov.au/sites/default/files/australias-national-action-plan-on-women-peace-and-security-2021-2031.pdf.

Figure 12.1 The cover of the Australian National Action Plan

Figure 12.2 Australia's 2014 Progress Report

can see two figures in camouflage uniform speaking to an Afghan woman dressed in a full black burqa. She has a young girl, possibly a daughter, at her side with her, wearing a vivid green headscarf over a colourful *salwar kameez*. The girl is carrying a child (a sibling?) on her hip, while a younger boy in traditional dress is visible between the woman and the girl. We see one soldier, machine gun slung over the shoulder, in profile, with a friendly expression, underlining the benign nature of the encounter. Most of the other uniformed person's face is obscured, but they appear to be wearing a headscarf under their helmet. The Afghans are only viewed from the back. The sex of the soldiers is not obvious from the image, but the photo credit informs us that this is 'Corporal Jenny Sapwell of Mentoring Task Force 2, and an interpreter, chat[ting] with local Afghan women' in Uruzgan Province in southern Afghanistan.

This image seems designed to emphasise Australia's progressive attitude to the inclusion of women in its armed forces on the same terms as men – here is a woman soldier serving in Afghanistan, smiling at the locals, yet carrying a powerful weapon as part of a 'Female Engagement Team' mission. Corporal Sapwell stands in contrast to the faceless, unnamed Afghan figures, whose clothing marks them as pre-modern and engulfed in custom. Despite the photograph's title, this is far from a 'chat', an encounter between equals. It seems rather a meeting of two different worlds: one of women who have apparently achieved equality with men and the other of a traditional society where women are veiled and apparently oppressed.[59]

The intention of the image might be to show that the military missions such as the International Security Assistance Force in Afghanistan can deliver peace and security for women, but it implies that this will be a top-down exercise. Corporal Sapwell's military weapon underscores the inequality of the engagement—she offers a type of friendship backed up by military superiority. The presence of children signals the Afghan women's peaceable natures. This image also anchors the WPS agenda firmly in foreign lands, where, according to the Australian NAP, 'women and girls ... face devastating human rights violations, including high levels of sexual and gender-based violence'.[60] Although this description can also readily apply to Australia, pursuit of the WPS agenda allows violence against women to be located offshore.

The photograph on the cover of Australia's 2014 Progress Report on the NAP, Figure 12.2, hews to a similar message. Once again, it is set in dusty rural Afghanistan. In the foreground are three (or possibly four) completely shrouded Afghan female figures sitting on the stony ground. Two young children with them have turned to regard the camera curiously. Four Australian soldiers (at least two of whom appear to be women) face the Afghan group and the camera. The Australians are in full camouflage gear; no weapons are visible, but they display a lot of military paraphernalia and equipment attached to their bodies. They crouch or kneel on the ground to be at eye level with the Afghan women. Although the eyes of two of the Australians are obscured by wrap-around army-issue sunglasses, their faces seem in sociable,

---

[59] *cf* Achilleos-Sarll's observation of 'agential' images of women in the UK NAPs (n 56).
[60] Australian Government, *Australian National Action Plan on Women, Peace and Security 2012–2018*, http://peacewomen.org/sites/default/files/Australia%20NAP%202012-2018%20(English).pdf.

conversational mode. The caption informs us that this is another Female Engagement Team speaking with women in the Karmisan Valley in southern Afghanistan.

Both these cover images illustrate apparently enlightened military women from the Global North who can travel abroad and deploy force along with their male colleagues, yet who have particular value through their special entrée with local women. The Female Engagement Teams, Australia's 2014 Progress Report tells us, are able to 'bridge the cultural gap where most Afghan women are not able to be engaged by the predominately male security forces'.[61] This view of women soldiers as less confrontational and thus able to get broader access to security issues across traditional societies is widely held within the UN.[62] The images suggest that the foreshadowed engagement is very limited, however. The Australian women soldiers seem inaccessible in their high-tech military cocoons, while the Australians' Afghan interlocutors appear as silent, shadowy figures, trapped in tradition. The overall visual message is that women from the Global South are the main victims of conflict and are the primary beneficiaries of the WPS agenda. They are the quintessential spectacle of victimhood. Women from the Global North appear only in guise of security-providers.

Figure 12.3 Women's Consultative Forum in Mogadishu

Image reproduced with the kind permission of AMISOM.

AMISOM, an African Union peacekeeping mission in Somalia, has used the image in Figure 12.3 in its publicity materials to depict its work in 'engendering' counter-violent

---

[61] Australian Government, *2014 Progress Report: Australian National Action on Women, Peace and Security* 25, www.pmc.gov.au/sites/default/files/publications/progress-report-2014-nap-women-peace-security-2012-2018.pdf. There are also Progress Reports for 2016 and 2018.

[62] UN Secretary General Antonio Guterres noted in 2019 that 'In patrol units women can better access intelligence to provide a holistic view of security challenges, and at checkpoints they promote a less confrontational atmosphere'. UN Secretary General, 'Secretary General's Remarks to Security Council on Women in Peacekeeping [as Delivered]' (New York, 11 April 2019) www.un.org/sg/en/content/sg/statement/2019-04-11/secretary-generals-remarks-security-council-women-peacekeeping-delivered.

extremism measures. The photograph shows participants at a 'Women's Consultative Forum on Countering Violent Extremism' held in Mogadishu in 2016. Eight people—five women and three men—sit around a table in a discussion group. Another discussion group is visible in the background. The men seem to be observers, while the women are more actively engaged in the discussion. One woman, in the foreground, is the notetaker, writing the discussion points, in English, on a poster-size piece of paper.

The image depicts a new role for women from the Global South. This presents women acting as early warning systems, detecting the nascent signs of violent extremism in their communities. Such a function is found in WPS resolutions from 2015 on, which assign women the special responsibility of being a bulwark against violent extremism and terrorism.[63] The idea is that women often have greater access to places and people that may reveal potential security risks.[64] So, women are presented as both 'vigilant mothers and neighbourhood experts' who can quickly detect people becoming radicalised, and are willing to inform the authorities about this.[65] They are, in the words of UNISOM, 'force multipliers' in responding to violent extremism.[66] The conference or classroom backdrop to many images of women in conflict zones indicates that women can be readily trained in the requisite skills of community sleuthing. The female subject of security has now become an agent of security.

Figure 12.4 NATO 'side by side' poster

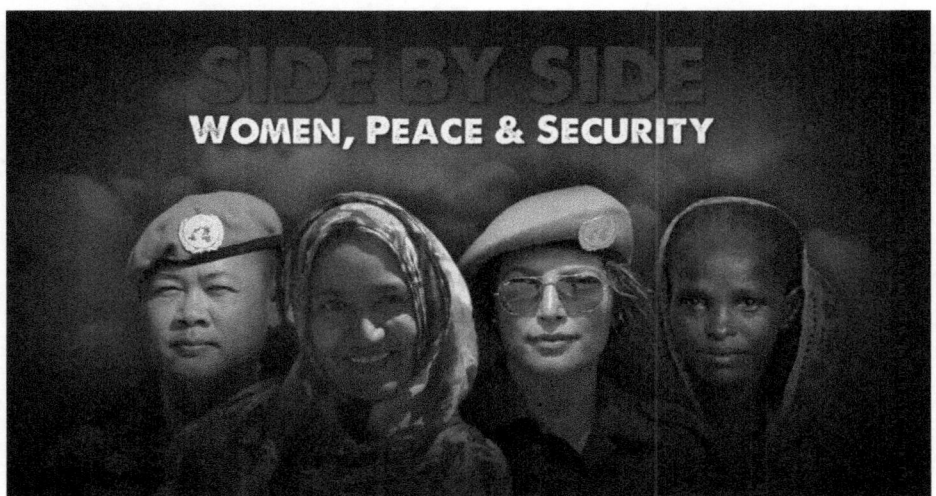

[63] eg UNSC Res 2242 (13 October 2015).
[64] Council on Foreign Relations (n 28).
[65] A Sancar, 'Women as a Tool for Preventing Violent Extremism?' (*swisspeace*, November 2016) www.swisspeace.ch/apropos/women-tool-preventing-violent-extremism/.
[66] AMISOM, 'AMISOM Holds Forum to Engender Counter Violent Extremism Efforts' (Mogadishu, 21 May 2016) https://amisom-au.org/2016/05/amisom-holds-forum-to-engender-counter-violent-extremism-efforts/.

NATO's Parliamentary Assembly used the image of the faces of a woman and a girl positioned next to the faces of two UN peacekeepers (Figure 12.4) to celebrate the sixteenth anniversary of the adoption of UNSC Resolution 1325 and to launch a new webpage to showcase NATO's work in support of the WPS agenda.[67] The illustration also appears on many websites of organisations concerned with the WPS agenda.

The image is a photomontage, depicting not the WPS agenda in action but the ideal. This is accentuated by the billowing clouds that surround the four heads, giving a transcendent air to the image. The woman, wearing a floral headscarf, could be from the Balkans. The girl looks African and her head is also covered. The woman and girl are smiling, while the two peacekeepers have more neutral expressions. They are wearing the blue beret of UN peacekeepers, with the UN insignia badge pinned on prominently. One peacekeeper appears to be female and is wearing reflective sunglasses, implying duty in a hot climate. Her long hair is loose, however, as if to underline the peacekeeper's femininity. The other peacekeeper appears male, possibly from Nepal, a regular contributor of peacekeeping troops.

The purpose of the image seems to send the message that peacekeepers and the local communities they serve are engaged in a partnership. This is made explicit in the slogan 'Side by Side' printed across the top of the image in large red letters. The words 'Women, Peace & Security' appear in white, in a smaller font, beneath it. This notion of local agency in peacekeeping generally and the WPS context in particular is undermined by the image's contrast between the detached professionalism of the uniformed peacekeepers and the trusting, vulnerable woman and girl. The image sends an optimistic missive about what the WPS agenda can deliver: saintly UN peacekeepers intervening in conflict and bringing smiles to the faces of downtrodden women and girls mired in their traditional cultures.

IV. WHAT WORK ARE VISUAL IMAGES DOING?

The visual plays an important role in the international circulation of ideas. Images of conflict follow a set of conventions regulating what can be shown and what cannot appear. For example, it is acceptable to show images of the injured or dead if they are from the Global South. The picture of three-year-old Syrian boy Alan Kurdi's body washed up on a Turkish beach in 2015 made headlines in media around the world.[68] This is not possible if the victims of violence are from the Global North. For example, no images of dead or wounded people were televised after the attacks on the USA on 11 September 2001 or after later attacks on London and Paris.[69]

---

[67] See, eg NATO, 'NATO PA Marks Anniversary of Landmark UN Resolution on Women, Peace and Security' (Brussels/Washington, 31 October 2016) www.nato-pa.int/news/nato-pa-marks-anniversary-landmark-un-resolution-women-peace-and-security.

[68] H Fehrenbach and D Rodogno, '"A Horrific Photo of a Drowned Syrian Child": Humanitarian Photography and NGO Media Strategies in Historical Perspective' (2015) 97 *International Review of the Red Cross* 1121.

[69] Abounadarra, 'Dignity Has Never Been Photographed' (*Documenta 14*, 24 March 2017) www.documenta14.de/en/notes-and-works/15348/dignity-has-never-been-photographed.

Visuality is critical to the WPS agenda, and WPS imagery has its own set of visual conventions. WPS visual imagery reproduces the limitations of the WPS agenda, reinforcing existing asymmetries of power.[70] In this way, it provides a narrative for international intervention. Each publication or website that deals with WPS includes striking photographs of groups of women in the Global South, usually engaged in some way with representatives of the UN or other international organisations. The imagery signals women's asserted innately peaceful nature sometimes by the presence of children and sometimes by presenting them as trainees or students, suggesting that they are not yet ready for an active role in world affairs. These photographs offer relief from the pages of printed text: they showcase the women's often highly coloured clothing in a manner reminiscent of tourist brochures, rendering the women emblems of exotic tradition.[71] The emblematic function of the photographs is highlighted by their limited captions: while the photographer's name and the location are often provided, most are undated. Women from the Global North appear in WPS visual images in a distinct manner. Some are presented as 'fly-in fly-out' experts on women, peace and security, dressed in more sombre 'professional' mode than the women they are advising or consulting with. Many are peacekeeping troops in military uniforms identical to those worn by men, suggesting women's equality with male colleagues. Their femininity is signalled, however, by details such as facial expression or hairstyle.

As the five images above show, men make only occasional appearances in the visual expressions of the WPS agenda, representing a safe pair of hands.[72] While the language of gender is omnipresent in the textual form of the WPS agenda, the texts make clear that it is simply a synonym for women, and this is reinforced through the WPS imagery. The resolutions that make up the WPS agenda refer fleetingly to men and masculinity, but they do not refer to masculine identities in times of conflict or violent patterns of conduct accepted because they are coded as male. The WPS agenda deploys gender as a static, monolithic category, centred on women as victims. So, 'gender security' means simply 'women in need of protection'.[73] The relational nature of gender, the contestability of categories of femininity and masculinity, as well as the role of power relations and the ways that structures of subordination and inequality are reproduced are invisible.[74] Also invisible are the ways that gender shapes the identification and resolution of international conflicts.[75]

---

[70] Hesford (n 54) 95. See also Achilleos-Sarll (n 56).

[71] One example is UN Women, 'Sourcebook on Women, Peace and Security' (2012) www.unwomen.org/sites/default/files/Headquarters/Attachments/Sections/Library/Publications/2012/10/WPSsourcebook-01-Overview-en.pdf.

[72] The UN Women's Sourcebook on Women, Peace and Security contains a rare exception. It includes an (undated) photograph of a Misseriya community meeting in South Sudan on resolving conflict with their Dinka neighbours where all the participants are men. The caption observes 'The absence of women is evident'. Ibid 7.

[73] L McLeod, 'The Women, Peace and Security Resolutions: UNSCR 1325 to 2122' in J Steans and D Tepe-Belfrage (eds), *Handbook on Gender in World Politics* (Cheltenham, Edward Elgar Publishing, 2016) 276.

[74] S Baden and AM Goetz, 'Who Needs (Sex) When You Can Have (Gender)? Conflicting Discourses on Gender at Beijing' (1997) 56 *Feminist Review* 3, 7.

[75] See Kreft (n 33).

The narrow account of gender deployed in international institutions and on display in the five images allows problems facing women to be understood as the product of particular cultures, lack of participation in public arenas, or lack of information or skills. Reducing 'gender' to a synonym for women empties the radical potential from the idea of gender. This is not only because it obscures the fact that men also have a gender and inhabit a gendered world, obscuring the role of masculinity in global politics. It is also because it implies that gender identity is fixed rather than constructed as a social and political practice. Gendering of identity intersects with factors such as race, class, sexuality and age. The international resort to the language of gender requires women to change or, alternatively, a change in the participation of women. The WPS images indicate that gender is above all a technical issue, a head count of women and men. Gender is also connected to vulnerability, dependence and the need of protection.

Like the written texts of the WPS agenda, its visual imagery alludes to the effects of conflict, but not its causes. Figures 12.2, 12.3 and 12.5, for example, give prominence to the role of international peacekeeping troops, suggesting that the use of force remains central to achieving peace and security. Local women can engage with and assist the international military endeavour by being a conduit into their communities. Feminist calls for disarmament, arms control and reducing military spending in favour of social investment are out of the visual frame.[76]

V. CONCLUSION

Each year, the UN Security Council considers the progress of the WPS agenda on the anniversary of the adoption of Resolution 1325. In 2020, the Secretary-General's report for the twentieth anniversary of Resolution 1325 urged states to implement the agenda fully.[77] The report listed many familiar techniques to achieve this: ensuring the participation of women in peace processes, including through 'mainstreaming a gender perspective', increasing the numbers of women in peacekeeping operations, promoting the rights of women, and creating safe and enabling environments for women in civil society. The UN's slow progress in achieving the WPS agenda goals suggests that the institution and its members have become practised at WPS rhetoric but are unwilling to go further. The five images I have discussed here mirror the limitations of the WPS agenda.

Does the WPS agenda retain any transformative promise? An arresting feature of Sally Engle Merry's work is its hopefulness. For example, she concludes *Human Rights and Gender Violence* by saying '[human rights] serves those in power but [are]

---

[76] UN Women, 'Remarks by UN Under-Secretary-General and Executive Director of UN Women, Phumzile Mlambo-Ngcuka, the UN Security Council Open Debate on Women, Peace and Security' (New York, 29 October 2019) www.unwomen.org/en/news/stories/2019/10/speech-ed-phumzile-open-debate-on-women-peace-and-security.

[77] UN Security Council, 'Report of the Secretary-General on Women and Peace and Security' (27 September 2021) UN Doc S/2021/827.

always in danger of escaping its bounds and working in a genuinely emancipatory way'.[78] Just as Sally observes of law, so the visual helps maintain power relations by 'defining categories and systems of meaning'.[79] Could visuality also offer techniques to deepen the emancipatory potential of the WPS agenda by destabilising its standard categories? The work of the Syrian film-making collective Abounadarra offers some hope that this is possible. Abounadarra's manifesto, 'The Right to the Image', draws attention to the politics of representation and the right to self-representation.[80] It has criticised the 'voyeurism that exploits the suffering of women and men in front of the camera' and the way that the media denies Syrians their diversity and reduces them to playing extras in television reports, victims without names or voices'.[81] Abounadarra has made visual works, including posters, graphic designs and videos, to counter the standard Northern view of oppressed Syrian women as perennial victims of conflict. The members of the collective use humour and satire to show the strength and creativity of Syrian women. This provides an intriguing and challenging model for WPS imagery in the next decade.

---

[78] Merry, *Human Rights and Gender Violence* (n 1) 231.
[79] ibid 362.
[80] S Kambarami, 'ABOUNADDARA: The Right to the Image' (*The New Context*, 7 December 2015) https://thenewcontext.org/abounaddara-the-right-to-the-image/.
[81] Abounaddara, 'The Murderer Returning to the Scene of the Crime' (*Documenta 14*, 2013) www.documenta14.de/en/artists/949/abounaddara.

13

The Seductions of Quantification Rebuffed? The Curious Failure by the CESCR to Engage Water and Sanitation Data

MARGARET L SATTERTHWAITE*

I. INTRODUCTION

SOME YEARS AGO, scholars noticed that the human rights field was turning towards metrics and quantification, seeking tools that might move the rights endeavour beyond its reliance on stories of suffering and towards the production of knowledge inflected by science. Chief among the tools practitioners began to embrace were human rights indicators, here defined as metrics calibrated to make empirical measurements related to specific norms. Rights indicators were said to be useful in understanding the scope, dynamics and relationships among human rights violations through population-based, quantitative and systematic qualitative monitoring methods.[1]

Indicators were also seen to allow advocates to access and deploy the political and cultural force of numbers in a world where what is measured is what counts.[2] They also

---

* I am grateful to Professor Sally Merry for her incredible scholarship, in addition to her generosity, wisdom and humour over the years. I thank Professor Benjamin Mason Meier for his collegial approach in sharing the code book he developed for qualitative coding of state reports that formed the basis for the one used in this chapter, discussed below in n 64. I acknowledge the following for excellent research assistance: Anika Ades, Camilla Akbari, Fontanne Chu, Philip Dalgarno, Chang Hahn, Julia Krusen, Caroline Marks, Rosa McKay Polaschek and Allen Wang. The preparation of this chapter was supported by the Filomen D'Agostino Research Fund at New York University School of Law.

[1] See, eg M Green, 'What We Talk about When We Talk about Indicators: Current Approaches to Human Rights Measurement' (2001) 23 *Human Rights Quarterly*, 1062; G De Beco, 'The Interplay between Human Rights and Development the Other Way Round: The Emerging Use of Quantitative Tools for Measuring the Progressive Realization of Economic, Social and Cultural Rights' (2010) 4 *Human Rights and International Legal Discourse* 265; EM Hafner-Burton, *Making Human Rights a Reality* (Princeton, Princeton University Press, 2013) 67; M Langford and S Fukuda-Parr, 'The Turn to Metrics' (2012) 30 *Nordic Journal of Human Rights* 222; P Vizard, 'Evaluating Compliance Using Quantitative Methods and Indicators: Lessons from the Human Rights Measurement Framework' (2012) 30 *Nordic Journal of Human Rights* 240.

[2] I Winkler, M Satterthwaite and C de Albuquerque, 'Treasuring What We Measure and Measuring What We Treasure: Post-2015 Monitoring for the Promotion of Equality in the Water, Sanitation, and Hygiene Sector' (2014) 32 *Wisconsin International Law Journal* 547.

presented the possibility of building human rights concerns into the very fabric of development, humanitarian practice and even security measures undertaken by states, inter-governmental organisations and other powerful actors. As Sally Merry explained in 2011, indicators were seen as 'objective', capable of 'set[ting] clearer standards for compliance with a convention'[3] and more concrete goals for advocates. As Rosga and I explained in 2009, 'the turn toward mechanics of measurement and notions of scientific objectivity may appear to offer a kind of authority that [human rights] bodies have never been able to achieve' in the eyes of mistrusting governments.[4]

While this embrace of quantification was celebrated as an advance by many, critics – with Merry prominent among them – also registered strong concerns.[5] Some of the negative impacts imputed to the use of indicators stemmed from risks inherent in quantitative ways of knowing. For example, while there were myriad methods for measuring – as well as a plethora of data on – some issues, in other places, there was a dearth of data on issues central to human rights.[6] Further, the enduring and irresolvable problem of venal political manipulation of data was acknowledged, as well as the predatory or abusive methods sometimes used to gather data.[7] Finally, the slippage between the concept one intended to measure and the choice of often-distant proxies was common but too often overlooked. Other unintended consequences related to the fact that the indicators phenomenon is an instance of power-through-knowledge,[8] or 'expert rule',[9] that empowered certain kinds of professional human rights expertise shared among an identifiable epistemic community[10] while ousting others. This empowerment sometimes came at the expense of grassroots, 'local' or embedded forms of knowledge.[11]

The 'deployment of statistical measures tends to replace political debate with technical expertise', Merry wrote in 2011.[12] In a piece published the same year, I explored similar dynamics in the use of rights-based indicators in crisis settings, concluding that indicators ended to 'render technical' very political debates over

---

[3] SE Merry, 'Measuring the World: Indicators, Human Rights, and Global Governance' (2011) 52 *Current Anthropology* S83.

[4] A Rosga and M Satterthwaite, 'The Trust in Indicators: Measuring Human Rights' (2009) 27 *Berkeley Journal of International Law* 253, 289; see also Merry, 'Measuring the World' (n 3) 170 (citing Rosga and Satterthwaite).

[5] See, eg Merry, 'Measuring the World' (n 3); SE Merry, *The Seductions of Quantification: Measuring Human Rights, Gender Violence, and Sex Trafficking* (Chicago, University of Chicago Press, 2016).

[6] See T Landman and E Carvalho, *Measuring Human Rights* (Oxford, Routledge, 2010).

[7] See W Seltzer and M Anderson, 'The Dark Side of Numbers: The Role of Population Data Systems in Human Rights Abuses' (2001) 68 *Social Research* 481.

[8] Merry, *The Seductions of Quantification* (n 5) 5.

[9] D Kennedy, 'Challenging Expert Rule: The Politics of Global Governance' (2005) 27 *Sydney Law Review* 5.

[10] P Haas, 'Introduction: Epistemic Communities and International Policy Coordination' (1992) 46 *International Organization* 1. The International Council on Human Rights Policy reported that in a workshop concerning human rights evaluation, some participants described 'evaluation' experts as an epistemic community. See ICHRP, 'No Perfect Measure: Rethinking Evaluation and Assessment of Human Rights Work' (January 2012) 5.

[11] See SE Merry and S Wood, 'Quantification and the Paradox of Measurement: Translating Children's Rights in Tanzania' (2015) 56 *Current Anthropology* 205.

[12] Merry, 'Measuring the World' (n 3).

human rights and accountability.¹³ Merry wrote in 2016 that the 'translation' of rights into numbers 'shifts human rights from a legal discourse with a broad and flexible vision of justice and rights to a technocratic one of economics and management'.¹⁴ This vison – which assumes the predictability of, control over and therefore possibility of rational management of social and political change – was a model for understanding the world that was seen as particularly ill-suited to human rights. The danger that states would seek to 'game' indicators instead of using them to measure rights enjoyment was also raised, suggesting an ever-increasing gap between the right being monitored and the metrics used to do so.¹⁵ This gap was especially problematic in relation to norms that had not yet been fully articulated by authoritative human rights bodies. These issues and others were explored in Merry's ethnographic accounts of indicator-creation, as well as in my work, and the work of Merry's collaborators, colleagues and those her work has influenced.¹⁶

A decade later, and in a datafied but increasingly 'post-truth' world, it seems useful to ask: have the concerns so eloquently articulated by scholars such as Sally Merry come to fruition in the human rights sphere? Has '"indicator culture" – marked by technical rationality, a pragmatic approach to measurement, and the magic of numbers'¹⁷ – taken root in the human rights field? More specifically, has the monitoring of rights become a system of technocratic audit?

To answer these questions, this chapter focuses on the use of indicators to measure fulfilment of the rights to water and sanitation, two of the rights arguably most amenable to quantification. Using a dataset designed for this purpose, the chapter examines the use of indicators, benchmarks and quantitative data concerning water and sanitation by the UN Committee on Economic, Social and Cultural Rights (CESCR, the Committee), the body charged with monitoring compliance with the International Covenant on Economic, Social and Cultural Rights (ICESCR, the Covenant). The chapter also draws on a second dataset assembled for this purpose that assesses the use by human rights NGOs of data and indicators in the context of advocacy to advance the rights to water and sanitation. What these data reveal is surprising: despite the relative ease of quantification and the broad use of rights-relevant data in the water and sanitation sector, the UN human rights experts charged with monitoring compliance with the ICESCR are not engaging in data-inflected assessments of these rights in a systematic way. Instead, they sporadically refer to data but do not deploy it or engage in datafied discussions that could simplify the tracking of progress or retrogression over time. The final section of this chapter explores some reasons behind this seeming rejection of the seductions of quantification. The chapter concludes that the analyses advanced by Merry in the past decade nonetheless retain

---

¹³ M Satterthwaite, 'Indicators in Crisis: Rights-Based Humanitarian Indicators in Post-Earthquake Haiti' (2011) 43 *New York University Journal of International Law and Politics* 865.
¹⁴ Merry, *The Seductions of Quantification* (n 5) 162.
¹⁵ Rosga and Satterthwaite, 'The Trust in Indicators' (n 4).
¹⁶ See, eg Merry, *The Seductions of Quantification* (n 5); Merry, 'Measuring the World' (n 3); Merry and Wood, (n 11); K Davis et al (eds), *Governance by Indicators: Global Power through Quantification and Rankings* (Oxford, Oxford University Press, 2012); SE Merry et al (eds), *The Quiet Power of Indicators: Measuring Governance, Corruption, and Rule of Law* (Cambridge, Cambridge University Press, 2016).
¹⁷ Merry, *The Seductions of Quantification* (n 5) 206.

II. THE CESCR'S TURN TO HUMAN RIGHTS INDICATORS

In a full-length article examining human rights indicators published in 2009, AnnJanette Rosga and I reviewed the history surrounding their use.[18] Here, I offer only a brief summary of key points, focusing on the CESCR as one of the key bodies eager to embrace indicators.[19] This embrace was part of wave of corrective moves following the sidelining of social, economic and cultural (ESC) rights for many decades, and was seen as necessary in light of the nature of state obligations in relation to ESC rights. On the whole, ESC rights as opposed to civil and political rights had suffered a long-term marginalisation, characterised by the late creation of a treaty-monitoring body for the ICESCR, a lack of infrastructure for their advancement and a sense that the rights were insufficiently specific to ensure accountability for their violation. In the early 1990s, human rights practitioners began searching in earnest for appropriate tools to turn the rhetoric of ESC rights into concrete reality. The CESCR searched for ways to measure states' efforts to comply with the ICESCR's Article 2 commandment that each ratifying state 'take steps' to the 'maximum of its available resources, with a view to achieving progressively the full realization' of ESC rights.[20] Without concrete ways to assess progress, this phrasing could be used as an 'escape hatch' by states that had done little to guarantee the rights of those under their jurisdiction.[21]

Early on, the Committee had reminded states that they must continually make good-faith efforts to guarantee ESC rights for all, and that these efforts should be measurable.[22] The turn towards indicators was an attempt to make such measurement systematic. While states were not obliged by the treaty text to adopt any particular method for documenting and monitoring their progress in implementing Covenant rights, the Committee suggested that they should use statistics as benchmarks or 'indication[s] of progress'.[23] Importantly, these benchmarks were to be created and applied by states, with the Committee in a supervisory, reviewing role. As Sally Merry wrote, such indicators were seen to help in 'translating the broad, often vague, terms of the treaty into specific policies, programs, and outcomes that make sense in the particular context and history of a country'.[24] Finally – and perhaps

---

[18] Rosga and Satterthwaite, 'The Trust in Indicators' (n 4).

[19] This subsection draws heavily on A Rosga and M Satterthwaite, 'Measuring Human Rights: UN Indicators in Critical Perspective' in Davis et al (n 16) 297.

[20] International Covenant on Economic, Social and Cultural Rights (New York, 16 December 1966) 993 UNTS 3, Art 2.

[21] E Felner, 'Closing the "Escape Hatch": A Toolkit to Monitor the Progressive Realization of Economic, Social, and Cultural Rights' (2009) 1 *Journal of Human Rights Practice* 409.

[22] CESCR, 'The Nature of States Parties' Obligations, General Comment No 3' (1990), reprinted in Compilation of General Comments and General Recommendations Adopted by Human Rights Treaty Bodies (26 April 2001) UN Doc HRI/GEN/1/Rev.5, paras 10, 11.

[23] CESCR, 'Reporting by States Parties: General Comment No 1' (1989), reprinted in Compilation of General Comments (n 22) paras 6, 14.

[24] Merry, *The Seductions of Quantification* (n 5) 165.

most significantly – while resource constraints could legitimately explain a state's inability to fully implement each right for all individuals, they would not be allowed to excuse a failure to monitor state efforts towards full realisation of ESC rights. In the years following these early requests, the Committee continually asked states to develop and apply indicators to monitor their own progress in implementing various provisions of the treaty. The duty to monitor was also examined from a sharper angle: in a General Comment published in 2000, the CESCR asserted that a state's failure to demonstratively monitor could itself amount to a violation of the Covenant.[25] And notably, in its 2003 General Comment on the Right to Water, the Committee specified that it was a 'core obligation' to 'monitor the extent of the realization, or the non-realization, of the right to water', and called on states to identify such indicators that address the many components of the right to water with data that is 'disaggregated by the prohibited grounds of discrimination'.[26] This General Comment explained that states would be invited to engage in a 'scoping' process, whereby they would set specific benchmarks for achievement using the indicators they had chosen and discuss any gaps between those goals and their achievement with the CESCR during the treaty monitoring process.[27]

Around this same time, the UN's Office of the High Commissioner for Human Rights (OHCHR) took on an international indicator-creation project intended to construct indicators for major rights guaranteed by the entire corpus of core human rights treaties. Members of the CESCR were part of this process, which became the focus of writings by Merry, Rosga, me and others; that project is not examined in this chapter. Alongside the OHCHR-led effort, the CESCR continued to insist that states should identify nationally relevant indicators for use as part of the monitoring process. This step taken by the CESCR – from suggesting to states that benchmarks might be 'useful' in 1990 to asserting that the creation and use of monitoring systems, including indicators, was a treaty obligation from 2000 onward – is striking. In effect, it ensured the onus of conceptualising and applying indicators was not only on the international community, but also rested – as a treaty matter – on states themselves. In relation to indicators, then, the Committee's most vital role was envisioned as the highly technical one of monitoring the state's monitoring.

III. STATES' CURIOUS FAILURE TO PROVIDE STATISTICS FOR MONITORING THE RIGHTS TO WATER AND SANITATION

How, then, did states respond to the CESCR's request for indicators and benchmarks? Did they supply the needed data to enable the CESCR to fulfil its auditing role? This section will examine that question, using the rights to water and sanitation as examples. These rights were chosen for several reasons. First, the normative framework for these rights was developed and made public at the same time that

---

[25] CESCR, 'The Right to the Highest Attainable Standard of Health' (11 August 2000) UN Doc E/C.12/2000/4, para 52.
[26] CESCR, 'The Right to Water' (20 January 2003) UN Doc E/C.12/2002/11, paras 37(g), 53.
[27] ibid para 54.

the indicators boom was in full swing. As mentioned above, the CESCR published a comprehensive General Comment on the Right to Water in 2003, clarifying state obligations to respect, protect and fulfil these rights, and made an authoritative statement about the contours of the right to sanitation in 2010; both embraced indicators.[28] The UN General Assembly and the Human Rights Council also affirmed the rights to water and sanitation – most notably in resolutions in 2010 – underlining the broad acceptance of these rights even among states that had not ratified the ICESCR.[29] Second, there is an existing international infrastructure for collecting, and a plethora of data concerning, water, sanitation and hygiene (WASH).[30] While not all WASH sector data is useful for rights monitoring, much of it is – and, as will be discussed below, WASH as a sector has been increasingly sensitive to human rights concerns.[31] Finally, human rights NGOs have called for the use of quantitative data in monitoring the rights to water and sanitation, and some of the early leading work on rights metrics can be traced to work on the rights to water and sanitation.[32]

Before turning to states' responses to the CESCR's request for WASH indicators, it's important to recall the procedures used by such UN treaty bodies in their monitoring of state compliance with human rights treaties. States are required to submit reports on their efforts to implement and protect the rights set out in a given treaty to the relevant UN mechanism – the 'treaty body' or 'treaty committee' – for the purpose of monitoring their compliance. Each treaty body, usually labelled with the name of the treaty (eg CESCR), examines the state reports as its main source of information, often supplemented by relevant information submitted by NGOs and sometimes UN development agencies. The committee then engages in a 'constructive dialogue' with state officials concerning the state's progress in implementing the treaty. These constructive dialogues have become increasingly formalised over the years, in part due to states' compliance with treaty-specific reporting guidelines, responsiveness to questions issued by the Committees prior to the dialogues and uniform formats for committee reports on the outcome of each review, including the treaty body's 'concluding comments' or 'concluding observations'. In 2006, the UN treaty bodies adopted 'harmonized reporting guidelines' concerning state reports across all treaties, with 'the aim being to strengthen State parties' capacity to fulfil their reporting obligations in a timely and efficient manner, including avoidance of unnecessary duplication of information'.[33] In addition, treaty bodies have issued

---

[28] ibid 'Statement on Sanitation'. While GC 15 called on states to use indicators to measure the right to water, the Statement on the Right to Sanitation simply used them, citing data revealing how far the governments of the world had to travel in order to achieve the sanitation-related target related to the Millennium Development Goal concerning water and sanitation. ibid paras 1–2.

[29] UNGA Res A/64/L.63/REV.1 (28 July 2010); UNHRC, 'Human Rights and Access to Safe Drinking Water and Sanitation' (6 October 2010) UN Doc A/HRC/RES/15/9.

[30] See, eg BM Meier et al, 'Examining the Practice of Developing Human Rights Indicators to Facilitate Accountability for the Human Right to Water and Sanitation' (2014) 6 *Journal of Human Rights Practice* 159.

[31] See discussion in Winkler et al (n 2).

[32] See V Roaf, A Khalfan and M Langford, 'Monitoring Implementation of the Right to Water: A Framework for Developing Indicators' (2005) 14 *Global Issue Papers*.

[33] OHCHR, *Reporting to the United Nations Human Rights Treaty Bodies Training Guide Part 1 – Manual* (United Nations, 2017) 34, www.ohchr.org/Documents/Publications/PTS20_HRTB_Training_Guide_Part1.pdf.

updated reporting guidelines related to the specific information they seek in reports forming the basis for country reviews under each treaty.

The 2006 harmonised guidelines recommended that states provide both 'demographic indicators' and a series of 'social, economic, and cultural indicators' seen as relevant to assessing compliance with the core human rights treaties.[34] These indicators are set out in an appendix to the guidelines.[35] Notably, the appendix does not list indicators concerning water and sanitation as ones that states are specifically requested to provide, though they could be seen as included – to a degree – in a request for data concerning household expenditures, dietary consumption and causes of death.[36] No matter the case, this lack of specificity was corrected by the CESCR in its 2008 revised guidelines for states reporting under the ICESCR. There, the CESCR requested that states provide information and data in relation to the substantive rights protected – whether explicitly or implicitly through authoritative interpretation, like the rights to water and sanitation – by the Covenant. In relation to the right to water, the Committee asked states to report on:

(a) The measures taken to ensure adequate and affordable access to water that is sufficient and safe for personal and domestic uses for everyone;
(b) The percentage of households without access to sufficient and safe water in the dwelling or within its immediate vicinity, disaggregated by region and urban/rural population and the measures taken to improve the situation;
(c) The measures taken to ensure that water services, whether privately or publicly provided, are affordable for everyone; and
(d) The system in place to monitor the quality of water.

[States should also provide] information on education concerning the hygienic use of water, protection of water sources and methods to minimize water wastage.[37]

Many types of information would be relevant to these requests, but the Committee's call for data specifically concerning access at the household level to sufficient, safe and affordable water can be seen as a solicitation for quantitative data. Further, by asking that this data be disaggregated by region and urban/rural populations, the Committee was implicitly suggesting that it sought to conduct comparisons across geographic spaces and between traditionally better-served urban communities and those often left out of water infrastructure in rural areas. Further, the Committee was not asking for this data in a vacuum.

Data concerning access to water and sanitation at the household level had been routinely gathered in a wide swathe of countries around the globe by national governments, or by governments working with development partners, since the 1980s and 1990s.[38]

---

[34] International Human Rights Instrument (IHRI), 'Harmonized Guidelines on Reporting under the International Human Rights Treaties, Including Guidelines on a Common Core Document and Treaty-Specific Documents' (10 May 2006) UN Doc HRI/MC/2006/3, paras 33–35 and Appendix 3.
[35] ibid.
[36] ibid Appendix 3.
[37] CESCR, 'Guidelines on Treaty-Specific Documents to be Submitted by States Parties under Articles 16 and 17 of the International Covenant on Economic, Social and Cultural Rights: Note by the Secretary-General' (24 March 2009) UN Doc E/C/12/2008/2, paras 48–49.
[38] L Van de Lande, *Eliminating Discrimination and Inequalities in Access to Water and Sanitation* (UN Water, 2015) 15–18.

Seeking more granular data concerning household consumption, the WASH sector had gradually turned away from reliance only on provider-based data in earlier years and towards collection and analysis of household data. These data were drawn from standardised surveys and censuses, including those conducted by national agencies in the Global North and by development partners and national agencies across the Global South. Over time, these agencies developed a set of 'core questions' on water and sanitation that were used across a wide variety of surveys in many countries.[39] The commonly used surveys include UNICEF's Multiple Indicator Cluster Surveys, USAID-funded Demographic and Health Surveys, the World Bank's Living Standards Measurement Study surveys and Core Welfare Indicator Questionnaires, and the WHO's World Health Surveys and Household Budget Surveys.[40] The household data these surveys provided were 'seen as an enormous improvement over provider-based data, which did not capture an accurate picture of the use of water and sanitation facilities, as distinct from their formal existence'.[41] Since 2002 – one year before the CESCR's General Comment on the Right to Water – the UN's Joint Monitoring Programme on Water Supply and Sanitation (JMP) had used 'survey and census data [as the] only primary source of data' for its analyses of the WASH sector.[42] During the Millennium Development Goals (MDGs) era, this data became even more important as it was used by JMP to track progress on the water and sanitation targets agreed to by the international community. Efforts were made to ensure that as many countries as possible had conducted reliable surveys to collect the needed information; by 2012, JMP was able to monitor 180 countries, up from about 70 in 1992.[43] Concerning the specific data used for MDG monitoring, JMP relied upon

> two proxy indicators: 'use of an improved water source' and 'use of improved sanitation facilities' to track progress toward the MDG target. JMP has defined specific sources of water as improved and others as unimproved, and particular types of sanitation facilities as improved and others as unimproved. These definitions and the methods for estimating coverage have been adjusted over time as information expanded and improved. In addition to providing these coverage indicators, JMP publishes national and global trend analyses. Relevant to understanding equality and equity, JMP disaggregates its findings by rural and urban areas ... [I]n 2004, it undertook trend analysis by wealth quintiles, and in 2010, the JMP report included extensive analysis of data disaggregated by wealth quintiles. In brief, '[th]e JMP has greatly expanded since its inception in 1990 ... International and national development partners recognize the JMP reports as the main source of reference data to support their decision-making'.[44]

Thus, by the time the CESCR asked states to provide data concerning 'the percentage of households without access to sufficient and safe water in the dwelling or within its immediate vicinity, disaggregated by region and urban/rural population', the data

---

[39] See WHO/UNICEF, 'Core Questions', Joint Monitoring Programme for Water Supply, Sanitation and Hygiene (JMP) https://washdata.org/monitoring/methods/core-questions.
[40] Van de Lande (n 38) 15–18.
[41] For example, provider-based data does not account for a wide variety of user-built, local and informal mechanisms for water and sanitation: ibid.
[42] ibid 15–18.
[43] ibid 17.
[44] ibid 17–18 (internal citations excluded).

needed to construct such indicators was widely available to governments. States in every region had the capacity to provide at least some of this data, which the state could use – with adjustments it may see as necessary – to illustrate the extent to which the rights to water and sanitation were being enjoyed. Oddly, the CESCR call too often went unheeded.

In an article published in 2015, Benjamin Mason Meier and Yuna Kim presented a comprehensive analysis of state reports submitted to the CESCR between 1999 and 2012, focusing specifically on the content of reporting concerning water and sanitation. Through systematic qualitative coding, the authors found that states increasingly reported on 'structure and process indicators' for water and sanitation, meaning that information about the legal framework and steps taken by the government to implement the rights to water and sanitation was increasingly made available to the CESCR.[45] However, as Mason Meier and Kim explain, 'in focusing reporting on structure and process, states have not linked these commitments and efforts to the ensuing results, neglecting consistent outcome indicators that are essential to determining the cause-and-effect dynamics of rights realization'.[46] Ironically, the JMP data discussed above is the type of data that is especially amenable to use as outcome indicators, since such data demonstrate the ability of households (and those within them) to access water and sanitation – often the outcome sought. If put together, information about government efforts to improve access and data about household enjoyment of such access could shed light on how effective such efforts have been, and where greater work is needed. Meier and Kim's analysis of state reports revealed that states have also largely failed to report on the obligation to ensure water and sanitation in a manner consistent with the human rights principles of non-discrimination and equality, participation and accountability.[47] They further found that, overall, 'there does not appear to be any consistent move toward quantification in state reporting' on water and sanitation, and that 'it appears that states are either unwilling or unable to apply the statistical data necessary to report on their implementation efforts for water and sanitation rights'.[48]

In 2016, Sally Merry reported similar results, finding that, on average, country reports submitted to major UN treaty bodies between 2007 and 2011 'included 4.6 references to indicators', though 'there was an above-average number of references to indicators in reports to the ICESCR'.[49] However, Merry's

> qualitative content analysis of 528 country reports to the six major human rights treaties from 2007 to 2013 showed that the indicators mentioned in these reports were primarily counts and ratios of basic social and demographic information rather than the full range of indicators [potentially relevant for human rights monitoring].[50]

---

[45] BM Meier and Y Kim, 'Human Rights Accountability through Treaty Bodies: Examining Human Rights Treaty Monitoring for Water and Sanitation' (2016) 26 *Duke Journal of Comparative & International Law* 141, 182–85.
[46] ibid 185–86.
[47] ibid 186–93.
[48] ibid 215–16.
[49] Merry, *The Seductions of Quantification* (n 5) 202.
[50] ibid 203.

Taking these findings together, it seems that country reports to the CESCR have included relatively few, surprisingly basic and largely unenlightening quantitative indicators. This is striking, since plenty of data were available in many countries that could have been presented to the CESCR in response to its call for countries to report on indicators concerning the rights to water and sanitation. In particular, the CESCR's request for data on the 'percentage of households without access to sufficient and safe water in the dwelling or within its immediate vicinity, disaggregated by region and urban/rural population and the measures taken to improve the situation' seeks the very type of data collected by the JMP, albeit with some analysis required by the country supplying the data to the CESCR.

In a 2014 study concerning the use of data to measure the rights to water and sanitation, Inga Winkler, Catarina de Albuquerque and I examined the datasets used by the JMP to assess the millennium development goals concerning water and sanitation.[51] We found that, far from being unhelpful for rights monitoring, the data – which was, at the time, available for roughly 180 countries around the world – includes not only extensive data on access to water and sanitation at the household level, but also 'a wide variety of equity and equality-related variables'.[52] These variables include 'data on race, national origin, language, and religion', as well as information that allows for disaggregation of populations by wealth.[53] We found that although these variables were underused at the international level, the JMP itself was starting to use these data to assess inequalities in access to water and sanitation – by comparing access by dominant social groups to access by those experiencing discrimination, or by presenting progress in accessing water and sanitation by wealth and income groups.[54] Certainly, there were gaps in the data that would be concerning for any human rights monitoring exercise, but those gaps could have been seen as an invitation for improved methods or invitations to contextualise the data with qualitative information instead of a reason not to engage with the data. For example, some marginalised populations, such as the unhoused or those living in informal settlements, were often excluded or systematically undercounted in such datasets.[55] These issues could be addressed through oversampling, engagement with community-gathered data and improved sampling. Water and sanitation data also tends to stop at the front door, failing to capture intra-household inequalities along the lines of gender, disability, age and other important axes of discrimination.[56] Further, the analysis that JMP did carry out that was aimed at examining inequalities was not 'integrated into routine monitoring or systematic analysis', meaning that it could not be relied upon without adjustment in the human rights monitoring setting.[57]

These shortcomings are not terribly surprising, since the JMP was set up by two international development agencies, where progress is measured using standardised

---

[51] See Winkler et al (n 2) 548 (internal citations omitted).
[52] ibid 575 (internal citations omitted).
[53] ibid (internal citations omitted).
[54] ibid 571 (internal citations omitted).
[55] M Satterthwaite, *JMP Working Group on Equity and Non-discrimination (END) Final Report* (2012).
[56] ibid.
[57] See Winkler et al (n 2) 583 (internal citations omitted).

economic and social metrics at the population level, not at the individual or community level, as is the tradition in human rights settings. Human rights experts and scholars worked hard to collaborate with development practitioners as the MDG era came to a close and Sustainable Development Goals (SDGs) were being formulated. The effort to broaden the focus from a narrow assessment of the aggregate good by integrating attention to human rights concerns like inequality into the SDGs had some remarkable successes. In the WASH sector, addressing inequalities was central to the sector-wide consultations on what became SDG 6.[58] This goal, 'Ensure access to water and sanitation for all', and its first target, 'By 2030, achieve universal and equitable access to safe and affordable drinking water for all', include the human rights imperatives of both achieving universal access and focusing efforts equitably on the hardest to reach and most marginalised groups. In the SDG context, the JMP routinely publishes data and analyses that are relevant for human rights monitoring.[59]

However, no matter how far the WASH sector may have come in embracing human rights principles, its work could never replace the role of the treaty bodies, which are obliged to monitor human rights. As Winkler, de Albuquerque and I concluded in 2014:

> Measuring development progress will never replace human rights monitoring, since human rights progress entails a wide variety of obligations and duties that are not captured by development goals and cannot be assessed solely using development indicators, no matter how rights-sensitive they are. Indeed, measurement can never replace the qualitative and judgment-laden processes of assessment required for human rights monitoring.[60]

To conclude, the fact revealed through careful study of state reports to the CESCR is that, even as governments and their development partners were increasingly producing and using standardised water and sanitation data in the WASH sector, they were not using these same data or creating relevant analyses for human rights monitoring and assessment. Were these data presented to the CESCR and analysed through a human rights lens, they could have served as the basis for monitoring, benchmarking and scoping exercises. Because the data were collected through standardised modules used across the world, the CESCR could have learned to work with these data fairly easily were the data provided. Such engagement might not only have shed a brighter

---

[58] The JMP created the 'Equity and Non-Discrimination Working Group', chaired by then-Special Rapporteur on the Rights to Water and Sanitation, Catarina de Albuquerque (and for which I served as rapporteur), which formulated recommendations for the SDG on water and sanitation, as well as for JMP's monitoring of the new goals and targets. The central insight emerging from these consultations was that 'eliminating inequalities' was the only way to achieve universal access in a human rights-respecting way. This insight has been taken on board by the WASH sector, even if it was not the centrepiece of the new SDG 6 or target 6.1. This uptake can be seen in reports from JMP and UN Water, as in eg the 2015 UN Water publication, *Eliminating Discrimination and Inequalities in Access to Water and Sanitation* (Van de Lande (n 38)), which concludes that 'a coherent approach based on human rights principles is needed if the aims and targets of sustainable development in relation to water, sanitation and hygiene, are to be realized'. Satterthwaite, *JMP Working Group* (n 55) 46.

[59] See WHO/UNICEF, 'Inequalities' (JMP) https://washdata.org/monitoring/inequalities.

[60] See Winkler et al (n 2) 554 (internal citations omitted).

light on the fulfilment of the rights, but could have exerted needed pressure on states and development partners to improve data gathering and analysis in line with human rights norms.[61]

It seems, therefore, that data availability at the country level is not the main obstacle to the CESCR's use of water and sanitation indicators. The WASH sector has begun to use existing databases to produce analyses that are inflected by human rights considerations – especially the obligation to dismantle inequalities and advance universal access to water and sanitation.[62] Ironically, the state agencies responsible for implementing rights treaties have seemingly fallen behind in providing the data and analyses needed by treaty bodies to monitor states' human rights obligations. The next section will examine the CESCR's efforts to monitor these rights despite state failures to provide indicators for the Committee to audit.

IV. THE CURIOUS LACK OF ENGAGEMENT WITH INDICATORS AND QUANTITATIVE DATA BY THE CESCR

To assess the CESCR's use of indicators and quantitative data in monitoring the rights to water and sanitation, a dataset was constructed for this chapter by coding the concluding observations (COs) made by the Committee concerning water and sanitation between 2003 and 2018.[63] The COs were chosen since they are the 'operative' portion of Committee reports published following state reviews. They form the basis for the Committee's follow-up procedure, and are often used by NGOs in advocacy efforts.[64]

The first step in creating the dataset was reviewing all COs published in the relevant years and entering the text of those COs that mentioned water, sanitation or related terms into a database. These WASH-related COs were then qualitatively coded for a variety of variables, including: use of the cross-cutting human rights principles of equality/non-discrimination, participation and accountability; specific populations addressed; the presence and type of quantitative data or indicators used; and the context of references to water and sanitation.[65] After the dataset was checked and cleaned, the data were analysed using Excel. This section presents the findings of this analysis.

---

[61] For examples of recommendations concerning rights-based data gathering, see Satterthwaite, *JMP Working Group* (n 55); OHCHR, 'Human Rights Indicators: A Guide to Measurement and Implementation' (1 January 2012) UN Doc HR/PUB/12/5, 46–51.

[62] See, eg Van de Lande (n 38).

[63] The year 2003 was chosen since it was the first year following publication of GC 15 on the Right to Water.

[64] CESCR, 'CESCR Note on the Procedure for Follow-Up to Concluding Observations' (2017) www.ohchr.org/Documents/HRBodies/CESCR/Follow-upConcludingObservations.docx.

[65] The code book used to develop this dataset was based on a condensed version of the one used by Meier and Kim. The author reduced the number of variables and then supplemented with specific questions concerning the use of quantitative data and statistics.

A. CESCR's Use of Indicators and Data in Assessing Water and Sanitation

Out of 192 country reviews for which concluding observations were published between 2003 and 2018, the CESCR referred to the rights to water and/or sanitation in the concluding observations for 130 reviews (amounting to approximately 68 per cent of country reviews during this period). While the CESCR's practice fluctuates a bit from year to year, the data reveals a rough upward trend in the Committee's engagement with water and sanitation over this 15-year period (see Figure 13.1). While the Committee made observations concerning water and/or sanitation in 60 per cent of the country reviews published in 2003, it did so 83 per cent of the time in 2018, with a nadir of 39 per cent in 2013 (see Figure 13.1).

Figure 13.1 Concluding observations

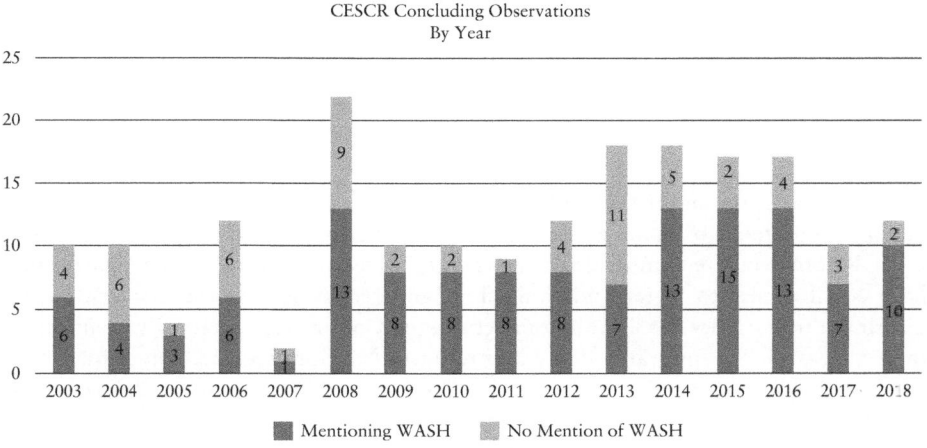

Substantively, the coding revealed that the CESCR engaged frequently on the issue of equality and non-discrimination in relation to water and sanitation and less frequently concerning other cross-cutting human rights principles. Roughly 50 per cent of the WASH-related COs mentioned equality and non-discrimination or deployed these concepts when examining WASH-related issues in the early years of coding. A gradual increase in the frequency of the CESCR's use of these principles in relation to WASH is observable until the final three years – 2016, 2017 and 2018 – when the Committee addressed equality and non-discrimination in 100 per cent of its WASH-related COs (see Figure 13.2). Discussion of accountability also increased over time, though the issue was less frequently included as compared with equality and non-discrimination. Accountability was addressed in fluctuating proportions, ranging from no mentions in some years to a steady integration between 2014 and 2018, when accountability was considered in 20 per cent to 60 per cent of WASH-related COs (see Figure 13.2). Inclusion of the principle of participation in WASH-related COs did not undergo a consistent change during the period of study, with mentions fluctuating between 0 per cent and 50 per cent of WASH-related COs (see Figure 13.2). CESCR's engagement with these cross-cutting human rights issues stands in contrast to state reports' general failure to engage them, as reported by Meier and Kim.[66]

Figure 13.2 Reviews

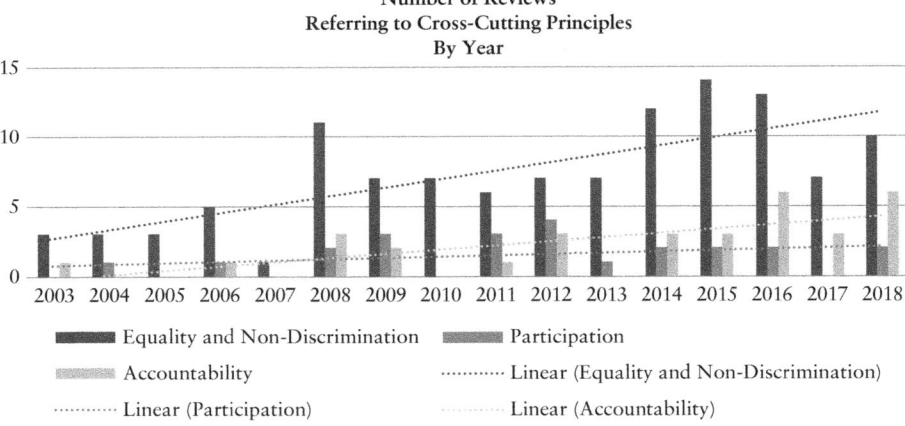

Reflecting both the importance of the principle of equality and the persistence of unequal enjoyment by some communities of the rights to water and sanitation, the CESCR commonly recommended that states take steps to ensure that specific groups have equal access to water and sanitation, and recommended the dismantling of discrimination in services. In this connection, the Committee specifically mentioned, inter alia, women,[67] migrants (including refugees[68]/asylum-seekers,[69] migrant workers,[70] internally displaced persons[71] and undocumented immigrants[72]), persons with disabilities,[73] indigenous peoples,[74] homeless persons,[75] those living in informal settlements[76] and rural areas,[77] smallholder farmers and agro-pastoralists,[78] religious and

---

[66] See discussion above (n 45) and accompanying text.
[67] CESCR, 'Concluding Observations on Niger' (4 June 2018) UN Doc E/C.12/NER/CO/1, para 17.
[68] CESCR, 'Concluding Observations on Lebanon' (24 October 2016) UN Doc E/C.12/LBN/CO/2, para 8.
[69] CESCR, 'Concluding Observations on the Philippines' (26 October 2016) UN Doc E/C.12/PHIL/CO/5–6, para 45.
[70] CESCR, 'Concluding Observations on Viet Nam' (15 December 2014) UN Doc E/C.12/VNM/CO/2–4, para 14.
[71] CESCR, 'Concluding Observations on Iraq' (27 October 2015) UN Doc E/C.12/IRQ/CO/4, para 47; CESCR, 'Concluding Observations on Kenya' (6 April 2016) UN Doc E/C.12/KEN/CO/2–5, para 11.
[72] CESCR, 'Concluding Observations on Italy' (14 December 2004) UN Doc E/C.12/1/Add.103, para 10.
[73] CESCR, 'Concluding Observations on the Central African Republic' (4 May 2018) UN Doc E/C.12/CAF/CO/1, para 11.
[74] CESCR, 'Concluding Observations Canada' (23 March 2016) UN Doc E/C.12/CAN/CO/6, para 43.
[75] CESCR, 'Concluding Observations on Chad' (16 December 2009) UN Doc E/C.12/TCD/CO/3, para 26.
[76] CESCR, 'Concluding Observations on Brazil' (26 June 2003) UN Doc E/C.12/1/Add.87, para 33.; CESCR, 'Concluding Observations on Thailand' (19 June 2015) UN Doc E/C.12/THA/CO/1–2, para 27.
[77] CESCR, 'Concluding Observations on Chile' (7 July 2015) UN Doc E/C.12/CHL/CO/4, para 27.
[78] CESCR, 'Concluding Observations on Niger' (n 67) para 17.

ethnic minorities (including Roma,[79] Bedouins,[80] the Amazigh population of Libya,[81] nomadic herders[82]), prisoners and other detainees,[83] as well as 'underprivileged and marginalized individuals and groups'.[84] For a snapshot of the most common populations addressed by the CESCR in WASH-related reviews, see Figure 13.3. Notably, the top two most frequently mentioned populations were rural and urban populations. As discussed above, WASH sector data are frequently disaggregated into urban and rural areas, since the MDG on water and sanitation demanded this. This means that states often have such data readily available, and could fulfil the CESCR's request, set out in the reporting guidelines, for household access data disaggregated by urban/rural population. Inclusion of such data would provide an easy grounding for the CESCR to comment on the enjoyment of – and gaps in fulfilment between – the rights to water and sanitation in urban and rural areas in its COs.

Figure 13.3 Populations addressed

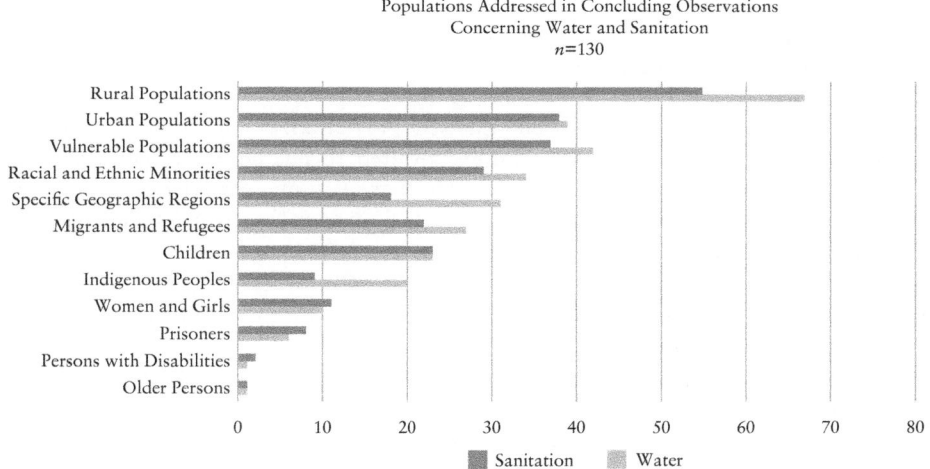

In its COs embracing equality and non-discrimination, the Committee frequently expressed concern about specific populations' lack of access to water and sanitation. It often failed to focus on the inequalities between dominant groups and groups that experience discrimination and/or marginalisation, though such a focus would

---

[79] CESCR, 'Concluding Observations on Serbia and Montenegro' (23 June 2005) UN Doc E/C.12/1/Add. 108, para 30; CESCR, 'Concluding Observations on Slovenia' (15 December 2014) UN Doc E/C.12/SVN/CO/2, para 21; CESCR, 'Concluding Observations on Montenegro' (15 December 2014) UN Doc E/C.12/MNE/CO/1, para 22; CESCR, 'Concluding Observations on Greece' (27 October 2015) UN Doc E/C.12/GRC/CO/2, para 33.
[80] CESCR, 'Concluding Observations on Israel' (26 June 2003) UN Doc E/C.12/1/Add.90, para 16.
[81] CESCR, 'Concluding Observations on Libya' (25 January 2006) UN Doc E/C.12/LYB/CO/2, para 18.
[82] CESCR, 'Concluding Observations on Mongolia' (7 July 2015) UN Doc E/C.12/MNG/CO/4, para 8.
[83] CESCR, 'Concluding Observations on Yemen' (12 December 2003) UN Doc E/C.12/1/Add.92, para 18; CESCR, 'Concluding Observations on Kyrgyzstan' (7 July 2015) UN Doc E/C.12/KGZ/CO/2–3, para 12.
[84] CESCR, 'Concluding Observations on Paraguay' (20 March 2015) UN Doc E/C.12/PRY/CO/4, para 25.

be especially amenable to quantitative illustration. For example, in COs concerning Serbia, the Committee made clear that it was 'gravely concerned about the poor conditions in which thousands of Roma families live in sub-standard informal settlements without access to basic services such as electricity, running water, sewage facilities, medical care and schools'.[85] Surprisingly, the Committee does not contrast these conditions with those of the dominant community in Serbia, much less embrace quantitative ways of exploring such gaps by, for example, contrasting coverage statistics in Roma communities with those of the ambient community.

With respect to accountability, the Committee made a broad range of recommendations aimed at encouraging states to ensure their own activities and those of private actors effectively advance the ability of communities to access adequate, safe and affordable water and sanitation. For example, the CESCR recommended that the government of Kenya ensure it was 'adequately controlling prices charged by private water services and water kiosks' in informal settlements, where the impunity of water vendors charging exorbitant prices may prevent communities living in poverty from accessing water of sufficient quality.[86] Notably, the Committee did not define adequacy here, despite the existence of numerous potential indicators for affordability in the water sector.[87]

The Committee sporadically emphasised participation by emphasising that individuals and communities must be empowered to engage in decision-making affecting their rights to water and sanitation. For example, the CESCR has called on states including Indonesia,[88] Mongolia[89] and Sweden[90] to respect the rights of indigenous communities to exercise free, prior and informed consent over activities that might harm their right to water. It is interesting to note that the Committee did not cite data establishing such harmful impacts, or examine data produced by the indigenous groups themselves.

While the focus of much WASH sector monitoring has been on the household, the Committee did look beyond this setting, expressing concern about access to water, sanitation and hygiene in schools,[91] workplaces[92] and places of

---

[85] CESCR, 'Concluding Observations on Serbia and Montenegro' (n 79) para 30.
[86] CESCR, 'Concluding Observations Concerning Kenya' (1 December 2008) UN Doc E/C.12/KEN/Co/1, para 30.
[87] See H Smets, 'Quantifying the Affordability Standard' in M Langford and A Russell (eds), *The Human Right to Water: Theory, Practice, and Prospects* (Cambridge, Cambridge University Press, 2017) 225.
[88] CESCR, 'Concluding Observations Concerning Indonesia' (19 June 2014) UN Doc E/C.12/IDN/CO/1, para 27.
[89] CESCR, 'Concluding Observations Concerning Mongolia' (n 82) para 8.
[90] CESCR, 'Concluding Observations Concerning Sweden' (14 July 2016) UN Doc E/C.12/SWE/CO/6, para 14.
[91] CESCR, 'Report on the Thirty-Sixth and Thirty-Seventh Sessions' (2007) UN Doc E/C.12/2006/1, para 479; CESCR, 'Concluding Observations on Sri Lanka' (9 December 2010) UN Doc E/C.12/LKA/CO/2–4, paras 29 (expressing concern about water and sanitation in schools for internally displaced persons) and 36 (expressing concern about lack of 'fresh drinking water' in rural schools); CESCR, 'Concluding Observations on Djibouti' (30 December 2013) UN Doc E/C.12/DJI/CO/1–2, para 35 (calling on the state to ensure water and sanitation services are available in schools).
[92] CESCR, 'Concluding Observations on the Dominican Republic' (21 October 2016) UN Doc E/C.12/DOM/CO/4, para 51 (discussing the lack of water and sanitation in sugarcane encampments); CESCR, 'Concluding Observations on South Africa' (29 November 2018) UN Doc E/C.12/ZAF/CO/1, para 37 (expressing concern about lack of water and sanitation for mineworkers and the dangers this poses, especially to women workers).

detention.[93] Following the adoption of the CESCR's Statement on the Right to Sanitation in 2010, the Committee began to refer to the statement in its concluding observations on the issue of sanitation.[94] The CESCR also expressed concern about the impact of large-scale development and industrial projects[95] and extractive industries[96] on the rights to water and sanitation. The Committee began to address the human rights impacts of climate change as well, including on the right to water.[97] Figure 13.4 illustrates the broad range of contexts in which reference was made to water and sanitation in the CESCR's WASH-related COs. This wide-ranging concern suggests that a broad swathe of datasets – including environmental, housing, food and agriculture data – would be potentially relevant to the CESCR's work monitoring the rights to water and sanitation. The Committee's engagement with such datasets was, however, negligible.

Figure 13.4 Context

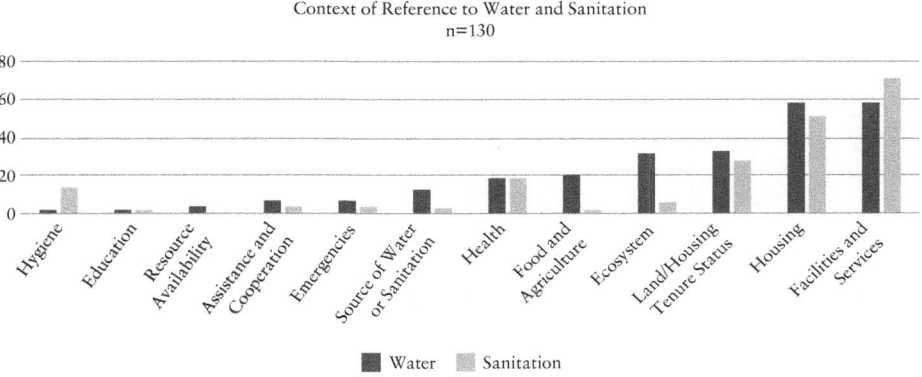

The coding undertaken for this study reveals that the CESCR made use of quantitative data in a relatively small portion of its COs concerning water and sanitation. As discussed above, some elements of the rights to water and sanitation are quite amenable to quantification. Despite this, and despite the CESCR calling on states to provide specific relevant data, the Committee itself refers to WASH data relatively

---

[93] CESCR, 'Concluding Observations on Ukraine' (4 January 2008) UN Doc E/C.12/UKR/CO/5, para 26; CESCR, 'Concluding observations concerning Kyrgyzstan' (n 83) para 18.

[94] CESCR, 'Concluding Observations on Yemen' (22 June 2011) UN Doc E/C.12/YEM/CO/2, para 26; CESCR, 'Concluding Observations on Cameroon' (23 January 2012) UN Doc E/C.12/CMR/CO/2–3, para 29; CESCR, 'Concluding Observations on Mauritania' (10 December 2012) UN Doc E/C.12/MRT/CO/1, para 29; CESCR, 'Concluding Observations on Romania' (9 December 2014) UN Doc E/C.12/ROU/CO/3–5, para 20.

[95] CESCR, 'Concluding Observations on Mexico' (9 June 2006) UN Doc E/C.12/MEX/CO/4, para 10 (expressing concern about the impact of planned hydroelectric dam on the rights of indigenous peoples to water); CESCR, 'Concluding Observations on Kazakhstan' (7 June 2010) UN Doc E/C.12/KAZ/CO/1, para 35 (expressing concern about impact on water of industrial waste).

[96] CESCR, 'Concluding Observations on Argentina' (14 December 2011) UN Doc E/C.12/ARG/CO/3, para 9 (expressing concern about the exploitation of lithium on the right to water of indigenous peoples); CESCR, 'Concluding Observations on Peru' (30 May 2012) E/C.12/PER/CO/2–4, para 22 (expressing concern about the impact of extractive industry activities on the right to health and water).

[97] CESCR, 'Concluding Observations on Cabo Verde' (27 November 2018) E/C.12/CPV/CO/1, para 8 (above noting with concern the impact of droughts caused by climate change).

rarely, even though its engagement with water and sanitation has increased over time (see Figure 13.5). Indeed, over the 15-year period examined here, there was no discernible trend towards more frequent citation of quantitative data in relation to water and sanitation (see Figure 13.5).

Figure 13.5 Annual variation

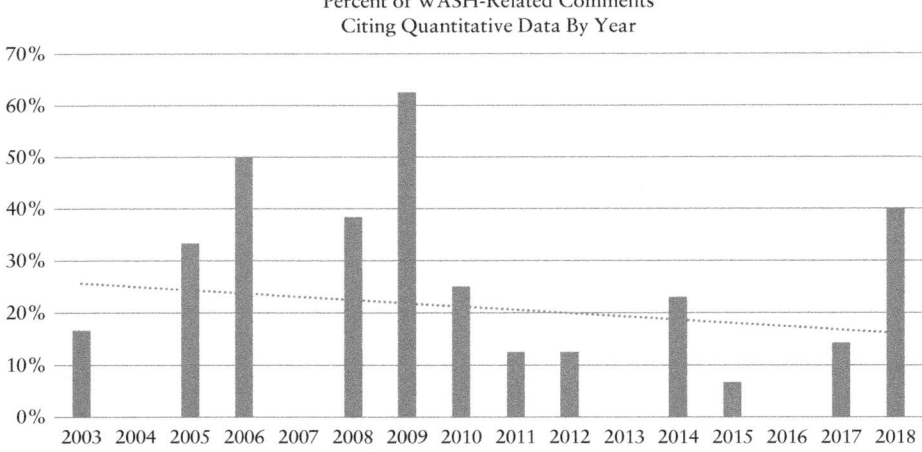

As illustrated in Figure 13.6, only 22 per cent of the WASH-related COs included any reference to quantitative data. Notably, as set out in Figure 13.7, about half of those statistics cited were not actually water and sanitation data, but were instead – for example – poverty or social security data.[98]

Figure 13.6 Provision of quantitative data

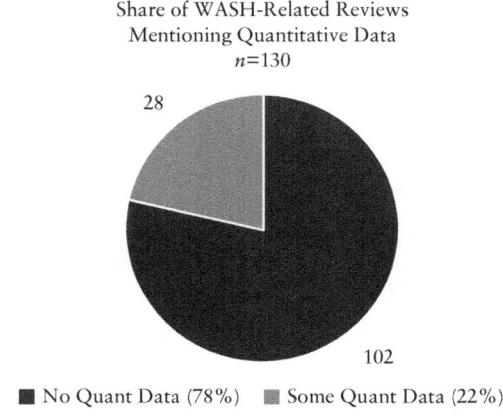

---

[98] See, eg CESCR, 'Concluding Observations on Korea' (17 December 2009) UN Doc E/C.12/KORE/CO/3, para 22.

Figure 13.7 Citation of quantitative data

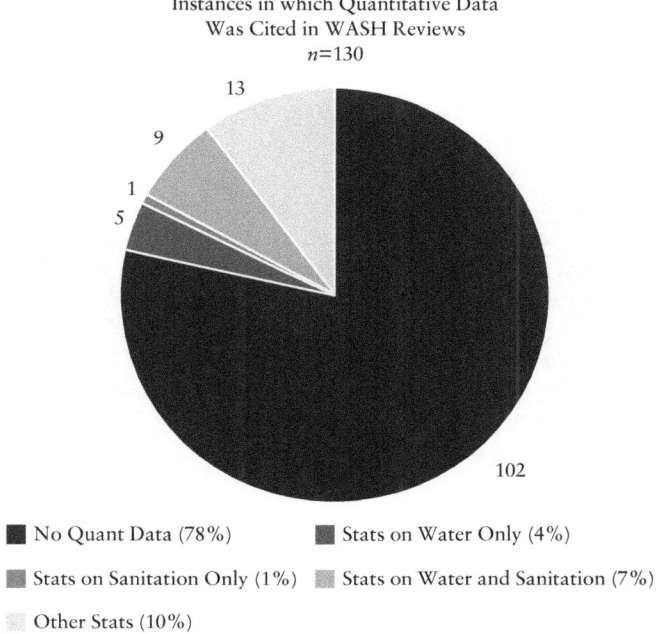

The water and sanitation statistics included in these concluding observations were, for the most part, extremely basic. Most often, they cited specific percentages of the population with – or without – 'access' to water and/or sanitation. For example, the CESCR cited with concern statistics about proportions of the population without access to 'improved', 'safe' or 'running' water:

- '28 per cent of the population do not have sustainable access to an improved water source'[99]
- '83 per cent of the population have no access to safe drinking water[100]
- 'over 10 per cent of households have no running water'[101]

In some cases, the Committee cited statistics about water in rural areas. For example, it expressed concern about the 'lack of direct access to safe drinking water in 17.5 per cent of rural households in Serbia' in 2005.[102] Concerning sanitation, the Committee cited statistics about the proportion of the population without access to toilets or sewerage, or to 'hygienic' or 'adequate' sanitation services:

---

[99] CESCR, 'Concluding Observations on Libya' (n 81) para 18.
[100] CESCR, 'Concluding Observations on the Democratic Republic of the Congo' (16 December 2009) UN Doc E/C.12/COD/CO/4, para 29.
[101] CESCR, 'Concluding Observations on Argentina' (1 November 2018) UN Doc E/C.12/ARG/CO/4, para 47.
[102] CESCR, 'Concluding Observations on Serbia' (n 79) para 30.

- '70 per cent have no access to hygienic sanitation facilities'[103]
- 'more than 70 per cent of the population lacked proper toilets, while only 24 per cent had access to an adequate sewage system'[104]

In a few cases, the same statistic was cited for both water and sanitation, as with this comment concerning Madagascar in 2009: 'about 50 per cent of the population of the State party has no access to clean drinking water and adequate sanitation facilities'.[105]

There were some instances in which the CESCR commented on statistics reflecting an improvement in access to water and/or sanitation between two periods of time, suggesting that it viewed such improvements as relevant to the state obligation of progressive realisation.[106] However, this was rare, and most of the time the Committee simply cited a statistic without explaining whether these percentages reflected improvements or declines over time.[107] While the Committee's practice is in part a reflection of the dearth of information included in state reports, this does not explain the CESCR's failure to engage in analysis of the data it does possess. For example, the Committee explained in General Comment (GC) 15, published in 2003, that it would engage in a 'scoping' exercise using indicators to monitor the right to water. This would involve the state identifying the indicators it felt were most salient to measuring the right to water, bringing forward baseline data for these indicators and engaging in a discussion with the CESCR to set goals for achievement against those baseline values.[108] It is unclear if this has happened; when formulating concluding observations, the Committee systematically fails to explain whether a given statistic was being cited as a baseline, an achievement or a benchmark for continued improvement or monitoring for retrogression.

However, the Committee does continually call on states to embrace and deploy disaggregated indicators for water and sanitation. For example:

- Serbia and Montenegro, 2005: The CESCR 'invites the State party to identify disaggregated indicators and appropriate national benchmarks in relation to the right to water, in line with the Committee's general comment No. 15 (2002), and to include information on the process of identifying such indicators and benchmarks in its next report'. Similar requests were made to Yemen in 2003, Bosnia and Herzegovina in 2006, Tajikistan in 2007, India in 2008 and the Dominican Republic in 2010.

---

[103] CESCR, 'Concluding Observations on the Democratic Republic of the Congo' (n 100) para 29.
[104] CESCR, 'Concluding Observations on Chad' (n 75) para 31.
[105] CESCR, 'Concluding Observations on Madagascar' (16 December 2009) UN Doc E/C.12/MDG/CO/2.
[106] See, eg CESCR, 'Concluding Observations on Argentina' (n 101): 'The Committee, while noting the reported overall increase in the percentage of households with improved drinking water between 2006 and 2016, remains concerned that access to safe drinking water and sanitation is much lower in rural areas than urban areas.'
[107] See, eg CESCR, 'Concluding Observations on Brazil' (n 76) para 33: 'The Committee notes with concern that, according to the State party's report, least 42 per cent of families currently live in inadequate housing facilities without adequate water supply, waste disposal and trash collection'; CESCR, 'Concluding Observations on Libya' (n 99): '28 per cent of the population do not have sustainable access to an improved water source'.
[108] CESCR, 'The Right to Water' (n 26) para 54.

- Turkey 2011: 'The Committee requests the State party to include in its next periodic report updated and detailed information on: ... (b) The physical accessibility and the affordability of water and sanitation, particularly for disadvantaged and marginalized groups, including statistical data disaggregated by region and urban/rural areas'. The Committee made a similar request to Moldova in 2011.

In conclusion, it is surprising that the Committee has not engaged in analysis to connect norms to specific indicators used by various countries, nor articulated a set of concrete recommendations for disaggregation beyond generic exhortations to 'disaggregate by prohibited grounds of discrimination' or mention of specific 'disadvantaged and marginalized' groups. Indeed, the impression one has after a systematic review of concluding observations is that the Committee either cannot or will not engage in tailored and searching assessments of or with data. It seems the Committee neither fully embraces its role as an auditor of the state's data nor takes up the tools of quantification as powerful ways of knowing whether states' efforts to advance human rights are effective and just.

B. The Data-Rich Environment of Advocacy for the Rights to Water and Sanitation

The Committee's abdication is especially remarkable given the extensive guidance available to the Committee from other UN agencies, especially the Office of the High Commissioner for Human Rights and the agencies that make up the Joint Monitoring Programme on Water Supply and Sanitation. The OHCHR, for its part, published a well-reasoned and extensive guide to using human rights indicators in 2012 after abandoning earlier, more problematic efforts to create universal, cross-body indicators.[109] While this guide did not include indicators for water and sanitation in particular, the OHCHR has more recently published a matrix of illustrative indicators for those rights that could be used as an analytical framework for linking the data supplied by countries and the norms the Committee is interpreting.[110] The Special Rapporteur on water and sanitation published a comprehensive manual on the rights to water and sanitation in 2014.[111] Comprising a series of nine booklets, the handbook embraces the use of indicators and provides extensive guidance for developing, implementing and reporting on such indicators.[112] The JMP possesses troves of data, and in recent years has produced analyses that are directly relevant to the Committee's work. For example, in addition to frequently comparing rural and urban WASH data, in the past several years, the JMP has used demographic variables to analyse the different rates of access to

---

[109] OHCHR, 'Human Rights Indicators' (n 61).
[110] OHCHR, 'Human Rights Indicators Tables: Updated with the Sustainable Development Goals (SDG) Indicators' (1 January 2020) www.ohchr.org/Documents/Issues/HRIndicators/SDG_Indicators_Tables.pdf.
[111] C de Albuquerque, *Realizing the Human Rights to Water and Sanitation: A Handbook* (UN Special Rapporteur on the human right to safe drinking water and sanitation, 2014) www.ohchr.org/EN/Issues/WaterAndSanitation/SRWater/Pages/Handbook.aspx.
[112] ibid 'Monitoring'.

improved drinking water and sanitation by wealth quintiles, ethnicity, language, literacy, religion and disability.[113]

When reviewing specific country performance under the ICESCR, JMP could be asked to provide data for country reviews on a regular basis. While UNICEF and WHO both have staff who work with countries to support their reporting to treaty bodies concerning the rights of the child and the right to health, respectively, the JMP apparently has no process for engaging affirmatively and directly with the treaty bodies (instead of country officials) absent a request for specific input – and such requests are apparently not common.[114] It may be the case that such engagement would be seen as inappropriate in the delicate world of treaty monitoring. In that case, perhaps the Committee could make better use of NGO-supplied data and approaches to its use.

Research suggests that such data would be available in many instances. A number of human rights NGOs have long embraced quantification as a tool for monitoring and advocacy related to water and sanitation. Specialist NGOs like the Center for Economic and Social Rights have engaged in research, analysis and reporting using WASH data for many years, publishing guides that embrace and use indicators even before the CESCR published GC 15 on the right to water.[115] Human rights NGOs have also advanced frameworks and methods for the creation and use of indicators for water and sanitation. The Centre on Housing Rights and Evictions produced an influential paper in 2005 titled 'Monitoring Implementation of the Right to Water: A Framework for Developing Indicators',[116] and produced an extensive *Manual on the Right to Water and Sanitation* in 2008.[117] More recently, the Danish Institute for Human Rights published an in-depth analytical framework for creating indicators for the right to water[118] and a user-friendly, rigorous manual on deploying these indicators in 2014.[119] Scholar-practitioners in the water and sanitation sector have also provided detailed guidance for conceptualising and constructing rights indicators.[120]

---

[113] See, eg WHO/UNICEF, 'Inequalities in Sanitation and Drinking Water in Latin America and the Caribbean' (JMP, 2016) https://washdata.org/monitoring/inequalities.

[114] Email communication between the author and JMP official (November 2019).

[115] See, eg Center for Economic and Social Rights (CESR), 'Ghana: Privatization and Water Sector Reform in Ghana' (17 August 2002) www.cesr.org/ghana-privatization-and-water-sector-reform-ghana (discussing the 2002 Report of the International Fact-Finding Mission on Water Sector Reform in Ghana); J King, *An Activist's Manual on the Covenant on Economic, Social, and Cultural Rights* (Law & Society Trust and Center for Economic and Social Rights, 2003) www.cesr.org/sites/default/files/CESR_s%20Activists%20 Manual.pdf. CESR's influential 'Visualizing Rights' and UPR submissions have routinely used data to inform human rights mechanisms about state performance under the ICESCR and other treaties. See, eg CESR, 'Visualizing Rights: Equatorial Guinea' (2009) www.cesr.org/sites/default/files/equatorial_ guinea_WEB_1.pdf.

[116] Roaf et al (n 32).

[117] COHRE et al, *Manual on the Right to Water and Sanitation* (2007) http://globalinitiative-escr.org/wp-content/uploads/2013/05/COHRE-Manual-on-Right-to-Water.pdf.

[118] MH Jensen, M Villumsen and TD Petersen, 'The AAAQ Framework and the Right to Water – International Indicators' (Danish Institute for Human Rights, 8 July 2014) www.humanrights.dk/publications/aaaq-framework-right-water-international-indicators.

[119] M Villumsen and MH Jensen, 'The AAAQ Manual and the Right to Water – Contextualising Indicators' (Danish Institute for Human Rights, 24 October 2014) www.humanrights.dk/publications/aaaq-manual-right-water-contextualising-indicators.

[120] See, eg UQ Amjad, G Kayser and BM Meier, 'Ced Indicators Regarding Non-discrimination and Equity in Access to Water and Sanitation' (2013) 4 *Journal of Water, Sanitation, and Hygiene for*

More broadly, experts have offered metrics for economic and social rights that are well rooted in both human rights norms and empirical reality.[121] Taken together, these initiatives provide comprehensive guidance for governments, advocates and human rights mechanisms to engage with data relevant to the rights to water and sanitation.

A dataset constructed for this chapter confirmed that a wide variety of organisations have been using and analysing quantitative data in the context of the rights to water and sanitation since the publication of GC 15 in 2003. While this dataset is necessarily incomplete, research assistants were able to locate more than five dozen human rights reports focusing on water and sanitation that analyse quantitative data published online in English between 2003 and 2018. Almost all of these reports engaged with secondary quantitative data, citing or analysing data collected by other organisations or agencies using a human rights framework. More than a third of the reports used primary quantitative data, which the organisation itself collected. While some of the reports' quantitative data were simple counts, other reports included extensive datasets that NGOs created through a variety of methods, presenting and analysing data about access to water and sanitation in formats familiar to the WASH sector. For example, in 2008, Zanmi Lasante, Partners in Health, RFK Human Rights and the NYU Center for Human Rights and Global Justice published 'Wòch nan Soley: The Denial of the Right to Water in Haiti', presenting the findings of a randomised survey, focus group discussions, and expert interviews on the right to water in northern Haiti.[122] In 2016, the Kenyan organisation Hakijamii/Economic and Social Rights Centre published 'State of Water and Sanitation Service Provision Performance in Mombasa County', which used the right to water to analyse quantitative data collected by the organisation using surveys, focus groups and interviews.[123] The indigenous South Rupununi District Council published a report in 2018 presenting information drawn from its own trained monitors who collect data using smartphones on the impacts of illegal activities on its traditional territories in Guyana, including mining's impact on water.[124] The Columbia Law School Human Rights Clinic and AC4 Earth Institute published 'Red Water: Mining and the Right to Water in Porgera, Papua New Guinea' in 2019, analysing data from site visits, interviews, focus group discussions and water and soil samples through the framework of the right to water.[125]

Development 182; J Schiff, 'Measuring the Human Right to Water: An Assessment of Compliance Indicators' (2019) 6 *WIREs Water*, e1321.

[121] See, eg S Fukuda-Parr, T Lawson-Remer and S Randolph, *Fulfilling Social and Economic Rights* (Oxford, Oxford University Press, 2015); Human Rights Measurement Initiative, 'Measuring Economic & Social Rights', https://humanrightsmeasurement.org/methodology/.

[122] Center for Human Rights and Global Justice et al, *Wòch Nan Soley: The Denial of the Right to Water in Haiti* (23 June 2008).

[123] Economic and Social Rights Centre (Hakijamii), 'State of Water and Sanitation Service Provision Performance in Mombasa County: Community Score Card' (2016).

[124] South Rupununi District Council, 'Wapichan Environmental Monitoring Report' (September 2018) http://wapichanao.communitylands.org/1548691773093-wapichan-environmental-monitoring-report-2018-v2.pdf.

[125] S Knuckey and B Hoffman, 'Red Water: Mining and the Right to Water in Porgera, Papua New Guinea' (Columbia Law School Human Rights Clinic and Advanced Consortium on Cooperation,

Even more traditional NGOs like Amnesty International and Human Rights Watch have integrated data analysis into their work on the rights to water and sanitation in recent years. For example, Amnesty International's 2009 report titled 'Thirsting for Justice: Palestinian Access to Water Restricted', combines primary qualitative data with analysis of secondary quantitative data to examine violations of the right to water. In a 2016 report titled 'Make it Safe: Canada's Obligation to End the First Nations Water Crisis', Human Rights Watch presented the results of a household survey and in-depth interviews examining violations of the right to water of First Nations persons living on reserves in Ontario.[126]

While human rights NGOs are usually not staffed by statisticians and data analysts, evidence suggests that they have increasingly used quantitative methods and data to advance their advocacy concerning the rights to water and sanitation.[127] This embrace is part of a broader move to expand methods and ways of knowing in the human rights field. As Satterthwaite and Simeone explain, 'human rights investigators increasingly supplement traditional testimonial strategies with social science methodologies, including quantitative data and tools'.[128] Between 2000 and 2010, reference to quantitative data in the executive summaries of research reports published by Amnesty International and Human Rights Watch increased substantially (see Figure 13.8).

Figure 13.8 The Seductions of Quantification Rebuffed? The Curious Failure by the CESCR to Engage Water and Sanitation Data – Margaret L Satterthwaite[129]

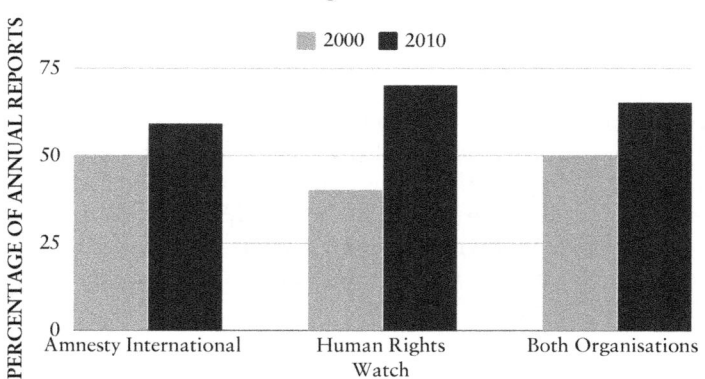

Conflict, and Complexity, February 2019) www.researchgate.net/publication/335589923_Red_Water_Mining_and_the_Right_to_Water_in_Porgera_Papua_New_Guinea.

[126] Human Rights Watch, 'Make It Safe: Canada's Obligation to End the First Nations Water Crisis' (7 June 2016) www.hrw.org/report/2016/06/07/make-it-safe/canadas-obligation-end-first-nations-water-crisis.

[127] See M Satterthwaite, 'On Rights-Based Partnerships to Measure Progress in Water and Sanitation' (2014) 20 *Science and Engineering Ethics* 833.

[128] M Satterthwaite and J Simeone, 'A Conceptual Roadmap for Social Science Methods in Human Rights Fact-Finding' in P Alston and S Knuckey (eds), *The Transformation of Human Rights Fact-Finding* (Oxford, Oxford University Press, 2016) 322.

[129] M Satterthwaite, A Sabele and J Simeone, 'The Emerging "Science" of Human Rights Fact-Finding: Reporting Trends, Investigatory Principles, & Advocacy Organizations in the 21st Century' (manuscript on file with author).

As Brian Root explains:

> [Q]uantitative analyses are a powerful tool in the human rights practitioner's methodology toolbox. Statistics allow researchers to reframe and examine topics in order to provide context or insights different from the information gathered in qualitative interviews, with the most common uses of data analysis being to demonstrate the scope, distribution (over geography and/or time), or variance of a human rights problem. As the supply of data increases, it becomes a more desirable component of high quality research and reporting.[130]

In the era of Big Data, quantitative reasoning and analysis is an important element of human rights work.[131]

So where is the disconnect for state reporting and review before the CESCR? If the development sector is increasingly using rights-inflected analyses of water and sanitation, and the advocacy world is using more data to advance these rights, why is the dialogue between states and the CESCR comparatively data poor?

V. CONCLUSION: QUANTIFICATION'S SEDUCTIONS REBUFFED

In an analysis of the use of data by the Committee on the Elimination of All Forms of Racial Discrimination (CERD Committee), Joshua Clark explains that the CERD Committee 'deploys its data-reporting requirements critically and differentially, taking into account wider concerns about what its efforts to know do':

> What makes it worthwhile to push states to produce their own indicators is if doing so sparks a wider state process – the establishment of targets, plans for achieving those targets, and subsequent measurement of success. That is, quantification is valuable inasmuch as it mobilizes state action.[132]

Is a similar dynamic at play inside the CESCR? During a discussion of indicators in 2008, a member of the CESCR emphasised that 'although it was important not to be overwhelmed by data, the Committee required more information on individual States parties in order to set goals and benchmarks for the promotion of human rights that took account of specific situations'.[133] Perhaps the Committee has been focused on pushing states to produce relevant data, encouraging 'state processes' inside ministries and agencies that would spur action, not only produce knowledge. Has the Committee refrained from using other UN agencies' data and eschewed engagement with non-state data in an effort to nudge the state towards better knowing and doing more with numbers? This is possible.

---

[130] B Root, 'Numbers Are Only Human: Lessons for Human Rights Practitioners from the Quantitative Literacy Movement' in Alston and Knuckey (n 128).

[131] See, eg J Aronson, 'Mobile Phones, Social Media and Big Data in Human Rights Fact-Finding', M Land, 'Democratizing Human Rights Fact-Finding' and P Meier, 'Big (Crisis) Data' in Alston and Knuckey (n 128); M Satterthwaite and D Kacinski, 'Quantitative Methods in Advocacy-Oriented Human Rights Research' in BA Andreassen, H-O Sano and S McInerney-Lankford (eds), *Research Methods in Human Rights: A Handbook* (Cheltenham, Edward Elgar Publishing, 2017).

[132] J Clark, 'Knowing and Doing with Numbers: Disaggregated Data in the Work of the Committee on the Elimination of Racial Discrimination' in D Keane and A Waughray (eds), *Fifty Years of the International Convention on the Elimination of All Forms of Racial Discrimination: A Living Instrument* (Manchester, Manchester University Press, 2017) 20.

[133] CESCR, 'Summary Record of the 2nd Meeting' (5 May 2008) UN Doc E/C.12/2008/SR.2, para 12.

Sally Merry sounded the alarm about the rise of indicators in human rights many years ago. Since then, the concerns – and claims – about quantified ways of knowing have outpaced the actual use of data by human rights mechanisms. What lessons can we draw from this mismatch, in a world moving beyond measurement and into datafication and the rise of artificial intelligence as technologies of governance? It is useful to recall that Merry suggested some of the apprehension about human rights indicators might not be warranted, explaining that whether they were taken up or not

> depends on what happens to the cultural enthusiasm for this technology and whether public trust in its claims to make a complex world knowable through 'indicator culture' – technical rationality, a pragmatic approach to measurement, and the magic of numbers – grows along with support for evidence-based governance and skepticism about political debate. If so, the human rights indicators may yet grow in popularity and influence.[134]

While the enthusiasm for the 'magic of numbers' has arguably not waned, support for 'evidence-based governance' and the rule of experts decidedly has. In a world of rising authoritarianism, crackdown on dissent and the replacement of technocrats with loyalists bent on remaking (or hollowing out) the state even in countries long seen as insulated from such takeover, worries about indicators seem almost quaint.

Rosga and I suggested that the use of indicators might provide advocates with an opportunity to join forces with the CESCR to hold states to account:

> Rather than trusting in numbers too quickly, those using human rights compliance indicators should embrace the opportunities presented by this new project, finding ways to utilize human rights indicators as a tool of global governance that allow the governed to form strategic political alliances with global bodies in the task of holding their governors to account.[135]

In other words, advocates could work with human rights bodies like the CESCR to insist that the state's techniques of quantified knowledge-as-power be open to scrutiny, and that the power wielded by these technologies are aimed at advancing rights. More than a decade later, these strategic alliances seem all too rare, but may – if taken up – become more important than ever. Such alliances would require treaty bodies, NGOs, UN agencies and practitioners to create more space for interaction, knowledge sharing and frank discussion of the impacts of knowing through data. What is required are spaces where rights bodies and practitioners can pry open the 'black box' of measurement[136] by engaging in discussions of what states' decisions – and their partners' decisions in development agencies – concerning what and how to *know through data* are impacting rights. What are these methods making visible, leaving out and distorting as they are used to govern? Without these engagements, the danger is that critiques of the unthinking embrace of indicators, now relevant to the dynamics of Big Data and algorithmic governance, may be lost in academic debates like these instead of usefully infusing efforts to harness the power of numbers for human rights.

---

[134] Merry, *The Seductions of Quantification* (n 5) 206.
[135] Rosga and Satterthwaite, 'The Trust in Indicators' (n 4).
[136] DV Malito, G Umbach and N Bhuta, 'Introduction: Of Numbers and Narratives – Indicators in Global Governance and the Rise of a Reflexive Indicator Culture' in DV Malito, G Umbach and N Bhuta (eds), *The Palgrave Handbook of Indicators in Global Governance* (Cham, Palgrave Macmillan, 2018) 5.

14

Strategising the World: Uncounted People in the Sustainable Development Goal on Health

SARA LM (MEG) DAVIS

IN PLATO'S *REPUBLIC*,[1] a group of friends visit Socrates during a festival, and over the course of a long conversation they imagine creating an ideal republic. Socrates tells the young men that they will need to invent a myth to give the republic's diverse citizens a shared sense of identity and purpose, a 'Noble Lie': 'We want one single, grand lie, which will be believed by everybody; including the rulers, ideally, but failing that, the rest of the city.' The Noble Lie, he says, needs to explain why, despite profound inequality, poor citizens should still go out to fight and even die for the republic.

Today, we lack a shared myth to explain why our globalised world remains so unequal. Instead, we have the Sustainable Development Goals (SDGs), a set of targets that give weight to a narrative about a global community united to end all forms of inequality by 2030.[2] The 17 goals, approved by UN member states in 2016, commit to ending hunger, poverty, illness, lack of education and more, with 'no one left behind'. The aspiration that inequality could end without any fundamental redistribution of wealth is made plausible through what Sally Engle Merry called 'the seductions of quantification'.[3]

In approving the SDGs, UN member states also launched the development of numerous global strategies to reach the goals. These strategies are increasingly linked to indicators used by UN agencies to monitor progress, part of the global rise of 'audit culture'.[4] We may not have a shared narrative, but we trust in numbers.

Merry, in her collaboration with Davis and Kingsbury, called on anthropologists to study the social and cultural practices linked to the development and use of indicators. Much of their work focused on indicators used in indices of such abstract

---

[1] A Bloom trans, *The Republic of Plato*, 2nd edn (New York, Basic Books, 1968).
[2] United Nations, *The Sustainable Development Goals Report* (New York, United Nations, 2022) https://unstats.un.org/sdgs/report/2022/The-Sustainable-Development-Goals-Report-2022.pdf.
[3] SE Merry, *The Seductions of Quantification* (Chicago, University of Chicago Press, 2016).
[4] M Strathern, 'The Tyranny of Transparency' (2000) 26 *British Educational Research Journal* 309.

phenomena as rule of law or corruption: they examined how these are premised on universalising concepts, reliant on aggregation of incommensurable data, and how indicators have become tools of global governance that increasingly have the power of law.[5] The process of producing indicators is, they observe, depicted as a pragmatic process whose political and interpretive work is hidden.

This chapter focuses on a different type of indicator from those used in indices, looking instead at indicators used in strategy implementation. Global health strategies and their related indicators, and monitoring, evaluation and learning (MEL) systems, are all on the rise in global health. The Joint United Nations Programme on HIV/AIDS (UNAIDS) now routinely produces global AIDS strategies, currently tied to SDG 3.3 on health.[6] The World Health Organization (WHO) has an End TB Strategy, its targets also aligned to SDG 3.3.[7] There are global strategies for efforts to end malaria and noncommunicable diseases.[8] In response to the COVID-19 pandemic, WHO launched a new strategy for improved pandemic preparedness.[9] The approval of each strategy is often followed by development of indicators and plans to periodically assess and report on progress.

Once approved, these strategies are incorporated into global health governance: they are used to determine global health agencies' budgets and resource allocations; to structure teams and work plans; and to write investment cases and fundraising proposals that generate funds to disburse to implementing agencies in low- and middle-income countries. The opinions and preferences of current and future funders, as well as the agencies that will be held accountable for implementing the strategy, inevitably come into consideration in strategy development: UNAIDS, for example, holds extensive consultations with civil society, donor agencies and UN member states. I have explored elsewhere[10] how these processes can become sites of negotiation and contest among diverse actors and agendas.

Thus, anthropologists who have studied indicators as tools of governance might further want to consider the development of strategies that precede and are used to develop the indicators. Drawing on the example of indicators used in the Global AIDS Strategy 2016–2021,[11] this chapter uses the challenges in meeting the strategy targets to explore some questions about strategising as a cultural practice, one that is situated in a political and economic context. In particular, it explores the combination of factors that can shape failure to meet ambitious goals, and asks:

---

[5] SE Merry, K Davis and B Kingsbury (eds), *The Quiet Power of Indicators: Measuring Governance, Corruption, and Rule of Law* (Cambridge, Cambridge University Press, 2015).

[6] Joint UN Programme on HIV and AIDS (UNAIDS), 'UNAIDS Strategy Development: Protect and Accelerate Progress Towards the End of AIDS: Ready, Set, Go!' (2020) www.unaids.org/en/Global_AIDS_strategy.

[7] World Health Organization, *The End TB Strategy* (Geneva, WHO, 2015) www.who.int/publications/i/item/WHO-HTM-TB-2015.19.

[8] World Health Organization, *Global Technical Strategy for Malaria 2016–2030* (Geneva, WHO, 2015) www.who.int/docs/default-source/documents/global-technical-strategy-for-malaria-2016-2030.pdf.

[9] World Health Organization, 'New WHO Strategy Aims to Strengthen Rapid Response to Health Emergencies' (October 2022) https://news.un.org/en/story/2022/10/1129272.

[10] SLM Davis, *The Uncounted: Politics of Data in Global Health* (Cambridge, Cambridge University Press, 2020).

[11] UNAIDS, *2016–2021 Strategy: On the Fast Track to End AIDS* (August 2015) www.unaids.org/en/resources/documents/2015/UNAIDS_PCB37_15-18.

what are some of the pressures that might spur an agency to create an ambitious strategy, knowing that it might not be realisable – that it might just be a Noble Lie? What interpretive work and assumptions might the apparently objective process of strategising involve? How might limited resources and ambitious goals shape the trade-offs needed to make programmes work in implementation?

I. THE GLOBAL AIDS STRATEGY 2016–2021

In 2016, the UN General Assembly approved the Global AIDS Strategy, which committed to ending HIV as a public health threat by 2030 using a 'Fast-Track' approach. Drawing on new evidence and mathematical models that showed the impact of accessing treatment on prevention of HIV transmission, the strategy proposed to fast-track the HIV response by focusing on 'locations, populations and interventions that will deliver the greatest impact', among other measures, using a set of ambitious new targets, '90–90–90', explained below. However, as briefly summarised here, implementation proved challenging due to insufficient funding and a need to ration resources: focusing on locations and populations proved difficult, given that some of the populations most likely to contract HIV are those for whom data is most sparse.[12]

As of 2016, while billions spent on the global HIV response had led to a sharp reduction in AIDS-related deaths, an estimated 22 million people living with HIV were still not accessing treatment.[13] The strategy was described by UNAIDS's then-executive director, Michel Sidibe, as:

> A bold call to action to get on the Fast-Track and reach people being left behind. It is an urgent call to front-load investments. It is a call to reach the 90–90–90 treatment targets, to close the testing gap and to protect the health of 22 million people living with HIV who are still not accessing treatment.[14]

The 90–90–90 targets were:

- 90 per cent of all people living with HIV are tested and know their HIV status;
- 90 per cent of all people with diagnosed HIV infection receive sustained antiretroviral therapy; and
- 90 per cent of all people receiving antiretroviral therapy have viral suppression.[15]

The targets were premised on evidence that universal access to treatment could also work as HIV prevention. People diagnosed with HIV infection who sustain antiretroviral therapy for long enough can live healthy lives and reduce their viral load

---

[12] This section summarises arguments made in more detail in SLM Davis, *The Uncounted: Politics of Data in Global Health* (Cambridge, Cambridge University Press, 2020); SLM Davis, 'Why Are We Failing to End HIV?' (*Med in Switzerland*, Medicus Mundi International, July 2020) www.medicusmundi.ch/en/advocacy/publications/med-in-switzerland/why-are-we-failing-to-end-hiv.
[13] UNAIDS, *2016–2021 Strategy* (n 11) 5.
[14] ibid.
[15] See, eg UNAIDS, '90–90–90 – An Ambitious Treatment Target to Help End the AIDS Epidemic' (1 January 2017) www.unaids.org/en/resources/documents/2017/90-90-90.

(the amount of HIV in the bloodstream) to the point where the virus is undetectable and cannot be passed on to others. In 2015, UNAIDS' infectious disease models of this approach, based in part on earlier 'Test and Treat' modelling, showed persuasively that a global scale-up of antiretroviral treatment to meet the 90–90–90 targets could trigger a phase change in countries where prevalence was highest, such as South Africa or Uganda.[16] Scale-up focused in specific geographic locations where HIV was most widespread could significantly reduce HIV transmission globally. The resulting 'Fast-Track approach', approved by the UN General Assembly, was one of the first global health strategies to be developed based largely on mathematical modelling.

It is worth pausing to reflect that in a context of increasing reliance on empirical evidence in public health, the case for the Fast-Track approach was predicated on mathematical models and not on empirical evidence. In part, this is because what was being proposed, as a global strategy, was orders of magnitude larger than the largest randomised controlled trials. Globally, public health had increasingly embraced the need for robust evidence, developing hierarchies of evidence and applying tools such as GRADE (Grading of Recommendations Assessment, Development and Evaluation) to assess the strength of evidence for specific interventions.[17] But strategies adopted at a global level were not required to – or pragmatically, perhaps could not – meet the same standards. An unexamined assumption of the Fast-Track approach was that interventions that had been successful for thousands of people in one setting would be as successful when applied to tens of millions of people globally.

The other issues the Fast-Track approach did not explicitly address were the cost of reaching 90–90–90 and the challenges of targeting locations and populations, given gaps in data.

II. DONOR AIDS FATIGUE

To meet the 90–90–90 targets, scale-up of treatment required a major increase in financial resources for HIV: what AIDS activist Matt Kavanaugh called implausible and 'magical thinking' in health finance.[18] Development assistance for HIV had risen globally in the early 2000s, dipped after the 2008 global economic downturn and begun to rebound in 2013–14. At the time that the 90–90–90 targets were set in 2016, it was a stretch, but not impossible, to believe that more funding could be mobilised to make one last push to the end.

---

[16] JW Eaton et al, 'HIV Treatment as Prevention: Systematic Comparison of Mathematical Models of the Potential Impact of Antiretroviral Therapy on HIV Incidence in South Africa' (2012) 9 *PLoS Medicine* e1001245.

[17] M Mercuri and REG Upshur, 'Evidence-Based Medicine and Public Health' in S Venkathapuram and A Broadbent (eds), *The Routledge Handbook of Philosophy of Public Health* (London, Routledge, 2022) 143–60.

[18] M Kavanaugh, 'Dear UNAIDS: Magical Thinking on Who Will Fund the AIDS Response Will Not End the Epidemic' (*HealthGap*, 6 April 2016) https://healthgap.org/dear-unaids-magical-thinking-on-who-will-fund-the-aids-response-will-not-end-the-epidemic/.

However, just as the Fast-Track approach was being approved by UN member states, a tectonic political shift hit the two leading donor countries in global health: UK citizens voted to leave the European Union and the USA elected Donald Trump president. Growing populism and preoccupation with internal issues led to cuts in financing for the global HIV response, which dropped by 3.3 per cent in 2018.[19]

In 2019, President Trump proposed sweeping cuts of 29 per cent to the Global Fund to Fight AIDS, TB and Malaria (the Global Fund), the largest international funder for HIV. The proposal was resisted by Congress.[20] However, from 2010 to 2018, HIV funding from other donors declined by more than $1 billion.[21] The COVID-19 pandemic had an even more devastating impact on the HIV response, diverting funds to other urgent needs.[22] The UK, formerly the second-largest donor to the Global Fund, significantly reduced its pledge in 2022.[23]

The governments of high-income countries (HICs) that fund the global HIV response faced increasing pressure to make the public case to taxpayers for overseas aid, and to demonstrate to the public that the investment was delivering progress. This created pressure on global health agencies to engage in rationing, debating which countries should be eligible for health aid at the Global Fund.[24]

The Fast-Track approach had promised that one day there could be an end to the need for billions to fund the HIV response: as a goal, ending AIDS would also free up resources to address other global priorities. But the Global AIDS Strategy had set ambitious targets as part of a narrative about creating an end to the epidemic, and had costed the targets only after they were approved. The unintended effect of ambitious targets and constrained funding was to implicitly require a less visible kind of priority-setting. Somewhere, someone would have to decide, in effect, what to prioritise and what to de-prioritise; or, who would be 'left behind'.

The imperative to target locations and populations led agenda-setting HIC donor agencies, such as the US President's Emergency Plan for AIDS Relief, to prioritise larger countries with high HIV prevalence and lower national income in sub-Saharan Africa, where investments could reach a larger number of people. This logic was grounded in principles of cost-effectiveness: targeting services in hospitals and clinics where HIV transmission rates were highest at the subnational level could deliver greater impact than would addressing HIV uniformly across the general population. Using epidemiological data to produce heat maps that showed

---

[19] Institute for Health Metrics and Evaluation, *Financing Global Health 2018: Countries and Programs in Transition* (Seattle, University of Washington, 2019) 14.
[20] Friends of the Global Fight, 'Q&A with Maurine Murenga, the Global Fund Board Member Representing Communities Affected by the Three Diseases' (25 May 2018) www.theglobalfight.org/qa-maurine-murenga-global-fund-board-member-representing-communities-affected-three-diseases/.
[21] J Kates, A Wexler and E Lief, *Donor Government Funding for HIV in Low and Middle-Income Countries in 2018* (San Francisco, KFF, 2019) https://files.kff.org/attachment/Report-Donor-Government-Funding-for-HIV-in-Low-and-Middle-Income-Countries-in-2018.
[22] S Brown, 'The Impact of COVID-19 on Development Assistance' (2021) 76 *International Journal* 42.
[23] RESULTS UK, 'RESULTS UK Statement on the UK Government's Pledge to the Global Fund to Fight AIDS, TB and Malaria' (Results, 14 November 2022) www.results.org.uk/results-uk-statement-uk-governments-pledge-global-fund-fight-hiv-tb-and-malaria.
[24] SLM Davis, *The Uncounted: Politics of Data in Global Health* (Cambridge, Cambridge University Press, 2020).

specific regions where the epidemic was concentrated, national health planners could better position services in HIV 'hot spots', where services could be 'tailored to the needs and contexts of specific populations'.[25] Aid-recipient countries were encouraged to use cost-effectiveness software to use data to target services, and to achieve maximum impact with lower costs.

From the global level to the most granular local level, donors began to shift their priorities to align with the logic of cost-effectiveness: divesting from smaller, middle-income countries where HIV was concentrated among criminalised and stigmatised 'key populations' (defined by the WHO as gay men and other men who have sex with men, sex workers, transgender people and people who use drugs), and instead concentrating funds in larger, lower-income countries where HIV was widespread.

Here, another unstated assumption was that middle-income countries that lost external aid would follow the same rational thinking: when external aid donors pulled out, middle-income country governments were expected step up and increase HIV financing domestically, targeting their funds to reach key populations. In practice, middle-income countries did not always have sufficient resources for health to dedicate more funds to the HIV response, nor have domestic political environments that would support health agencies to prioritise funds for stigmatised and criminalised groups. (This should have been evident from the launch of the Fast-Track strategy: at the very high-level meeting where UN member states voted to approve the Fast-Track approach, some member states blackballed key populations-led organisations and groups of people living with HIV from participating.[26])

This global strategy of scale-up and targeting to end HIV was justified, as noted above, by mathematical models that had predicted success. But the assumptions used to shape these models did not consider, or quantify, on-the-ground realities – stigma, discrimination, marginalisation – or economic realities that could make some middle-income countries either reluctant or unable to fill the gaps left by donor divestment. The models left out what Seaver calls 'the unquantified remainder that haunts math';[27] in particular, the gaps in data for key populations.

III. UNCOUNTED PEOPLE

As a result of stigma, discrimination and criminalisation, many countries have little or no accurate data on key populations, creating a 'data paradox': 'Decision-makers deny that most affected populations exist ... so no research gets done on these populations; the lack of data feeds the denial; and so on.'[28] Of 140 countries assessed by

---

[25] P Piot et al on behalf of the UNAIDS–Lancet Commission, 'Defeating AIDS: Advancing Global Health' (2015) 386 *The Lancet* 171.
[26] A Holpuch, 'UN Pledges to End AIDS Epidemic but Plan Barely Mentions Those Most at Risk' *The Guardian* (8 June 2016) www.theguardian.com/society/2016/jun/08/un-hiv-aids-summit-gay-transgender-groups-excluded.
[27] N Seaver, 'The Nice Thing about Context Is That Everyone Has It' (2015) 37 *Media, Culture and Society* 1101.
[28] S Baral and M Greenall, 'The "Data Paradox"' (*Where There Is No Data*, 5 July 2013) https://wherethereisnodata.wordpress.com/2013/07/05/the-data-paradox/.

UNAIDS and Global Fund researchers in 2016, 41 had no key population estimates to report since 2010, and even these estimates were often assessed as inadequate.[29] Absence of evidence is taken as evidence of absence by governments in denial about the existence of criminalised and stigmatised groups. Gaps in data on key populations can sometimes result in cost-effectiveness software failing to prioritise them for life-saving services. Cost-effectiveness analysis software helps health planners to use mathematical models to forecast the future of the epidemic among sub-populations, and to decide where investments will have the biggest impact. It is exercised as a tool as if it were neutral, but the context in which the data is produced and used to make decisions is not neutral.

Before the devastating effect of the COVID-19 pandemic on health systems, the Fast-Track approach did achieve remarkable success in Africa, where AIDS-related deaths dropped. However, HIV incidence increased among key populations, especially in middle-income countries where donors divested. Since 2016, the global share of new infections has increased among key populations and their partners by at least 10 per cent each year, reaching over 60 per cent in 2020.[30] The Fast-Track approach and its related 90–90–90 targets did help to inspire action in sub-Saharan Africa. However, as a global approach it was not successful, in part because the climate of scarcity required trade-offs and rationing that had not been explicitly considered in the strategy narrative. Such a frank conversation might be unsavoury, even disastrous: as one veteran AIDS activist wryly joked when we discussed this, 'No one wants to go to a meeting titled *Let's decide who we are going to leave behind*'. This reluctance is understandable, but absent a transparent, accountable and ethical discussion of trade-offs, those calculations and choices are more likely to be made behind closed doors.

In 2021, the UN Secretary-General acknowledged that the SDGs would not be attained, including the global effort to end HIV by 2030. While he correctly pointed to the COVID-19 pandemic as having undermined progress towards the SDGs, UNAIDS had already warned in 2019 that the world risked falling off track to ending HIV.[31]

Strategies inherently require difficult choices. The process of planning is not only a decision about what to do; it requires an admission that one cannot do everything and that something will have to be dropped. In this case, the drafters of the Global AIDS Strategy faced an extremely difficult task, given the need to both develop a plan that diverse global actors could implement together to address an ongoing humanitarian crisis and inspire fatigued funders in a context of growing complacency. Ending AIDS is a noble goal, and 90–90–90 worked in some contexts and to some extent.

---

[29] K Sabin et al, 'Availability and Quality of Size Estimations of Female Sex Workers, Men Who Have Sex with Men, People Who Inject Drugs and Transgender Women in Low- and Middle-Income Countries' (2016) 11 *PLoS ONE* e0155150.

[30] UNAIDS, 'UNAIDS Strategy Development' (n 6).

[31] UNAIDS, 'Global Aids Update 2019 – Communities at the Centre: Defending Rights, Breaking Barriers, Reaching People with HIV Services' (Geneva, 10 December 2019) www.unaids.org/en/resources/documents/2019/2019-global-AIDS-update.

But HIV persists globally, not only because millions of individuals lack access to treatment, but because of profound structural inequalities among and within countries. The case study of the Global AIDS Strategy 2016–2021 raises larger questions about strategising as a practice in global governance that might merit further study and reflection.

IV. STRATEGISING THE WORLD

The mental discipline of strategising is itself a cultural and rhetorical act which locates its protagonist, the strategic thinker, somewhere outside and above the field of action, able to objectively assess strengths, weaknesses, opportunities and threats; a bird's-eye view that Jurgenson[32] calls a 'view from nowhere'. In reality, of course, the strategist always has a view from somewhere: a background and lived experience, a set of available data, and dependence on political and social pressures, including from current and potential funders. All these factors may shape assumptions in the crafting of a narrative.

In her formative article, 'Measuring the World', Merry advocates 'an ethnographic approach to understanding the role and impact of indicators'.[33] To do so would mean:

> Examining the history of the creation of an indicator and its underlying theory, observing expert group meetings and international discussions where the terms of the indicator are debated and defined, interviewing expert statisticians and other experts about the meaning and process of producing indicators, observing data-collection processes, and examining the ways indicators affect decision making and public perceptions.[34]

Numerous thoughtful analyses of indicators have followed. Perhaps now we might also begin to consider the strategic thinking that undergirds them as an object of ethnographic study and reflection. An ethnographic consideration of strategy development might consider, first: what are the social, linguistic and cultural practices that produce a global health strategy? How have the practices and discourses of military and business strategising shaped the way this practice is done in global health? What kinds of authority and social capital do strategies confer on strategisers?

Second, what are the kinds of evidence used to develop global health strategies, and how is evidence constructed and applied? What are the standards of evidence used, and how are gaps considered or addressed?

Third, how can we more precisely situate in time, space, socioeconomic class and other grounded specificities the actors who engage in strategising: ranging from consultants who conduct stakeholder interviews, to modelers who create projections, to the things that are considered or left out of a SWOT (strengths, weaknesses, opportunities, threats) analysis? What are the steps and discourses used in strategy

---

[32] N Jurgenson, 'The View from Nowhere' (*The New Inquiry*, 9 October 2014) https://thenewinquiry.com/view-from-nowhere/.

[33] SE Merry, 'Measuring the World: Indicators, Human Rights and Global Governance' (2011) 52 *Current Anthropology* 583, 585.

[34] ibid.

development? Who is in the room when strategies are drafted, shared, revised and validated, and what roles do these actors play?

V. CONCLUSIONS

The SDGs were written to create a narrative that unifies diverse countries around a common set of objectives; they are what Bauman calls a 'species of situated human communication' whose meaning is shaped by external factors.[35] The SDG on health tells a story about global unity in pursuit of an end to crisis, one meant to inspire collaboration in the face of persistent inequalities. But if we make a virus the opponent to be vanquished with strategies, indicators and targets, while leaving the broader climate of inequality an afterthought, do we design a strategy that will win battles while losing the war?

While the Fast-Track approach to 90–90–90 helped to mobilise significant resources and political action, progress in one geographic region has been undermined by backsliding in another. Economic pressures and a global climate of scarcity forced trade-offs that effectively decided which people would be left behind in the global HIV response.

As constrained global resources for health face ever-more pressing demands, including from new outbreaks and pandemics, the future choices global health agencies will face are likely to become increasingly difficult. It may be more crucial than ever to have a clear-eyed picture of how those choices get made, and how the hidden assumptions behind strategic plans may shape outcomes.

---

[35] R Bauman, *Verbal Art as Performance* (Prospect Heights, IL, Waveland Press, 1977) 8.

Index

accountability of human rights offenders, 12, 44–45, 51, 52–53, 58–59, 77, 248–49
   Committee for economic, social and cultural rights
   water and sanitation rights, 250, 255, 258–60, 262
   transitional justice, 119
acquired immunodeficiency syndrome, *see* HIV/AIDS
Afghanistan, 125, 233, 238–40
   accountability for human rights offenders, 52–53
   international tribunals and reparations claims mechanisms
   British trials of soldiers accused of torture, 49–50
alternative dispute resolution, 44–45
ambiguity of quantification, 18–20, 171–72
anthropological ethics, 71, 101, 115–16, 153, 161, 197
anthropology:
   anthropology/law disconnect, 10–12
   engagement with law and social ordering, 26–27, 43–46
   legal pluralism, 24, 26, 43–44, 46, 48, 60, 100
anthropology of human rights, 101–2
   customary and colonial law, 43–44
   deterritorialised ethnography, 105–6
   dispute resolution, 44
   human rights in conflict zones, 45
   legal consciousness of working class, 45
   post-conflict justice, 44–55
   truth and reconciliation commissions, 44–55, 119
anti-slavery campaigns, 31–32
   personal stories, 154–65
      text and staged photography, 165–67
      vanishing points, 159–67
   prevalence estimates, 154–58, 170–72
      banalisation of survivor stories, 159–65
      over-reliance on, 168–70
   qualitative studies, 168
   quantification, 154, 155–59
   personal stories and representational context, 154–55
apologies:
   social integration, 30, 141–44

Cambodia:
   accountability for human rights offenders, 44, 52–53
   Extraordinary Chambers of the Courts
   international tribunals and reparations claims mechanisms, 49–50, 56–57
conceptualising human rights, 48–50, 115–16
   cultural sensitivity requirement, 10–11
   dynamic social processes, as, 189–90
conflict zones and human rights, 45–46, 241
conflicts over rights:
   cultural property, 93–94, 98–100
   cultural rights, 93–97, 98–100
   customary and colonial law, conflicts between, 93–97, 98–100
   localisation of international norms, 70–72
   rights shaming, 66–70
consensus-building, 28–29, 83–84, 86–87, 115, 146
   UPR documentation process, 193, 195, 196–97, 200
consultation:
   Indigenous peoples
      free, prior and informed consultation, 79–80, 81, 86–91
   social integration, 145–47
Convention for the Safeguarding of the Intangible Cultural Heritage, 94–95
Convention on the Elimination of All Forms of Discrimination against Women (CEDAW), 57, 104, 106–7, 108, 214, 217
COVID-19 pandemic:
   HIV/AIDS, impact on, 39, 274, 277, 279
   truth-telling, 134
   xenophobic/racist tendencies, impact on, 125
criminal law, 54
   international tribunals, 45, 58
   People's International Tribunal for Native Hawaiians, 48
   rules of evidence and procedure, 58
cultural appropriation, 94–95, 100
cultural constructions of social life, 37, 229–30
cultural property, 93–94
   revelation of restricted knowledge, 96–97
   customary and colonial law, conflicts between, 98–100

cultural relativism/universalism debate, 10–11, 47
cultural rights, 10, 66, 93–97
   articulation of cultural rights, 98–99
   circulation of culture, 96–99
      customary and colonial law, conflicts between, 98–100
   cultural appropriation, 94–95, 100
   cultural property, 93–94
      customary and colonial law, conflicts between, 98–100
      revelation of restricted knowledge, 96–100
culture-based approach to human rights norms, 15–17, 28, 64
   illiberal movements, 65–66
   "naming and shaming", 66–70
   non-liberal cultural lenses
      professionalism effect, 65
      traditional religious effect, 65
customary and colonial law, relationship between, 43–44, 98–100

"deterritorialized ethnography", 28, 77, 83, 105–6
dispute resolution, 44–45
domestic violence, *see* violence against women

Ease of Doing Business indicators, 174
   domestic political pressures, 176
   reforms, relationship with, 177–78
   reputation, impact on, 176
   state policy, influence on, 175–77
   see also global performance indicators
empowerment:
   quantification/indicators, through, 26, 248
   vernacularization, through, 108–15, 116
   women's courts, 106–7
ethics, 279
   document production, 192–98, 201
   see also anthropological ethics
ethnography and international justice, 56
   benefits and inadequacies of international accountability institutions, 58
      documentation of events, 58–59
      lack of knowledge/expertise, 58
      specialised evidence, 58
      testimony of survivors, 58–59
   "deterritorialized ethnography", 105–6
   International Criminal Court, 56–57
   Nuremberg trials, 56
evidence:
   belief versus evidence, 160–61, 165, 167, 168–69, 171–72
   environmental destruction, 91
   evidence-based governance, decline of, 272

   global health strategies, 276, 280
   Grading of Recommendations Assessment, Development and Evaluation, 276
   post-truth politics, 156–59, 160–61, 165, 167, 168–69, 171–72
   rankings and reforms, link between, 177–78, 186
      Indian political strategy, 181–85
      rankings and domestic competition, 178–80
   rules of evidence and procedure international tribunals, 58–59

failure of quantification, 20–21
failures of social integration:
   political polarisation, 120–23
   transitional justice lessons, 132
      apologies, 141–44
      consultation and participation, 145–47
      enhancing trust, 147–50
      memorialisation, 136–40
      truth-telling, 132–36
   trust, 127–32
   xenophobia and racism, 123–27
flexible universality of international human rights standards:
   apolitical nature of human rights, 8–9
   flexibility requirement defined, 7–8
   incontestable universality, 10
   living instrument concept, 8
   normative certainty and human rights, 9–10
   resistance to, 12–13
free, prior and informed consultation (FPIC):
   Indigenous peoples, 79–80, 81, 86–91
funding:
   HIV/AIDS 90-90-90, 276, 281
   failure of models, 278
   fast track approach, 276–77, 281
   Global Fund to Fight AIDS, 277
   populism, impact of, 277
   US President's Emergency Plan for AIDS Relief, 277–78

Global AIDS Strategy 2016–2021, 274, 275–76, 280
Global North versus Global South, 37–38, 75–76, 78, 214, 254
global performance indicators, 32–33, 173–74, 175, 186
   domestic political pressure, impact on, 176
   domestic regulatory reforms, 181–85
   global competition, 178–80
   Ease of Doing Business indicators, 174
      domestic political pressures, 176, 178–80
      reforms, relationship with, 177–78
      reputation, impact on, 176
      state policy, influence on, 175–77

India's engagement with EDB, 181
  2014 election, 181
  Modi initiatives, 181–82
  national politics, 184–85
  subnational EDB rankings, 182–84
  see also indicators
globalisation of human rights:
  framing theory, 89–90
  reframing of rights, 90–91
  Global North-centred human rights, creation of, 75–76
  Indigenous rights, 85–86
    consensus building, 86–87
    localisation of transnational knowledge, 87–88
    transnational programme transplants, 87
  social movement theory, 88–89
Guatemala:
  accountability for human rights offenders, 52–53
  international tribunals and reparations claims mechanisms
  genocide trials, 49–50

HIV/AIDS:
  COVID-19, impact of, 279
  ending the AIDS epidemic, 39
    see also Sustainable Development Goals
  funding 90-90-90, 276, 281
    failure of models, 278
    fast track approach, 276–77, 279, 281
    Global Fund to Fight AIDS, 277
    populism, impact of, 277
    US President's Emergency Plan for AIDS Relief, 277–78
  Global AIDS Strategy 2016–2021, 274, 275–76, 280
  Joint United Nations Programme on HIV/AIDS (UNAIDS), 274
  uncounted people, 278–80
Holocaust:
  accountability for human rights offenders, 52–53
  international tribunals and reparations claims mechanisms, 49–50
human immunodeficiency virus (HIV), *see* **HIV/AIDS**
human rights language:
  interpretation, 2, 34–35, 83
  LGBTQ+ community, 113–15
  vernacularization, 29–30, 61–63
    defined, 1–2, 15–17
    criticisms, 27–28, 63
    language of duties, use of, 63
    watering down of message, 63
    unidirectional nature, 29, 79, 84–85
  legal realism, 26, 43, 48–50, 51–52, 57
  transnational human rights talk, 46–47
  UPR process, 212–16
  women's rights, 104–8
human rights monitoring, *see* **Universal Periodic Review**
human rights norms, 1–2
  culture-based approach, 16–17, 28–30, 64, 70, 76, 79
    illiberal movements, 65–66
    "naming and shaming", 66–70
    non-liberal cultural lenses, 65
    professionalism effect, 65
    traditional religious effect, 65
  economic and social rights, 257–58, 268–69
  transplanting into domestic legal systems, 28, 83–85, 87
  vernacularization process, 83–85, 107–8

independence principle, 36–37, 53
indicators, 216–17, 247–48
  AIDS/HIV, 273–74
    see also Sustainable Development Goals
  competition, 175
  concerns about use of indicators, 248–49, 272–73
  production of indicators, 22–23
  quantification compared, 21–26
  rights to water and sanitation
    datasets, 249
  UPR, 217–18
  see also global performance indicators
Indigenous peoples:
  cultural property, 93–94
    customary and colonial law, conflicts between, 98–100
    revelation of restricted knowledge, 96–100
  cultural rights, 93–97
    circulation of culture, 96–100
    customary and colonial law, conflicts between, 98–100
    cultural property, 93–100
  customary and colonial law, conflicts between
    cultural property, 93–94, 98–100
    cultural rights, 93–97, 98–100
  empowerment through vernacularization, 108–13
  framing theory, 89–91
  free, prior and informed consultation, 79–80, 81, 86–91
  globalising Indigenous rights, 85–86
    consensus building, 86–87
    localisation of transnational knowledge, 87–88
    transnational programme transplants, 87

reframing of rights, 90–91
UN Declaration on the Rights of Indigenous Peoples, 29–30, 94–95
intermediaries:
UPR secretariat, 36–37, 193, 204–5
see also Universal Period Review; UPR secretariat
vernacularization, 2, 3, 28–29, 113, 117–18
intermediaries as translators, 34–35, 46–47, 51, 212
localisation of transnational knowledge, 83–84, 106–7, 111, 187
international accountability institutions, 58
documentation of events, 58–59
lack of knowledge/expertise, 58
specialised evidence, 58
testimony of survivors, 58–59
see also individual courts and tribunals
International Covenant on Civil and Political Rights (ICCPR), 15–16
International Covenant on Economic, Social and Cultural Rights (ICESCR), 15–16, 38, 249, 250–53, 255–56, 268
see also UN Committee on Economic, Social and Cultural Rights
International Criminal Court, 49–50, 52–53
International Criminal Tribunal for Rwanda (ICTR), 49–50, 52–53, 56–57
International Criminal Tribunal for the Former Yugoslavia (ICTFY), 49–50, 52–53, 56–57
International Tribunal for East Timor, 49–50, 52–53
interpretation:
approaches to language
linguistic advances, 15–16
complexities, 15–17
human rights language, 2, 83
intermediaries as translators, 34–35, 46–47, 51, 212
intermediaries
UPR secretariat, 36–37, 193, 204–5
see also Universal Period Review; UPR secretariat
uncertainties, 16
vernacularization, 2, 3, 28–29, 113, 117–18
intermediaries as translators, 34–35, 46–47, 51, 212
localisation of transnational knowledge, 83–84, 106–7, 111, 187

Joint United Nations Programme on HIV/AIDS (UNAIDS), 274
Global AIDS Strategy 2016–2021, 275–76
uncounted people, 278–79

legal anthropology, 82–83
anthropology/law disconnect, 10–12
customary and colonial law, 43–44
dispute resolution, 44
engagement with law and social ordering, 26–27, 43–46
human rights in conflict zones, 45
legal consciousness of working class, 45
legal pluralism, 43–44
post-conflict justice, 44–55
truth and reconciliation commissions, 44–55
legal consciousness of working classes, 45
legal globalisation from below, 29, 88–90
reframing of rights, 90–91
legal knowledge, 57–58, 80, 194
legal pluralism, 24–26, 43–44, 46, 60, 100, 116, 212
customary and colonial law, conflicts between, 98–100
legal realism:
vernacularization, 26, 43, 48–50, 51–52, 57
LGBTQ+ rights:
empowerment through vernacularization, 113–15
living instrument concept, 8
localisation of international norms, 70–72, 80–83, 211–12
cultural vernacularization, relationship with, 72–73, 83–85
UPR process, 212–16
localisation of transnational knowledge, 28–29, 83, 87–88

memorialisation:
social integration, 136–40
Millennium Development Goals (MDGs), 23–24, 214, 254, 257, 261
misconceptions surrounding human rights regimes:
apolitical nature of human rights, 8–9
incontestable universality, 10
normative certainty and human rights, 9–10
slippery slope argument, 12–13
modern slavery, 18–19, 31–32, 165, 167, 168
prevalence estimates, 38, 154, 159–60, 163, 169
see also anti-slavery campaigns

neoliberalism, 51–53, 55
global values package, 64
neutrality principle:
UN officials, 36–37, 193
UPR secretariat, 188, 191–92
new legal realism, 46
Convention on the Elimination of All Forms of Discrimination against Women, 57 vernacularization of legal realism, 47–50

Office of the High Commissioner for Human
     Rights (OHCHR):
  Compilation, 34, 191, 198–99, 206, 215, 217
  indicator-creation project, 251
  neutrality, 188–89
  Stakeholder Summary, 34, 191, 196, 206, 208,
     211, 215, 217
  see also Universal Period Review

participation:
  social integration, 145–47
People's International Tribunal for Native
     Hawaiians (Hawaiian People's
     Tribunal), 27, 48
political polarisation, 120–21
  growth of, 121–23
  trust and trustworthiness, 128–31
     polarisation and democratic erosion,
        131–32
power relationships, 37–38, 197, 230, 243,
     244–45

quantification:
  anti-slavery campaigns, 31–32
     banalisation of survivor stories, 159–65
     over-reliance on, 168–70
     prevalence estimates, 154–72
  concerns, 248–49
  defined, 2, 17–20
  prevalence estimates, 154–58, 170–72
     banalisation of survivor stories, 159–65
     over-reliance on, 168–70
  water and sanitation data, 247–73

racism, racist violence and xenophobia
  growth of, 124–27
rankings and league tables:
  global performance indicators, 173–74, 175
  Ease of Doing Business indicators, 174,
     175–78
retributive justice, 53–54, 58
right to sanitation, *see* rights to water and
     sanitation
rights shaming, 28, 57, 62, 66–70, 76, 203
rights to water and sanitation:
  datasets, 249
  UN Committee on Economic, Social and
     Cultural Rights, 38
     access to water and sanitation, 253–55
     information gathering, 253–55
     lack of engagement with indicators, 258–71
     request to states for indicators, 251, 254–58
  UN Joint Monitoring Programme on Water
     Supply and Sanitation, 38, 254–58,
     267–68

Rwanda:
  accountability for human rights offenders, 52–53
  international tribunals and reparations claims
     mechanisms
     Gacaca courts, 49–50
     International Criminal Tribunal for Rwanda,
        44–50, 56–57

sanitation, *see* rights to water and sanitation
"shaming", *see* rights shaming
Sierra Leone:
  accountability for human rights offenders, 52–53
  international tribunals and reparations claims
     mechanisms
     Special Court for Sierra Leone, 49–50, 56–57
     Sierra Leone Truth Commission, 49–50
social integration:
  political polarisation, impact of, 120–23
  transitional justice, 132
     apologies, 141–44
     consultation and participation, 145–47
     enhancing trust, 147–50
     memorialisation, 136–40
     truth-telling, 132–36
  trust, 127–32
  xenophobia and racism, impact of, 123–27
South Africa:
  accountability for human rights offenders,
     49, 52–53
  apartheid-era crimes
     international tribunals and reparations
        claims mechanisms, 49–50, 195, 132
strategizing, 280
  ethnographic approach, 280–81
  evidence, 280
  see also Global AIDS Strategy 2016–2021
Sustainable Development Goals (SDGs), 23–24,
     72, 257, 267, 273, 281
  ending the AIDS epidemic, 39, 274

targeting:
  HIV/AIDS, 276–77
terrorism:
  international tribunals and reparations claims
     mechanisms, 49–50
torture:
  quantification, 17
  vernacularization, 63, 64–65
transitional justice, 30, 44–55, 118–19, 119–20
  apologies, 141–44
  consultation and participation, 145–47
  enhancing trust, 147–50
  failures of social integration
     political polarisation, 120–23
     transitional justice lessons, 132–50

trust, 127–32
xenophobia and racism, 123–27
memorialisation, 136–40
truth-telling, 132–36
translation of human rights language:
intermediaries as translators, 34–35, 46–47, 51, 212
see also vernacularization
transparency, 21–22, 39, 64, 182
UN officials, 193, 199–200
transplanting human rights norms into domestic legal systems, 28, 83–85, 87
trust and trustworthiness, 127–28
interpersonal, generalised trust, 127–28
institutional or political trust, 128–31
polarisation and democratic erosion, 131–32
social integration, 147–50
truth and reconciliation commissions, 44–55, 132–33
accountability for human rights offenders, 52–53
unofficial truth commissions, 135
truth-telling:
social integration, 132–35
limitations, 135–36
truth and reconciliation commissions, 44–55, 132–33, 135
accountability for human rights offenders, 52–53
unofficial truth commissions, 135

UN Charter, 81, 206, 232
UN Commission on Human Rights, 4–5
independence principle, 36–37
neutrality principle, 36–37
see also Office of the High Commissioner for Human Rights
UN Committee on Economic, Social and Cultural Rights (CESCR), 38
access to water and sanitation
accountability, 250, 255, 258–60, 262
information gathering, 253–55
lack of engagement with indicators, 258–71
duty to monitor, 251
lack of engagement with water and sanitation indicators, 258–71
monitoring procedures, 252–53
guidelines, 253
request to states for indicators, 251
states' response, 251–58
water and sanitation data, 254–58
use of data, 38–39, 249–50, 258
assessment of water and sanitation, 259–67
benchmarks of progress, as, 250–51
extensive nature of data, 267–68
lack of engagement with water and sanitation indicators, 259–67

UN Committee on the Elimination of All Forms of Racial Discrimination (CERD Committee):
reporting requirements, 271
use of data, 271
UN Declaration on the Rights of Indigenous Peoples, 29–30, 94–95
UN Education, Scientific and Cultural Organization (UNESCO), 4–6
UN Joint Monitoring Programme on Water Supply and Sanitation (JMP), 38, 254–58, 267–68
UN General Assembly (UNGA), 4
Global AIDS Strategy 2016–2021, 274, 275–76, 280
UN Security Council (UNSC):
Women, Peace and Security (WPS) agenda, 37–38, 231
see also Women, Peace and Security (WPS) agenda
United Nations:
monitoring procedures, 252–53
see also individual bodies, conventions and declarations
Universal Declaration of Human Rights (UDHR), 4–7, 81
flexible universality, 7–10
Universal Periodic Review (UPR), 34–37, 203–5, 226–27
cultural translation, 35, 187, 212–16
drafters, 187–90
see also UPR secretariat
guiding principles, 190–92, 206
implementation of recommendations, 208
indicators, 217–18
information gathering, 206
localisation of international norms, 212–16
objectives, 205–6
origins, 190–92
public audit rituals, 207–8, 227
quantification, 35–36
recommendations
focus on recommendations, 208–9
form of recommendations, 209–10
identification of, 218–22
implementation, 208, 210–11
monitoring implementation of, 210–11
ranking recommendations, 222–26
terminology, 210
translation/vernacularization, 212
universality, 190, 191–92, 203–4, 206
voice/ownership, 198–200
universalism/cultural relativism debate, 10–11, 47

UPR secretariat, 187–90
    "bureaucratic stamina", 194–95
    conflicting responsibilities, 193
    drafting process, 195–97
        parrhesia, 197–98
    guidelines, 194
    impartiality, 191–92, 194, 199–200
    intermediaries, as, 193
    neutrality, 188, 191–92, 193–4, 201

verifiable data, 32, 157
vernacularization, 61–63
    defined, 1–2, 15–17
    criticisms, 27–28
        language of duties, use of, 63
        watering down of message, 63
    dilemmas, 63
    legal realism, 26, 43, 48–50, 51–52, 57
    transitional justice, 30, 118–19, 119–20
        apologies, 141–44
        consultation and participation, 145–47
        enhancing trust, 147–50
        failures of social integration, 120–50
        memorialisation, 136–40
        political polarisation, 120–23
        trust, 127–32
        truth-telling, 132–36
        xenophobia and racism, 123–27
    transnational human rights talk, 46–47
    unidirectional nature, 29, 79, 84–85
    UPR process, 212–16
    women's rights, 104–8
violence against women:
    anthropological research, 104–5
    women's courts, 106–7

women's rights mobilisation, 104
see also Convention on the Elimination of All Forms of Discrimination against Women; Women, Peace and Security agenda

water and sanitation, *see* **rights to water and sanitation**
Women, Peace and Security (WPS) agenda, 37–38, 231, 244–45
    images and visual illustrations
        effects, not causes, of conflict, 244
        importance of, 242
        visual conventions, 243–44
        women as victims, 236–40
        women from Global North, 239–41
        women from Global South, 236–40
    language of gender, 243–44
    militarism and conflict, 235
    progress, lack of, 232–34, 244
    scope, 232
    Security Council Resolution 1325, 231–32
    women/girls/gender, 234–35
        language of gender, 243–44
World Bank:
    Ease of Doing Business indicators, 25, 32–34
    see also Ease of Doing Business indicators; global performance indicators
    Women, Business and the Law indicators, 25

xenophobia and racism:
    growth of, 124–27